CH00663140

B12/6

The Diplomatic
Diaries of
Oliver Harvey
1937–1940

Oliver Harvey
from a drawing by M.A.H.

The Diplomatic Diaries of Oliver Harvey 1937-1940

Edited by John Harvey

COLLINS
St James's Place, London, 1970

ISBN 0 00 211472 0
© John Harvey 1970
Printed in Great Britain
Collins Clear-Type Press:
London and Glasgow

For M. A. H.

by H. A. F.

Editor's Note

These diaries, which my father regarded simply as historical material, were given by him to the British Museum in 1964 with instructions that they should not be opened until 1980. However, during the last few months of his life he decided that he should alter this to conform with the shortening of the ban on publication of Government papers to thirty years. He also indicated that he had no objection to publication provided he was no longer alive, and suggested that—if they were published—they should come out in two parts: the first to run from Feburary 1938 until the fall of France in June 1940—which is this volume; and the second, to appear in 1976, from July 1940 to April 1946.

The original manuscript is written in exercise books and on odd sheets of paper, and there is a typescript copy which is the text given here in its entirety. I have omitted a few sentences of no general interest and changed one or two phrases which might have caused offence to living persons.

Included with the diaries in the British Museum are various memoranda, letters and records of conversations. All of these are relevant to the text, and were obviously intended to complement it, but it has not been possible to include them in full. I have inserted as much as I can amongst the diary entries and have given extracts in the Appendix.

I wish to express my thanks for the help given me by the authorities of the British Museum.

J.H.

Contents

Introduction

I was appointed Private Secretary by Anthony Eden shortly after he became Foreign Secretary. I came over from Paris, where I had been Head of the Chancery, arriving in January 1936 on the day King George V was dying, the end of another chapter.

It was some time before I began my diary. Owing to pressure of new work, I was too busy to think of it, but as time went on it seemed to me that it might be valuable to set down day by day the course of events and our first reaction to them as they struck us at our particular centre of things. The diary was thus written down "hot" at the time, sometimes hour by hour, rarely a few days or a week or so after the events, and it has in no case been written up or adjusted subsequently. Indeed, its whole value, if it has a value, lies in its "hotness", in the immediate impression and atmosphere. I am the first to recognise how many of the first reactions and impressions and judgments were proved wrong and would be admitted wrong by myself now, but that is not the point. This is how we saw things at the time.

Eden gave me his confidence most fully and I endeavoured to return it in the same spirit, loyally and to the best of my ability. I was Private Secretary to him from January 1936 until he resigned in February 1938, when I continued in the same office with Lord Halifax until December 1939. I then went to Paris as Minister and was an eye witness at the Fall of France. These events are also described as I saw them in the diary. On returning home, I worked in London at the Ministry of Information until in June 1941 I was again appointed Private Secretary to Eden. Our old association then resumed on exactly the old footing, although in November 1943 I was appointed to be an Assistant Under-Secretary as I was really getting too old for this particular post. With the defeat of the Churchill Government in July 1945, Eden resigned as Foreign Secretary and was succeeded by Ernest Bevin. My diary finally closes in April 1946.

My diary therefore presents only a chapter in a longer story, but a chapter written by one who then held a privileged position as observer and confidant. I have not wished to alter it or expurgate it, and so I do not want it to be published or quoted until after a long delay, so as not to hurt personal feelings. The more light that can be shed on the circumstances in which impressions were formed, decisions and action taken, the better.

Harvey of Tasburgh
May 1958

Part One
February 23rd - May 4th 1937

Italy invaded Abyssinia on October 3rd 1935. The League of Nations –
prompted by Anthony Eden, then Minister without Portfolio in Baldwin's
Government – recommended a policy of sanctions against the aggressor.
In the British General Election which took place the following month,
Baldwin reaffirmed his support of the League's action and his National
Government of Conservatives, National Liberals and National Labour
was returned to power with a slightly reduced majority of 247 over the
Labour Party, the I.L.P. and the Liberals. In December the Foreign
Secretary, Sir Samuel Hoare, joined with Pierre Laval, the French
Prime Minister, in a plan for the ending of the Abyssinian war which
involved the virtual dismemberment of Abyssinia. The ensuing public
outcry forced his resignation on December 18th 1935, when he was
succeeded by Anthony Eden who thus became Foreign Secretary for the
first time at the age of thirty-eight.

But progress towards enforcing the sanctions policy was not achieved and
soon the Abyssinian crisis was overshadowed by Germany's reoccupation
of the Rhineland in March 1936. British and French reactions to
this violation of the Locarno Treaty were divided and ineffective. Be-
hind them Mussolini pushed on with his conquest of Abyssinia, which
was completed on May 9th 1936. By early June Neville Chamberlain
was calling the sanctions policy midsummer madness, and on June 18th
Eden had to announce its abandonment to the House of Commons.

On July 18th Civil War broke out in Spain, after the failure of an
attempted coup by right-wing elements under General Franco against
the newly elected Republican Government which was supported by the
Socialists and Communists. At the end of August a Non-Intervention
Agreement was signed between Britain, Germany, Italy, Russia and
other powers, and the first meeting of the Non-Intervention Committee
took place in London on September 9th. By October violations of this
by Germany, Italy and Russia, in contrast to the strict self-enforcement
practised by Britain and France, had begun to tilt the policy in favour
of the rebels.

In December 1936 *came the midwinter distraction of the Abdication. Baldwin's handling of this crisis increased his prestige, but increased also his disinclination for foreign affairs during the last months of his Premiership. But if he gave little support, at least he did not directly interfere with the efforts of the Foreign Secretary and the Foreign Office to construct an effective policy against totalitarian aggression.*

On January 2nd 1937 *came the "Gentleman's Agreement" with Italy whereby both countries disclaimed their intention of altering the* status quo *in the Mediterranean or of indulging in unfriendly activities or hostile propaganda. On the day after its signature news came of a further large contingent of Italian soldiers arriving in Spain.*

The attempt to control these floods of "volunteers" and to enforce the Non-Intervention Agreement, and the question of British recognition of the Italian conquest of Abyssinia preoccupied the Foreign Office, and at this point the diary opens.

February 23rd 1937

A.E. returned to work today after fortnight's holiday on Riviera – looking very well. He was much disturbed at reading latest account of state of air re-armament and our inferiority to Germany in bombers. This account does not appear to tally with previous more favourable Air Ministry figures.

Lunched at his house. A.E. much interested and amused at German reports that there would be a change of policy when Baldwin went and that he, A.E., would go to another office.

This afternoon he expressed anxiety at unsatisfactory attitude of Belgium[1] who seemed to be slipping into the German camp largely owing to anti-French feeling. King Leopold very pro-Nazi. Belgian Ambassador[2] was sent for and confirmed rather than allayed this by speaking of Belgian nervousness at possibility of France wishing to go to help of Czechoslovakia and to send troops through Belgium, and even of French aggressive designs on Belgian territory!

February 24th

A.E. much touched at being cheered in the House of Commons this afternoon after his holiday – especially by the Labour benches.

Meeting to consider Belgian question – A.E., Van,[3] Cranborne,[4]

1. Belgium was a signatory of the Locarno Pact (1925) which guaranteed Germany's Western frontiers and the demilitarisation of the Rhineland – which Germany had re-occupied the previous March.
2. Baron Cartier de Marchienne.
3. Sir Robert Vansittart (later Lord Vansittart), Permanent Under-Secretary at Foreign Office.
4. Lord Cranborne, M.P. (now Lord Salisbury), Under-Secretary for Foreign Affairs.

Sargent,[1] Cadogan,[2] Malkin,[3] Strang[4] – danger of Belgium agreeing to bilateral non-aggression treaty with Germany unless restrained by Great Britain if situation allowed to drift. It was agreed (a) to ask King George if he would agree to receive King Leopold on a private visit of two or three days in early future so that opportunity would be afforded of talking to him (and Van Zeeland,[5] who might accompany him) and (b) to consider further possibility of offering Belgium a multilateral pact of non-aggression and non-interference in forestalment of bilateral pact with Germany and in place of Locarno guarantee by France and Great Britain which she no longer wanted.

February 25th

Italian press and opinion very excited at invitation to Emperor of Abyssinia to be represented at Coronation. Question of invitation had been carefully considered and it had been decided that in spite of obvious disadvantages it must be issued as Emperor was still *de jure* ruler and represented at Court: at King's recent reception of Heads of Missions, Dr Martin[6] had been allowed to present his credentials. Italy had not then objected: to omit him from Coronation would be to depart from rule of inviting representatives of *all* sovereigns recognised at Court: any such action moreover would have led to much criticism in Left circles here. A.E. and Bobbety quite firm that this decision was right. Van and Southern Department very anxious to find means of soothing Mussolini and of hastening recognition. A.E. determined to do nothing until after next Assembly at Geneva when question must be decided by Credentials Committee. An explanatory telegram sent to Drummond.[7]

A.E. wrote to Inskip[8] to suggest possibility of Air Defences of London being strengthened by addition of units of regular Army (at present they are undertaken by Territorials) with a view to increasing deterrent effect *vis-à-vis* Germany. At Cabinet yesterday he called

1. Sir Orme Sargent, Assistant Under-Secretary.
2. Sir Alexander Cadogan, Deputy Under-Secretary.
3. Sir H. Malkin, Legal Adviser to the Foreign Office.
4. William Strang (now Lord Strang), Counsellor at Foreign Office.
5. Paul Van Zeeland, Belgian Prime Minister.
6. Abyssinian Ambassador.
7. Sir Eric Drummond (later Lord Perth), Ambassador in Rome.
8. Sir Thomas Inskip (later Lord Caldecote), Minister for Co-ordination of Defence.

attention to apparent shortage of long-range bombers, but Swinton[1] explained that disparity was not actually so great owing to 200% reserves and to steady expansion of output.

We had a meeting this morning (A.E., Van, Bobbety,[2] Cadogan, Craigie[3] and myself) to consider message sent by Morgenthau, U.S. Secretary of Treasury, to Chancellor of Exchequer[4] inquiring what U.S.A. could do in conjunction with H.M.G. to avoid danger of war. A.E. had already discussed it with Chancellor and both agreed on importance of responding in spite of its vagueness and of unorthodox method employed (message given personally to Bewlay, Financial Counsellor at H.M. Embassy at Washington, who was told not to show it to anybody but to bring it straight to London – Morgenthau even offered him a destroyer to come in). A.E. very anxious to find means of co-operating with U.S.A. A draft reply is to be prepared.

A.E. spoke to Lord Wigram[5] about possibility of King inviting King of Belgians.

February 26th

Ribbentrop[6] came this morning. A.E. urged him to send a reply to our Five-Power Proposals[7] to which both France and Belgium had replied. Ribbentrop suggested possibility of dealing with Belgium first and independently and asked whether H.M.G. would object. A.E. said he would not object to anything in advance and urged that proposals should be put forward in writing. Ribbentrop undertook to try and secure this. (He returns to Germany on Monday.) A.E. was careful not to mention idea of a multilateral non-aggression pact but was struck by evident eagerness to deal with Belgium. Ribbentrop also referred to what he had said about Colonies to Halifax[8] ten days ago: A.E. said this question was governed by his statement in House of Commons last July which was not a personal statement of his but one carefully drafted and approved by whole Cabinet.

1. Lord Swinton, Secretary of State for Air.
2. Nickname of Lord Cranborne.
3. Sir Robert Craigie, Assistant Under-Secretary.
4. At this time Neville Chamberlain.
5. Lord-in-waiting to King George VI.
6. German Ambassador.
7. Proposals for the Locarno Nations in view of Germany's re-occupation of the Rhineland.
8. Lord President of the Council in Baldwin's Government.

February 27th

The King having agreed to receive King Leopold if he came on a private visit to London now, A.E. saw Belgian Ambassador, who said he felt sure he would like to do this but hoped that it would be possible to have a *State* visit in the autumn. He said King Leopold was staunchest friend of England. Ambassador said he had also seen Ribbentrop, who had spoken of importance of pressing on with a settlement at least as regards Belgium. Baron Cartier was unfavourably impressed by Ribbentrop's demeanour which smacked of "the spider and the fly".

The action of Franco in handing over to Germany the copper from the Rio Tinto mines which should all be sent to England where it is needed for our own re-armament was discussed today. A.E. annoyed at not having heard of it before, proposes to bring it before Cabinet on Wednesday with a view to drastic measures.

Discussion about Czechoslovakia (A.E., Van, Bobbety, Sargent, Cadogan, self). Should we urge Benes[1] to make terms with Germany? Bentinck[2] had reported that he believed agreement would be possible, but Phipps[3] was strongly opposed to our "butting in". Latter did not feel that Germany had at present any immediate designs on Czechoslovakia as she was not ready; obviously she wished, if she could, to detach Czechoslovakia from France: German policy aimed at concluding bilateral pacts with all her neighbours. There was some evidence that Benes was giving it out that he was refusing to make terms with Germany out of loyalty to his Western friends, although it was also understood that Jan Masaryk[4] (Czech Minister here) was in some sort of discussion with Ribbentrop. It was decided to let matters alone, but that if Benes should take this line with Newton,[5] our new Minister, he might indicate that we would like Czechoslovakia to be on good terms with all her neighbours. We should not take the responsibility of urging agreement as Benes might interpret this as encouragement to desert from France and

1. President of Czechoslovakia.
2. Sir Charles Bentinck, British Minister to Czechoslovakia 1930–1937.
3. Sir Eric Phipps, British Ambassador to Germany 1933–1937. Ambassador to France 1937–1939.
4. Son of Thomas Masaryk, first President of Czechoslovakia.
5. Basil Newton (afterwards Sir Basil), British Minister to Czechoslovakia 1937–1939.

Russia or as committing Great Britain to stand by him if negotiations failed.

A.E. feels fairly satisfied with general situation. Spain better owing to agreement on Non-Intervention and apparent desire of dictators to cut their losses there. Germany to all accounts playing for time as she is not yet ready – sobering effect of British Defence Loan abroad, although progress of re-armament especially in air leaves much to be desired – in France our excellent relations with Blum,[1] although we are very anxious about financial situation, the only threat to Blum – in America the inestimable value to us of goodwill of Roosevelt.

March 1st

We heard today the Emperor of Abyssinia is sending his son, the Crown Prince, to represent him at the Coronation. Whilst A.E. is opposed to giving way to the Italians over this, he and all feel that the presence of the Crown Prince (who would have to take precedence with other Royalties) as opposed to that of Martin would really be unnecessarily embarrassing. P.M. is anxious to find a way of dissuading Emperor from sending him. It has been decided that Cranborne should see Collier, who acts as an adviser to Emperor, and put to him the desirability of the Crown Prince not coming in all the circumstances and ask him if he could say a word to the Emperor.

The Belgian Ambassador came again and spoke of desirability of a British Minister visiting Brussels shortly.

Instructions sent to Ronnie Campbell[2] at Belgrade regarding Italo-Yugoslav negotiations. The Italians want an alliance but Yugoslavs wish to water this down. We suggested that they should take Anglo-Italian Declaration as a model, but they feel they must go rather further than this and at least agree to a treaty, although the terms should be as vague as possible.

March 2nd

Debate in the House of Commons on Foreign Affairs. A.E. very effective, especially about Spain and our obligations under Covenant

1. Léon Blum, French Prime Minister of the *Front Populaire*, 1936–June 1937.
2. Sir Ronald H. Campbell, British Minister to Yugoslavia 1935–1939.

and Locarno. Austen Chamberlain also – rather heavy and hard to hear. Bobbety wound up – not a very good speech.

March 3rd

Strang and I lunched with A.E. who wanted to discuss Leith-Ross[1] – Schacht[2] conversation and whether any further steps should be taken in this direction. A.E. thought of sending Schacht a written statement of our policy. Both Strang and I opposed to making any further use of this channel since we did not know how far Schacht really represents Hitler, who could at any moment disown him, whilst Leith-Ross had necessarily a Treasury rather than a Foreign Office view. Hence danger of Leith-Ross getting us involved in a negotiation behind the backs of the Wilhelmstrasse. Essence of Schacht's case was a demand for colonies – on that issue it was useless and dangerous to give him any encouragement, unless H.M.G. were prepared to cede colonies. If we were ready for any negotiations on such a basis, they should be taken up through the Ambassadors. Moreover, no British Government would cede Tanganyika; the only possibility was Cameroons, but that was a very small area and would pre-suppose France giving up her own much larger ex-German areas there. British policy required no fresh statement – it was contained in recent correspondence for Five-Power conversations as regards European settlement and in statement in House of Commons in July last as regards colonies. A.E. inclined to agree and favoured sending Schacht a simple message of thanks and saying that British policy had already been defined as above; at same time Cabinet should again consider question of colonies and make up its mind definitely. A.E. rather worried at way in which colonial question is being worked up in Germany (Hitler, Ribbentrop, Goering, Schacht, etc.). Strang said he thought that it was a sort of intermediate objective between rectifications of treaty provisions which only affected German territory (and which were now exhausted) and violation of foreign territory and that campaign was largely intended for home consumption, to blame the hardships of the Four Years' Plan on the foreigners and possibly to alienate sympathy abroad from Great Britain as the largest colony-owner, whilst German preparations were pushed on.

We also discussed danger to Blum Government in France arising

1. Sir Frederick Leith-Ross, Chief Economic Adviser to H.M.G.
2. President of Reichsbank and German Minister of Economics 1934–1937.

from financial situation. A.E. had talked to Chancellor yesterday about possibility of helping, but he had seen none. Blum unlikely to abandon *Front Populaire*[1] and form a National Government *à la* Ramsay MacDonald. If Blum resigned or were overthrown and a National Government were formed without him, most serious "troubles" might be expected as working classes would not stand a repetition of February 1934. Only hope seemed to be that Blum should impose a pause in social legislation on his Government.

March 4th

A.E. saw Leith-Ross this morning, when it was decided that the latter should send only a brief interim reply to Schacht to the effect that he had reported the upshot of their conversation to the Chancellor, that Eden had been away and that after Leith-Ross himself had returned from his trip to Geneva for the Raw Materials Committee, he hoped to send him a message. Meanwhile, A.E. contemplates drawing up a statement of British policy which would be sent to Neurath[2] in reference to the Schacht talks. He wishes to stop the Schacht–Leith-Ross exchanges and to bring any discussion into regular channels.

March 5th

A.E. said he regretted Neville Chamberlain's aggressive speech on Imperial Preference with its attack on Sir A. Sinclair.[3] He feared that when Neville Chamberlain became Prime Minister affairs would go less smoothly in the country than with Baldwin – there would be better administration and more discipline in the Cabinet, but he would not be able to resist scoring off the Opposition.

We discussed a draft Cabinet Paper on Belgium prepared by Strang on the pros and cons of a general guarantee pact of Belgian independence by all her neighbours (which is what Belgium wants) and a general pact of non-aggression and non-interference without a guarantee. We agreed that what must be avoided is a bilateral

1. Name for the parties of the Left who had combined during the election; the Communists later refused to join Blum's Government, which was a coalition of Socialists and Radical-Socialists.
2. Baron Von Neurath, German Foreign Minister.
3. Leader of Liberal Party 1935–1945. (Later Lord Thurso.)

German-Belgian guarantee pact which is what Germany wishes to give, but A.E. is rather divided in his mind as to merits of other two; Malkins now favours the former. He thinks of paying a visit to Brussels in April. Continued anxiety about French financial situation. I hear via Elisabeth Bibesco[1] that Blum himself is now seriously concerned. Leith-Ross is lunching with Blum on Sunday.

March 6th

A fuss over the Duke of Kent who, after going to his sister-in-law in Munich, is now going on to Florence and may be going on to Rome, although the King knew nothing about it, and the Foreign Office had asked them not to. After consultation with Lord Wigram we sent a telegram to Consul at Florence to find out his intentions and to warn him that a visit to Rome might cause comment.

A.E. preparing speech for Aberdeen on Monday.

March 7th

I prepared a memo for A.E. on our German policy.[2]

I went to his house this evening to go through the final version of his speech. He has much improved it.

A.E. spoke about his lack of confidence in Van's judgment and said he thought it quite likely that Neville Chamberlain when he became Prime Minister would retire him. He did not think he was any longer in a fit state of health for his work. He feared, however, Van's retirement would be interpreted in Germany as foreshadowing a change of policy. I said I doubted this and in any case I didn't see that it mattered: there would in fact be no change of policy. Van's refusal to go to Paris when offered it, and urged by both A.E. and the P.M. in December and January last, made his position a weak one. A.E. said he wished he could find him another job.

He mentioned that he had discovered that it was Van, and not Simon[3] (who was in Scotland), who had issued a statement in the papers that A.E. "had no authority to negotiate when he was on his visit to Berlin".[4]

1. Princess Bibesco, daughter of H. H. Asquith.   2. See Appendix B.
3. Sir John Simon, at that date Foreign Secretary.
4. This refers to A.E.'s visit to Berlin in February 1934 as Lord Privy Seal. He was to explain H.M.G.'s Memorandum of January 1934, which was a

No sooner had I left than I was rung up from the Foreign Office with a message from Paris asking me to show A.E. the latest telegrams about the new French Loan and the wish of the French Treasury for certain facilities on the London market. Leith-Ross and the Embassy urged that these should be given, but the Chancellor and the Treasury officials saw difficulties and were refusing. Gwatkin[1] and I took the telegrams to A.E., who was dining with Philip Sassoon[2] before leaving for Aberdeen at 10 p.m. He rang up the Chancellor and asked him to do what he could to help in view of political importance of stability in France. Latter undertook to do what he could, but did not like it and believed the Loan would fail in any case.

March 10th

A.E. returned last night – very satisfied with Aberdeen meeting – hall quite crowded, loudly applauded: very good articles in provincial papers. He wonders whether he should not give up Liverpool meeting next month as he has not anything particular to say. Roger Lumley[3] inclined to favour this, but I urged him to hold it as he need not always make a topical speech and I think it important that he should speak regularly and be seen in different parts of the country, especially in view of German hopes that he is in process of being "liquidated". Rex Leeper[4] thinks this too. I am sure it is most important that he should build up as broad a popular backing as possible. You cannot conduct a Foreign Policy in a democratic country without popular understanding and approval. These speeches strengthen his position in the country, in the House, and also abroad: they also strengthen his hand in the Cabinet, where all are not too pleased at his growing strength.

He was pleased with my memo and said he had read Trevelyan's *Life of Grey* in the train and was much struck by the similarity of their problems, also that my advice to him was exactly what Grey

---

reply to Hitler's walk-out from the Geneva Disarmament Conference and from the League of Nations the previous October.

1. F. T. A. Ashton-Gwatkin, Counsellor at Foreign Office.
2. Sir Philip Sassoon, M.P., later Minister of Works.
3. M.P. (later Lord Scarbrough), P.P.S. to Anthony Eden until appointed Governor of Bombay.
4. Sir Reginald Leeper, then Head of Press Department at Foreign Office.

had himself thought. What Belgium was then, Czechoslovakia is now. I think he is really fairly confident now that he is on the right lines – an honest and clear policy steadily pursued. He is worried, however, that re-armament, especially the Air Force and anti-air defence, is not proceeding faster.

He went to see the King[1] today and found him looking much better than before – very keen and taking great interest and much more self-assured. The King said the Italians were behaving ridiculously over the Coronation.

Foreign Affairs Committee of the Cabinet met at 6 to consider Belgium. They decided in favour of general pact of non-aggression rather than general treaty of guarantee – but were opposed to A.E. going to Brussels himself. A.E. is not now anxious to go and is convinced that the country dislikes such visits abroad.

March 11th

Discussion about Spain this morning. A.E., Plymouth,[2] Cranborne, Mounsey,[3] Leeper. A.E. disturbed at slowness with which control scheme[4] is being brought into force and at likelihood of Franco taking Madrid very shortly – anxious to establish whether Italians are still sending men into Spain.[5] He is still convinced that Non-Intervention was the right policy and that the alternatives of intervention or warning-off of Italians last summer would have created grave risk of war in a case where no British interests were involved.

Discussion about Yugoslav-Italian negotiations this evening. A.E. very anxious to prevent Yugoslavia being dragged into Italian camp, feels that Prince Regent[6] is weak and nervous and that he requires soothing treatment, but sees difficulty of being too categoric with him. He wonders whether a Mediterranean Pact might be a solution by merging Yugoslav-Italian relations into something bigger. Italy is

1. King George VI succeeded Edward VIII on December 11th 1936.
2. Lord Plymouth, Under-Secretary for Foreign Affairs (in House of Lords).
3. Sir G. A. Mounsey, Assistant Under-Secretary at Foreign Office.
4. The Non-Intervention Committee's scheme of March 8th for Spanish borders to be watched by international observers, all foreign troops to be withdrawn, observers to be stationed on ships trading with Spain, and for the coast to be patrolled.
5. By this time an estimated 80,000 Italians and 30,000 Germans were serving in the Nationalist Army.
6. Prince Paul of Yugoslavia.

at present asking Yugoslavia for consultation before Yugoslavia concludes any arrangement with any other state and no further fortification on Italo-Yugoslav frontier (Italian side is already heavily fortified, but Yugoslav side has no fortifications).

March 12th

Discussion about Abyssinia and method by which Negus[1] is to be excluded from League Assembly next May. A.E. hates the business, but all feel that it is necessary. In any case, unlike last July, it can now definitely be said that Negus exercises no control over Abyssinia: this would not necessarily involve recognition of Italian conquest. Everybody disgusted at Italian atrocities at Addis Ababa following attempt on Graziani.[2] Feeling is very high against Italians in House of Commons as well as in country. *Times* is to publish a most damaging report from its own correspondent tomorrow, and Archbishop of Canterbury,[3] who came to see A.E. today, said he was going to raise it in the Lords.

We heard today that German reply about Five-Power conversations had been handed to Phipps – a first fruit of our firmer German policy?

A.E. rather worried about Spanish situation – the fall of Madrid seems imminent and Italian troops are prominently active on Franco's side. The Spanish Ambassador[4] came today to say that his Government wished to raise question of intervention by these regular Italian military forces.

March 13th

Ribbentrop came this morning and brought a copy of German reply with him, but as neither he nor A.E. had had time to read it yet, they did not discuss it, although Ribbentrop took credit for expediting its arrival. Ribbentrop said Hitler was still most anxious for settlement with Great Britain, but worried at situation. A.E., speaking personally and not officially, recalled how in years before 1914 Germany had antagonised opinion here by challenging our position at sea and said there was a danger that present German campaign about return of colonies, which was now being so vociferously conducted against

1. The Emperor of Abyssinia. 2. Italian Viceroy in Abyssinia.
3. Cosmo Gordon Lang. 4. Señor Azcarate y Florez.

Great Britain, might have a similar effect: colonial question was not one which affected Great Britain alone. Ribbentrop said he realised that time was needed but hoped that two, three or even four years would see change in opinion here. A.E. gained impression that Germany was both puzzled and rather anxious.

A.E. fairly satisfied about position as regards Germany and confident that our present policy is right and must be persistently and calmly pursued; annoyed and disgusted with Italy – fuss over Negus and Coronation on which he refuses to be apologetic, atrocities in Addis Ababa, press polemics of Gayda,[1] etc., regarding our re-armament programme, Mussolini's attempt to blackmail Yugoslavia into exclusive alliance, behaviour in Spain – but convinced that she must be over-reaching herself economically and that we must not run after her, but keep her "lean" by refusing any credit facilities; pleased at signs of better feeling in Japan afforded by Sato's[2] speeches.

March 15th

Discussion of draft Cabinet paper regarding possible reply to Schacht proposals. I emphasised danger of encouraging discussion of colonies with Germany – we can never give up Tanganyika and have very little to offer in the Cameroons, where the principal beneficiaries were the French. Both Imperialists and Labour would unite to oppose cession; Dominions would also strongly oppose. Germans want *full* sovereignty, moreover, and not merely a mandate. To offer settlement in Cameroons would be to ask France to bear chief loss and might play into German hands by making bad blood between us. A.E. inclined to agree. He and Strang think German reply on Five Power proposals quite unsatisfactory as it would rule out League of Nations and prevent anybody helping anybody in event of sudden aggression.

Sandler, Swedish Minister for Foreign Affairs, arrived today on official visit. A.E. was very pleased with their talk.

March 16th

Meeting on question of advisability of attaching a British agent to Franco in Spain. (A.E., Cadogan, Cranborne, Mounsey, self.) Pro-

1. Virginio Gayda, mouthpiece of Mussolini in *Giornale D'Italia*.
2. Japanese Foreign Minister.

posed to appoint Sir R. Hodgson[1] – not to involve recognition but for protection of British interests. A.E. satisfied that this could be defended in House of Commons – decided to ask Chilton's[2] views as to Franco's probable attitude to this.

Official dinner at Foreign Office to Sandler – just before dinner we heard Austen Chamberlain was dead. Neville had rung up A.E. to tell him of it and to say he could not come to dinner. A.E. very shocked.

I had a long talk to Dalton[3] after dinner. Dalton expressed anxiety lest Neville Chamberlain when he became Prime Minister would favour idea of direct Anglo-German agreement: I assured him that he need have no fear of this and that on the contrary he fully shared A.E.'s views on Foreign Policy and would back them up much more vigorously than Stanley Baldwin. I said that Neville Chamberlain would be much more aggressive to Opposition on Home affairs – this Dalton said he did not mind – but that on Foreign Affairs there was really nothing to divide them. A.E. was working for a national Foreign Policy: if we were to impress foreigners we must have a continuity of Foreign Policy which went on whatever party was in power: this was largely the case now. Dalton said he fully supported re-armament but he would like us to undertake to defend Czechoslovakia. He thought clarity most important element in foreign affairs. I said I agreed but danger was that if we said as much as that we should split country. There were, after all, the Londonderrys[4] on one side and the Lansburys[5] on the other who would not stand for this policy. Dalton said Lansbury was of no importance. I said I thought the Protocol was undoubtedly right but there must be no doubt about the willingness of all to fulfil it: we had now built up a clear foreign policy during the past year based on certain definite undertakings – Leamington – we did not feel we could go further yet. Dalton, speaking of France, said Vincent Auriol[6] was like

1. Sir Robert Hodgson, British Agent to Nationalist Government 1937–1939 and Chargé d'Affaires at Burgos February–April 1939.
2. Sir Henry Chilton, British Ambassador to Spain 1935–1938.
3. Hugh Dalton (later Lord Dalton), M.P. and Chancellor of Exchequer in post-war Labour Government.
4. Marquess of Londonderry, Minister for Air 1931–1935, apologist for Hitler.
5. George Lansbury, Labour M.P. and noted pacifist.
6. Socialist Minister of Finance in Blum Government. President of France 1947–1954.

Snowden[1] and did not understand economic and financial questions which Blum did. He asked whether it was true that H.M.G. had put pressure on France to loosen her ties with Soviets. I said certainly not: they well realised importance of keeping Soviets in line. He expressed some anxiety lest, if Franco won in Spain, Germany would use him to squeeze France; I said we doubted whether on a long view it made much difference which side won because we did not believe that Spain would ever depart from traditional aloofness and neutrality although, on a short view, Franco's victory would be a fillip to dictators. Dalton spoke of Denmark and hopeless situation in which she was as a result of her weakness: he hoped if Stauning[2] came here we would impress this on him. A useful talk – which Dalton told A.E. afterwards "had taught him a lot"![3]

After all had gone, I sat up with A.E. while he wrote to Lady Chamberlain[4] and Neville Chamberlain – he is going to broadcast tomorrow night.

March 18th

A.E. went to D.P.R.[5] and spoke to me afterwards of the incredible slowness of War Office in carrying out their re-armament programme. Admiralty and Air Ministry doing well but Anti-Aircraft defences, which are under War Office, very backward.

Foreign Affairs Committee of Cabinet this afternoon to discuss possible reply to Schacht proposals and question of policy as regards German colonies.

A.E.'s chief anxiety now Spain and complications of Italian troops. I mentioned danger of Italian troops being severely defeated and risk of Mussolini, who can scarcely admit their defeat, then intervening directly against Valencia. If Mussolini really did this, then A.E. thinks he would have to be rounded on and made to climb down. He is convinced of fundamental weakness of Italy and is always regretting the lost opportunity afforded by Abyssinia of pulling him up. We heard today that Prince of Piedmont[6] will probably not come

1. Philip Snowden, Labour Chancellor of Exchequer 1929–1931.
2. Danish Foreign Minister.
3. O.H. discusses some of these issues in a memo given at Appendix C.
4. Widow of Sir Austen Chamberlain.
5. Defence Policy and Re-armament Committee of the Cabinet.
6. Eldest son of King of Italy, later King Umberto.

to Coronation because of the Emperor having been asked. A.E. rightly holds this to be a matter of complete indifference. He is simply horrified and disgusted at the Italians' behaviour in Addis Ababa: we now hear they have shot poor old Dr Martin's two sons.

The proposal to appoint a British agent to Franco – to facilitate protection of British interests and collection of intelligence – is still under consideration – it would, of course, be informal and not involve recognition – but I am doubtful whether this would not provoke undue hostility in Parliament where feeling runs very high. A.E. himself now rather uncertain.

March 19th

Spanish Ambassador called to complain that Italians were now importing Eritreans into Spanish Morocco.

Further hitch over control scheme owing to difficulties about nationalities of resident controllers at ports – Palermo, Cherbourg, Gibraltar, etc. A.E. decided it would be simpler to have nationals of small states only and saw five Ambassadors this afternoon – ten minutes each – to urge this solution on them.

Foreign Affairs Committee yesterday decided that we could never cede Tanganyika, but we might, as part of a general settlement, cede our bits of Cameroons if French were ready to cede their West Africa ex-German colonies – this is to be explained to the French – not with a view to urging them to do so but to make clear our own position. A.E. insisted that before we go further we must clear our own minds and there can be no question of pressing France (who have got much less colonial area than Great Britain) to pay the principal price.

Grandi[1] called to complain of Dean of Winchester[2] having called Mussolini a madman. A.E., whilst expressing regret at *any* polemics of this sort, countered by inquiring what Mussolini meant by speaking of us in his last speech in Tripoli as "a more or less great democracy".

March 20th

O.H. to Secretary of State

Dr Weizmann,[3] who is an old friend of mine, came to see me yesterday

1. Count Grandi, Italian Ambassador 1932–1939. 2. Dr Selwyn.
3. Dr Chaim Weizmann, scientist and British subject, who became first President of Israel.

as he wanted to lay before me certain considerations in connection with the forthcoming report of the Royal Commission on Palestine.[1] From what Dr Weizmann had gathered during his last hearing before the Royal Commission and also from a private conversation he had had with one of the Royal Commissioners, the Commission may eventually recommend the following solution of the problem: that the boundaries between Palestine and Transjordan should be changed and that the hill country of Palestine, which was almost entirely Arab in population, should be included in Transjordan, leaving the plains where all the Jewish settlements are in Palestine, whilst Jerusalem, Nazareth and Hebron should be in a special category of holy places under a special regime. This solution would have the advantage of leaving Palestine, as reconstructed, almost entirely Jewish, where the principal of the absorptive capacity of the country could be applied to Jewish immigration, whilst in the Arab areas there would be no threat of Jewish domination or immigration. Dr Weizmann was extremely interested by this suggestion, but had not yet been able to study it in all its aspects. At first sight he was rather attracted by it, and he was anxious that the Foreign Office should also turn it over in their minds. He was inclined to think that it could be made acceptable to the Jews, and from such investigations as his people had made among the neighbouring Arab countries they would also probably be prepared to welcome it, since each of these countries, Egypt, Syria and Iraq notably, were now largely concerned with their own internal affairs and did not wish to be involved in difficulties with His Majesty's Government over Palestine.

I must say that I myself am rather attracted by the idea at first sight, as it would seem to have the elements of permanent solution. We should then have the two mandates side by side, one almost entirely Jewish, the other entirely Arab. The effect of the alteration of the boundaries would be to leave some 200,000 Arabs in the Jewish part of Palestine, whilst the remainder of the Arab population, some 600,000, I think, would be in the hills. Obviously provision would have to be made for Customs and economic arrangements between the two territories, but it would have this advantage, that both sides would then have removed from them the nightmare of domination by the other, and would have equal access to the holy places, and the unequal clash between two cultures based on conceptions differing from each other by centuries would be removed. It strikes me, again at first sight, as a very statesmanlike attempt at a permanent solution which deserves very careful consideration.

1. Appointed following Arab disorders in Palestine April–October 1936 in protest against continued Jewish emigration. The Jews retaliated with terrorist activity. The Commission reported in July 1937.

March 22nd

In view of defeats of Spanish insurgents before Madrid, and especially of Italian contingent, A.E. is now disinclined to proceed with appointment of British agent to France, which he feels, rightly I am sure, would not justify the outcry it would be certain to cause here. A.E. received deputation of T.U.C. (including Citrine[1] and Bevin[2]) this evening: they expressed misgivings about Spain and lack of energy shown by H.M.G. in implementing control scheme. They were very anxious for more drastic action against dictators, especially against Mussolini, if he now broke Non-Intervention agreement. A.E. replied very sympathetically and convinced them, I think, of the sincerity of his efforts to make the control scheme work. He insisted on uselessness of a policy of threats unless we were prepared to carry them out – viz. by war – T.U.C. leaders quite agreed and assured him of support of bulk of Labour Movement in a vigorous policy.[3]

Woermann (German Counsellor) raised with Bland[4] today question whether representatives of Germany at Coronation would not go in front of Royal representatives of smaller power; when told that they would probably not, he said Ribbentrop would come to see the Secretary of State about it.

A.E. dined at Belgian Embassy to meet King Leopold who arrived today.

March 23rd

A.E. very favourably impressed with King Leopold. He found him well informed about Treaty position but inclined to be anti-French.

Crisis in Non-Intervention Committee owing to refusal of Mussolini to agree now to any discussion of withdrawal of volunteers (although he originally proposed it) or to answer about proposed

1. Walter Citrine (later Lord Citrine), General Secretary of T.U.C. 1926–1946.
2. Ernest Bevin, General Secretary of Transport and General Workers' Union. Foreign Secretary 1946–1950.
3. The Labour Party in Parliament had begun to oppose Non-Intervention.
4. Sir Neville Bland, at this time head of Treaty Department at Foreign Office.

31

employment of representatives of smaller states instead of Great Powers as observers in ports. Mussolini has returned unexpectedly from Libya in a towering rage at defeat of Italians before Madrid. French Ambassador very worried, says France will almost certainly denounce Non-Intervention if Italy holds up operation of control scheme. A.E. says we should do so too.

I lunched with A.E. today and discussed political situation here. He fears for health of Neville Chamberlain and feels it is perhaps a pity that a younger man is not available. He agreed with me that Sam Hoare[1] would be fatal, Walter Elliot[2] not very effective, Inskip a possibility, Duff[3] disappointing at War Office and will probably be shifted, Kingsley Wood[4] very bad influence in foreign affairs and cynical professional politician. I spoke of A.E.'s own very strong prospects in two or three years' time when Neville Chamberlain goes, if peace is preserved. He would have confidence of country in foreign affairs and by being Prime Minister could still carry on his policy, whilst he would bring a fresh mind to internal affairs which would then require driving forward. A.E. said he had no wish to move from Foreign Office. I said that just as Stanley Baldwin[5] had confidence of wider public than his own party in home affairs, so he, A.E., had the same position in foreign affairs. Whereas he had been made use of to catch votes in last election, he had now outgrown those who had put him in and who now found in him a master – hence these tears at his speeches which were making him stronger and stronger. I think he realises this.

We spoke of the weakness of the Labour Opposition – he likes Dalton and thinks him a bigger and better man than Attlee,[6] although he has very bad platform manner. He likes Grenfell.[7]

I said that when new Government is formed, Harry Crookshank[8] ought to be included. He would be first-class at War Office – gets on with soldiers, very able and active. A.E. said that might be a good

1. Sir Samuel Hoare, M.P. (later Lord Templewood), First Lord of Admiralty in Baldwin's Government.
2. M.P. (later Lord Elliot), Secretary of State for Scotland.
3. Alfred Duff Cooper, M.P. (later Lord Norwich), Minister for War.
4. M.P., Minister of Health.
5. Prime Minister since 1935. He resigned May 1937.
6. (Later Lord Attlee.) Leader of the Opposition 1935–1940.
7. David Grenfell, Labour M.P. for Gower 1922–1959.
8. Captain H. F. C. Crookshank (later Lord Crookshank), Conservative M.P., Secretary for Mines 1935–1939.

idea; H.C. had done so well over coal-mines. He wants Colville[1] also to be pushed on – would like to see Bobbety in Cabinet but difficult as Plymouth ought to be promoted first being much senior. I said Bobbety had anyway an assured political future before him and plenty of time. Roger Lumley will probably leave us, he said, to go to Bombay – we agreed what a great loss this would be.

March 24th

Just before Cabinet we learnt from Italian Embassy that Mussolini agreed to the appointment of neutral observers for Spanish control scheme, thus allowing scheme to come into force. This much relieves tension as question of withdrawal of volunteers can be left now for a few days while we hope Mussolini cools down.

A.E. saw Corbin[2] and handed him our reply agreeing to French proposal to release Belgian Government from Locarno obligations – Cabinet decided to hold up all question of appointing a British Agent to Franco.

March 25th

Dined with Francis Rodd,[3] who thought our appointment of Nevile Henderson to Berlin was excellent. Lord Rennell[4] there too, who spoke of our lack of contact with Hitler, and said he believed that Hitler, unlike Mussolini, was a man one could influence and work with if one could make a contact with him. Both he and Francis agreed as to hopelessness of Ribbentrop. Francis said that he thought Mussolini would soon have to be brought up short or we should have great trouble with him. Rennell reiterated importance of making some friendly reference to Germany – we were too cold and too remote.

March 26th

A.E. went to see Chancellor who is in bed with gout, although this is not known. He found him in very good spirits and looking forward

1. D. J. Colville, M.P., Financial Secretary to the Treasury.
2. Charles Corbin, French Ambassador 1933–1940.
3. Now Lord Rennell. Formerly in the Foreign Office.
4. First Lord Rennell of Rodd. British Ambassador to Italy 1908–1919.

D.D.O.H.—C

to becoming Prime Minister. He told A.E. he intended to give him much more support at F.O. than he had had hitherto. He had also been impressed by memo A.E. had sent him on necessity of relaxing our Ottawa obligations somewhat in order to facilitate foreign economic relations. Chancellor agreed as to necessity of some relaxation, although he believed trade ties did help to keep the Dominions with us. I asked A.E. if Neville Chamberlain had made up his Government yet but he said that he had not mentioned it and A.E. thought it better not to ask. He did not believe Neville Chamberlain had spoken to anyone about it. Neville Chamberlain had not anyway suggested a change at F.O. A.E. thought Neville Chamberlain had makings of a really great Prime Minister if only his health held out. I said "if he isn't too grim": but A.E. thought this need not necessarily matter: he had a grip of affairs which Stanley Baldwin had never had.

A.E. gave instructions to damp down press as much as possible over Mussolini. The press is playing into his hands at present by attacking him so vociferously and he is using it to strengthen himself at home, just as he was able to do over sanctions. I hear opinion in House of Commons is almost bellicose about Italy.

March 31st

A.E. goes off to Yorks. tomorrow. We lunched with him and Mrs Eden. A.E. in good spirits, believes general situation getting slowly better in spite of occasional setbacks. Germany strangely quiet – is this due to increasing realisation of our re-armament? Franco's side in Spain doing less well. A.E. definitely now wants Government side to win. He had a long talk this morning with Ogilvie-Forbes,[1] who also believes a Government win would be best result but says it is impossible to forecast. Government side are now in much better fettle and a real army is being formed. Ogilvie-Forbes confirms that Italians had run like hares in recent defeat near Madrid, but he is nervous how Mussolini will take it. Del Vayo[2] was doing all he could to prevent Press from saying too much about it and so dangerously fanning Italian wrath. Rex Leeper is to pass this on to our own Left

1. Sir George Ogilvie-Forbes, at this time British *Chargé d'Affaires* at Madrid.
2. Alvarez del Vayo, Minister of Foreign Affairs in the Spanish Government.

34

press. A.E. very anxious to get control scheme in operation as soon
as possible, but this apparently cannot be for at least another ten days
owing to administrative difficulties.

April 5th

A.E. returned from Yorkshire today. He was horrified at reading
dispatches from Bond[1] at Addis Ababa describing massacres. He
would like to withdraw all our Consuls and publish the dispatches.
He is sending them to the Prime Minister personally.

He sent for Cartier and told him that Prime Minister had authorised
him to visit Brussels on April 26th. Corbin also came on his return
from Paris and confirmed that French Government saw eye to eye
with us about Spain – viz. that if Italy were to send further volunteers
in spite of Non-Intervention Agreement, a most grave situation
would arise requiring consultation, but Paris had some hope from
what Italian Ambassador had said that Mussolini might now be
willing to discuss withdrawal of volunteers.

A.E. undertook to see Grandi tomorrow and urge this course.

April 6th

Foreign Affairs Committee of Cabinet met this morning to consider
question of pursuing Schacht – Leith-Ross discussions and general
question of colonial restitution. A.E. found his colleagues disappointing and discouraging. They all harped on need of "getting into
contact" with Germany as if we hadn't been trying to do that for the
past year! It was decided to take French Government into our confidence first by explaining frankly our views for a general settlement.
As regards colonies, Great Britain would not return Tanganyika,
but would be prepared to return small West African colonies if France
were prepared to return Cameroons and Togoland; we would be
prepared to consider economic concessions to Germany instead of
colonial restitution.[2] A.E. very anxious to deal in future with Neurath
and not Schacht, whose official position is uncertain and whom
German Government might repudiate as soon as they had learned
what we were prepared to do. Altogether, A.E. believes his colleagues
to be in too much of a hurry and too flabby. They profess to be afraid

1. W. L. Bond, British Consul-General at Addis Ababa.
2. See Appendix D.

for the consequences of bad winter in Germany owing to internal difficulties if no agreement is reached.

A.E. found House of Commons very noisy and critical at question time today; atmosphere very hostile to Italy and tendency to regard our policy as weak. House of Commons getting very bellicose, as though voting for re-armament is same thing as being re-armed.

Grandi came. A.E. found him very unforthcoming on subject of withdrawal of volunteers. We began preparation of Liverpool speech. A.E. thinks he should put in a warning to Italy about Spain, also statement of what we can *not* agree to with Germany (viz. exclusion of League).

April 7th

A move in Cabinet this morning by Hoare and Simon to secure appointment of British agent to Franco and to give him belligerent rights owing to difficulties arising from his blockade of Bilbao. Question was referred to Cabinet Committee this afternoon when, however, it was again decided not to appoint agents. I am sure this is right as such a move at present moment when Franco is doing less well would be regarded as giving him encouragement.

April 8th

I lunched with Tyrrell[1] and Walford Selby[2] – both insistent on importance of doing nothing to loosen Franco-Soviet or Franco-Czech pacts as they hear Soviet and German General Staffs are ready to get together again. A.E. very anxious over slow progress being made in getting Spanish control scheme into force. It is now only a question of getting the observers on to the spot, but this will take another ten days. Delay very dangerous owing to risk of Mussolini sending in more "volunteers" on one pretext or another.

Brussels visit announced tonight.

1. Lord Tyrrell, formerly Ambassador to France and Under Secretary at Foreign Office.
2. Sir Walford Selby, Minister in Vienna 1933–1937.

April 10th

A.E. in bed with a cold, but he had to get up for a meeting with Hoare and Runciman[1] about Bilbao. Franco now threatens to stop any British ship entering port; ships are therefore being ordered by our Navy to stay at Bayonne pending a decision. A.E. in favour of refusing to recognise blockade and of concentrating overwhelming British forces to act as escort and overawe Franco. Runciman also favours this. The Admiralty as usual are for doing nothing and accepting blockade. It was decided to refer matter to a special Cabinet tomorrow and meanwhile send for *Hood*[2] from Gibraltar.

He put finishing touches to Liverpool speech.

Grandi came and offered to agree to discuss withdrawal of volunteers at Non-Intervention Committee provided Soviet Ambassador agreed to withdraw offensive note sponsoring Spanish Government's accusation that Italy had sent in more volunteers.

April 11th

Meeting at Foreign Office at four (Cranborne, Van, Mounsey, Howard,[3] Fitzmaurice,[4] self) about Bilbao. We rang up Ambassador at Hendaye and found that Santander is still open to shipping and the land communications between Santander and Bilbao are also open. Therefore, it is proposed to divert shipping to Santander. Further problem how to get iron ore belonging to British interests from Bilbao which is being bombed daily.

Cabinet met from six to eight and decided to divert shipping as above and to warn Franco at same time that we cannot recognise his right to interfere.

April 12th

Prime Minister sent for A.E. this morning and said he must ask him to stay over question time in House of Commons in case Opposition

1. Sir W. Runciman (later Lord Runciman), President of Board of Trade until Chamberlain became Prime Minister in May.
2. The Battlecruiser *Hood*, then our largest warship.
3. Sir Douglas Howard, then First Secretary at Foreign Office.
   Sir Gerald Fitzmaurice, Third Legal Adviser to Foreign Office.

move adjournment when Prime Minister makes his statement on decision regarding Bilbao, as Prime Minister does not feel able to take it. If no adjournment is moved, A.E. can go to Liverpool by aeroplane and yet be in time for his meeting. A.E. very annoyed at this further instance of lack of help given by Prime Minister who, however, confessed to him that he had not been able to take in the question at all!

I lunched with A.E. at Carlton. He spoke, as he has often before, of his reluctance to continue his life in office which now leaves him no leisure for reading or for anything he wants to do. I sympathised but said there could be no question of retiring at this stage. He would not really be happy if he were in the Lords or held a sinecure office like Halifax. If he were not in an executive position like Foreign Office he would be merely chafing, and if he went altogether out of politics, he would soon miss it. He complained of the extra burden thrown upon him now by Parliament, quite different from what it was only a few years ago; if only he were able to devote himself to Foreign Office work, he would be happy, but continual debates and harassing P.Q.s made life almost intolerable. He admitted, however, that he could not possibly go now because it would be letting Neville Chamberlain down with a bump. I told him, as I have told him before, that he will probably find himself Prime Minister before very long. He said he would at least like to be Foreign Secretary when this country has re-armed.

We discussed a little the question whether H.M.G. should publish the Consul's reports on the Addis massacres. A.E. would like to publish but feels really no useful purpose would now be served. Ramsay MacDonald favours publishing: Halifax also, and urged on A.E. that on a long view H.M.G. do stand for decency and morality and they must not be like the Pope. He would publish in spite of any immediate political disadvantages. Neville Chamberlain, however, is opposed to doing anything. (We have ascertained that neither U.S.A. nor France intend to publish.) I said to publish would mean finally burning our boats as regards Italy and goodbye to any hope of facilities or concessions to British interests; I doubted whether it was worth it as it could not help the Abyssinians.

The Opposition in the end asked not for an adjournment but for a day to discuss Bilbao, so A.E. was able to leave by air for Liverpool.

April 13th

A.E. flew back from Liverpool: very satisfied with meeting – most enthusiastic reception – noted especially loud applause at all references to keeping out of entanglements in Spain.

Debate fixed for tomorrow. Prime Minister refuses to take part and it has been decided that Simon shall speak first and A.E. wind up.

April 14th

Debate. Attlee opened with attack on Government on grounds of cowardice and pro-Franco sympathy for failing to use Navy to enable British ships to use Bilbao. Simon followed, very much interrupted, with strong case on behalf of Government showing that exactly same procedure of non-protection had been followed at Ceuta with roles of Government and insurgents reversed last summer. Best speech that of Winston[1] on behalf of strict non-intervention. A.E. wound up – promised that shipping would be protected up to three-mile limit.

April 15th

A.E.'s misgivings regarding Admiralty attitude towards Bilbao partly confirmed by telegram from *Hood* saying that blockade not effective. He thinks shipping must now be authorised to proceed. Accounts of mines also seem to have been much exaggerated.

Non-Intervention Committee met to fix midnight next Monday for entry into force of scheme.

April 17th

A.E. still not satisfied with Admiralty over Bilbao. It was decided yesterday that British ships must be protected up to three-mile limit, although they should be advised not to proceed to Bilbao at present. A.E. does not wish Bilbao to starve and very doubtful how far blockade exists in reality. It is very difficult to get facts out of Admiralty at all.

I lunched with Paul Emrys-Evans[2] who was very anxious to get

1. Winston Churchill was then back-bench Member for Epping.
2. Conservative M.P. for South Derbyshire 1931–1945.

Conservative Central Office to issue Leamington and Bradford speeches in pamphlet form as he finds they are not sufficiently known in the country, and speakers are always asking for such guidance. Hacking[1] at Central Office strangely inactive about A.E.'s speeches which are the best propaganda the Party could wish for. He said he was convinced public opinion here was now united on two things – determination to keep out of trouble in Spain and opposition to any cession of colonies to Germany.

April 19th[2]

Opposition moved adjournment of House of Commons over Bilbao again – debate to take place tomorrow – all due to Hoare's handling of P.Q.s and impression he gave of wishing to *prevent* ships from going to Basque ports (which is, in fact, what he really wants to do). I begged A.E. to refuse to take part in debate again and to insist on it being taken by Hoare – Board of Trade – as it is not a matter of foreign policy but of technical execution – everyone is of same opinion – even L.G.![3] Hoare is most reluctant to speak.

April 21st

Hoare put his case badly in House of Commons last night and quite failed to disarm Opposition of their suspicion of his pro-Franco sentiments. A.E. finally decided to wind up. A.E. convinced today that less discouraging warnings must be given to British shipping. He is sure, as we all are, that Hoare and Admiralty have not been frank and have made much more of danger of mines than was justified by facts. We heard today from our Consul at Bilbao of large numbers of ships which have successfully entered port without any mishap. As a result, Cabinet today decided not to treat Bilbao any longer as more risky than the Basque ports. "This Government would be more reactionary if I were not in it," A.E. said to me today.

Ormsby-Gore[4] told A.E. that Sam Hoare was now saying he

1. Sir Douglas Hacking (later Lord Hacking), Chairman of Conservative Party.
2. The Non-Intervention Control Scheme finally came into force on this day.
3. Rt. Hon. David Lloyd George, later Lord Lloyd George, Independent Liberal M.P. for Caernarvon Boroughs.
4. Hon. W. Ormsby-Gore, M.P. (later Lord Harlech), Secretary for the Colonies 1936–1938.

could not remain on in New Government at Admiralty "unless foreign policy was changed and we ceased to be on bad terms with Germany, Italy and Japan at the same time"!

April 23rd

A.E. had been to Windsor for the night and was very impressed by the King and especially by the Queen, who has great character and common sense and encourages the King. Queen Mary told A.E. she had only seen Mrs Simpson once.

Nevile Henderson was also at Windsor and A.E. was rather aghast at the nonsense he was talking about what he was going to do in Germany. It seems quite to have gone to his head. He spoke of an idea of going off to see Prince Paul of Yugoslavia at Munich immediately after he gets to Berlin to receive some special message which Prince Paul wishes to give him. A.E. was horrified and told him pretty sharply that he was now Ambassador in Berlin and that if Prince Paul (whom he was not particularly pleased with) had any messages he could send them through Ronnie Campbell. A.E. asked me to speak to Van about this, and Van is to give him a talking to on Monday. I hope we are not sending another Ribbentrop to Berlin. Nevile Henderson may steady down when he sees what he is up against, and there really is not anybody else obvious to send.

Situation at Bilbao for the moment fairly satisfactory. Three food ships got through today after being escorted up to three-mile limit by *Hood*, although challenged by Franco cruiser about five miles off coast. Franco's ship claimed six miles territorial waters and this *Hood* refused to recognise. Shore batteries also opened fire against Franco ship. This will ease situation in Bilbao for the present: it also shows that there is substance in Franco's claim that there is a blockade and therefore risk for shipping to justify some warning.

April 25th

Flew to Brussels, arriving 6.30 – Mr and Mrs Eden and I, Strang and Peake[1] went by train – met at station by Spaak[2] and Ambassador.[3] Dinner at Embassy with staff only. Discussion after with Military

1. Sir Charles Peake, later Ambassador to Yugoslavia and Greece.
2. Paul-Henri Spaak, Belgian Foreign Minister.
3. Sir Esmond Ovey, Ambassador to Belgium 1934–1937.

and Air Attachés about Belgian attitude towards military co-operation. Military Attaché said, since King Leopold's speech, information was being withheld reluctantly by his friends on staff in consequence of instructions from higher authority which he believed to be General Nyhtens, who is military adviser to the King and a former dismissed C.G.S. Air Attaché said he had nothing to complain of as Belgians wanted to know about us and they had nothing of particular interest to show us. Both agreed that Belgians would never have staff conversations with Germany. Military Attaché said from our point of view it should always be possible to obtain all information we need by personal informal contacts between officers of two staffs without formal staff conversations. Noel Charles[1] said he didn't believe that if Belgian air were violated, say, by German machines flying high and going to attack us or France, the Belgian people would come in – although Belgian Government have given most formal assurances that they would not tolerate this.

After dinner A.E. prepared speech for tomorrow.

April 26th

Talks between A.E. and Belgian Ministers in morning.

Lunch at Embassy – Van Zeeland, Spaak, etc.

Further talks between A.E. and Van Zeeland.

Banquet at Ministry of Foreign Affairs. A.E.'s speech very successful.

April 27th

More talks in the morning. Luncheon at Van Zeeland's house – sat next Spaak and talked after to Langenhowe (Secretary-General of Ministry of Foreign Affairs).

Flew back in the evening.

I think the Belgian visit has been an undoubted success. The Belgians were very gratified at A.E. going and he neither lectured nor hectored them, but told them frankly our views and policy and asked for theirs; the Belgians like frank discussion and relations with Van Zeeland could not be easier. The Belgians are having a bad anti-French reaction due to their dislike of the Franco-Soviet Pact which they think may involve them in war, to the *Front Populaire*

1. Sir Noel Charles, at this time Counsellor at Brussels Embassy.

Government in France which they believe on the verge of Communism, and to the bad tactics employed by the French in handling them. They have in no way changed as regards us, and wish to be as close and friendly as possible, and they are determined not to allow German interference inside Belgium. They are determined to be more independent, however, i.e. neither a province of France (as since 1920) nor a neutralised state (as under 1839 treaty): they adhere to the League of Nations: they are determined to defend themselves. But they will not agree to staff conversations which they regard as compromising, for they believe – rightly or wrongly – that if they do not so compromise their independence Belgian soil may escape the next war. We were assured, however, that they will keep us informed of their state of defence – which is, of course, not the same thing as staff conversations and exchange of plans.

The French have behaved with unusual restraint. They agreed without too much difficulty to the exchange of notes releasing Belgium from her Locarno obligations. They have let Belgium know, however, that without close previous military collaboration it may not be possible for France to come effectively to her defence.

The Belgians have undertaken to study our plan for a multilateral pact of non-aggression in regard to Belgium with independent declaratory guarantees from those who care to make them. The French are doing so too.

Bilbao has occupied us incessantly since we got back. The Admiralty are strangely reluctant to help, either in defending British ships on the high seas or by co-operating in the evacuation of refugees, but they have been obliged to do both. Yet the impression of ill will remains.

May 4th

A.E. had Norman Davis[1] to luncheon when the latter said he hoped either A.E. or Neville Chamberlain would visit the United States in the autumn. He also said he thought the autumn or winter might prove a favourable moment for restarting the disarmament question. He insisted on the paramount importance of an Anglo-American Trade Agreement as a prelude to this. He confirmed A.E.'s view that the European situation showed improvement. The U.S. Am-

1. U.S. Ambassador-at-Large and U.S. Representative at the Geneva Disarmament Conference.

43

bassador[1] has also strongly urged a visit by A.E. We have written to Lindsay[2] to ask his views.

A.E. spoke to Chancellor about Van and necessity of replacing him. Chancellor agreed to such action being taken but said that it would obviously be wise to wait a little. He asked A.E. who he wanted instead. A.E. said "Alec Cadogan". Chancellor said Warren Fisher[3] strongly opposed to this and wished to see Findlater Stewart[4] from the India Office appointed. Chancellor added he did not favour A.C. A.E. told me afterwards he could not possibly have an outsider not a trained diplomat and would insist on A.C.

1. R. W. Bingham, U.S. Ambassador to Great Britain 1933–1937.
2. Sir Ronald Lindsay, British Ambassador to U.S.A. 1930–1939.
3. Sir Warren Fisher, Permanent Secretary at Treasury and Head of Civil Service.
4. Sir Findlater Stewart, Permanent Under-Secretary at India Office.

Part Two
September 22nd 1937 - February 27th 1938

There is a gap here in the diary which begins again on September 22nd 1937. In the meantime, on May 12th 1937 George VI was crowned and on May 28th Baldwin resigned and handed over the Premiership to Neville Chamberlain. Anthony Eden continued as Foreign Secretary. On May 29th the German battleship Deutschland *was bombed by Republican planes and in retaliation the Germans bombarded Almeria. On June 19th the Germans claimed a cruiser of theirs had been attacked and asked for support from Britain and France in a counter-demonstration.[1] When this was refused, Germany and Italy withdrew their patrols in the Mediterranean and the Portuguese did the same along their land frontier. The Non-Intervention Committee continued to sit in London.*

Against a background of disorder caused by increasing Jewish emigration in face of Nazi persecution, the Royal Commission on Palestine reported in July 1937 recommending a partition into three – an Arab State, a Jewish State and a mandated territory of the Holy Places with a corridor to the sea at Jaffa. This pleased nobody and the matter was referred to a further Commission.

Relations with Italy were still entangled in the question of British recognition of the conquest of Abyssinia. In July Mussolini sent through Grandi a message for Chamberlain who replied in a friendly personal letter which he did not show to the Foreign Secretary. In August submarine and air attacks of Italian origin took place against British and other ships in the Mediterranean, and Mussolini openly congratulated his troops for their part in the taking of Santander.

As the submarine attacks increased, the British and French Governments summoned a Conference of Mediterranean Powers at Nyon on September 10th. Though the Germans and Italians refused to attend, Britain, France, Greece, Yugoslavia, Russia and Turkey reached

1. See Appendix E.

agreement within twenty-four hours on a plan for destroyer patrols with orders to sink any submarine caught attacking a non-Spanish ship or found in the vicinity of one just attacked. The attacks ceased: it was the first and last success the democracies would enjoy for some time.

O.H. discussed most of these problems in a memorandum of July 25th to the Secretary of State, which is given at Appendix F.

September 22nd 1937

Back from Geneva after Nyon.[1] A.E. saw the P.M. today (he had already had a very satisfactory letter from P.M. congratulating him on his success). A.E. anxious to ascertain his reactions as regards the next step *vis-à-vis* Italy, found him "fed up" with the Italians and not at all disposed to run after them. The P.M. then said he was very annoyed to find A.E. was addressing a meeting at Llandudno on October 15th and wished him to cancel it as he would tire himself out; that he wouldn't allow his Foreign Secretary to be used as a "party hack" and had forbidden the Central Office to ask him. A.E. protested that his health was all right and that he rather enjoyed it, and that 18,000 people had applied for seats. P.M. very firm and obstinate and said Llandudno in any case a bad place. When A.E. told Jim Thomas[2] and me we were aghast and begged A.E. not to agree to cancel it as it would encourage rumours of difference between A.E. and P.M., apart from the fact that three or four speeches by him a year were invaluable and indeed indispensable for keeping public opinion informed of his foreign policy. A.E. agreed, and when lunching with P.M. later told him so. Jim Thomas meanwhile ascertained from Miss Maxse[3] at Central Office that she was horrified at this veto and put the worst construction on it, viz. that the P.M. wanted to deal with Foreign Affairs himself and to keep A.E. out of the picture. The P.M. had seen Hacking and was apparently most obstinate and had said that anyhow October 15th was a bad date as he, P.M., meant to devote his Scarborough speech on October 12th to Foreign Affairs! Anyway, it has now been decided that Llandudno is to stand, but this episode is disquieting for the future.

1. The Nyon Agreement was signed on September 17th 1937.
2. J. P. L. Thomas, M.P. (later Lord Gilcennin), succeeded Roger Lumley as P.P.S. to Anthony Eden.
3. Miss Marjorie Maxse, Chief Organisation Officer, Conservative Central Office 1921–1939.

A.E. had shortly before this, on his return from holiday, discussed P.M. with me and said that there was no doubt a difference as to methods between them, that he believed P.M. *au fond* had a certain sympathy for dictators whose efficiency appealed to him (much as was the case with Austen and Muss and Primo[1]) and that he really believed it would be possible to get an agreement with Muss by running after him. A.E. disapproved of his precipitate reply to Musso's letter offering conversations (sent without asking A.E. first), and there is no doubt now that it was a mistake, since we offered conversations and as we cannot yet do anything about Abyssinia we cannot really usefully discuss anything.

October 2nd

A.E. went to Yorkshire on September 30th for a long weekend. Before he left he had agreed on terms of our draft for Anglo-French note to Muss regarding tripartite conversations for withdrawal of volunteers, etc.

The French Embassy subsequently produced their draft which was more elaborate and more tricky, but agreement was finally reached on practically our own terms and the note was to be delivered today.

P.M. and A.E. agreed that this was the right course although P.M. was reluctant and had some misgivings after Wednesday's Cabinet when A.E. and P.M. had to some extent to impose it on an unwilling Cabinet who disliked our taking joint action with the French. Kingsley Wood was particularly obstructive.

Far East.[2] Owing to growing pressure of public opinion on Government to take economic action against Japan in conjunction with U.S.A. and other states concerned, A.E. decided he must approach the U.S. Government to ascertain their views as to joint action. This point is certain to be raised in Parliament when it reassembles. He discussed with Van a draft telegram to Washington just before he left to catch the train. Van then took draft over to P.M. who rewrote final paragraph to effect that "we were not convinced

1. Primo de Rivera, Spanish Dictator 1923–1930.
2. The Japanese invasion of China, begun in February 1933, had recently flared up. Shanghai, Nanking and the Yangtse valley had been attacked in July, and Chiang Kai Shek's Government had been forced to flee to Chungking. China had then appealed to the League.

48

any such action would be effective but we would be ready to examine matters with the U.S. Government if latter thought it worthwhile." A.E. only saw the telegram (which went off on September 30th) today, and immediately rang me up in great annoyance at this ending which he regarded as an invitation to America to reject idea and one which U.S. Government would seize on in order to say that it was *we* who did not think action would be effective. He was in no way appeased when told that these were the *ipsissima verba* of the P.M. and complained that he should have been told at once of such a change. We rang up Washington but found that action had been taken yesterday so that it was impossible to cancel it. He therefore decided to send a second telegram instructing Mallet[1] to go again to State Department under pretext of impressing them with urgency for an early reply and to say that "whether or not action would be effective was obviously a matter for examination and we should be very glad to join in such examination with U.S. Government if they felt able to do so." In other words, to emphasise that the British attitude was an open and unprejudiced one on the subject and that we really were anxious to examine possibilities with the U.S.

The truth is that here again there is a divergence between A.E. and P.M. as latter is strongly opposed to any sort of economic boycott in the Far East even with U.S.A. A.E., on the other hand, would welcome joint action with U.S.A.

October 5th

A.E. returned to London tonight. I went to see him and he discussed Spain and the fresh evidence we have that Muss is already breaking his undertaking given since Nyon by sending further men and aeroplanes, the risk of Valencia collapsing before the winter and the evident intention of Muss to try and force a quick victory for Franco. A.E. feels we cannot go on restraining the French from opening the frontier which is also what Valencia itself wants, although we ourselves may doubt whether in fact such a course will work out to Valencia's advantage. He is extremely anxious to find some means of helping Valencia, whose survival he is convinced is now to our interests, and of putting a bar to Muss's progress. How to do this? I said I was sure public opinion, though anti-fascist, would not approve anything approaching war in or for Spain and that was what

1. Sir Victor Mallet, then Counsellor at Washington Embassy.

any sort of ultimatum to Muss to withdraw his volunteers would amount to. At the same time, the way in which Italy broke every pledge she took showed the futility of any conversations with her. A.E. thought we should try and hasten Musso's reply to the Franco-British invitations, as if it were a refusal, we should agree to France opening frontiers and we ourselves should sell arms: if Muss accepted discussion provided it was in Non-Intervention Committee, we should agree but allow frontiers to be opened all the same, as otherwise Valencia might collapse during protracted discussions.

October 10th

A.E. went to Balmoral on Friday night: Italian reply received yesterday. A.E. returns on Tuesday; he is working meanwhile on Cabinet paper on our policy for Wednesday's Cabinet. French Cabinet meet tomorrow so we shan't get their reactions till the afternoon.

The reply, as anticipated, is completely negative: refusal of Three Power conversations, suggestions of rediscussion in the Non-Intervention Committee, refusal to participate in *any* discussions without Germany. To agree to reference back to Non-Intervention Committee means futile delay while Muss sends more help in to Franco. To open French frontier, as I see it, means almost certainty of Muss himself denouncing Non-Intervention and sending in massive reinforcements openly; yet that is what Valencia and the French desire. Thompson[1] just back from Hendaye believes that Valencia in advocating this hopes for a general conflagration which is their only chance.

October 15th

A.E. went to Llandudno today for his speech . . . 18,000 have applied for seats to hear him! There is no doubt he has more appeal than any of his colleagues. He has the H. of C. behind him as well as the country, but in the Cabinet he is criticised and thwarted by half his colleagues who are jealous of him and would trip him up if they had half a chance.

The worst ones are Hoare and Swinton: the first is consumed with ambition to be P.M., though God knows he'd land his party on the rocks in six months, and has never forgiven A.E. for succeeding him.

1. Sir Geoffrey Thompson, then *Chargé d'Affaires* at Hendaye.

Swinton is anyway a very second-rate politician. Simon is slippery and evasive, a moral coward; yet incredible as it may seem, he also believes that he can become P.M.

Hailsham[1] has had a stroke and should have been dropped at the reconstruction: he is a diehard and an obstructionist (he was responsible when Minister of War for appointing Massingbird C.I.G.S.[2] as he was a fellow-Ulsterman, instead of a younger and better man). Kingsley Wood is a severe critic of A.E. and is a pushing professional politician. De La Warr,[3] Malcolm MacD.[4] (a good man), Ormsby-Gore, Elliot, Stanley[5] are all lightweights, though on A.E.'s side. Duff Cooper is bone-idle. Halifax is idle and pernickety. Most of the colleagues are "dictator-minded" and hate to see us associate with France. A.E. had a very difficult time in the Cabinet on Wednesday, when it was a question of our joining with France in a common attitude on the Italian reply. The Cabinet are in fact far to the right of the H. of C. and the country.

A.E. very worried about Spain, as we all are: he feels all the difficulty of allowing ourselves to be hoodwinked by Muss without any counteraction, and yet there is no *effective* counteraction which we can take short of a direct challenge to Muss. The idea of a temporary occupation of Minorca in conjunction with the French coupled with an offer of international neutralisation appeals to him rather and he is discussing it with the P.M.

October 17th

A.E. returned from Wales tonight and I went round after dinner to see him. Rex Leeper and Jim Thomas also there. Llandudno meeting the greatest success, enormous crowds and great enthusiasm. A.E. delighted and heartened by it. We hope he'll now agree to another meeting in December.

We discussed Spain and meeting of the N.I. Committee next Tuesday when A.E. is to take the chair in Plymouth's absence. I had

1. 1st Viscount Hailsham, Lord Chancellor.
2. Field-Marshal Sir Archibald Montgomery Massingbird, C.I.G.S., 1933–1936.
3. Lord De La Warr, Under-Secretary of State for Colonies 1936–1937, Lord Privy Seal 1937–1938.
4. Malcolm MacDonald, Secretary of State for Dominions 1935–1938.
5. Oliver Stanley, M.P., President of the Board of Trade.

received a message from Margerie[1] that the French Government had had no success in their efforts to make Soviets helpful. We agreed that A.E. should make a further appeal to Litvinoff[2] and should make it clear that if Soviets were responsible for breakdown of Committee again he would be obliged to go for them and pillory them in public. In fact, he should take a firm line with Italy or Soviets, whichever was obstructive. We also agreed that he should ask if all accepted principle of proportionate withdrawals, numbers to be ascertained by commissions whose figures should be accepted by proportions, and if they would agree to H.M.G. deciding when sufficient progress had been made to justify grant of belligerent rights. I urged the pacifist and non-interventionist frame of mind of the British public as reason for going very slow and refusing to commit ourselves to any interventionist action and also the fact that the Labour Front Bench – Attlee, Baker,[3] etc. – represent nobody but themselves. He should go for Opposition in debate on Thursday and accuse them roundly of seeking to bring about intervention and war.

We must be very careful about Minorca so as not to give Muss any bad example. We must leave it to Muss to take a false step and only turn on him when we are absolutely sure of our ground and he has attacked a British interest.

October 20th

At Non-Intervention meeting yesterday Grandi behaved intolerably, prevaricating and wasting time by seeking to transfer discussions from French proposals to British plan of last July. A.E. very firm and stiff and insisted on bringing him back to agenda, finally pinning him down to the fact that he had not budged from attitude of last July when he had refused to agree to withdrawal of volunteers unless belligerent rights were first granted. He decided, however, not to break up meeting then and there but, whilst drawing attention to deadlock, to adjourn for twenty-four hours in case dangers of breakdown should induce a more reasonable frame of mind, failing which he would have to report failure. Grandi was supported like an echo

1. Roland de Margerie, First Secretary at the French Embassy in London 1933–1939.
2. Maxim Litvinoff, Soviet Foreign Minister 1930–1939.
3. Philip Noel-Baker, Labour M.P. for Coventry.

by Woermann,[1] the German. The Portuguese made an interminable speech attacking the Soviets. Maisky[2] said very little.

This morning Corbin telephoned to say his Government were prepared to go further in the path of conciliation and agree to reference of point to two parties in Spain. At the Cabinet A.E. found colleagues strongly in favour of keeping the Committee going and greatly alarmed at the consequences of opening the French frontier: they all agreed if France did so, we could *not* sell munitions to Valencia. I lunched with A.E. to discuss possibility of asking for agreement on token withdrawal of equal numbers from each side but including all foreign airmen. He decided to spring this on the Committee if a fresh deadlock was reached. We both thought the prospects pretty hopeless but felt it necessary to keep farce alive as the alternative of French opening frontiers would be worse and merely lead to a speedy Franco victory.

Just before the Committee met at 3.30, Grandi came to see A.E. and said he had instructions to accept all points proposed at the last meeting (immediate departure of commissions to count volunteers, withdrawals to be proportionate based on their figures, belligerent rights to be granted *after* beginning of withdrawal when our authority decided the time had come, and an immediate token withdrawal of men from each side)! When the Committee began, Grandi read out a statement to this effect. Woermann said the German attitude was the same.

Atmosphere now completely changed, though we were not out of the wood as Grandi then proposed that the Committee should accept immediately British plan of last July which Corbin could not do without instructions from Paris. The meeting finally adjourned till Friday on this less good note but with Grandi pinned down at least to his original statement of acceptance.

As A.E. said, it always pays to be firm with Italians, but he is at a loss to know whether this is genuine (as Grandi told him, because they really wanted to get their men home) or merely manœuvring.

October 24th

Our optimism – never very confirmed – was soon dispelled. At the next meeting of the Non-Intervention Committee on Friday – after a

1. Counsellor at the German Embassy.
2. Ivan Maisky, Soviet Ambassador 1932–1943.

successful debate in the House of Commons on Thursday when A.E. and the P.M. had explained what we understood to be the Italian offer – Grandi, to the general amazement, in conjunction with the Portuguese, took the line that Italy could not bind herself now to accept the figures for volunteers on each side to be found by the commissions as establishing the proportions for the withdrawals. This of course meant that Italy intended, after the commissions had reported, to reopen the whole question of these figures in the Committee, thereby securing endless further delay. It was the slipperiest business I've ever seen and Grandi behaved like a little Italian lawyer. Compared with this the Soviet attitude, which was that Russia could not agree now to give belligerent rights when a certain stage in the withdrawals had been reached, was at least honest because it had never been dissembled. Moreover, it was made clear that if necessary the French and we were prepared to proceed without the Russians if their intransigence was maintained. If the Italians had been sincere in their wish to withdraw, they would have seized on this opening in order to isolate the Russians and secure agreement with the French and ourselves without them. They could have made us choose between losing our plan and maintaining solidarity with the Russians. Alternatively, they could have insisted that their offer was dependent on acceptance by all, including the Russians. Grandi did, in fact, make this demand, thereby placing all onus on the Soviets. As it is, by going back on his offer of last Wednesday he has given the whole show away . . . i.e. that Italy does not want agreement, she only wants to gain time and she is afraid that we would abandon Soviets and be ready to make agreement over their heads.

Meanwhile, Gijon has fallen and it is evidently hoped that troops thus released will enable Franco to win in the East. Next meeting is fixed for Tuesday and we shall then have to threaten a break-up and reversion to freedom of action. Italians don't want this, we believe, as it would probably entail their sending still more troops to Spain; whereas they hope to be able to secure Franco's victory without further cost with their existing "volunteers".

November 2nd

Arrived Brussels 9 a.m. A.E., Malcolm MacDonald, Cadogan, had a talk with Norman Davis[1] this morning. The latter then made clear

1. Now U.S. Delegate to the Brussels Conference on the Far East.

that Roosevelt hoped to be able to make use of the Conference[1] for the education of his own people to realities of the international situation. Roosevelt felt that Japan, if not tackled soon, would mop up first British possessions in the Far East, then Dutch, and after that U.S.A. would have to tackle her alone. He hoped that if the Conference, after exhausting the possibilities of conciliation, finally had to report failure owing to Jap obstruction, then U.S. opinion would react and he, Roosevelt, would be able "to do something more".

Danger of this attitude is that it involves great risk of U.S. public opinion not reacting sufficiently to enable Roosevelt to act, and also risk of proposed U.S. action being inadequate. We feel after the Abyssinian experience that it is no good applying sanctions at all unless *effective* sanctions are applied, and that means all must be prepared for war AT ONCE – no bluffing. Would U.S.A. be prepared for such 100% sanctions and also to join in naval guarantee of Far Eastern territories of all those applying them? I much doubt it. If the Conference breaks down, and if we report failure to League of Nations, the latter will then wish to proceed to Articles 16 and 17 and sanctions. If at that point we find U.S.A. only ready to join in partial sanctions without military guarantees, then we must refuse to go on and Anglo-American relations may suffer from the reaction (the U.S. delegation here have already told us they doubt usefulness of an oil sanction).

On the other hand, prospects of mediation seem most unpromising; the idea is that two or three Powers on the Conference, e.g. Great Britain and U.S.A., might be delegated to undertake soundings. If this fails, as is almost certain, then it is inevitable that we shall have to refer back to Geneva with consequences as above.

November 3rd

A.E. had a further conversation with Norman Davis today, together with Malcolm Macdonald and Alec Cadogan, when he put straight to him our difficulty as regards sanctions . . . viz. that they must be

1. The Conference was composed of the signatories of the Nine-Power Pact signed at Washington in 1922. (G.B., U.S.A., Belgium, China, France, Italy, Japan, Netherlands, Portugal.) The Pact recognised the independence, territorial and administrative integrity of China. The Conference was the result of China's appeal to the League.

effective or we cannot agree, and if effective then there is some risk of war for which we must all be prepared to offer mutual guarantees. Owing to the situation in Europe we cannot send the whole fleet to the Far East. Norman Davis professed to understand this.

A.E. has an ovation wherever he goes; crowds outside the hotel and the Conference buildings. The Italian representative's speech at the Conference today was received in icy silence. The isolation of Italy here could not be more marked.

Long talk with Jim Thomas about A.E.'s position in the Cabinet. On the day of A.E.'s speech in the House of Commons last Monday the P.M., who was still in bed with gout, sent a message through Lord Dunglass[1] to Jim "that he hoped he would say nothing to upset the Dictators"! (Jim didn't deliver this message.) J.T. and I feel he must sooner or later have a frank explanation with the P.M.; he must either support A.E. or A.E. must resign and the Government would then fall. The Cabinet cannot use A.E.'s popularity and sabotage his foreign policy. The majority of the Cabinet are against A.E. and the Cabinet are far too right both of H. of C. and of Country. His supporters in the Cabinet are flabby or unassertive, i.e. Stanley, MacDonald, Elliot, De La Warr; his opponents, Simon, Sam Hoare, Kingsley Wood, Swinton, Hailsham, are important and effective. A.E.'s last speech brought him the greatest ovation he has ever had; it was also his firmest speech; yet the Cabinet would certainly have prevented him making it if he had shown it to them. A.E., very worried over slowness of re-armament campaign, especially anti-aircraft defences, has written to the P.M. about this today; the Cabinet seems unable or unwilling to face realities and lives in an atmosphere of complacent unreality.

November 5th

A.E. had further talk to Norman Davis today before returning by air to London. Davis then said U.S.A. would not put on any sanctions beyond refusing to buy Jap goods – that was all they would do; they wouldn't refuse to sell to them. A.E. explained that this had been done in the case of Italy without success. There were two kinds of sanctions, effective and ineffective: to apply the latter was provocative and useless. To this Davis agreed. To apply the former meant some risk of war; we were quite prepared to examine this, but if so we

1. His Parliamentary Private Secretary, later Sir Alec Douglas-Home.

must be ready to share the risks. N.D. appeared to think the Japanese were unlikely to do anything in reply to sanctions.

November 7th

After thinking over the whole position as regards A.E. and the Government, I decided to write to him as I saw it, viz. that he was being exploited by them in public and hampered in private and that he, as the only indispensable member of the Cabinet, must insist on more support or else must seriously consider resignation.[1]

We had a meeting at his house at 5.30. Leeper, Cadogan, Sargent, Strang, Cranborne and self, to consider policy towards Germany and Italy. Leeper had seen Grandi last week and had heard from him strong appeal for immediate approach to Italy "as this was the eleventh hour", and otherwise Italy would be finally wedded to Germany. Leeper, much impressed by this, had strongly urged A.E. immediately to recognise Abyssinia and to start conversations at once without waiting for position in Spain to clear up. He (Leeper) was also much impressed by criticism by Horace Wilson[2] of negative policy of F.O. and failure to make approaches to dictators. Moley[3] supported Rex in urging pro-Italian policy.

Bobbety and I and A.E. were opposed to doing any more with Italy until Spain cleared up; we had made approach last Christmas and it had led nowhere; it savoured of the old policy of running after Muss. On the other hand, we all favoured approach to Hitler and offer of a bilateral declaration of our policy, although none of us liked the idea of the Halifax visit: if Hitler confirmed Aga Khan's report of conversation, then approach regarding Czechoslovakia could also be made (i.e. possibility of German-French-English guarantee if Czechoslovakia gave autonomy to Sudeten).

A.E. much interested by my letter which he showed to Beatrice,[4] who fully agreed with it. He later talked to Bobbety, who also agreed with diagnosis though he didn't show him the letter. He proposes to see P.M. on Monday and speak strongly about re-armament, etc.[5]

1. The text of this letter is at Appendix G.
2. Sir Horace Wilson, Chief Industrial Adviser to H.M. Government 1930–1939, seconded to Treasury for Service with P.M. 1935.
3. Nickname of Sir Orme Sargent.
4. Mrs Eden.
5. Appendix H contains a memorandum from O.H. to the Secretary of State of this date about the Palestinian problem.

November 8th

A.E.'s conversation with the P.M. went very badly. P.M. stiff; never even mentioned A.E.'s speech; complained that F.O. never made genuine effort to get together with dictators. A.E. said it was useless and impossible to do so unless and until we were strongly armed, complained of the spirit in which re-armament was being undertaken and urged the necessity for buying abroad. The P.M. promised to hold Cabinet Committee later in the week to consider foreign policy and hear A.E.'s complaints.

At a small meeting at 6 p.m. (P.M., Simon, A.E., Inskip, Malcolm MacDonald) A.E. carried completely his view of the necessity of purchase of A.A. guns abroad, and action is to be taken accordingly.

Debate at eight on the appointment of British agent at Salamanca. If P.M. had been firmer, no debate would have been given. After debate, Van, Rex and Moley returned again to the charge about Italy and begged A.E. to send personal appeal to Ciano[1] to come to Brussels. A.E. refused, but agreed to Van seeing Grandi and letting him know that it would be a good thing if Ciano came. Rex and Van are now quite frantic on this subject – how they change!

November 9th

Left London for Brussels again by air. A.E. talked to me about P.M. and expressed doubts about his health. "Sixty too old for a P.M. nowadays." Who could succeed? Not Simon nor Hoare. Inskip not the man for wild times, too easy-going. There would probably be a Cabinet split. We also spoke of the danger of the Halifax visit producing plausible and vague account of Hitler which would have a soporific effect on the Cabinet.

A.E. had spoken to the P.M. about Far East conference. The latter said, "On no account will I impose a sanction!" A.E.: "Do you want me to say that to Norman Davis?" The P.M. agreed no. A.E. said we must say we cannot impose ANY sanction unless we receive guarantee.

1. Count Ciano, Italian Foreign Minister and Mussolini's son-in-law.

November 11th, Brussels

News of Halifax's proposed visit to Germany has leaked into the *Evening Standard*, and the P.M. is anxious to announce at once in the House of Commons that he is going. A.E. very annoyed at the indecent haste with which the P.M. and Halifax are pressing on with it and insists on twenty-four hours' delay so as to enable a communiqué to be agreed with Germans and insists that it must say that H. has been invited by Hitler to see him. A.E. is opposed to the visit anyway, as having seen Halifax's notes for proposed talks he finds them very feeble and based on the idea of the Four Power Pact. A.E.'s original conditions were that H. should go to Berlin during the Hunting Exhibition, that if he saw Hitler it should be at Berlin during the Exhibition and that Hitler should invite him. Now Henderson ascertains that Hitler would not be in Berlin during that period and will not arrange to return there to see H. but would receive Halifax at Berchtesgaden. This puts an entirely new aspect on the visit which will have greater publicity and will look almost like a Canossa. Finally, Germans insist that terms of communiqué, while speaking of an invitation by Hitler to Halifax, shall make clear that initiative comes from Halifax. Bobbety, who has telephoned about this, says P.M. and Halifax are absolutely determined that visit shall take place regardless of fact that H. is forcing himself on Hitler, and of the impression it will produce on the Germans of our anxiety to run after them immediately after the Tripartite Anti-Communist Pact has been announced.

We here (Malcolm MacDonald, Cadogan, Jim Thomas and I) discussed it with A.E., who finally and reluctantly agreed to the visit taking place in these circumstances, but said that he must have time to discuss with the P.M. and H. on his return what latter is going to say to Hitler. Owing to leakage, to have refused now and so stopped visit would have caused a fresh German grievance and made more bad blood just at the moment when we are anxious to make a fresh start with Germany. Nonetheless, the precipitancy with which the P.M. and Halifax have pressed on with this visit in A.E.'s absence, knowing that A.E. did not favour it, shows shocking lack of solidarity and even of common decent behaviour. A wobble of this kind following A.E.'s firm speech last week may undo all the good then done.

November 14th

A.E. and I left Brussels for London by train; arrived 4 p.m. and found Bobbety and Van at 17 Fitzhardinge Street[1] waiting to discuss Halifax visit before A.E. and Van see P.M. and Halifax himself at 6.30. They went through Halifax's notes and pruned them.

On A.E.'s instructions, I told Rex to see that *The Times* denied that there were to be any simultaneous conversations with Italy, in respect of which the position remained unchanged; viz. as soon as withdrawal of Italian volunteers in Spain had taken place, conversations could begin. Later I saw Paul Emrys-Evans who was greatly agitated at what was going on behind A.E.'s back in the Cabinet. He was insistent that he should not return to Brussels and said that opinion in the H. of C. was perplexed and there was a fairly strong tendency to favour approach being made both to Germany and to Italy. (A.E. himself by this time had come to regard Halifax visit as not necessarily a bad thing as H. would impress Hitler, provided always visit was kept informal and no negotiations were started, and it was a concession to his colleagues which would put him in a stronger position for later.)

November 16th

This morning's newspapers (especially *Times* and *Daily Telegraph*) contained the most exaggerated account of scope of Halifax visit, whilst the note which Rex gave out, emphasising its informal and limited character and the fact that it implied no change in the present policy of H.M.G., was not even published. A.E. (who had been in bed with slight flu since Monday) was extremely annoyed and got up to come down to F.O. to see Halifax at 11.30. H. was himself much worried at press accounts and felt it had made his visit extremely difficult owing to the great expectations which had been aroused. A.E.'s interview with the P.M., as he put it, "couldn't have gone worse", although the P.M. also deplored exaggerated press accounts and undertook to see the Press himself and correct them. The P.M. also expressed annoyance at the Brussels Conference. A.E., who was evidently fairly roused, also spoke of slowness and lack of imagination shown in re-armament by colleagues and their depart-

1. Anthony Eden's London home.

ments. P.M. for his part advised A.E. to go back to bed and take an aspirin!

On returning to the F.O., A.E. at once wrote to P.M. to recapitulate his views of the limited and informal nature of the H. visit, and to repeat again what he had said about the re-armament programme and the importance of greater efforts IMMEDIATELY to improve our situation now by purchase abroad, since the next six months were the vital time. The P.M. replied the same evening in a letter full of friendly sentiments, but completely missing the point by attributing A.E.'s concern at re-armament and the general situation to the flu!

November 17th

Jim Thomas saw Horace Wilson whom he knows well and had a frank talk about the relations between A.E. and P.M. and the intrigues of Simon, Hoare and Kingsley Wood. H.W. maintained that P.M. was devoted to A.E. and regarded him as first man in his Cabinet and that there was no question of any personal hostility or jealousy; but that at same time P.M. DID think his own policy of using every opportunity of getting together with the dictators was right and that he was determined to go on with it. P.M. genuinely thought A.E. was wrong and that "he was saving A.E. from himself".

Jim told H.W. how Cartland had told him that Beverley Baxter[2] (Atticus in *Sunday Times*) had been visited by both Simon and Hoare separately to explain that A.E.'s flu was the beginning of the end for A.E., that strain was too great and he would soon go. Hoare had added that as time had now shown that Hoare-Laval proposals had not been so wrong, he would now be prepared to take F.O. again! H.W. said P.M. was aware of these intrigues.

November 22nd

I met Halifax at Victoria on his return from Berlin. He came to see A.E. at F.O. and then both went to P.M. at six. Record of his conversation showed that Hitler had spoken of Colonial Question as only outstanding point between H.M.G. and Germany, but that he was in no hurry about it. He showed great distrust of democracies as

1. Ronald Cartland, Conservative M.P., a supporter of Eden's policy in the House of Commons.
2. Sir Beverley Baxter, M.P. and journalist.

impossible to deal with owing to strength of party forces. Halifax was quite firm in talking to him. No suggestion of a deal over colonies and Central Europe was made. Indeed, Hitler said he was satisfied with his own bilateral arrangements with Poland and Austria and he believed he could do the same with Czechoslovakia, provided Czechs would allow Sudeten tolerable conditions. He failed to see how disarmament could now be handled and deplored failure to take advantage of his previous offers. He regarded return of colonies as a RIGHT, not to be bartered against other things.

Halifax got definite impression both from Hitler and from Goering that they were in no hurry and were not contemplating any warlike adventures in immediate future; they thought time was on their side and the adjustment and changes they wanted would come of themselves.

November 23rd

A.E. had a satisfactory talk with P.M.

Decided to invite Delbos[1] and Chautemps[2] to come on November 29th and 30th.

November 25th

A.E. received Press to explain purport of French visit. P.M. dined with him to discuss agenda of meeting with French tomorrow.

December 5th

Events of last ten days – Halifax visit to Berlin and French visit here have much clarified position. Negative results of Halifax mission and fact that it demonstrated that no immediate deal for peace with Germany was possible has evidently impressed P.M. who now admits that no immediate action is possible, but that the colonies issue must next be carefully studied. The French visit left the best impression; the P.M. was very good in the conversations and removed all their suspicions. They saw P.M. and A.E. in close harmony, while they in turn created good impression on the P.M. by their

1. Yvon Delbos, French Foreign Minister.
2. Camille Chautemps, French Premier from June 25th 1937, following the fall of Blum's *Front Populaire*. The new Government contained M. Georges Bonnet, for the first time, as Minister of Finance.

common-sense attitude. Thus I think the P.M. and A.E. are now together again, the former having learnt much from this experience. The intrigues in the Cabinet – Simon, Hoare, Swinton – continue actively, however, but I fear them less, or indeed not at all, so long as P.M. and A.E. see eye to eye. Halifax, though not an intriguer, is tiresome and a captious critic – he hasn't learnt much from the German visit and is very much in the German camp. A.E. complains bitterly of defeatist attitude of all his older colleagues, including Inskip, in matter of re-armament and of attitude towards dictators generally. He says there is little doubt that his policy – now shared by P.M. – is that of a minority in the Cabinet. He wonders whether he could not serve his country better outside the Government. I told him I did not think it had come to this yet – so long as A.E. found himself in agreement on main lines with P.M., but if latter definitely joined dissentients, then he would have to reconsider his position seriously.

A.E. is hoping to take six weeks' holiday and go to West Indies just after Christmas. P.M. to take on F.O. in his absence. This is rather alarming in view of intrigues, but as P.M. is now in agreement with A.E., perhaps all will be well. In any case, A.E. MUST have a holiday and now is a quieter season diplomatically than any other.

December 7th

A.E. had a very satisfactory talk with P.M. and they were in absolute agreement about Germany – viz. no settlement except a general European settlement. It was agreed that Foreign Affairs Committee of Cabinet should consider Colonies Question in the first instance. A.E. told P.M. he did not at all like the idea of any swapping round of colonies, or any arrangement by which France would be expected to pay major share by concession in West Africa: in fact, if any concession had to be made, and if a general settlement were secured in exchange, he would prefer to return ALL ex-German colonies, including Tanganyika itself.

P.M. raised question of Van's future and was quite determined that he should be removed from his present post. He proposed to A.E. that he should become "Chief Diplomatic Adviser" to H.M.G., a post to be created similar to those of Leith-Ross and Horace Wilson, who are Chief Economic and Chief Labour Advisers respectively. He would no longer hold executive functions and would be available for duty at C.I.D.[1] meetings, missions abroad and conferences. Alec Cadogan would succeed as Permanent Under-Secretary. A.E. asked me what I thought of it. I said I doubted whether Van would accept as it seemed rather too obvious a way of removing him, also that it would be very necessary to safeguard Alec's position as executive head since Van was very active.

December 18th

It has now been agreed that Van shall become Chief Diplomatic Adviser to H.M.G. He did not dislike the idea as much as had been expected, but was anxious chiefly that the appointment should be so announced as to make it clear that he was not being *dégommé* and that there was no change of policy, also that his status as senior to the P.U.S. (though with no executive functions) should be preserved. The appointment is to be announced in January and will take effect in February.

A.E. is to go to Madeira for a holiday on December 28th till the end of January. The P.M. will take over.

Meanwhile, German questions having calmed down as a result of Halifax visit and French visit, Spanish questions having also become less tense owing to continued delay in Franco's offensive and consequent loss of prestige by his Italian backers (while Hodgson has now got to Salamanca as British agent), Far East has blown up afresh with bombing and sinking of U.S. ship *Panay* and bombing of British ships in Yangtse. We had already told Lindsay of our readiness to send ships to Far East if U.S. would do likewise, although, with Europe as it is, we could not act alone as this would involve sending practically the whole fleet and denuding Mediterranean. Now we have authorised Lindsay to tell Hull[2] that we would in fact send up to eight-nine capital ships if U.S. would send equivalent force. U.S. opinion has been deeply stirred by this last attack and has moved considerably since Brussels Conference days.

Lindsay saw Roosevelt late on December 16th when latter was in a most expansive mood and talked of blockading Japan by means of U.S. and British fleets, undertook to send a naval officer to England to discuss plans, and was in fact prepared for fullest co-operation with H.M.G. in F.E. He seemed to think, however, that it would be

1. Committee of Imperial Defence.
2. Cordell Hull, American Secretary of State 1933–1944.

possible to blockade Japan without a war, though it might take eighteen months and that cruisers alone would suffice.

A.E. is much encouraged by this response. He feels strongly the need of bringing the Japs up short before they get further into China and make the position of Shanghai and Hong Kong untenable. His idea is to arrange for French to take over watch in Mediterranean, if we send fleet to Singapore.

December 19th – 23rd

A.E. began to doubt wisdom of going so far away as Madeira in view of forthcoming negotiations with U.S. over joint action in Far East. I felt bound to agree with him that it was essential that he should be in London when U.S. naval representative arrived, i.e. just after Christmas. As he said, this development of Anglo-American relations was the most important thing that had happened and what he had been working for for years. The P.M. is heavy-handed and has no touch for dealing with delicate situations and might easily upset the Americans for good. A.E. has a natural "flair" which enables him to say and do exactly what is needed. It is a great bore as he is very tired and badly needs a holiday, but he proposes to go to South of France in January instead. He also feels he must put in an appearance at Geneva – the first meeting after Italy's withdrawal.

In view of Italy's withdrawal[1] and Musso's last speech he feels it is hopeless to expect the League of Nations ever to take the initiative towards recognition of Italy's position in Abyssinia. How can it be expected to? On the other hand, he feels we may be in danger of cutting off our nose to spite our face by too negative an attitude. He told me when we lunched together on December 23rd that he always felt he must be particularly careful to prevent his personal prejudices in regard to Musso from colouring his attitude too much. He said he regarded Muss as anti-Christ! I said I did too. He has now directed the Department to draw up a list of our *desiderata* which we would demand of Muss in return for *de jure* recognition, supposing it were decided to go ahead independently of the League of Nations. He would in any case act only in conjunction with the French. I told him my own view was that we could not even expect to get Muss to co-operate sincerely with us or with League of Nations whatever we gave him, as his whole system was hostile to ours. Similarly, we

1. From the League of Nations.

couldn't expect to get Hitler to agree to the general settlement we wanted. In such a situation it became a question of expediency whether we really must buy off Muss or whether we could afford to let matters drift. But if we did try to buy him off by *de jure* recognition, we must not have any delusions that it would change his heart.

In debate on December 22nd the P.M., whom A.E. had persuaded to speak first, made satisfactory speech, particularly in reference to Germany and to our wish for a general European settlement. Although a sincere speaker, he is dull and very uninspiring. A.E. wound up. A dull debate except for fireworks by Winston.

January 1st – 13th 1938

Owing to leakage in Press about Van being about to get a "high honour" and an Embassy, it was decided yesterday to bring out announcement of his new appointment as "Chief Diplomatic Adviser to H.M.G." today, together with honours list in which he gets G.C.B. A tremendous puff of him appeared in the Press (which we all think he has worked himself!). No one so much as hints at the truth, which is that he has been sidetracked. In fact, the suggestion is so much the other way – that he is now permanently and exclusively to advise the S. of S. that I think something must be done through Press to restore the balance and show that Alec will be what the P.U.S. has always been, and Van a supernumerary adviser *en marge* of the machine who will advise and function ONLY IF AND WHEN ASKED. Otherwise this may react unfavourably on position both of Alec and of S. of S. himself. Alec being by nature the most retiring and simple of men, hating all this publicity, will do nothing himself to enhance his own position. Gladwyn Jebb[1] is to become his Private Secretary.

A.E. saw Ingersoll, the U.S. Naval representative sent over by Roosevelt, on January 1st. He did not turn out to have any definite plans or proposals to submit for moving U.S. ships to Far East, but he has authority to show us all their dispositions and to discuss plans, but the idea still seems to prevail in the U.S. that we must wait for the next incident before it will be possible to take any action, whereas we would like to take some joint action NOW by way of demonstration, which we believe would prevent any fresh incident. Lindsay is to return to the charge about this with Roosevelt. Meanwhile, Ingersoll remains here and will consult with Admiralty.

1. Now Lord Gladwyn. Ambassador to France 1954–1960.

On December 31st we had a discussion with A.E., Alec and Moley Sargent on merits of (a) giving recognition of Abyssinia in return for a hard bargain, or of (b) giving it as a gesture to which would be coupled an Anglo-French Declaration of collaboration in the Mediterranean and an invitation to Italy to negotiate outstanding questions. We all preferred latter course and regarded a bargain as too repugnant after all that has been said. A.E. very doubtful still as to wisdom of giving recognition yet in view of Muss's weakness and difficulties, which it would help to exorcise. (I had sent him a paper about this which I had written over Christmas and which he said had interested him.[1]) He finally decided to write to the P.M., sending him details of BOTH alternatives and telling him of his preference for (b) and of his doubts about expediency of either. He proposes to discuss it all with Delbos at Geneva on January 16th.

A.E. left for South of France on January 3rd (1938) and proposes to go from there direct to Geneva, where I shall go to meet him. Meanwhile the P.M. is in charge of the F.O.

P.M. replied to A.E. and expressed strong preferences for (a), the bargain, although he does not admit the word but regards it as a "general statement" to which all sides must make contributions. This was forwarded to the South of France and A.E. replied saying that he would discuss the position with Delbos at Geneva on January 16th. The F.O. see great difficulties in (a) and papers have been sent to A.E. to read before he reaches Geneva.

Meanwhile yesterday and today (January 12th and 13th) Lindsay has telegraphed particulars of a plan Roosevelt proposes to launch next week for a world discussion of the underlying causes of the present discontents. His idea is (a) a general appeal and invitation which, if accepted, will be followed by (b) the appointment of a sort of drafting committee of the U.S. and certain minor powers (Holland, Belgium, Sweden, Turkey, Hungary, Jugoslavia) to draw up the agenda which at a final stage (c) would be submitted to ALL the other powers. The objective is to discuss disarmament, raw materials and other broad questions. He wants us to let him know by January 17th whether we approve and support it. Alec Cadogan has discussed it with the P.M. and proposed to reply to Roosevelt notifying him of fact that we are about to discuss *de jure* recognition of Abyssinia with French with a view to attempting settlement with Italy, and to examine Colonies Question with a view to attempting general settlement with

1. See Appendix I.

Germany, that R's plans would seem to cut across this and he may wish to hold it up to see how much progress is made, but if he STILL prefers to go ahead, we will give wholehearted support. He proposed to send this draft to A.E. to approve. The P.M. was not very favourably impressed by R.'s plan which he regarded as woolly and dangerous and has decided to leave out Cadogan's last paragraph offering our support, and to end with inquiry to R. who can still reply before the 17th. This is being sent off as instruction to Lindsay tonight and a copy is being sent to A.E. by air. The latter will get it tomorrow, Friday evening, and can telephone in time to give his views before the final reply is sent when we get R.'s answer.

It is most unfortunate A.E. is away. This is a vital decision and may affect whole future of Anglo-U.S. relations. It is hard to understand why Roosevelt should insist on reply by 17th; at same time most important not to give cold douche which P.M. is inclined to do.[1]

January 14th

Read in *Times* this morning that French Government has fallen. Obviously, then, Delbos won't be able to go to Geneva to meet A.E. on Sunday, and latter can be brought back without causing sensation of having cancelled meeting. I rang up Cadogan and suggested this; he quite agreed and said he would speak to P.M. He saw P.M. at 11 a.m., who also agreed, and we rang up A.E. at once. He will catch train from Cannes tonight and arrive here on Saturday morning by air from Paris. Bag with telegrams will be handed to him at Marseilles tonight at ten. P.M. is going to Chequers and wants him to go down there on Saturday afternoon for the night. I was to have started for Paris myself this morning en route for Geneva but have given it up.

Meanwhile the French Government have asked for postponement of Council meeting till January 26th because of their crisis – this will be a great help because it enables A.E. to stay here during next week instead of going back to Geneva on Sunday or Monday.

I'm thankful A.E. is returning. The more I think of Roosevelt's proposals the more convinced I am that we must clinch with them and co-operate for all we are worth in spite of the risks they contain. I feel sure A.E. will want to do this and that P.M. will be most reluctant. (Why did Roosevelt launch this just when A.E. is out of

1. It is worth noting that the U.S. Embassy was at this time between Ambassadors; Bingham had died and Kennedy had not yet taken up his post.

the country? He must be extremely badly informed as to relative receptiveness of A.E. and P.M. At same time it really is very short notice to hurl it at us.) Alec says he feels sure P.M. will wish to refuse because he regards it as woolly and because he really believes his German and Italian initiatives will lead us somewhere. P.M. is being advised also in this sense by Horace Wilson. I discussed it very confidentially with Rex Leeper, who strongly favours immediate acceptance. I've jotted down a few points for A.E. I fear a very stiff fight with P.M. We should never be forgiven if we turned this offer down.

Notes for A.E. on Roosevelt Plan

Contra

Proposed discussion of Arms Limitation and Raw Materials obviously opens up dangerous possibilities (e.g. danger of British public wishing to slack off Re-armament – danger of Great Britain being called upon to pay lion's share of sacrifices in respect of Colonies and Economic Concessions).

No guarantee that Roosevelt will bring U.S.A. into a reformed League – in fact, it is almost certain that he would *not*; or that he would accept any definite commitment to help us in Europe – in fact, he says he won't accept any political involvement!

The unsatisfactory way in which the Far East seems to be fading out of his interest in favour of this vaguer plan just when we are getting to grips with the Far Eastern problem.

Danger of American public again repudiating President (cf. Wilson) and leaving us to carry the baby – though Roosevelt is a far astuter politician than Wilson.

Pro

Scheme is one which public opinion here will certainly approve – i.e. the Press, *The Times*, the House of Commons (what members would dare oppose such co-operation with America?).

The fact that so wise and cautious an Ambassador as Lindsay urges us to back it.

The fact that no real progress is anticipated by us in Foreign Office from our own attempts at "general settlements" with Germany and Italy. We only hope to gain time thereby pending our re-armament. In any case, Roosevelt's initiative is admittedly parallel to our efforts.

We must accept some risks. Roosevelt is on side of democracies and we must pay some price whether by colonies or economic concessions for peace.

The only fatal risk for us is to antagonise Roosevelt and America: with-

out his backing we might be overwhelmed in a war. The scheme, if nipped
by us in the bud, will certainly leak out and then what will U.S.A. and
world say of us? Unthinkable that we should assume such responsibility.

We may try and persuade Roosevelt to delay or modify scheme, but if
he persists we should heartily concur and co-operate for all we are worth.
We should not be forgiven if we turned it down.

And please don't underestimate your influence in the Cabinet and your
importance to the Government! You can afford to take a *very* strong line –
they couldn't let you go on this!

January 15th

All our arrangements have gone wrong. A.E. missed the bag at
Marseilles as the train was in two parts, and when he reached Paris
the air service was interrupted because of the gale and he is coming
on by train due in London at 5.20 p.m. Alec Cadogan and I decided
to go down and meet him at Folkestone with the papers. The boat
was very late and A.E. didn't in fact land till five. We only got to
London at seven, which was too late to think of going down to
Chequers, and he is to go tomorrow for lunch, by which time we
should have Roosevelt's answer. We discussed the proposals in the
train and A.E. took the view we expected, viz. that we MUST accept.
He regarded P.M.'s reply as much too chilling and would himself
have accepted outright, whilst at the same time suggesting certain
amendments to the wording of R.'s appeal to make it less dangerous
from our point of view. (Before going down to Folkestone I showed
the papers to Bobbety after consulting Alec, and he also said at once
that we must accept outright – he has been asked to dine with Alec
tonight to talk it over with A.E.)

A.E. has returned from his holiday much fortified in his instinct
against giving Italy *de jure* recognition. He had seen Lloyd George
and Winston in South of France and they were both strongly
opposed to recognition.

January 16th

I was woken up about 1 a.m. by a messenger from the F.O. with
two telegrams. One, from Lindsay, saying that Roosevelt was rather
disappointed with the P.M.'s reply, that he consented to hold up his
plan "for a while" and that he was writing to the P.M. on Monday.
The other, a reply sent off by A.E. from Alec Cadogan's house saying

that he had only just returned to London, that the P.M. had brought him back to consult him and that he hoped Roosevelt would not regard reply as negative, which it was not intended to be.

I went round to A.E.'s house at 10.30, when Alec and Rex Leeper came also. On receipt of the telegram from Washington last night, A.E. had rung up Lindsay himself, and the latter had confirmed Roosevelt's disappointment. We are all very much concerned at the effect of this cold douche which the P.M. has administered. A.E. is motoring down for luncheon at Chequers and will try to get him to agree to send a further message to Roosevelt confirming A.E.'s telegram.

A.E. rang me up at about 6 p.m. on his return. He said he found the P.M. personally very friendly, but he evidently did not much like A.E.'s telegram of last night and he refused to send a further telegram but preferred to await Roosevelt's promised letter on Monday. A.E. said he found he apparently sincerely believed that our initiatives with Germany and Italy were likely to lead very soon to real settlements! When expostulated with, P.M. could only say that F.O. weren't sincere in their efforts.

I'm afraid the P.M. may have committed a colossal blunder which it is too late to retrieve. A.E. will have to consider his position very carefully, for he obviously cannot remain responsible for foreign policy if the P.M. persists in such a line. He cannot accept responsibility for a policy which will antagonise America.

The P.M. is being advised in this folly by Horace Wilson who knows nothing about foreign affairs. He, the P.M., is temperamentally anti-American, but he is also, I'm afraid, moved by some vanity over his own ventures with Hitler and Muss. If Roosevelt's letter isn't too bad, we may still perhaps retrieve situation, but I'm very much afraid the first shock will have been too much for him.

January 17th

A.E. wrote to P.M. this morning to make his position clear. He wrote that after reading the telegrams and going over again what had been said at Chequers yesterday, he felt more and more convinced of the importance of Roosevelt's offer and of the necessity of accepting it fully. He feared that the first telegrams of reply must have had a discouraging effect and was certain that a very grave mistake would have been made if R. were deterred by us from pursuing his plan.

If R.'s reply showed any opening, we should afford it all the possible measure of support.

Shortly after Horace Wilson came to see A.E. and said P.M. was much disturbed at this difference, more especially over recognition of Italy in Abyssinia, which P.M. and Wilson still regard as of greater importance than the Roosevelt initiative! A.E. said he failed to make any impression and was in fact much annoyed at Wilson's attitude.

I had a talk with Bobbety who agreed that the difference was of the most fundamental kind and that A.E. couldn't stay in the Government if the P.M. refused to agree to accept R.'s plan if it still proved to be open, and that he also should resign if it was found that the P.M. had killed it.

A.E. and I lunched alone together at the Savoy to discuss the position. He feels himself that he cannot go on like this. "The old gang" will do him down, if they can get him to swallow such treatment. He is the most important person in the Cabinet and if he went the Government would fall. It is most important to prevent him being compromised by this gaffe – which he will be if the P.M. gets his way and the Roosevelt initiative is killed and A.E. still stays on. He has a loyalty to his supporters in the country which is of greater importance than that to his colleagues. If he is firm, moreover, I think the P.M. will give way, especially if he insists on a Cabinet.

Directly after lunch he decided to ring up Lindsay and tell him that he, A.E., entirely agreed with Lindsay's view of importance of accepting scheme, that if Lindsay could prevent Roosevelt from "chucking his hand in", A.E. would do all he possibly could to get acceptance here. Lindsay was just going to State Department and said this would help him a lot. (We felt that the issue was so important in itself that almost any means were justified which might revive Roosevelt plan after the shock it had received.)

I also discussed it all with Jim Thomas, who is profoundly disturbed and fully agrees with our views.

Bobbety is dining with A.E. tonight. We can only wait now for R.'s reply tomorrow.

January 18th

Roosevelt's reply arrived this morning. He said that he was willing to defer his appeal but he took grave exception to our idea of granting *de jure* recognition to Italy in Abyssinia: he felt that such action would arouse disgust in America where opinion could only agree to co-operation with other peace-loving nations on a basis of legality. Lindsay had also seen Hull, who also objected strongly to idea of *de jure* recognition. There was no doubt that the President was disappointed by our reply, although he agreed to defer action.

A.E. at once saw his way clear, viz. that we must on this decide to drop any idea of proceeding with *de jure* recognition in deference to Roosevelt and we must tell him that we would back his initiative in the fullest possible measure. He is to see the P.M. at five, and in preparation drafted a considered minute in this sense. Bobbety, Alec, Jim and I all agreed in this.

He returned from his interview with the P.M. about seven. It had gone very badly. The P.M. had refused absolutely to accept A.E.'s view and to endorse Roosevelt's proposal. He held that we were in such a dangerous position with three dictator states lined against us that it was essential to make terms with Italy. He had received letters from Lady (Austen) Chamberlain saying that this was a "psychological" moment, and Muss was ready for a settlement. He wanted to send a reply arguing with the President as to why he wished to proceed with *de jure* recognition, and asking him to hold up his plan until after he had started his negotiations with Italy.

He admitted that there was a fundamental difference between him and A.E. and left the impression that one or the other must go. The matter is to be referred to the Foreign Affairs Committee of the Cabinet on Wednesday.

A.E. very calm though rather distressed at interview. He feels there can be no compromise between the two points of view and that everything must give way to primary importance of good relations with Roosevelt and America. We discussed it before dinner and he has begun writing brief for tomorrow's Committee. Jim dined with him and Bobbety went after. Although he would, I think, have been prepared to agree to *de jure* recognition in return for 100% co-operation with Roosevelt plan, the attitude of Roosevelt and U.S.A. towards *de jure* as now just revealed to us, has entirely changed position. The P.M., on the other hand, remains firmly wedded to the idea of recognition and to the belief that this will lead to far-reaching settlement with Italy. A.E. feels there is no alternative for him but to resign unless his view is accepted, as no compromise is possible.

January 19*th*

A.E. prepared his notes for meeting this afternoon. Hankey[1] came to see him and put in a strong plea for making peace with Italy in spite of the Americans, on the ground of our weakness. Van takes the same view! (It is amusing that Van is the ONLY person in the F.O. who takes the same view as the P.M., who was chiefly responsible for removing him from the post of P.U.S. last month because his advice was so bad!) A.E. saw Oliver Stanley and put facts before him, and Bobbety saw Ormsby-Gore.

At this point A.E. received a letter from Grandi to say that he had just returned from leave and would like to see him and the P.M. together for an informal talk. A.E. decided he must see him first, and he came this afternoon: A.E. felt that he might have some proposal to make which would have a bearing on discussions. Grandi, however, had nothing definite to say except that Italy was very anxious for discussions to start at any place at any time and that *de jure* must really be included if they were to lead anywhere.

The Committee met from 5–7.30. The P.M., Halifax, Simon and Inskip all ridiculed the plan and opposed acceptance on the ground that America would do nothing for us and that there was a real chance of a real agreement now with the dictators. P.M. quoted long extracts from Lady Chamberlain! Malcolm MacDonald spoke up a little for acceptance, as did Ormsby-Gore and Stanley. Simon was at his worst and played up to the P.M. The P.M. produced a draft telegram for Roosevelt re-explaining his hopes of *de jure* recognition and ending up with an appeal to R. to use his influence with Italy to help us get an agreement, not a word about accepting the R. plan. A.E. is to let P.M. know his views on this draft in the morning.

We met at A.E.'s house after dinner. Alec, Bobbety, Jim and myself; and Malcolm MacDonald came later. Alec undertook to prepare a fresh telegram to Roosevelt putting the facts as we see them about the situation in the Mediterranean and the Far East, and the risk that if there is trouble with Italy in the Mediterranean we should be unable to do anything in the Far East – and then offering to waive our Italian negotiations and support the Roosevelt plan

1. Sir M. Hankey (later Lord Hankey), Secretary to Cabinet, and Committee of Imperial Defence.

100% if R. still dislikes the idea of negotiating with Italy. Bobbety feels there is a fundamental difference and that no telegram can be drafted to bridge it. A.E. thinks so too and feels strongly that there is grave risk of riling Roosevelt by further questioning such as P.M. desires. He doesn't think you can have a stronger expression of R.'s views than F.O. have already got from Lindsay, and nothing we can say will persuade him otherwise. He is prepared to see the draft, but he believes it is right to stand firm and refuse any further concession, and resign. Malcolm favours another telegram to R. in order to elicit once more that he hates the idea of *de jure* recognition: this, Malcolm thinks, would much strengthen A.E.'s friends in the Government. A further aspect is that of France and the Dominions. How can A.E. urge Delbos at Geneva next week to agree to *de jure* recognition of Italy and withold from him knowledge of R.'s intended appeal and of his dislike for such recognition?

Similarly, how can MacDonald urge the Dominions to do so and not let them know of America's attitude? This seems a final argument against any further hesitation in accepting R.'s plan.

January 20th

Alec produced his draft and A.E. went through it. He is more and more convinced of the undesirability of sending any further communication to R. which isn't a definite acceptance. He proposes to tell the P.M. and Committee that he has a draft telegram but he doesn't propose to produce it, as he is opposed to any further arguing with the President. (Bobbety, Alec, Jim and I all favour this. Alec is anxious to prevent a breach if possible as he fears the effects of A.E. resigning in such circumstances in which Anglo-American relations become a political issue: he also sees difficulty for A.E. in defending his action in resigning when his lips must be sealed about the extent of American co-operation we are hoping for in the Far East.)

Jim saw Horace Wilson this morning. The latter defended P.M.'s policy of coming to terms with dictators and condemned the F.O. attitude which he represented as obstructing this. He admitted there was a fundamental difference between P.M.'s and A.E.'s policies and seemed prepared for a break: he let it be known that if A.E. did go there would be an onslaught on him and the F.O. for their attitude. (We think Wilson must evidently have been working up P.M. and not vice versa.) He regards U.S. policy as pure bunk and believes the world will greet Roosevelt's scheme with screams of laughter. What ignorance!

A.E. saw P.M. alone at 12.15. He felt at once that P.M. was no longer so sure of his case, although he still argued fiercely. He thinks he would now agree to parallel action – i.e. that R. should go on with his scheme and P.M. with his Italian negotiations. We all agree that this is not possible; in view of R.'s attitude to *de jure*, we must now allow R. to make his effort first.

Cabinet Committee met again from 3–4.30. A.E. found his colleagues noticeably less stiff. The P.M. had clearly been shaken by feeling that A.E. would resign: Stanley and MacDonald spoke up more, while Halifax, Inskip and Hailsham were no longer easy in their minds. It was finally agreed that A.E. should produce three telegrams: (I) to Roosevelt asking him to defer plan no longer, (II) also to R. explaining why we had been considering *de jure* recognition but saying we intended to defer this negotiation now, and (III) to Lindsay instructing him, if he thought possible, to ask for certain modifications in the wording of R.'s appeal. In other words, an almost complete reversal of P.M.'s and Committee's previous attitude – a very great triumph for A.E., although we are not out of the wood yet and we may still have difficulty over telegrams, etc. as to degree of warmth with which we bless R. plan, and as to extent to which we agree to defer our Italian negotiations. As to latter point, Alec feels this isn't any longer important as he believes announcement of R. plan will completely change the situation, and it will be clear to all that this particular negotiation must be merged in wider questions. I am a little doubtful how far this triumph is really a blessing – so are Jim and also Bobbety – we feel there is a fundamental difference and A.E. would be better outside the Government as the "old gang" will watch to trip him again. Anyway, he can afford to be as firm as he likes as now they realise he would resign on it they are afraid of him. Next time he may not have such a good wicket. We know now that the P.M. hates American co-operation and wants to make peace with the dictators.

January 21st

Cabinet Committee at 11.30 when A.E. produced his three draft telegrams. P.M., who had been to Birmingham for the night, returned in a bad temper and the meeting went very badly; agreement was not reached on the drafts because they weren't felt to have given fully enough the arguments for *de jure* recognition or to have shown that H.M.G. could not hold it up indefinitely. Halifax rather more helpful this time, Simon as bad as usual. It was decided that Stanley and MacDonald should try to re-draft telegrams before a further meeting at three. These drafts were finally agreed about 4.30, viz.:

(I) Telegram containing a message from P.M. to President asking latter to go ahead and promising warm welcome. (This telegram is very satisfactory.)

(II) Telegram to Lindsay himself explaining that H.M.G. weren't enthusiastic about plan but didn't wish to do anything to stop it: it expressed doubts about its success and indicated points we would like changed. Lindsay had authority, however, to use this or not and he can be trusted, I think, to pay little attention to it.

(III) A second message from P.M. to President giving a long argument of reasons which obliged H.M.G. to contemplate *de jure* recognition, and inviting R.'s further views.

(IV) A further telegram to Lindsay emphasising the danger we felt ourselves to be in in the Mediterranean and need for improving relations with Italy, but adding that we would not start conversations for at least a week. (This is a thoroughly bad telegram as well as III and calculated to make the worst impression on R., who may think H.M.G. want to start negotiations with Italy immediately after his appeal has been launched and thereby dish prospects of support by public opinion in U.S.A. – he may even now refuse to go on.)

On the other hand, A.E. extracted agreement from the Committee that whole question of *de jure* must be reconsidered in light of R.'s appeal and he is not committed now to start conversations then.

I dislike this solution; it seems to me to run grave risk of antagonising R. and I wish A.E. had insisted on his own terms, if necessary resigning. His colleagues are almost in a panic about the Mediterranean – just like Hoare-Laval over again – without any reason, as A.E. is convinced. But they will be even more frightened of letting him go because they know in their hearts they can't afford to lose him unless they have first discredited him – which is now their main object. The P.M. believes himself a man with a mission to make peace with dictators. He is both vain and obstinate and continually flattered by Simon and Hoare.

January 23rd

Two telegrams from Lindsay arrived, both describing conversations with Sumner Welles[1] when he handed him P.M.'s messages. Latter said definitely he thought replies would please President, who would be relieved that *de jure* recognition was not intended in the immediate future and then only as part of a general settlement. He said recognition was a "bitter pill" which it would be better that Great Britain and U.S.A. should swallow together, and that whereas Great Britain contemplated recognising as part of a general Italian settlement, the President contemplated doing so as part of a general European settlement. Lindsay brought out various points in R.'s appeal which we didn't care for. Sumner Welles said he thought the President would probably not bring out his appeal this week while Geneva was going on, but would want to put further points to us.

This prospect of further questions and delay is bad, as I fear it will re-open the whole issue with the Cabinet Committee. However, there is nothing to be done until we get the reply of R. himself.

January 24th

I talked to Bobbety who was rather worried and feels that A.E. may have committed himself too far on principle of *de jure* as result of continuous and wearing discussions in Committee. I rather feel so too.

Foreign Affairs Committee of Cabinet met again this afternoon to consider Colonial question in reference to a German settlement. Here, too, P.M. seems to favour precipitate action in sense of agreeing to discussion of colonial redistribution without first deciding what WE are prepared to give. As first step it was decided to consult Henderson on how best to approach Germans. (I feel sure P.M. is running into trouble over this.)

Cabinet met at 6.30 to hear statement by A.E. on Roosevelt message. I gathered it went only moderately well, although Zetland[2] and Morrison[3] felt that P.M. had been unduly precipitate in sending his first reply.

1. U.S. Under-Secretary of State 1937–1943.
2. Second Marquess of Zetland, Secretary of State for India 1935–1940.
3. W. S. Morrison, M.P. (later Lord Dunrossil), Financial Secretary to the Treasury.

January 25th

Just before we left for Geneva we received a telegram from Lindsay saying that Roosevelt was "deeply gratified" by the P.M.'s two messages, that Lindsay would be having further conversations with Sumner Welles on procedure and that there would probably be a further written message from Roosevelt. This is satisfactory as far as it goes, but I wish R. would now bring out his scheme as I dread the prospect of further discussions. Also the delay seriously handicaps our talks with the French and others at Geneva on *de jure* question.

We were very reluctant to leave London at all in view of all that has passed, but A.E. feels he must attend Council meeting and see French Ministers. We've left Bobbety behind till Wednesday afternoon, and we intend to be back Sunday. Jim Thomas is remaining home all the time to watch the situation.

On arrival in Paris, we went to the Quai d'Orsay (A.E., Ambassador,[1] Hugh Lloyd Thomas[2] and myself) and were received by both Chautemps and Delbos and afterwards dined with them, catching Geneva train after at 10.30. Very friendly and satisfactory talks on all subjects.

They asked about Italy and the recognition question. A.E. told them that H.M.G. had taken no definite decision yet, but were contemplating conversations on basis of a general appeasement in the Mediterranean, in return for which *de jure* recognition might be granted. French Ministers did not object to this idea but expressed the wish that Spain should also be covered by proposed agreement.

A.E. asked them to let him know their *desiderata* which might eventually be included in our own. They agreed to do this. They also believed Muss to be in serious difficulties and didn't exclude possibility of some act of folly: they weren't seriously alarmed, however, and were much more anxious for an agreement with Germany.

Geneva – January 26th–28th

New Rumanian Minister of Foreign Affairs, Micescu, who came to see A.E., makes a bad impression. Although obviously a Jew, he is in a Government with strong anti-Semite programme; he, however,

1. Sir Eric Phipps, Ambassador to France 1937–1939.
2. H.M. Minister in Paris.

79

is at pains to assure us that the Government for all their violent words will take no serious ACTION against the Jews. I can't believe that such a Government will survive the elections which are to be held in March. They may then be succeeded by an Iron Guard (Fascist) Government, or by some sort of dictatorship; in either case a very bad prelude to King Carol's visit. We've asked Rex Hoare[1] if there is any prospect of postponing elections.

A.E. had Burckhardt, High Commissioner for Danzig, to lunch on 27th: he gave us very interesting sidelights on Germany. Factions led by Goering[2] and Goebbels[3] respectively might, he thought, lead to a *blutbad* this year. Goebbels inclined to *rapprochement* with Soviet Russia, and even Goering might not be unwilling if the Nationalist element in Russia were to dominate the Communists there; which seems to be the development which Stalin is now bringing about. Germany didn't take Italy very seriously and would still prefer agreement with us and Western Powers.

On January 28th we received repetition of telegram to Henderson in Berlin saying that P.M. wished him to return at once to consult on question of conversations with Germany. Henderson had meanwhile answered request for his view on probable German attitude towards P.M.'s ideas for a middle zone in Africa where frontiers might be redrawn and areas redistributed, some kind of convention regarding treatment of natives and free trade being applicable to whole zone. He said that he couldn't say what German reaction would be until it was known how much territory Germany would receive. (This is exactly the reply we expected and is exactly what the P.M. won't face.) Here again the P.M. is pushing ahead too fast; he is determined, I feel, to get in before Roosevelt, and we shall have fresh trouble as soon as we return, and a fresh drive to start *de jure* discussions with Italy. The P.M. didn't even refer to A.E. before summoning Henderson back. Cadogan has meanwhile asked Lindsay if he can say what the present position is as regards Roosevelt's appeal.

January 31st

We got back to London last night. A.E. saw P.M. after dinner and found him much less optimistic of prospects of agreement with

1. Sir Reginald Hoare, H.M. Minister in Rumania 1935–1941.
2. Nazi Air Minister.   3. Nazi Propaganda Minister.

Germany, having just read *The House that Hitler Built*[1]; he even suggested that, if we couldn't reach agreement, we should have to go in for encirclement and perhaps have an arrangement with Russia! What a man! I can't keep up with these changes.

A.E. is now convinced that conversations with Italy must include Spain if *de jure* recognition is to be given. If foreign troops could be withdrawn from Spain as part of an agreement, everybody would welcome it as a real appeasement. A purely Anglo-Italian settlement of Anglo-Italian questions would be regarded as a shady bargain and would not be acceptable either to Geneva or to Roosevelt. Moreover, if as he fears likely, the Italian troops were only withdrawn from Libya to be sent to Spain, or if the bombing of Barcelona by Italian aeroplanes continued, any good aspect of an Anglo-Italian *détente* would be destroyed. He put this to P.M. who apparently agreed. Meanwhile, we've heard from Lindsay that Roosevelt's reply may be expected any day now.

We had a meeting this morning with Nevile Henderson to discuss German negotiations. He said he thought that Germany, though refusing to give any undertaking about Austria as being an internal German question, would be ready to sign a non-aggression pact with Czechoslovakia, to return to a reformed League and to reach an agreement for "humanising" war. He felt sure that Germany would be most reluctant to come in against us even if the fleet had to be sent to the Far East, but there was a danger of Muss dragging Germany in as a result of an act of folly of his own. He also said that there were serious internal squabbles inside the regime. German opinion was completely divided on Far East question.

As regards Far East, our own position seems now to be this: can we safely send a fleet to Far East (which must be strong enough to cope with the Jap fleet and include seven or eight battleships), thereby reducing our strength in the Mediterranean? Chiefs of Staff fear not with our present relations with Italy. A.E. not so sure and inclines to the view that we could safely take this risk as French would watch the Mediterranean. If Japan attacked us, we should have to do so. But obviously we should be careful not to send it out otherwise unless absolutely essential to protect British interests. The difficulty seems to me that once out there it might have to stay months or even a year or two; until, in fact, Chino-Jap war came to an end.

1. By Stephen Roberts.

February 6th

A busy week.

To take our troubles in turn, in the Far East there seems to be some easing of tension. The Jap Minister of Foreign Affairs has made a conciliatory speech, believed to be the result of the recent clash between the Army extremists and the moderates, as a result of which the Emperor came down on the side of the latter. Although not involving any change of fundamental aims, Jap policy seems now to aim at the GRADUAL instead of the brutal elimination of foreign interests in China, and the avoidance of anti-foreign incidents. This, we think, must be the first fruits of Anglo-American "invisible" co-operation and can cause us qualified satisfaction. The Japs are evidently feeling the magnitude of the job they've taken on in China and are going slow.

In Spain there have been developments – both good and bad. The sinking of the British ship *Endymion* at the beginning of the week by a submarine and then, while this was being considered, the sinking of another by aeroplane attack, caused intense indignation as everybody believes here, rightly or wrongly, that both are due to Italian action.

At Cabinet on Wednesday it was decided to resume full Nyon patrol (which had been relaxed owing to complete absence of any submarining for some months) and to inform both parties in Spain that we in our area will take steps to sink any submarine which is submerged. A.E. saw French and Italian Ambassadors and told them what we intended to do. Meanwhile, the Admiralty, after first saying it was a submarine, now say that it might equally have been a mine and are most reluctant to take action proposed because it will impair the relations they have established with Franco's Admiral Moreno, as a result of which apparently he informs our Admiral confidentially of where all his submarines are working. A.E. rightly feels that this cannot be allowed to stand in the way, and the country would tolerate nothing less than the action proposed. As a result a Cabinet Committee met on Saturday and the instructions to the Navy and the warning to the two parties in Spain were sent off. On Friday evening Grandi came to say the Italian Government agreed to take similar action in their area. The French Government had already agreed. The Italian acceptance made any going back in the sense desired by the Admiralty quite impossible.

When Grandi came to see A.E. on Friday and brought this un-expected acceptance, the former to his surprise himself spoke of Spain as the great stumbling block in the way of improvement of relations between us and said he wished we could work together in some way to bring about appeasement there. He readily agreed to two points A.E. put to him, viz. that a stalemate had been reached there and that there was far less danger of either bolshevism or fascism. A.E. said that if we could together clear up the position in Spain, all the immediate difficulties in the way of an Anglo-Italian settlement would be removed.

This conversation has much encouraged A.E. who thinks, if Grandi really represents Muss, that Italy may perhaps be anxious now to find a way out of Spain owing to her many difficulties, and it may be possible to achieve useful Anglo-Italian conversations after all, involving a really comprehensive settlement. If Spain could be liquidated as part of it, we need have no fear of an Anglo-Italian settlement with *de jure* recognition so far as public opinion in this country or even probably in the U.S.A. is concerned. A.E.'s view of the necessity of including Spain or, indeed, as he holds now, of making it a condition precedent has been much strengthened by a memorandum written by Bobbety on his return from Geneva on Thursday, in which he said that as a result of his contacts there he was convinced that it would be a disastrous mistake to rush ahead and give *de jure* recognition right away (which we know would be repugnant to Roosevelt), apart from a comprehensive settlement. We have now a strong moral position which, taken with our re-armament, is bringing us increasing prestige in the world, while everybody believes that Muss's position is getting weaker. We ought to go very slowly and do nothing without Roosevelt's approval.

Earlier in the week we received a cryptic message from Lindsay in answer to our inquiry, saying that the President wished us to "hold back our horses" a little longer and he would send us a public com-munication about his plan. But (and here the telegram was contra-dictory) there was no objection to our going on with our Italian conversations on the lines proposed, although the President main-tained his views about the ill-effects of *de jure* recognition.

The P.M. naturally seized on this as entitling us to go ahead and wanted A.E. to summon Grandi at once and tell him we would start conversations. A.E. refused to be rushed and has sent a further telegram to Lindsay asking for a clearer statement of what exactly the President means. Does he or doesn't he approve of our starting our discussion with Italy for a general settlement including *de jure?*

P.M. returned to the charge again on Friday, when as he had gone to Birmingham, he sent a message through Horace Wilson to ask A.E. to summon Grandi to a joint meeting with P.M. and A.E. on Tuesday next. A.E. pointed out that by the Cabinet decision the matter of opening conversations has to be RECONSIDERED after Roosevelt's reaction has become known, and insists that it must go before the Cabinet again first next Wednesday.

A.E.'s own views may now be summarised as follows:

(i) He feels that so long as British ships are being sunk by Spaniards (whom the public believe are Italians or instigated by Italians), so long as the bombing of civilians by Italian aircraft continues and so long as there is likelihood of further Italians going to Spain, no Anglo-Italian settlement can have any lasting effect in improving Anglo-Italian relations.

(ii) We must therefore deal with Spain in connection with the conversations, preferably as the indispensable prelude.

(iii) Grandi's conversation shows that he and possibly Muss also realise this.

(iv) We must get it quite clear from Roosevelt that he does not object to our going ahead on these lines.

(v) If we can secure the evacuation of Spain, we can safely agree to *de jure* recognition of Abyssinia so far as public opinion at home and at Geneva is concerned.

In the meantime we believe we are on the point of bringing off a mass exchange of prisoners and hostages in Spain under purely British auspices – a great tribute by Spain to British impartiality, and also incidentally to the rightness of our non-intervention policy. We are also appealing to both sides and offering good offices to limit bombing in the war areas. Valencia has already accepted this; Burgos hasn't yet replied.

Finally Germany. Here, after much preliminary rumbling, the explosion has occurred and Blomberg[1] and other generals,[2] etc. have been thrown out. The result is not yet clear but seems an uneasy compromise between the Party leaders and the Army. We believe that the storm was started by demands from Muss for guarantees to back him in further efforts in Spain, that the Army objected and that

Nazi War Minister.   2. Including Von Fritsch, the C.-in-C.

Hitler has had to give way. (This refusal may be connected with Grandi's change of attitude towards Spain, and possible Italian anxiety to climb out of Spain gracefully by means of Anglo-Italian conversations: Muss may have felt that he must either send many more men to Spain, which would be very unpopular in Italy and might lead to a European conflagration, OR that he must let Franco down and clear his men out.) Anyway, it is too soon to see yet whether the moderates in Germany are strengthened or weakened by these events.

During the week discussions took place between P.M., A.E. and rest of Foreign Affairs Committee of Cabinet with Nevile Henderson on how to open negotiations with Germany, including Colonial question. P.M.'s idea of allowing Germany a redistribution of Colonial territory in Central Africa, under certain restrictions as to raising armies, free trade and native rights to be controlled not by League of Nations mandates but by African Powers, was further discussed – opinion turned more to view of returning Germany her original colonies, as being fairer and more practical than a reshuffle. Henderson returned to Berlin and instructions are being drafted for him to sound German Government as to their willingness to contemplate a settlement on some such lines, no details as to exact territory being given them, in return for a general settlement to include something about Austria, Czechoslovakia, arms limitation (or "humanisation" of bombing) and possible return to the League of Nations.

I see no harm in such negotiations being proposed, but I am confident Germany will not look at return of colonies with such restrictions. An offer of negotiations can only do good provided we insist on a general settlement. A.E. fears, and I think he is right, that the P.M., Halifax and Simon, etc. would throw colonies away as a sop apart from any general settlement, just as they would throw *de jure* recognition of Abyssinia away to Italy out of sheer funk; but this must be resisted. (Sam Hoare is quite firm about the need of a general settlement with Germany.) I believe that opinion in this country and Germany is not yet ripe for any transfer of colonies; we must insist on conditions which Germany couldn't accept; but there is no harm from our point of view in making our position clear. In time, conditions in Germany may change and so make a transfer possible.

A.E. spoke to the P.M. on Tuesday about a report of conversation at a luncheon, which has reached Van from a friend who had taken it down, when Swinton had openly said Van had been "kicked upstairs" and foreign affairs were now going to be run by the P.M. and a small committee (of which Swinton would be one) and that A.E. would either have to fall in or else he too would go! P.M. expressed astonishment that even Swinton, conceited as he is, could have expressed such sentiments. (Nonetheless, there is more than a grain of truth in it!) P.M. and A.E. also spoke of the "defeatism" of the Chiefs of Staff and have agreed to see Inskip together so as to insist on their agreeing to more adequate staff conversations with the French.

February 8th

A.E. complained of the constant obstructiveness and, indeed, double-crossing of his colleagues. He feels that there is a really fundamental difference between him and the P.M. as to policy. He was particularly annoyed to hear from Perth that Lady Chamberlain had again been hobnobbing with Muss and Ciano, reading to them letters from the P.M. implying that we are passionately anxious for a settlement "and negotiations are to begin in February!" He wrote to the P.M. objecting strongly to this and asking him to tell Lady Chamberlain not to engage in any further such conversations, which could only confuse the position. He spoke bitterly of the position and would in many ways welcome resignation. The "old gang" have probably killed Roosevelt's initiative and may now ruin prospects of new Eden-Grandi talks by appearing to run after Muss. He discussed the situation with both Walter Elliot and Malcolm MacDonald who, I gather, agreed with his reading of it. I told him I thought he must insist on getting his way on what he regarded as important or go – he must above all avoid compromising himself by acquiescing in policies of which he profoundly disapproved. Whenever he took a firm line, the Cabinet gave way because they couldn't face his resignation. I spoke to him of the great importance of his speech at Birmingham on Saturday next. The country believed passionately in what he believed in himself; it was anti-defeatist, pro-League, anti-dictator, but it was bewildered and looked to him for leadership and guidance. It had no faith in the P.M. or the older colleagues, but it was ignorant of the real position and feared it might really be so weak that we couldn't stand up to the dictators.

Later in the day we went across to see the P.M. and Inskip about a particularly defeatist C.I.D. report to the Chiefs of Staff in which they criticise foreign policy and urge against our holding any staff talks with the French for the implementing of our Locarno commitment or for better co-ordinating our naval movements (which the French have proposed) for fear of annoying the Germans! A.E. was furious and Inskip collapsed: the offending report is to be withdrawn.

The attitude of the Service departments is most disturbing. Whenever ANY action is proposed they produce nothing but difficulties. The Admiralty (under Chatfield[1]) is particularly bad. The Navy never seems to be able to do anything unless it is kicked into it.

February 9th

A.E. very annoyed at a press campaign bearing all the marks of authoritative inspiration crying up the prospects of early and complete agreement between us and the Italians; this is exactly the way to arouse exaggerated hopes and to make the Italians more difficult, because they will think we are so eager we will pay anything for agreement. According to the News Department, this campaign (initiated by an article in the *Daily Mail*) can only have come from No. 10. A.E. saw the P.M. just before the Cabinet; the latter, however, denied that anything had been put out from there and he summoned Horace Wilson who confirmed this. Even Grandi, we hear, is alarmed at this exaggerated boosting.

February 10th

A.E. saw Grandi again. The latter reported that the Italian Government were ready to open conversations at any time on as wide a basis as possible, including *de jure* but not excluding Spain. He said the number of Italian volunteers there has been reduced. A.E. spoke of the difficulty of *de jure* for us; we must act as loyal members of the League of Nations. If the two Governments could make a real contribution not only to Anglo-Italian but also to European appeasement, world opinion would approve, and hence the importance of dealing with Spain. A.E. also handed Grandi a summary of recent

1. Admiral Lord Chatfield, First Sea Lord and Chief of Naval Staff 1933–1938.

Bari broadcasts, and also gave him details of the scheme for withdrawing volunteers and establishing the question of "substantial progress" which A.E. proposes to refer to parties in Spain. If he can get Italian concurrence (Grandi will refer it to Rome), this will show Italy is in earnest and rapid progress should be possible.

February 11th

Lindsay (who had already reported that he was satisfied the President would not object to our proceeding with our negotiations with Italy on broad basis proposed) telegraphed that Hull, but not President, had impression H.M.G. were lukewarm towards his plan. A.E. wished at once to instruct Lindsay in reply to leave Hull with no delusion that they did not welcome it. There was the usual wrangle with the P.M. who wished to water this down, of course, and in the end only a moderately satisfactory telegram went off. (I'm afraid this initiative of Roosevelt's has been effectively killed by the P.M. The great danger now is that he should give it up and lay the responsibility at our door.)

I hear that the report on Civil Aviation which is shortly coming out contains such damning evidence against the Air Ministry that Swinton will have to go. The P.M. is inclined to defend him, but I understand it will be quite impossible for him to remain. If this is so and he should go, this may precipitate a Government crisis involving even the P.M.: it will in any case be most damaging to the old guard.

February 12th

Fleet Street is full of rumours of the division in the Cabinet between the P.M. and A.E. This is, of course, the inevitable result of Whitehall speaking with two voices – i.e. recent accounts of our negotiations with Italy (whether put out by No. 10 or by some other Cabinet Minister) independently of, and in conflict with those of, the F.O. News Department. I can't believe the P.M. can have put them out, though Rex has very circumstantial evidence from journalists that they did come from No. 10 at any rate; but I'm not sure of Horace Wilson. In any case, I feel it is no bad thing that the public should realise that a division exists, for it can then range itself on one side or the other and we shall see who has the big battalions. The country is unenthusiastic about the P.M. and it is a good thing that it should realise that there are two minds in the Government itself. What is bad is when these fundamental divisions are patched up and hushed up inside the Cabinet and nobody knows what is going on. The House of Commons is also uneasy and guesses where the trouble lies. Now if Swinton has to go we may have a landslide.

February 13th

I hear A.E.'s speech at Birmingham last night was the greatest success; it certainly reads very well and contains some very shrewd good points. "We want peace not only in our time but in your time" (he was speaking to the Junior Imperial League), "no shirking of responsibilities to obtain quick results." This appeal to youth couldn't have come off at a better moment for us. The whole tone is anti-defeatist.

The Sunday Times today has a formal *démenti* "from the highest authority" of any difference between the P.M. and A.E. – no one will believe that!

February 14th

The P.M. and A.E. had a meeting today with the Chiefs of Staff to discuss staff contacts with the French and need for arranging air-bases in France if we are to fulfil our obligations under Locarno. The Chiefs of Staff persist in regarding the problem as though we had three enemies – Germany, Italy and Japan – who all might attack us together and we should have no one to help us. They are terrified of any co-operation with the French. Chatfield, who has the brains of the three Chiefs, leads the other two and is most unhelpful. However, the P.M. agrees with A.E. on the necessity for co-operation with France which can only have a salutary effect on Germany and Italy, and it has been decided to have further contacts and to ask for air-bases, while we are to explain that we can't undertake to send an army in the first instance.

Instructions sent to Henderson to let Hitler know before February 20th, when he is to make a speech, that he has a communication to make to him arising out of Halifax visit.

A curious story reaches me that press campaign about Italy was given out by Sir Joseph Ball[1] at Conservative Head Office, NOT from No. 10. By whose authority, I wonder?

February 15th

News was received this morning of the conditions imposed by Hitler on Schuschnigg[2] when he was summoned to Berchtesgaden last week. Obvious attempt at blackmail, crucial point being insistence on Pan-German and pro-Nazi Seyss-Inquart[3] becoming the Minister of the Interior with control of Police, together with admission of Austrian Nazis to Patriotic Front. Schuschnigg, who went alone with Schmidt,[4] was confronted by Hitler, Ribbentrop and Papen[5] as well as by various high Nazi and Army personages.

He held out as much as he could and it remains to be seen whether the Austrian President will ratify the agreement. Possible compromise is to give Seyss-Inquart the post of Minister of the Interior but to keep the police separate (police control in Austria is key position). We had a meeting at the F.O. about it all this morning. A.E. determined not to get into the false position of giving the Austrians advice and then being saddled with the responsibility if they accept advice and the situation gets worse. We cannot fight for Austria and we must be careful not to raise false hopes in Vienna. France equally can do nothing for Austria. After all, it is more Musso's funeral than ours! We have telegraphed to Palairet[6] at Vienna to ask what prospects there are of compromise and we've told Henderson at Berlin to ask what is happening and to say we'd like to know because we take an interest in Austria, and Austria is mentioned in the communication which he has been instructed to make arising out of the Halifax visit. I think this is all we can do. Van wanted to make our inquiry much more searching and imperative but was overruled. It would only be to lead the Austrians up the garden path to do more.

The situation is full of uncertainty. It looks as if Hitler – who they

1. Sir Joseph Ball, Director of Conservative Research Department 1930–1939.
2. Kurt von Schuschnigg, Austrian Chancellor 1934–1938.
3. Artur von Seyss-Inquart, Leader of Austrian Nazis, Wartime Gauleiter of Holland.
4. Guido Schmidt, Austrian Foreign Minister.
5. Franz von Papen, former German Chancellor, Hitler's Ambassador to Turkey during the war.
6. Sir Michael Palairet, Ambassador to Austria.

say spoke like a madman – felt he must bring off some "coup" to reassure himself after his recent and damaging internal crisis, and he has chosen Austria which is the pet subject of the Nazis. It seems clear proof anyway that Muss has abdicated in Austria. If the Austrians accept Seyss-Inquart as Minister of the Interior with Police, this looks very much like the thin edge of the wedge. On the other hand, if Austria resists or insists on compromise, can Hitler now accept it?

February 16th

Austrian Government has accepted Hitler's conditions, including control of Police under the new Minister of Interior. No further news except that Muss was apparently not told in advance by Hitler of what he was intending. My instinct is not to take this too tragically; the prohibition on the Anschluss has been wrong from the start: it was a flagrant violation of principle of self-determination and perhaps the weakest point in our post-war policy. Crowe[1] always thought it wrong. One way or another an Austrian majority has always been in favour of Anschluss, Catholics, Socialists, Nazis, according to the ruling colour in Germany. Anschluss (which hasn't yet occurred), or at least a satellite Austria, is probably inevitable, and to stop it from outside is impossible and indefensible. First of all it is a blow to Muss and must weaken and possibly break the axis; we may soon hear as much about the S. Tyrolese as the Sudeten. After that we cannot tell. I can't believe the absorption of Austria will strengthen Germany; it should put much water in the Nazi wine.

A long fight in Cabinet today over closer Staff contacts with the French. P.M. and Simon both backed up A.E.: Halifax and Kingsley Wood strongly against but finally overruled.

P.M. told A.E. he had heard Grandi was in the depths of depression (a) because of Austria, and (b) because of his personal position, and wished to see P.M. and ask for immediate opening of conversations. P.M. would like to see Grandi with A.E. and ask him about Austria. A.E. ready to do this but insists that to announce opening of conversations now would be playing Muss's game of trying to play us off against Hitler. He wishes to go on lines already embarked on of dealing with Grandi informally and of clearing up Spain first. Muss is even weaker now than he was before, but we must go slowly if we

1. Sir Eyre Crowe, Permanent Under-Secretary at Foreign Office 1920–1925.

are to get what we want. He has proposed to P.M. to see Grandi alone tomorrow and ask for his reply about the Spanish withdrawal scheme and then arrange a joint meeting with P.M. next week.

I have now heard of three separate opinions all spontaneously given about A.E.'s position, and they are all practically the same. Lloyd George says he has still to show he has the courage to resign and the ball will then be at his feet: old Jim Thomas[1] told young Jim T. that he must be careful to resign on a good wicket before he is compromised by the old men: Willie Tyrrell told Charles Peake that he mustn't hesitate to resign regardless of consequences and of the immediate future because he will be sure to come back eventually in time to save the situation. Miss Maxse, however, put in a warning that he must be absolutely sure of his ground because the country will not forsake a Chamberlain lightly.

February 17th

A.E. very worried over Austria and the impending Italian talks. Grandi has refused to come to the Foreign Office for the last two days but now he has been summoned to meet both the P.M. and A.E. at No. 10 tomorrow in order to force him into the open. He has been apparently waiting for some instructions which will presumably contain a pressing appeal for immediate opening of conversations with us. A.E. feels we must go very slowly indeed over this in view of great uncertainty of situation. He feels Spain must still be *sine qua non* of any settlement and, in fact, Italians must be out of Spain before negotiations are begun. He feels P.M. will be sorely tempted to rush into immediate conversations and he has written to warn him against danger of this. A.E. feels more and more the difference between colleagues and himself. I said I thought he must insist on Spain being cleared up first as ONLY after that had been done could it be possible to make *de jure* recognition acceptable here. And if the P.M. won't agree to this, he (A.E.) must go. We do not know what, if any, secret understanding exists between Musso and Hitler. Has Hitler bought Musso off in Austria by any offer to back him in Spain later? If so, we should be fools to negotiate with him now if Spain is to be stoked up again in two months' time. Alternatively, if he has no arrangement with Hitler and wishes to use a conversation with us to

1. J. H. Thomas, National Labour M.P. for Derby, and former Colonial Secretary.

scare Hitler, then we are in a strong position to get the Italians out of Spain at our price. At Conservative Foreign Affairs Committee in the House of Commons this evening opinion was almost unanimous in opposing any talks with Italy just now, still less *de jure* recognition. This violent anti-Italian feeling is very significant and shows that opinion would back A.E.'s own instinct in this.

February 18th

P.M. and A.E. received Grandi this morning. He came to say that Italy wondered whether Great Britain really meant to open conversations, that Italy couldn't have both Germany and G.B. against her, and that if we didn't make haste Italy would become still more wedded to Germany. He said "there was very little time left". The P.M. referred to Ciano's messages of readiness to open discussion. Grandi said conversations should include everything and be held in Rome. When pressed, he said he had no instructions to mention Austria and he wasn't authorised to agree to Spanish plan. At conclusion, P.M. asked Grandi to return at three. P.M. then told A.E. he thought right course was to agree to immediate conversations in Rome and to announce it that afternoon! P.M. said "you've lost chance after chance with Italy", Musso was obviously in earnest; the announcement of the opening of conversations would be welcomed throughout Europe and America.

A.E. said he couldn't agree; he thought it would have the worst effect; look like capitulation to blackmail or panic. Musso was asking all the conditions from us, he had played us false so long and so often that we must insist on acts such as progress in Spain before we could possibly safely begin talks.

A.E. came back at 1.30 and talked it over with Bobbety, Alec Cadogan, Jim and me at lunch. We all agreed that it was impossible to announce conversations now: the question must anyway go to the Cabinet first, where he must state his views.

A.E. saw the P.M. again at 2.30 and it was agreed to hold Cabinet tomorrow Saturday afternoon and to tell Grandi when he called again that he was consulting his colleagues and would see him again on Monday.

A.E. had to go to Leamington at 5.30 so had little further time to discuss. He feels he cannot agree to formal opening of talks in such circumstances. He is very bitter at the way his colleagues treat him

93

and feels he cannot go on like this. We all feel he is right. He had a talk with Walter Elliot. It is really a completely different interpretation of events. We believe Muss is not sincere and is only gaining time. P.M. and No. 10 think Austria (Schuschnigg) interview at Berchtesgaden has changed everything![1]

February 19th

A.E. came back from Leamington about 11.30 and then started preparing his brief for this afternoon's Cabinet. Bobbety had prepared him a note taking the line that this was not the moment for opening any formal conversations with Muss. We must insist first on acts to convince us of his sincerity, i.e. in Spain and propaganda. Alec and Rex held that he might offer to agree to open conversations in Rome provided that they were tied up with settlement in Spain. I thought he might agree to open provided it was made clear that Muss had asked for conversations, that he accepted the Spanish plan and that it was understood nothing would be signed until the Italians were out of Spain. A.E. felt strongly that there should be no opening of conversations at all at present owing to uncertainty of situation (Hitler's speech on Sunday and Roosevelt plan probably due at the end of the week) and that they shouldn't in any case begin until progress had been made in Spain. Moreover, while P.M. thinks Muss is in earnest and effect of opening of conversations in Europe will be good, A.E. thinks the opposite. He proposes to take this line and to offer to resign if he is overruled.

We all lunched at F.O. together again (A.E., Bobbety, Alec, Jim Thomas, Rex Leeper, Caccia[2] and I). He saw Malcolm MacDonald, who thought No. 10 had treated him disgracefully. Simon came round, typically enough, to say that he couldn't see that any principles were involved and it was merely a question of timing. I walked across to No. 10 with A.E. He was cheered by crowds outside. Cabinet lasted till well past six. When A.E. returned to F.O. he said he'd resigned, but there was to be a further meeting at three tomorrow. He had stated his case but nearly all were against him, especially, however, the older ones . . . P.M., Simon, Sam Hoare,

1. See Appendix J for letter and note from O.H. to A.E. setting out position on possibility of talks with Italy.
2. Harold (later Lord) Caccia, then Assistant Private Secretary to Secretary of State.

Hailsham, Swinton: MacDonald and Elliot very close to A.E., Zetland close too (because he thought it would prejudice negotiations with Germany); Billy Gore, Burgin[1] and Brown[2] against: Shakespeare Morrison fairly close. Simon sought to prove no principles involved, but this had been too much for P.M. who had snubbed him. Halifax at the end had suggested compromise of announcing conversations now but saying nothing was to be delivered until Spain cleared.

A.E. felt more and more opposed to P.M.'s policy the more he heard of it. P.M. had no idea of what he wanted or where he was going. At the end of it A.E. announced that he must go.

We had a short talk on his return on the possibility of accepting some such compromise as Halifax suggested. Alec Cadogan, from official point of view, thought this would be good enough; A.E. would safeguard himself from charge of surrender to Muss, but he thought it very doubtful whether Muss could accept. A.E. feels himself that he would rather go as there is really a profound gulf between him and his colleagues. A genuine difference of outlook.

He went to dine with Malcolm MacDonald at Hampstead; and Bobbety and Jim were seeing him later. When I rang him after dinner he told me he hadn't changed his mind as to going . . . had I? I said no, all my feelings led me to say he had better go. He might have endeavoured to accept compromise if this had been the first instance, but I was convinced we should have exactly the same thing in a week over something else. He agreed.

February 20th

A.E. rang up at eleven and asked if my views had changed. I said "No." He said his hadn't either.

I went round at 11.30. W. Strang was there. Sunday papers have full and satisfactory accounts of deep division and expect resignation. We all feel no case for compromise and he must go. A.E. said Malcolm MacDonald, with whom he dined last night, thought that the P.M. realised this and wanted him to go. (MacDonald was then with P.M.) Alec Cadogan came round and feels same; there are two different policies and P.M.'s will have more chance if A.E. goes.

The P.M. sent for A.E. at 12.45. We drove down together. He

1. Leslie Burgin, Minister of Transport.
2. Ernest Brown, Minister of Labour.

feels certain in his own mind that the right course is to go, but much hates the prospect. He doesn't believe any colleagues will go too.

The P.M. told A.E. he wouldn't press him to stay, there was a real difference between the two, but a number of colleagues would put a great deal of pressure on him to remain. But he, the P.M., couldn't. Simon had for instance the idea that he should carry on for ten days and then go on health grounds!

A.E. also talked to Van on the telephone. He was very much concerned at European aspect of resignation.

I walked across with A.E. to the Cabinet at three.[1] The street was crowded and he received loud cheers. It lasted till 6.30. Papers were sent for and we, who were waiting in the Private Secretaries' room at F.O., felt alarm lest he should be giving way under the third degree methods of the Cabinet. He rang me up quite exhausted at about 6.30 and said a sub-committee had been at work on a compromise and he was being very strongly pressed to accept. I begged him to insist on time to consider calmly over at the F.O. what exactly the compromise amounted to. He then came over. He said his colleagues had all made difficulties when he had said that there were more differences than that over Italy. They took the line that A.E. couldn't go and there wasn't any such great difference between P.M. and himself. A sub-committee was set up of P.M., Halifax, Shakespeare Morrison, Stanley, Inskip and MacDonald to find a compromise. It was suggested that he should agree to the formal opening of conversations provided Italy accepted withdrawal formula and that though this agreement should be signed, no *de jure* should be given until Spain had been cleared up.

Malcolm MacDonald came across to the F.O. and urged this strongly. He said A.E.'s friends in the Cabinet all thought he ought to agree; they had moved far to meet him, he was putting his personal considerations before the National Government. MacDonald admitted that there would be sure to be another row with the P.M. in ten days and said he could go then. He (A.E.) said he really couldn't agree to a policy which he was absolutely convinced was wrong and would lead nowhere. He would have to defend it to the H. of C. the very next day. He was convinced the compromise wouldn't work and it represented in fact no advance on his original position of no conversations until there had been performance and not only promises. There were only two alternatives in reality – either the

1. See Appendix K for notes for this meeting.

P.M.'s of immediate formal conversations and no conditions, or his own of informal talks while Spain is being cleared up. A *via media* would be the worst of both and wouldn't be acceptable even to Musso.

He went back to the Cabinet again at 7.30 and resigned. When he had done this, Stanley said to Cabinet in his presence that he must reconsider his position if A.E. went. Halifax was very angry and said "you've put us in a most impossible position".

A.E. then drafted his letter of resignation and we went home and dined.

A.E., though unhappy at parting, is, I think, really glad to be out of it. He then began to prepare statement for H. of C. tomorrow with Bobbety and Jim. Bobbety fully agreed with his decision and is, of course, resigning too. We learn there is to be a further Cabinet at ten. A.E. fears they may still come after him. However, the P.M.'s letter accepting resignation arrived at twelve. (We think it bears evident signs of having been drafted by Simon.)

February 21st

I went and saw A.E. who was preparing his speech. He has no doubts. Large crowds outside his house. Jim Thomas and Bobbety came and we all lunched together. We hear Grandi is with the P.M. and that Simon is to take P.Q.s. Later we drove to the H. of C. Loud cheers from large crowds outside the House. We also heard that Roosevelt story was known in Fleet Street.

Statements of A.E. and Bobbety were first rate. They were side by side on the upper back benches and nothing could have been more impressive than the way these two young men got up in turn and announced that they had resigned for their principles. The House was bewildered and the P.M., who followed, was most unimpressive. Attlee made a biting attack and the ensuing debate was very disturbed. Harold Nicolson[1] attacked the Government and so did Paul Emrys-Evans who followed. The story was spread by the Whips that A.E. was ill; this is, of course, Simon's effort. We hear the Cabinet are furious at the veiled reference in A.E.'s statement to the Roosevelt business. Harry Crookshank gave me dinner; he was very troubled indeed, but having been completely ignorant and as his chief Oliver Stanley has not resigned, feels it very difficult for him to do so alone as it would look as if he had only done it to get out of his Coal Bill.

1. National Labour Member for West Leicester.

I believe the House is genuinely bewildered and in the face of no other resignation from the Cabinet feels obliged to stand by the P.M., but with many it is *à contre coeur* and the whole Government side looked most uncomfortable and sheepish. I think we must trust that the real issues will be taken up in the provinces later. There is to be a vote of censure tomorrow, when Winston and Lloyd George are to speak.

February 22nd

I went to F.O. A.E. came at eleven and said goodbye to the Office: most affecting as everybody is heartbroken. He discussed with Bobbety and Jim whether or not to reply to P.M. on the "threat" issue.[1]

I went to H. of C. at four. Vote of censure. P.M., who answered Greenwood,[2] had a very bad reception, many interruptions, and when he went on to speak of the League of Nations as a thing to be laid aside for better times, he horrified many of his supporters, besides giving a terrific opportunity for the Opposition. David Balniel[3] told me he was aghast at what he had said and believed there had been a tremendous miscalculation by the Government of the effect of A.E. going. Harry Crookshank also very worried. Winston and Lloyd George both spoke, not at their best however. I witnessed a scene between Ellen Wilkinson[4] and Lady Astor[5] in the corridor. A.E. attended the debate, partly to show that he wasn't ill as the Whips were kindly saying, and partly in case it was necessary to correct any further mis-statements of his case. He did, in fact, intervene once about Grandi's message of acceptance of the British withdrawal plan. P.M. said, in reply to Lloyd George, that he had received an intimation on Sunday from an unofficial friend that Grandi had instructions to accept the plan and that the document was not received till Monday. A.E. intervened to say that no such message

1. In his resignation speech, A.E. said: "It is seldom right to depart from the traditional method of diplomacy which has been tested by time and experience. It is certainly never right to do so because one party to the negotiations intimates that it is now or never. Agreements that are worthwhile are never made on the basis of a threat."
2. Rt. Hon. Arthur Greenwood, Labour M.P., Deputy Leader of the Opposition.
3. Now Lord Crawford; M.P. 1924–1940.   4. Labour M.P. for Jarrow.
5. Lady Astor, M.P. for Sutton Division of Plymouth 1919–1945.

or document had reached the F.O. while he was there, but in any case had he received it, this would not have affected his decision. (A.E. didn't intervene about the threat issue which the Government go on denying because he thinks he will deal with it later in a speech in the country.) But the P.M. and Lloyd George were at cross purposes. Lloyd George was seeking to prove that the P.M. had held back this message which he received on Sunday from A.E. But he hadn't because he told A.E. at lunch-time on Sunday that he had had it. The real points to bring out should of course have been (a) that GRANDI almost certainly held up the message until A.E.'s resignation was practically certain, and (b) the incredible fact that the P.M. ACCEPTED a message through an unofficial friend from a foreign Ambassador in London on a major issue of policy as sufficiently authoritative to place before his Cabinet instead of insisting on the Ambassador himself delivering his message or sending a document. But this perfect example of the new methods we must expect was completely lost on the H. of C.

Philip Sassoon took A.E. and me back to dine at Park Lane. We discussed his meeting in his constituency, which we all think should be held as soon as possible, and A.E. decided to have this on Friday. A.E. said he was now in an extremely difficult position as he had to decide what his future attitude should be. I said he should make his speech, setting out his faith once more, and then wait and see; either there might be an immediate reaction from the country, which would upset the Government, or there would be no immediate reaction and in that case A.E. should sit back, give the P.M. his run and then attack when he was getting on the rocks. We discussed the disastrous effects which the P.M.'s speech may be expected to have on Central Europe and France: it was an open intimation that Great Britain would do nothing to protect the small nations from the dictators. A.E. was delighted with his reception by the King today when he had delivered up his seals. The King had said he had great sympathy with his point of view and he didn't think it would be long before he saw him again.

We returned to H. of C. again after dinner to hear Morrison wind up for the Government. The Whips are exerting the utmost pressure to get people to vote for the Government and were even saying that A.E. *wished* members to vote for the Government! Morrison had been put up to wind up because doubtless he represented the younger men in the Cabinet and, as they didn't resign, they are to be made as responsible as possible for the new turn of events; to be thoroughly compromised in fact. Morrison's reply was in fact a light bantering after-dinner sort of speech which didn't attempt to deal with the real issues raised.

Afterwards I drove back with A.E. to Fitzhardinge Street. He was in very good spirits and feels absolutely justified. As he said, if he hadn't resigned on Sunday he would have had to resign tonight, after the P.M.'s speech about the League. He is disappointed with his colleagues, although he always said he never expected any of them would go. (I hear privately that Stanley is again wobbly and also Crookshank.) We hear the result of the divisions and think it pretty bad for the Government.

February 23rd

Halifax, who has been put temporarily in charge, came to F.O. today. He showed me the draft of his speech in the Lords for tomorrow and asked me to read it and see whether it was fair to A.E.

The facts seem fairly stated, but it really turns on *appreciation* of the facts, and here, of course, he must put his view which is the opposite of that of A.E. I pointed out that A.E.'s insistence on performance was because we had had two previous attempts at an Anglo-Italian *rapprochement* ("Gentlemen's Agreement" of January 1937 and P.M.'s letter of July), both of which had flopped owing to Spain and propaganda; a third flop might make things worse still.

Referring to the "threat" issue, H. proposed to say "the Cabinet were unaware of any threat except that of the Foreign Secretary's resignation", I said he couldn't really say that and he took it out.

He discussed the F.O. work in case he accepted. (He told me P.M. had offered it to him.) He said he was very lazy and disliked work. Could he hunt on Saturdays? I said there was a lot of work but much of it could be done at home or in the train and we agreed that he needn't see as much as A.E. used to do. (The difficulty always was to prevent A.E. seeing so much as he followed everything with a passionate interest.)

The Whips are evidently scared to death. (A.E. told me yesterday that both Hacking and Miss Maxse were aghast – as indeed they should be – at turn of events.)

February 25th

Halifax's appointment is announced today. R. A. Butler[1] is to be Under-Secretary.

Discussions with Perth and Alec on agenda for Rome conversations proceeded all day.

H. asked if we three Private Secretaries would stay on with him. I had previously talked to Alec about my position and he had strongly urged me to remain if asked. Alec had since spoken to H., whereupon the latter had said he would like to keep us.

I lunched with Charles Peake who told me Harry Crookshank has been in close contact with A.E. and helping with speech; likewise David Balniel. Van is using present change to try and increase his position. He has told H. that A.E. had agreed he should have access to P.M. and this was a condition of his taking it on. I'm certain this is not the case and told H. so. I said it would be best to be quite firm with Van from the start . . . viz. that H. should tell him that he would consult him when he wanted his advice but that he couldn't agree to his seeing P.M. unless he, H., especially wished him to do so.

Otherwise Alec's position, which was very difficult anyway, would be made impossible and the whole system would break down. H. agreed with this. I told him my view that the arrangement really was an unworkable compromise and that Van should have been sent abroad but that neither S.B. nor the present P.M. had faced this. Alec had put up with a great deal and wasn't in the least attached to outward forms but he must insist, for the sake of his post, on being directly responsible to the Secretary of State, and whilst quite prepared that H. should consult Van whenever he wanted to, he couldn't accept that Van should also be advising No. 10. I think H. quite saw this.

February 26th

Discussions of Perth's instructions continued. H. had Alec, R. A. Butler, Perth, Ingram[2] and other heads of departments concerned. I had asked him if he minded my being present at such meetings in

1. Now Lord Butler of Saffron Walden. Conservative M.P.
2. Maurice Ingram, Counsellor at Foreign Office. Previously Counsellor in Rome.

his room as it helped me to follow what was going on. He said no, and so I was also there. The idea is to consider instructions at Foreign Affairs Committee of Cabinet on Tuesday and then at the Cabinet itself on Wednesday so that Perth can go back to Rome on Saturday.

A.E.'s speech at Leamington yesterday is in all the papers; very dignified, not a fighting speech. He made it clear he supported the "National Government", though not *the* National Government. At the same time reaffirming with conviction that he had been absolutely right to resign and that he stood by all that he had said in the debate about the "threat". There was a good dig about our place being with the great democracies. I hear the Cabinet are much relieved. Halifax told me he thought it was "an awfully good speech".

February 27th

To sum up situation as I see it. It is quite evident that A.E. was right to go as he disapproved absolutely of the method proposed. But even if he could have agreed to compromise here, he had every reason to go on general record of P.M.'s treatment of foreign affairs, of which this was a typical instance. No Foreign Secretary could go on being responsible in circumstances to which he was being continually exposed (i.e. P.M.'s original letter to Muss . . . Halifax visit . . . Roosevelt plan). A Foreign Secretary must have continual and unquestioning support of P.M. and colleagues. A.E. never had this from P.M., and many colleagues were actively intriguing against him.

The Government were in a great fright at what they had done, as indeed they had every reason to be, and took every possible step to secure the London papers. *The Times*, of course, was on their side already. *Daily Telegraph* came heavily in against A.E. (Victor Gordon-Lennox[1] was in tears at the way his paper had behaved). The B.B.C. was told to say nothing that night about Germany and Italy. At the same time frantic telegrams have been sent to Paris and Washington to assure those Governments that there is "no change". But every act and utterance of the new regime proclaims the contrary. They cannot have it both ways . . . if there hadn't been a change A.E. would not have gone, and no propaganda nor pressure will alter this.

One sound element has been the provincial press, which alone is

1. Foreign Correspondent of the *Daily Telegraph*.

relatively free, e.g. *Birmingham Post, Manchester Guardian, Yorkshire Post*. The London press is rotten. All the London Conservative papers have toed the line. The Left press, *News Chronicle* and *Daily Herald*, naturally support him, but that is an embarrassment rather than an asset . . . like the Opposition cheers in the House.

What will happen next? The immediate effect has been to rejoice every dictator and to cause dismay in every democracy. The foreign press bears witness to this. In America and in the Dominions too, as far as can be seen, A.E.'s resignation has caused a profound and disagreeable shock.

Will Muss now play up and really deliver the goods? And will Hitler do the same? Or will they lead the P.M. up the garden path, keeping us in play until the democratic front has disintegrated? It is impossible to say. What seems certain is that all the worst elements in the Government (which A.E. had kept down) are now rampant again. Sam (and even Londonderry!) very much to the fore. All those, in fact, who are dictator-minded and defeatist.

I feel myself profoundly miserable at the turn events have taken. They have let our best man go at such a moment as this! Whilst more than ever convinced that A.E. had to go, I fear it is going to be worse before it is better. Thank God, though, that he is out of it and free to come back uncontaminated! All the worst elements in the Conservative Party are loose again. But the country is NOT Conservative and the floating vote upon which the National Government depends and which S.B. and A.E. held is now adrift. What will the country have to pay for this? A bitter experience. The Cabinet is now in the hands of six old discredited pre-war politicians and six young men who hadn't the courage of their inmost convictions. What is one to think of those wretched young men? Malcolm MacDonald (who could have ensured survival for his party by resigning), Elliot, Shakespeare Morrison (supposed to be a future P.M.!) and Oliver Stanley ("the Stanleys have been trimmers ever since Bosworth", as Lady Cranborne said when she heard he wasn't resigning). I believe they will never live this down.

I heard a nice story of a lady who had in her house an Austrian servant girl whom she found weeping. She asked her what was the matter. The girl replied that she was crying because Mr Eden had resigned and she didn't know now what would become of her mother who was a Jewess in Vienna.

We dined with A.E. and Beatrice just back from Leamington. He looked extraordinarily well and in very good spirits. He thinks of going now to Yorkshire and possibly America later. He'd had a tremendous reception in Leamington and a unanimous vote in his favour. We discussed what would happen now. He thinks himself the Government will stagger along more and more discredited, politics getting much more bitter, losing by-elections and all support from the "floating vote", and further resignations coming later.

Part Three
March 5th - September 30th 1938

With Eden's departure, the Prime Minister was free to pursue his policy of appeasement. His new Foreign Secretary, Halifax, had served in all the Conservative administrations since the War. He had been Minister for Education (twice), Minister for Agriculture, Minister for War, and Lord President of the Council under Chamberlain. From 1926 – 1931 he had been Viceroy of India. He was now aged 57 and known to be in sympathy with Chamberlain's views.

But the pursuit of an Agreement with Italy was once again overshadowed by Hitler who annexed Austria on March 11th. After the initial shock Chamberlain continued to believe that this would make Italy more anxious for British favours and he resumed his courtship of Mussolini.

In Palestine the Government were having to suppress a full-scale Arab rebellion, to the unconcealed delight of the totalitarian powers.

At the same time the Nazi presence in Austria brought Czechoslovakia into the forefront of the European scene, and the first Czech crisis took place in May.

Part Three
March 31st – September 30th 1938

March 5th

A depressing week. On Tuesday the Cabinet Committee approved Perth's instructions. Efforts are being made to influence the Press and the B.B.C. to refrain from anti-Italian or anti-German comment; at the same time all steps are being taken to reassure America and foreign opinion, as well as our own that there has been "no change".

On Wednesday the Cabinet itself approved Perth's instructions and he is to start off on Saturday taking Ingram with him. The instructions are extremely vague although covering all questions and it is hoped to reach agreement with Muss in some ten days. The results will be recorded in a series of *procès-verbaux*. Spain though figuring formally on the agenda, is to be left to the Non Intervention Committee and will only be taken up with Ciano if difficulties are encountered at the London Committee.

Halifax received the Negus, at the latter's request, on Wednesday. The Negus had written an appeal to the P.M. and had been persuaded not to publish it as had been his intention. (The Negus behaved extremely well over this.) He now came to urge that his country should not be made the subject of a deal. A pathetic interview in which the Negus showed great dignity.

A statement has been prepared in the Office for use by the P.M. explaining and reconciling as far as possible the different accounts which have been given by A.E., P.M., and Halifax about the League. It is intended that it should be used in a speech in the H. of C. on Defence Debate on Monday. (We heard later that P.M. thought it too apologetic and proposed to make his own version . . . if he does this he will probably again make matters worse!)

We had a discussion on Thursday (H., Butler, Mounsey, Plymouth) as to how far it will be possible in practice to link up the Spanish settlement with the Anglo-Italian Settlement. It is probable that the latter, on the basis of Perth's instructions, will be concluded in ten days, but there is little or no hope of any serious progress

107

having been made with withdrawal from Spain by then. The Russians and the French are obviously very suspicious and are beginning to make difficulties, but even if there is no hitch, it is calculated that ten days are necessary to complete the evacuation once the scheme is adopted and put into operation. The P.M. and H., however, are desperately anxious to secure some sort of release authorising recognition of Abyssinia *de jure* from Geneva in May. Nonetheless they have pledged themselves to Parliament to include a settlement of the Spanish Question in the Anglo-Italian agreement.

They are indeed in a fix. They want a quick success with Muss and will certainly not wait if it can be represented – as well it may – that delay in Spain is due not to the Italians but to the Soviets and French. But I doubt if that will carry conviction with opinion here, still less at Geneva. (They are also pledged to proceed with the League in the matter of recognition.)

H. saw Reith[1] of the B.B.C. on Thursday to ask him not to proceed with a series of talks on the subject of the return of the German Colonies. Reith asked H. pointblank whether H.M.G. wished him to stop them – to which H. replied that was so but he would deny it if challenged in public!

On Friday we received Henderson's telegram describing his conversation with Hitler on the previous day. He had carried out his instructions to sound him as to a settlement of the colonial question on the basis of a middle zone in Africa being made open again in which Germany with others should participate on principles such as those provided by the Congo Basin Act; such settlement being dependent upon assurance of good behaviour as regards Central Europe. (These instructions had been held up on account of the Schuschnigg interview at Berchtesgaden and then of Hitler's speech. They were practically the same as those approved in A.E.'s time except that the references to Austria had been toned down.) Hitler was in a mad mood and after Henderson had said his piece, he started raving and attacked the British press, the British Bishops and the British Government for interfering in German affairs and stiffening resistance to Germany in Central Europe. He said the Colonial question could wait, there was no hurry for that; but he was determined to protect the ten million Germans outside Germany in Central Europe and to secure for them equal conditions "even if it

1. Sir John Reith (now Lord Reith), Director of the B.B.C. 1927–1938.

meant war". In fact we could not have received a more complete rebuff . . . even on the question of limitation of armaments or at least of "humanising bombing", on which Hitler had previously held out some hopes, he was absolutely negative on the ground that this would involve Soviet Russia. Henderson himself in reporting the conversation was forced to admit that the prospect seemed hopeless and that we could only console ourselves with the fact that we had made a further effort and that it was not our fault if it had failed. The position is to be considered on Monday morning. Meanwhile H. left Yorkshire for the weekend . . . he wants to hunt tomorrow!

What I am sure the Government would like to do is to have an election in the Autumn on the claim that they have made peace with Hitler and Mussolini and that the armaments bill can now be reduced. They will strain every nerve to get some specious success for this purpose. They *may* get an agreement with Muss but without Spain and they have now got a flat refusal from Hitler. But even full agreement with Muss including Spain would be valueless to justify disarmament without agreement with Hitler.

But what is so dangerous now is the state of mind of Hitler and his determination to have his way in Central Europe. A.E.'s departure has unsettled the whole world and our friends are full of suspicion at what the P.M. may do next: the dictators are encouraged in the belief that we are becoming isolationist and disinterested. A.E. was a symbol for a certain policy which all alike had come to understand. It had steadied our friends and it had kept the dictators guessing; this was the utmost it could do to make our influence felt. Granted, as I always have, that nobody would fight for Austria, what will happen now if Czechoslovakia is challenged and she resists as Hodza[1] says she will? France has said she will stand by her ally, and if she does, it will mean a European war. Will Hitler be tempted to make a fresh "coup" because he believes the P.M. and H. would stand aside and France would not dare to move without us? That is the danger of the situation as I see it.

March 6th

We had supper with the Edens who returned from Yorkshire today and go to the South of France for a fortnight on Tuesday. He looked very well. He much hopes the French Government will be firm over

1. Milan Hodza, Prime Minister of Czechoslovakia.

Spain, etc. and generally refuse to be rattled in the present situation as he is sure opinion here will back them up. He had had a very satisfactory letter from Mann[1] of the *Yorkshire Post* and also from Rupert Beckett the proprietor: Mann had also written to Halifax. Shoals of letters continue to reach him and give him much pleasure. A good one from the Archbishop of Canterbury. He proposes to speak in his constituency in April; then he has his broadcast on "England" on St George's Day, and also a speech to the Brotherhood later in the Summer. In the South of France he will be seeing Baldwin which will be valuable. The Whips have asked him if he will publicly disown the Council of Action's Referendum on his resignation. He has refused to do so, quite rightly, I think, because although he has had nothing to do with it and may disapprove of some of its promoters, the movement itself comes from those who support him and want to help him – why should he discourage them? He is still playing with the idea of a short visit to America in May – if the situation here permits. I am in favour of it if it is possible as I would like him to meet Roosevelt and make clear his position about the Plan.

March 7th

Discussion in H.'s room on Hitler's reception of Henderson's instructions (Alec C., Van, Butler, Sargent, Strang and me). H. proposes to read Ribbentrop a lecture in tone between sorrow and anger correcting Hitler's grossest misrepresentations and warning him also of the dangers of precipitate action in Central Europe. He would like to revive what he calls the "guessing Position" of the Leamington speech[2] under which Germany could never be sure that H.M.G. would not intervene in Central Europe and the French could never be sure that we *would* – thereby discouraging both from forward policies. He would like to say to Ribbentrop that no one in Great Britain wants to fight for Czechoslovakia but if Czechoslovakia were attacked, there would be very great risk of a general conflagration in which we should be inevitably dragged in. A draft brief is being prepared in this sense and he will show it to P.M. He is to see Ribbentrop on Thursday (R. is coming over for three days to say goodbye).[3]

1. A. H. Mann, Editor of *Yorkshire Post* 1919–1939.
2. Of Eden on November 20th 1936.
3. Ribbentrop had just become German Foreign Minister.

Hardinge[1] asked whether the King ought to give him a luncheon: he was not particularly anxious to do so as R. had taken no trouble to reside here as Ambassador and had moreover been conspicuously unhelpful during Henderson's conversations with Hitler, but was prepared to do so if P.M. and H. thought it desirable. Both P.M. and H. thought this would be excessive and the P.M. is to give the R.'s lunch instead and the King will just receive him.

March 8th

H. received the British press today, a difficult business as he appealed to them to refrain as far as possible from reporting "rumours" which might embitter relations with Germany and Italy. Press are of course profoundly suspicious and will remain so, whatever the Government say, until they are convinced by acts that the Government are not going to run after the Dictators and abandon Central Europe and the League. H. was questioned about the linking of Spain to the Italian conversations and about our attitude to Czechoslovakia. His replies could hardly be very reassuring.

March 9th

Cabinet today approved the line H. proposes to take with Ribbentrop tomorrow.

We received telegrams from Perth on his first contacts with Ciano. Latter seemed ready to go ahead with us on all points in our proposals, but he raised at once the question of how soon H.M.G. intended to take up recognition of Abyssinia at Geneva. He did not wish to wait for May Council since he thought agreement could be reached on all questions in two to three weeks. When Perth mentioned Spain, he objected strongly to implementing of agreement being held up for this. He asked exactly what P.M. had meant by "a settlement of the Spanish question" (this is of course exactly what A.E. expected would happen. Italy will try and get a settlement from us without giving us anything in Spain).

Later H. discussed with Alec C., Mounsey, Plymouth and Van at what point H.M.G. would be justified in disassociating Italian negotiations from Spanish question. He is preparing a paper for

1. Sir Alexander Hardinge (later Lord Hardinge of Penshurst), the King's Private Secretary.

Cabinet on the subject. If he is personally satisfied of Italian good faith and if delay in withdrawals is not due to Italian obstruction, he would favour telling H. of C. frankly that H.M.G. propose to depart from P.M.'s undertaking to link up Anglo-Italian agreement with settlement of Spanish Question. But this is going to be very difficult as after recent crisis opinion will be very suspicious and P.M. will be charged with bad faith and with being fooled again by Italian assurances. Again it will be very difficult to get Geneva to move unless there is marked progress in the Spanish question. H. however means to proceed with recognition with League of Nations if possible but without it if necessary and if he is satisfied with Italian *bona fides*. Meanwhile French Government are becoming very sticky as regards withdrawal scheme itself. We are in danger of an Anglo-French row over this from which Mussolini will take the profit.

News came tonight of Schuschnigg's intention of holding a plebiscite in Austria next Sunday. It looks as if we might be in for a Nazi putsch there now, whichever way the vote goes. The French Government have sent us a further note pressing us to give Germany a vigorous warning against high-handed procedure not only as regards Austria but as regards Czechoslovakia also, and making it quite clear, as Delbos has already said in his speech, that France means to fight for Czechoslovakia.

March 10th

Ribbentrop came to see H. this morning. He was greeted with cries of "Release Niemöller![1]" on arrival from a considerable but orderly crowd outside the Foreign Office. When he left the crowds were larger and shouted "Ribbentrop get out" in chorus.

He stayed for two hours and H. saw him with Alec. He said much the same as Hitler had said about Germany's attitude towards Colonies and Central Europe and the Press. H. gave him his lecture according to plan but it is doubtful if it made any impression on him. About Austria Ribbentrop made plain that he much disliked plebiscite and asked H. to use his influence to get it cancelled. H. said it was a tall order to suggest that the P.M. of an independent country could not have a plebiscite if he wanted and urged that everything should be done to ensure that it should be held in calm and free conditions.

1. Pastor Martin Niemöller, imprisoned by the Nazis since May 28th 1937.

March 11th

We learned today of German troop movements in Bavaria in connection with the Austrian plebiscite. When H. saw Ribbentrop yesterday he had given him a warning that we should expect Germany to do all she could to ensure that the plebiscite was free and undisturbed. Nevile Henderson was instructed at once this morning to repeat this warning to Hitler immediately. H., however, has no delusions that this will have any effect. "The only thing they understand is force," he said to Cadogan and me, "a warning will be useless unless accompanied by a threat to use force which we cannot do." At the same time he thinks Schuschnigg's action in calling plebiscite foolish and provocative.

Ribbentrop was lunching today at No. 10 and as the party were talking after luncheon news came of the German ultimatum to Austria demanding cancellation of the plebiscite and Schuschnigg's resignation. S. was willing to accept former but refused latter. P.M. and H. took Ribbentrop to another room and spoke sharply to him about this. Latter professed ignorance of the facts but claimed that Austria had been provocative and that anyway we should welcome "a peaceful solution". R. made the worst impression on P.M. Schuschnigg had meanwhile asked our advice as to what he should do. Reply was sent that we had spoken to Ribbentrop and also to Berlin but that as to Schuschnigg's position we were unable to advise in a matter affecting the safety of his country in respect of which we could offer no guarantee.

H. afterwards agreed with me that situation was "bloody" and complained bitterly of these highwaymen's methods. He went to German Embassy at 5.15 to say goodbye to Ribbentrop where he stayed an hour and again spoke most severely to him. Ribbentrop had heard that Schuschnigg had resigned (although this turned out to be premature) and claimed that now this question was out of the way Anglo-German relations would be easier! H. left him under no delusion in this respect – he said such methods would set back our relations indefinitely. The whole British press tomorrow would stigmatise this German action as "a surrender to naked force" and would declare that if it was Austria today it might be Czechoslovakia or what next tomorrow. Ribbentrop said that countries had sometimes to be strong and hard and instanced Great Britain and Ireland. H.

said there could be no worse analogy. At that time Ireland was as much part of England as London or Yorks: but what would the Germans have said if we, Great Britain, had sent Belgium an ultimatum saying that her Prime Minister was anti-British and must resign by 5 p.m. or we'd bombard Antwerp? That was a much closer analogy. Ribbentrop is so dense however that H. does not feel that anything said to him has the least effect.

Meanwhile we had heard of a second German ultimatum demanding Schuschnigg's resignation by 5.30, failing which German aeroplanes would fly over Vienna. On his return from Ribbentrop, H. sent off a further telegram to Henderson to protest in the strongest terms against such use of coercion which was incompatible with the independent status of Austria.

Messages came in continually by telephone, and telegrams from the Press, from our Legation and the Austrian Legation, mainly contradictory. Our Legation reported the advance of German troops into Austria on the authority of the Austrian Government but later the Austrian War Office said they could not confirm this. We also had a report that Goering was in Vienna. Finally we heard that Schuschnigg had resigned and was broadcasting farewell and asking the country not to resist the act of force and that Seyss-Inquart had been made Chancellor.

We all returned to Foreign Office after dinner to see any further telegrams. A telegram was sent to Washington for information of Roosevelt describing the course of events and what we had done. We admitted the failure of our effort at conversations with Germany "one of the two matters because of which we'd asked the President to hold up his plan" but added that H.M.G. still hoped to reach results with Italy.

March 12th

Cabinet met from 10.30-12.30 after which a full communiqué was issued full of warnings.

Cabinet is to meet again on Monday to make up its mind on the statement to be made in Parliament and whether it should also be announced that we are increasing our Air Force Programme in consequence.

Today's news is that German troops are pouring into Austria and aeroplanes are over Vienna. It has been given out in Germany that German forces had been sent in at request of Austrian Government to maintain order and to protect Austrian Nazis!

H. saw Attlee whom he described as very sensible and intelligent and who did not press for a debate.

He also saw Corbin and Masaryk. The former urged that the two Governments should consult with a view to a policy of common action. H. asked him how exactly France contemplated bringing support to Czechoslovakia. Delbos had also seen Phipps and told him that German aggression against Czechoslovakia would mean France going to assist the Czechs: he urged that H.M.G. should agree to a joint warning to Germany. Masaryk reported the assurances given to the Czechs by Goering: he said Benes was not apprehensive of immediate trouble and suggested that we should take note of Goering's assurances.

The Press is unanimous in condemning Germany's behaviour. Even *The Times*, though reluctantly so but H. had spoken to Dawson[1] who will do whatever H. tells him. I dined with Harry Crookshank who was very worried about the situation and has no confidence in the P.M. He thinks the party's chances are ruined for years unless A.E. can be brought in but does not see how this can be done. He told me of his letter to the P.M. complaining about his attitude towards the League and how the P.M. had sent for him and assured him that the Government had not changed its attitude. I also had a letter from Jim Thomas who is with A.E. in the South of France describing S.B.'s fury at what Neville C. had done – "all my work in keeping politics national instead of party undone," "Anthony could have done nothing else". "He has added immeasurably to his reputation". The Baldwins and Edens had been seeing a great deal of each other down there – the best possible thing. S.B. is the one man who may one day be able to turn the scales for him.

March 13th

Austria now declared a German "Land".

We've decided to recall Palairet at once or else we may be presented with a German demand for his recall.

Perth reported his interview with Ciano whom he had asked for Italian views. Latter made it quite clear that Mussolini would do

1. Geoffrey Dawson, Editor of *The Times* (1923–1941).

nothing. We also received a note from Neurath rejecting our protests as inadmissible in a dispute between German nations.

March 14th

Cabinet at eleven which approved draft of statement for Parliament this afternoon. There is to be a debate in the House of Commons after all tonight and in the Lords on Wednesday. Government intend to announce increase in armament programme.

News from France of formation of a narrow Radical and Socialist Government under Blum with Boncour[1] as M.F.A. Very disappointing. Apparently the formation of a real National Government from the Right to the Communists was only blocked by that snake Flandin.[2] But I do not feel this Government will last and will thus make way for a genuine National Government.

March 15th

Foreign Policy Committee of Cabinet met today to consider H.'s paper on relation of Anglo-Italian negotiations to Spanish question which recommended (a) not holding up Anglo-Italian negotiations because of Spain if we were satisfied that delay wasn't Italy's fault and (b) proceeding with *de jure* recognition of Abyssinia at Geneva by unilateral declaration if a general resolution could not be obtained. Committee felt however that in view of Austria it would be impossible to secure public opinion here for such a policy and that we must insist on some performance by way of a gesture to prove Italy's good faith in Spain. A telegram is being sent to Perth to explain this to Ciano who is objecting strongly to any idea of subordinating agreement or recognition etc. to Spain in Geneva. In fact we are very nearly back where A.E. said they would stick!

Moley has put up a paper urging that we should give an indirect guarantee to Czechoslovakia viz. that we should announce that if France is attacked by Germany as a result of her going to the support of Czechoslovakia against unprovoked German aggression, Great Britain would support France. This is the furthest probably that we could go. I do not believe a direct guarantee of Czecho-

1. Paul Boncour, former Prime Minister, Permanent French Delegate to League of Nations.
2. P.-E. Flandin, French Premier, November 1934–1935, and Foreign Minister 1936 in Sarraut's Government.

slovakia is possible – but this is also the least we should do if we are to stop the rot. I lunched with Paul Emrys-Evans who was much less despondent than I was. He thought people, even in the City, felt that events were rapidly proving A.E. right.

What I feel is that the Austrian crisis has come as a godsend to the Government. Their approach to Hitler had completely failed and this rebuff would have had to be revealed – their approach to Mussolini would almost certainly get them into difficulties over Spain and Geneva – therefore by the end of 2-3 months P.M. would have had to admit failure on both points of his policy. Now, however, Austria has come as a red herring and they are able to cover up their own failure with Hitler with the general indignation at the rape of Austria, which they trust will also help their case in public opinion for speedy negotiations with Italy. Government obviously intend to use the crisis to save Swinton in spite of the Cadman report on the ground that he must handle the increased air programme. In the meanwhile we know that Italy has been pouring further munitions into Spain and Franco looks like taking Barcelona.

We heard yesterday from Washington that Roosevelt has now decided to postpone his plan indefinitely as the moment had passed, although he had thought a favourable opportunity had offered in January. So that initiative has been effectively killed as we feared. If only that plan had been launched in January, I can believe that these events in Austria would not have occurred. This is perhaps the worst of the P.M.'s blunders. But I still think he will come to grief over Musso.

I am convinced that only a vigorous policy with France embracing some indirect guarantee of Czechoslovakia plus more and faster rearmament especially in the air, can now stop Europe stumbling into war. But I am also certain that this Government without A.E.'s appeal cannot put such a policy across the country and secure Labour (T.U.C.) support (indispensable for making labour available for accelerating armament). For it must never be forgotten that with A.E.'s departure they have lost "the floating vote" and the confidence of the Left – and this applies as much at home as abroad where the small "floating" states are now full of mistrust.

Rex Leeper told me today of an amazing message he had heard had been sent by S.B. through a third party to Mann of the *Yorkshire Post*, saying that he was so disturbed at P.M.'s action in letting A.E. go and destroying the whole basis of the National Government and at the danger to the country that the Government must go and give way to a new Government with S.B. himself as Lord President, Winston as P.M. and A.E. as Foreign Secretary! I can hardly believe it, especially as regards Winston as P.M., but I hope at least it means that the old man is at work on something.

March 16th

Grave news from Spain where Franco's offensive aided by German and Italian aircraft and tanks now threatens to break through to the sea and cut off Barcelona from Valencia. The French are increasingly nervous and want H.M.G. to mediate, failing which Boncour says he will be compelled to open the frontier and intervene on the side of the Spanish Government. H.M.G. in a quandary because they want to maintain Non-Intervention and because they feel mediation now offers no prospect of success. They are toying with the idea of a meeting with French Ministers to discuss whole situation both Spain and Central Europe (which French Government also want) but feel – rightly – that it is useless to talk to present Blum-Boncour Government which will fall in a few days and want to await formation of real National Government in France with which talks would be fruitful.

Paul Emrys-Evans tells me the City is getting alarmed at last and has lost confidence in P.M. and Co.

I spent afternoon in H. of L. for debate on Foreign Affairs – what a contrast after H. of C.! A perfectly dead atmosphere, Cecil,[1] Crewe,[2] Snell[3] and Strabolgi[4] attacked Government: Lothian[5] and Londonderry supported. Cecil impossible as always. Strabolgi beat the box and tried (unsuccessfully) to put a little feeling into the debate. Londonderry pure pro-Nazi apologist, Lothian very washy. H. wound up in a not very impressive speech – full of lofty sentiments but nothing much else.

In the H. of C. the Opposition moved the adjournment on Spain. P.M. had to speak again and Simon wound up. Latter had a very rough passage.

1. Lord Cecil of Chelwood, President of the League of Nations Union.
2. Marquess of Crewe, former Secretary of State for India, War, etc.
3. Lord Snell, Chairman of the L.C.C. 1919–1925. Labour M.P. 1922–1931.
4. Lord Strabolgi, Opposition Chief Whip in House of Lords.
5. Marquess of Lothian. Ambassador to U.S. 1939–1940.

In Cabinet this morning as in Foreign Affairs Committee yesterday there was a good deal of plain speaking by younger members of Cabinet. Belisha[1] complained of lack of policy and need for vigour. Stanley and MacDonald were also critical (why did they not speak up like this three weeks ago?).

Attempts to draft telegram to Perth about Spain unsuccessful and it is still held up. Mounsey and Plymouth feel they've been set an impossible task.

March 17th

I lunched with Nigel Law[2] who confirmed what Paul said about City being now violently anti-P.M. and insisting on broader Government with Winston in it.

Position about a guarantee to Czechoslovakia now is (i) That Chiefs of Staff have been asked to advise on military aspect of (a) our giving a contingent guarantee to France to protect her if attacked in consequence of her going to support of Czechoslovakia, and (b) a Grand Alliance *à la* Winston of Great Britain, France, Russia, Little Entente, etc., etc., based on League of Nations and directed against any and all aggression: (ii) That Foreign Office have produced a draft Cabinet paper on political aspect recommending a contingent guarantee to France as above coupled with a requirement that Czechoslovakia should allow an Anglo-French or a purely British Commission of inquiry to visit Czechoslovakia and report on Sudeten position.

P.M.'s thoughts are apparently moving on these lines and H. has been discussing this with him. Meanwhile great pressure is being put on him in H. of C. to make a pronouncement of policy in this respect and Butler told me today that he, the P.M., showed signs of being rather rattled by it, although in H. of C. this afternoon, as it turned out, he wasn't pressed overmuch.

We had a discussion in H.'s room this evening about telegram to Perth about Spain and H. dictated a bit proposing Anglo-Italian mediation – but we all feel this would not possibly work and telegram is still held up. H. said Cabinet would not stand for mere Italian assurances in respect of Spain now. H. also feels we shall not get any performance out of them until Franco has won, so we are in

1. Leslie Hore-Belisha, Minister for War.
2. Formerly of the Foreign Office.

a complete jam – hence the mediation idea – but of course Franco won't look at mediation now.

Evening papers this evening are full of reports of division in the Cabinet and in the Government majority in H. of C. over delay in giving guarantee to Czechoslovakia. This must mean the breakdown is in sight – far sooner than I had expected.

Press people are talking now as if the Government could not carry on as it is even over the week-end. What they will do of course is to appeal to the outsiders to come in and help in the National Emergency and the greatest pressure, I expect, will be put on Winston and A.E. – but I hope and believe these two will refuse to come in with the present P.M. because as long as he is there he will try to run foreign policy and the country will be suspicious. I think Stanley Baldwin might be brought back as President of Council to assure the Apostolic Succession, then A.E. could be P.M. or Foreign Secretary. I would like to see Winston as Air Minister or Minister of Co-ordination – but definitely not P.M.; I would rather see A.E. as Foreign Secretary than P.M. at this stage provided always he had his hands free and the loyal support of a P.M. – but who is to be P.M.?

March 18th

Foreign Policy Committee of Cabinet meet this evening to consider F.O. memo on Czechoslovakia situation and possibility of H.M.G. accepting a further commitment – also the telegram to Perth about the relation of Spain to the Anglo-Italian conversations. We had a further discussion about the latter in H.'s room first as a result of which the idea of suggesting mediation in conjunction with the Italians has been dropped; instead it is proposed to tell the Italians frankly of H.M.G.'s dilemma, namely that they cannot secure the acceptance here of an Anglo-Italian agreement whilst events in Spain continue as they are, and to ask whether the Italians have any suggestions to make.

Poland has addressed an ultimatum to Lithuania demanding establishment of diplomatic relations within 48 hours in consequence of recent frontier incident (Lithuania has hitherto refused any diplomatic relations with Poland much to the latter's annoyance, owing to Poland having seized Vilna years ago as a result of a perfectly outrageous military coup which was never redressed). Lithuanian Minister came to see H. today and said his Government seemed disposed to accept. H. urged acceptance, as also the French have done. After all, monstrously as Poland has behaved in the past, she is not asking very much now, certainly not enough to justify bloodshed.

March 19th

Polish-Lithuanian dispute has been settled with acceptance of Polish ultimatum.

Foreign Affairs Committee is to meet again on Monday to continue discussion of Czechoslovakia memo. Very divided counsels. The telegram to Perth about Spain has been held up again. (What the Government hope for now of course is an early victory by Franco so that they can then get Italy to withdraw.)

We've received further secret information that the Italian aircraft are being ordered from Rome to intensify the bombardment of Barcelona. A telegram is now being sent to Rome telling Perth to refer to "rumours" to this effect and emphasise disastrous effect on Anglo-Italian conversations if they were confirmed.

H. told me he could quite understand German action in regard to Austria but he did not regard it as likely that Germany meant to use this as a first step towards recreating a vast Empire in Central Europe and the Balkans (which is Van's idea). Nazi Germany's whole policy was based on race. There was in any case no objection to Germany having economic hegemony in Central Europe. What H. objected to was the methods employed and the fact that Germany did not realise the effect of such methods on us and world generally, or that, if she did, she did not care. I said that all anti-German feeling here and wish to block Germany only went back to beginning of Nazi regime; if the Brüning[1] regime had continued Germany would long ago have received her colonies, etc.

H. said he was very suspicious of Soviet Russia and convinced that a direct guarantee to Czechoslovakia was impossible; he feels something, though not much, should be given to France. He thinks opinion is now influenced by events and anti-dictator feeling and demands a lead but does not know where it wants to go and may bitterly regret commitments entered into in a hurry. He is much impressed by military weakness of France and ourselves. I said I thought we wanted something between a guarantee to Czecho-

1. Dr Heinrich Brüning, German Chancellor 1930–1932.

slovakia and present situation – viz., a greater guarantee to France – we ought to try and restore "the guessing situation" by making it more uncertain in Hitler's mind that we would *not* intervene whilst making France rather more certain that we would stand by her. After all, weak as we might be, Germany must also take Russia into account with her air force, though we need have no illusions ourselves about Russia coming to our help. Germany was very vulnerable in the East. I was myself convinced Hitler would not do anything if he was certain it would involve a European war.

March 21st

Foreign Affairs Committee today considered further the Czech memo and a draft statement for Parliament to be made on Thursday. Also the telegram to Perth about Spain. As regards the former it is now proposed, contrary to what I had hoped and to some extent expected, to do absolutely nothing, i.e., to tell the French and the Czechs that we cannot increase our existing commitments and merely to repeat the Leamington speech (they can never do anything without quoting A.E.!). It is of course as good as an invitation to Hitler to step into Czechoslovakia. It is just possible that the Cabinet (which is to decide tomorrow) may recoil from the consequences internal and external of this. The decision is based on the Chiefs of Staff report which gives the most pessimistic account of our state of defence compared with Germany's. There could be no more damning document to the Government – what has been done with all the money voted for re-armament and why should Germany by now have a larger air force than France and ourselves combined? And why should we have no A.A. defences? For the last two years A.E. has been writing to the P.M. of the need for greater speeding up and of the importance of the early years.

Again and again the F.O. have warned the Cabinet and the Air Ministry that the German figures on which the latter were working were false. When A.E. took office, he was told that if he could keep the peace for two years we should then have the defences necessary for a more positive policy. And now this!

The telegram to Perth about Spain has at last been approved and sent off. It amounts to a confession to Mussolini that H.M.G. cannot implement any Anglo-Italian agreement including recognition of Abyssinia until progress has been made with actual withdrawal from Spain.

March 22nd

Cabinet today approved proposed policy in regard to Czechoslovakia; alterations of drafting are to be made in the statement to Parliament and the communication to the French Government (to be made in Paris tomorrow evening) so as to make it less bleak.

I talked to Moley today. He really feels that all is lost. A mixture of utter contempt for the Government and profound anxiety as to the consequences.

March 24th

As a result of almost continuous tinkering the statement for Parliament today has now been considerably improved, largely as a result, it appears, of the efforts of the other members of the Cabinet who insisted on the P.M. making it less negative and more friendly to France. Whilst we still say we refuse to give guarantees either to Czechoslovakia or to France (beyond Locarno) we repeat Leamington speech and say definitely this *might* apply to Czecho. In our note to French Government we've also suggested holding immediate air staff conversations.

March 25th

I was not in H. of C. yesterday but hear that P.M.'s statement went well except for the references to Italy and Spain which flopped badly. (F.O. were opposed to putting this in which was H. Wilson's idea.) The general impression seems to have been that it was better than was expected. Winston made a great oration, the main point of which was that we were getting the worst of both worlds – although we admitted that in certain circumstances we should *have* to come in, we failed to use this necessity to its full deterrent value by saying we *would* come in. Reception abroad has been fairly good, even in France. Boncour, however, objected strongly to idea proposed by us of bringing Germany into negotiations with ourselves and France and Czecho over Sudeten. He said that if Germany attacked Czecho, France would first call Council of League and only intervene after that body had pronounced that an act of aggression had been committed. He clearly contemplated invasion of Rhineland in such circumstances.

I am inclined to agree now that statement was not too bad and perhaps as much as could have been expected of Government in view of defence position. But it all depends on how it is carried out. Will they really expedite re-armament now so that we shall be in a position to stand up for ourselves and our friends? Trouble is I do not trust them to do this. H. is terribly weak where resistance is required and neither he nor P.M. have such an abhorrence of dictatorship as to overcome their innate mistrust of French democracy and its supposed inefficiency. I am amazed that H. with all his High Church principles is not more shocked at Hitler's proceedings – but he is always trying to understand Germans. He easily blinds himself to unpleasant facts and is ingenious and even jesuitical in rounding awkward corners in his mind. "My colleagues are dictator-minded!" as A.E. used to say, and it is true. Again, I gravely doubt their determination, without A.E. to drive them, to press on with the re-armament, staff talks, etc. Inskip has no drive whatever. The General Staffs are defeatist especially Admiralty. How can one have confidence in Swinton after the mess he has made of civil aviation (vide Cadman Report) and after the way we at F.O. know Air Ministry have always allowed themselves to be hoodwinked by false German air figures?

Baldwin returns to London tomorrow and H. has asked to see him on Monday night. He wants to give him his version of A.E.'s resignation.

There is to be a meeting of Foreign Affairs Committee of Cabinet on Tuesday to consider procedure at Geneva regarding Abyssinia. The idea is that we are to go ahead at Geneva and try (a) for a resolution leaving us all free to recognise, and failing unanimity necessary for this method, we should (b) proceed by unilateral declaration. We are going to tell French and other members of Council in advance of our intention in regard to (a) and enlist their support. Once we've dealt with Geneva by one of these alternatives we shall hold ourselves free to recognise when we think the moment has come, i.e., when Anglo-Italian conversations are complete and when "a settlement of Spanish question allows." Whatever that may mean but probably in fact when Franco has won. Despairing of hope of any progress on Non-Intervention withdrawal scheme, we are now endeavouring to pin Ciano down to undertaking that his volunteers will be withdrawn as soon as Franco has won. It looks in fact as if poor Republicans would not now last more than a month or so. I had a long talk with William Strang – looking back on it all, we agreed that there had been a regular conspiracy to drive A.E. out. The "old gang" were prepared to keep him so long as he toed the line and they ran the policy but as soon as they saw he would not do this, they made life as intolerable for him as possible by continual interference and sabotage – not a pretty story. We both were very bitter about it but anyway there was no doubt between us that A.E. had been right to go.

March 31st

Cabinet yesterday agreed on instructions to be sent to Perth regarding League and Spain, viz., that it was hoped that Anglo-Italian agreement could be signed in a few weeks, that meanwhile on April 9th H.M.G. would give necessary month's notice of their intention of raising Abyssinian question at Geneva with a view to some liberating action, but that Anglo-Italian agreement should not be brought into force until H.M.G. were satisfied sufficient progress had been made in Spain. Ciano is to be told that we consider he should regard our action on April 9th in regard to Geneva as sufficient guarantee of our intentions and should not require any written document as well.

April 1st

We had a meeting today in H.'s room to consider what concessions we might urge on Czech Government to make to Sudeten. Extremely difficult to know what to suggest especially as in addition to Sudeten there are the other minorities all round the perimeter of the State; geographically they are hardly suitably placed for autonomy unless perhaps through a cantonal system like Switzerland, though here again any cohesive element such as common patriotism or common fear is lacking. It was felt that we had not sufficient information to justify our recommending any specific course of reform. It was agreed however that we ought to speak strongly to the French with a view to our both speaking firmly to Benes and insisting on the

125

necessity for him meeting Henlein[1] and doing all he could to reach agreement with him. A paper on these lines is to be prepared for the Foreign Policy Committee of Cabinet.

Perth has now replied pressing strongly that we should agree to give Ciano a letter defining our intentions at Geneva in return for which Ciano should put in writing his assurances about Spain. Drafts have now been prepared in this sense (a) taking note of Italian assurances *re* withdrawal of men after war is over and respect for *status quo* in Spain (b) describing our intended action on April 9th at Geneva and (c) adding a reminder that a settlement of Spanish question must remain for us a prerequisite of putting agreement into force.

April 13th

I have been away for ten days. We went to Paris and met Anthony and Jim there on their way home from Cannes on April 4th. We spent the day together. Both in very good spirits. We discussed the situation. They had seen a great deal of the Baldwins who both fully approved A.E.'s action in resigning and were horrified at the line the P.M. was pursuing – conducting the Government on pure Tory party lines and destroying its national character which S.B. regarded as his life's work. I said that I thought A.E.'s line should be acceptance of the Government statement so far as it concerned Central Europe – he quite agreed with this – and insistence on need for speedy moral and material re-armament to implement it. He should not attack National Government as such but should become the leader of all those elements in majority who are dissatisfied with present leaders of National Government and their defeatist trend. The conversations between T.U.C. leaders and Government to secure speeding up of re-armament by dilution of labour etc., should be watched closely and if Government cannot secure T.U.C. co-operation they should be attacked mercilessly. I told him of Winston's intended Midlothian campaign on behalf of re-armament which might prove rather embarrassing. A.E. had been invited to go to America in May by Lamont[2] for a lecture. Beatrice was anxious that he should accept but we were all very much against his going abroad again in May when so much would be happening in England,

1. Konrad Henlein, Leader of the Sudeten Germans.
2. T. W. Lamont, U.S. banker and millionaire.

and his absence would not be understood by his supporters – Michael Wright[1] who knows America was also insistent that he ought not to go under the auspices of any private individual such as Lamont.

On my return to London I lunched with Jim Thomas on April 13th, A.E. having now gone to Yorkshire. Jim had seen the P.M. and been in the H. of C. and had collected all the gossip. The Conservatives in H. of C. were hysterically behind the P.M. and applauding his partisan speeches. The loss of Fulham by-election[2] had been a great blow and was, according to Miss Maxse, typical of what the position was in the whole country at the moment. Jim had seen Horace Wilson who reported the P.M. as full of confidence in himself and expecting to win the next election as the man who had preserved peace in face of the dictators and lead the Government on for a further five years on the ground that although he would be 75, he was really ten years younger than his age! He had also seen W. Tyrrell who is being very active and in touch with T.U.C. leaders who had apparently been consulting him. Tyrrell said he had advised them to insist on P.M. showing them re-armament figures before they consented to any agreement and these would be so damaging that they would then be able to insist on his widening the Government by taking in A.E. again as Foreign Secretary and Winston as Defence Minister and two T.U.C. leaders. These should in fact be the conditions of their co-operation in the re-armament campaign. Tyrrell is obsessed, probably rightly, by the shortness of time before Germany is too strong for us and feels that we cannot wait for the Government to fall in the normal course; and whilst he despises the P.M., he believes the only chance is to keep him on as P.M. because the Conservatives won't yet follow any other leader but to make him a prisoner by placing A.E., Winston and the T.U.C. in the Cabinet. As I told Jim Thomas and Rex Leeper who also knew of it, I did not believe this possible because the P.M. was not the sort of man to accept the role of prisoner in his own Cabinet and if A.E. and he were together they would clash again in three months because their views were opposed on every question of foreign policy. I believed he would battle on alone with or without T.U.C. support until he fell from the defection of his own side. Jim had seen S.B. again who told him how everybody had been to see him since he got back including the P.M. – who however kept to polite generalities –

1. Sir Michael Wright, then First Secretary at Paris Embassy.
2. Won by Dr Edith Summerskill (Labour) from the Government.

and Halifax who said he still could not understand why A.E. had resigned, to which S.B. had said he had perfectly understood, and the only thing he did not understand was why he had not resigned before! Jim said that S.B., who before the crisis had regarded Shakes Morrison as the future P.M., now regarded A.E. as the only possible leader. I hope to go and stay with A.E. in Yorks next week.

Nothing much going on in the F.O. The Italian agreement[1] is to be signed on Saturday and published on Sunday. Halifax has gone away for ten days. We are lucky in the new French Government – Daladier,[2] Bonnet[3] – and should be able to get them to do what is wanted at Geneva. I saw Phipps in Paris and he talked of the importance of a meeting with British Ministers and when I saw H. today he suggested inviting them over the week after next for a first conversation here. This has now been done.

April 22nd

I went up to Yorkshire to stay with A.E. on 20th and returned today. A.E. was looking extremely well and in very good spirits – it is always heartening to see him. When I arrived he had just spent the morning with Halifax who had come over to see him. He said he was very worried over the internal situation as he quite realised that the Government had lost touch with the floating vote and that the P.M.'s methods were unlikely to retrieve this. H. said he had been told by S.B. years ago that A.E. was the only successor to Neville as P.M. H. felt that the future would be much easier for all concerned if A.E. were to return to the Cabinet, in about six months' time say, as First Lord of the Admiralty. A.E. had replied that he was not like Sam Hoare and he was not prepared to accept office again with the P.M., nor did he believe the P.M. would want him. H. had also talked about the Office and said how he had come to appreciate Alec Cadogan whom he had at first thought rather a light-weight. He was apparently much relieved when A.E. told him that he had heard the F.O. liked him (H.) very much! He also talked about sending Lampson[4] to Washington when Lindsay left: A.E. told him he thought it

1. It was little more than the "Gentleman's Agreement" over again.
2. Edouard Daladier became French Premier on April 10th 1938.
3. Georges Bonnet was his Minister of Foreign Affairs.
4. Sir Miles Lampson (later Lord Killearn), Ambassador to Egypt 1936–1946.

might be more important to keep him in Cairo where his prestige was very great and the situation was going to be very difficult: he thought it better to keep people where they were doing good work rather than to change them round. A.E. also told H. that he thought Loraine[1] would do well in Rome. H. was apparently no longer so satisfied with Henderson in Berlin as he had been. (A.E. and I agreed how bad an appointment that had turned out.) A.E. did not find H. at all happy about Central Europe and Czechoslovakia; A.E. mentioned to him his own idea of a reformed Czechoslovakia guaranteed by Great Britain, France and Germany.

A.E. and I discussed Willie Tyrrell's idea of his returning to F.O. as part of enlargement of Government – Jim Thomas had spoken to S.B. about it over the week-end – and his reaction had been exactly what A.E.'s (and mine) had been, viz., that P.M. would not agree and A.E. could not accept. S.B. favoured his staying outside and occupying his time by studying the oppressed areas and unemployment. I said I thought this an excellent idea and strongly urged it. A.E. likes it too, I think, and said he could begin in his native Durham. S.B. thought the P.M. would break down physically under the strain of the one-man show he is running. It seemed to me impossible to foretell how the crisis would come – there might be an Air Arms scandal over the purchases in America and at the moment this looked imminent – or there might be difficulties in the Cabinet over a further approach to Germany which the younger ones – Stanley, Elliot, Malcolm MacDonald would not stand for – A.E. thought it possible that the P.M. would get away with Italian agreement and with luck stagger on to general elections and then be defeated owing to country's dislike of humiliating approaches to Dictators, and even Labour might come in, much as the country might deplore the alternative. I said it seemed clear to me that his role was to constitute himself the leader and spokesman of that floating vote which the Government had now lost and thus become an alternative head of National Government for all those, and they were a majority, who did not want the P.M.'s present Conservative trend any more than a Labour Government. He should make speeches on the theme of "moral and material re-armament", higher and broader speeches than the P.M. made; study of industrial conditions would all be part of this campaign, he needn't, and perhaps had better not make any

1. Sir Percy Loraine, Bart., Ambassador to Turkey, who was transferred to Rome in May 1939.

purely foreign affairs speeches at all at present. A.E. doesn't intend to return to H. of C. until after debate on Italian agreement. He is going to stay week-end with S.B. and then come to London for two nights (he is making his St George's Day speech on Tuesday night) and then back to Yorkshire for another week. He showed me the draft of his speech and we went through it. I think it very good – praise of democracy and what it stands for in England and the need for it to make greater efforts if it is to hold its own with the Dictators. There is nothing too offensive to Dictators in it; he has to be careful not to get into position of becoming a symbol for war on dictatorship all round – Eden *à la guerre*! – whilst separating himself from the truckling attitude of the present Government.

A.E. asked what I thought about his writing for Press. He was being asked to do so. I said I thought it would be excellent. It would be just as good as his making speeches: he could say the same sort of things and could make his position known to his supporters, and he would also be able to earn a little money.

I said he should certainly also write occasionally in American papers – most important for the future that he should be understood there. He is still toying with the idea of a visit to U.S.A. in autumn. I told him that it seemed to be rather tricky as an electioneering period was soon opening there and Roosevelt was being very much attacked: A.E. would have to be very careful to avoid being exploited or misrepresented by party forces there. A.E. will, I think, consult Lindsay first.

A.E. was very worried about Spain, and hates the way in which the Government are making peace with Mussolini on the back of the Spanish Government. He says he could not possibly have sponsored Italian agreement in House of Commons and believes that much trouble is coming to H.M.G. because of it. He thinks the country will loathe it, especially if there are more Italian bombings or anti-democratic speeches by Mussolini. He said "You have saved Mussolini," just when the Anschluss added to all his other difficulties had shaken his position fatally.

We spoke a lot of unsatisfactory state of our armaments, especially Air and Anti-Aircraft and how he must continually urge speedier re-armament. I said I regretted now he had not said more about it in his resignation speech – as well he might have done in view of all the warnings he had given while in office.

Jim Thomas (who was also there) said he had seen Shakespeare

Morrison who had wished to talk to him about A.E.'s resignation. At that moment he said he was himself on point of resigning over Irish negotiations[1] and effect on English agriculture – this issue, however, had become eclipsed in A.E.'s crisis – and Morrison had been made to make winding-up speech – how he had loathed it and how much he had tried to avoid it. What had been the effect on A.E.? Did he mind it very much?

A.E. is now much more reconciled and accustomed to idea of No. 10. I think he feels it inevitable now. What he would have liked best, I think, would be to remain at F.O. with a P.M. he could work with, but there is no one else now. Inskip is no good – he has no popular appeal and no drive. Sam Hoare is out of the question. Of the young men there is none now who can compare with A.E. I told him that when he was P.M., I thought his Foreign Secretary would have a rotten time. He laughed but denied this and said it would not be so if either Malcolm MacDonald or Bobbety were Foreign Secretary. He realises immense importance of Stanley Baldwin's approval and is obviously extremely thankful to have it; I'm sure he will be guided by him in his attitude henceforward. Stanley Baldwin will be essential for the "switch-over", however it may come, from Neville to A.E. I also urged him now that he has more time, to see more of his younger colleagues and M.P.'s, especially Crookshank. (I believe if he had not lived so secluded a life with his work at Foreign Office and if it had been possible for him to be more in the House of Commons and even see more of his younger colleagues in off-hours, then there might have been more resignations when he left.)

I said what a pity it was P.M. and Co. now seemed to go out of their way to throw mud at the League of Nations. A.E. more than agreed and spoke of the danger that Labour would once more become pacifist and refuse to co-operate in armament production if the Government went on repudiating the League of Nations and making up to Dictators – the country might then be split on Foreign Affairs. We spoke of the fatal mistake made when H.M.G. had failed to press on with Sanctions against Italy after Sam Hoare's speech. Mussolini would have been broken, the League of Nations immensely strengthened and Germany correspondingly impressed. A.E. said how much responsibility Van bore for this runaway because of the frantic

1. The negotiations leading to the Agreement of April 25th 1938.

minutes he wrote while A.E. was at Geneva, prophesying war and saying that we had no armaments. A.E. agreed with me when I said that I did not believe any real peace was possible between Mussolini's system and ours.

April 25th–26th

Daily meetings with department to discuss agenda for French conversations. On Czechoslovakia prevailing view is that the military position is untenable and Czechoslovakia can really only be preserved against Germany if latter fears a general war. We are not prepared for a general war. It is thought we should press Benes to go as far as possible to meet Henlein but we should not assume responsibility for recommending any given scheme or we should be expected to guarantee it. What is desirable is to keep Germany guessing and at the same time not allow Benes to think he need do nothing. The ideal settlement would be one guaranteed by Germany, France, Russia (and by us?).

Staff talks with French also discussed. Chiefs of Staff are of course dead against any talks. As we can only promise two divisions, War Office do not want any army talks. Admiralty do not want any naval talks because they say dispositions can quickly be made at last minute. Air Ministry are prepared to have talks about bases in France.

Scandal over lack of performance of Air Ministry is gradually blowing up in consequence of decision to send mission to purchase in U.S.A. – letters in *Times*, etc. Today I saw the minute sent by Warren Fisher to P.M. (copy to Halifax) saying Air Ministry hopeless, our airforce is being increasingly outclassed by Germany in spite of soothing syrup given out by Air Ministry and "now for the first time in history we are at the mercy of a foreign power!" This at last should precipitate events.

We listened in today to A.E.'s St George's Day speech (Tuesday). Most impressive and even minatory. No mincing of words. Stanley Baldwin had put in one paragraph himself about danger of democracy ending if allowed to deviate too much to Right or Left.

April 27th

H. and I drove out to Croydon today to meet Daladier and Bonnet on their arrival. H. said he did not see any possible alternative policy to what we were pursuing as regards Czechoslovakia. The great thing to avoid was having bluff called if we cannot do anything. I said Czechoslovakia could only be preserved if Hitler was convinced that there would be a European war if he attacked her and that we could not threaten in our present state of armament. H. said he was doubtful if dictatorships could last indefinitely. He thought they ended by creating their own difficulties and *hubris* in international affairs brought its own revenge. I agreed and said Fascist Italy and Nazi Germany were essentially one-man shows and I doubted whether Hitler and Mussolini would find successors. Modern dictators had nothing to fall back on like the tradition of autocratic monarchies and they had personally to be supermen or fail. I doubted whether a brutal blusterer like Goering could ever capture and hold the German people like a mystic such as Hitler. He agreed.

April 28th

The French delegation told our people last night that they were most disappointed at our refusal to agree to naval talks. We were the great naval power – they were the great military power. We were ready to have staff talks regarding the army (to help us) but not about the navy (to help them over their transports to North Africa). At Windsor Daladier and Bonnet impressed on H. that, bad though the situation was, France would have to honour her obligations if Czechoslovakia were attacked but she would welcome and press on Benes any solution, even a Federal one, and neutralisation which would hold the situation.

At midday something of a deadlock was reached over Czechoslovakia but it was thought that if we could agree to naval talks the French would accept our view about Czechoslovakia. (Daladier's brother-in-law, an Englishman named Hodgkisson, told me however – contrary to what Léger[1] was telling Van and Sargent – that Daladier was very well pleased indeed last night with the results of the conversations. Are the French bluffing to try to get more out of

1. Alexis Léger, Secretary-General at the Quai d'Orsay.

us?) Anyway, agreement was finally reached and the French left in high spirits, having got us to concede naval staff talks (which I think was a perfectly justifiable request) but also having got us to go a good long way over Czechoslovakia – further I think than the P.M. and H. intended to go – largely in consequence of Van's pressure on our people. It has in fact been agreed (i) that we should both speak in Prague and urge on Benes the greatest possible concessions to meet the Sudeten, and (ii) that we should speak alone in Berlin and point out what we and French were doing at Prague, say that France had told us that she meant to fulfil her treaty obligations if Czechoslovakia were attacked, recall P.M.'s words in Statement in House of Commons that if war began there, we might well be brought in, and conclude by expressing our hope therefore that Germany will not attempt any violent solutions.

I have a feeling that we have gone rather far. It is very doubtful whether France in fact (under Daladier and Bonnet) would fight. Both Charles Mendl[1] and Mrs Hyde[2] have said that there was no question of it. We have laid ourselves open to a snub from Hitler by offering him advice about Czechoslovakia. It is true that if France fights, we shall probably be drawn in but I believe Germany thinks this a very doubtful contingency and she knows how weak we are. We want to keep the Germans guessing as much as possible – as H. himself says – but I feel very doubtful of the wisdom of speaking in Berlin in Hitler's present mood.

I heard today that Sir M. Hankey and David Margesson,[3] the Government whip, are to be the two Government directors of the Suez Canal – so Hankey is to go. I cannot help feeling that this is satisfactory. Hankey who has been running the C.I.D. since 1912, is tired and now only immersed in the ramifications of his own machinery: he is out of touch and rather reactionary.

May 2nd

H. saw Masaryk today and told him of what we had undertaken to do as regards Czechoslovakia. The latter surprised H. by saying that

1. Press Attaché at H.M. Embassy in Paris.
2. Mrs James Hazell Hyde, formerly Mme. André Thome, a well-known French political hostess of the time.
3. David Margesson, M.P. (later Lord Margesson), Conservative Chief Whip.

Benes not only now fully realised the need of going to the very limit of reconciliation as regards the Sudeten but was even in fact prepared for a "Swiss solution". He said that his father, the old President, had never wished to have the Sudeten in Czechoslovakia but that Lloyd George had insisted on their being incorporated. Even if the Sudeten now were to "plebiscite" themselves out of Czechoslovakia, he did not believe the other minorities would follow.

May 3rd

I lunched with Miss Maxse and had a long talk. I told her of anxiety of Government to get A.E. back – except for P.M. Her advice was that he should keep out of it at present. She thought he should also keep off foreign affairs and speak on some other subject: the "England" speech had been first-rate: the Right hated him and were thankful at his going but they could be safely ignored as they were helpless. She quoted a remark of Lady Maud Hoare[1] on A.E.'s departure: "It has taken us years to do it!" She said A.E. had been very slow to realise P.M.'s determination to get A.E. out. It became plain to Central Office when he tried to stop the Llandudno speech. Swinton was the P.M.'s evil genius (like Davidson[2] to Stanley Baldwin). She had been anxious for years to get old party labels abolished: they no longer carried weight with the country but the diehards had been too strong. We discussed the future P.M.; she asked my view about Sam Hoare: I said he was an able administrator but nothing more. He would wreck the party in six months as P.M. She agreed. Simon was unthinkable; Inskip no good; there were only A.E. and Morrison. She said the Government would lose Lichfield and might lose the General Election to Labour. The P.M. was hitting up Labour just when their support was necessary for his re-armament policy. Government now a purely one-man show.

May 9th

We arrived Geneva yesterday morning and H. began his interviews with those members of Council who had already arrived. As regards Ethiopia the plan is to secure agreement on a resolution (liberating

1. Wife of Sir Samuel Hoare.
2. Viscount Davidson, Chancellor of Duchy of Lancaster 1931–1937, previously Private Secretary to Bonar Law and Baldwin.

each member to do as he likes) if possible, failing which, to proceed by declaration – each member of Council making a statement of his views, and Avenol[1] summing them up. The prospects of a resolution seem very doubtful owing largely to China's dislike of compromising the doctrine of non-recognition in regard to Manchukuo. We do not know for certain that the Negus is not coming in person, but his delegation has arrived. Are they to be treated as officially entitled to sit at the Council table when Ethiopia is being discussed? This raises the old question of credentials. We feel they should be invited to sit as an act of courtesy only.

H. is taking the rather unaccustomed atmosphere very well. He is as calm and detached as ever, very dignified. He rather liked Litvinoff (whom he thought he would hate). I met King-Hall[2] of News Letter fame today – just back from Rome – very interesting about the unpopularity of the Axis in Italy and of the fantastic expense and precautions in connection with the Hitler visit. Charles Peake is going to arrange for us to dine together and I am sure he ought to meet A.E.

Phipps, as we passed through Paris on Saturday night, spoke to H. (and Michael Wright to me) of the anxiety which some members of the French Cabinet (notably Patenôtre,[3] I think) feel at Royal Visit[4] and danger of an *attentat* by Gestapo. It is of course a terrific risk and the chance of ruining Anglo-French relations for a generation might well tempt the Nazi gangsters. But to call it off now would be almost as bad. Daladier is well aware of the risk but Sarraut[5] (who was Minister of Interior when King Alexander was assassinated at Marseilles) is said to be careless.

Dined last night with Charles Peake, Ingram and Vernon Bartlett.[6] The last recently back from China says he thinks China can hold out indefinitely against Japs.

1. Joseph Avenol, Secretary-General of the League of Nations.
2. Commander Stephen King-Hall.
3. Minister of National Economy in Daladier Government.
4. The Royal Visit to France arranged for July 19th 1938.
5. M. Albert Sarraut, Minister of Interior.
6. Vernon Bartlett, broadcaster and journalist on staff of *News Chronicle*.

May 10th

Long secret meeting of Council last night at which procedure in regard to Abyssinia and presence of Abyssinian delegates was approved. H. is to open with his speech, then the Abyssinian Representative (who will be admitted as the Representative not of Abyssinia but of the Emperor Haile Selassie) will speak, then any others. All was arranged for this to take place today but this morning the Abyssinians have asked for a second day so as to enable them to consider the speeches and reply appropriately. H. is very anxious to avoid any such adjournment, and is prepared to agree to the discussion itself taking place on a later day provided it is all over in one day. (This procedure was finally adopted at a further secret meeting tonight and the appointed day is to be Thursday.) It is now reported that the Emperor himself intends to appear in person.

May 11th

Ingram and I dined with H. last night. We discussed beginnings of Abyssinian affair. We all agreed that one of the turning points was Stresa Conference[1] when British Delegation failed to mention question at all to Mussolini who was expecting it. H. said he had never understood why this was. I said, if A.E. had been there, he would have insisted on bringing it up but in his absence (he was ill after the aeroplane journey) I supposed neither Ramsay[2] nor Simon wished to do so for fear of annoying Mussolini, and Van, who should have made them do it, was unwilling and let it slide for fear of harming his special child, the Stresa front. Ingram (who was in Rome at the time) thought this was the last chance of stopping it before Mussolini had committed himself too far. Ingram said that if full sanctions (i.e. including oil and Suez canal) had been applied at the outset, Mussolini would have collapsed, although to save his face, he would probably have had to go to war. The Italians were terrified at that time. Speaking of Hoare-Laval proposals, H. blamed Van for allowing Sam Hoare to go ahead as he did. Sam Hoare ought never to have signed anything without referring to the Cabinet: he should have insisted on referring it home. The Cabinet moreover had given

1. In 1935 between Britain, France and Italy.
2. Rt. Hon. Ramsay MacDonald, at that time Prime Minister.

him no authority to agree to anything: they only thought he would have a general discussion with Laval of the boundaries of Ethiopia. (I was there at the time and Van, far from restraining S.H. was in a wild state of excitement and wanted to give everything away – it was my first eye-opener as to Van's bad judgment and weakness as a negotiator.)

H. told us the story (which I had already heard from A.E.) of how Sam Hoare had told H. that his wife could never forgive him for one thing he'd said in his speech in the House of Lords on the Hoare-Laval proposals. When H. asked what it was, Sam replied that it was H.'s saying that "Sir Samuel Hoare had gone to Paris not to sign an agreement but for *quite different reasons!*"

H. said after his experience of Sam Hoare[1] during the India Bill, when he'd shown both wisdom and astuteness, he would never have believed that he could have slipped up in such a way with public opinion.

He said he believed it would now be wise to take all coercive measures out of the Covenant as they were only irritating to those to whom they were applied and humiliating to those who applied them. His constant theme, to which he returns again and again, is the need for adapting ideals to facts in this hard world.

I dined with Charles Peake and Ewer.[2] Latter said he thought Sudeten would have to go.

May 12th

A grim day. The Council met this morning and the little Negus came in to take his place, full of dignity in his black cloak. H. made the first speech, a reasoned statement of the case for facing facts and freeing ourselves from any obligation to act together in the matter of recognition, rather too sermonising and moralising in tone. The Negus followed, his speech, after the first few words, being read for him by his secretary, an appeal to international Law and sentiment. Then the rest of the Council followed on, moving in favour of our view, only China and New Zealand being definitely opposed, old Jordan[3] being painfully honest and idealistic though quite unpractical.

1. Then Secretary of State for India.
2. W. N. Ewer, Editor of the *Daily Herald*.
3. The New Zealand Prime Minister.

Finally, Munters, the Latvian, who is President of the Council, summed up and the session closed. A tragic and humiliating performance.

I lunched with King-Hall. He has idea of Centre Party. He is standing for Liverpool as National Labour and is anxious to get in touch with A.E. He also regards Central Europe as written off but contemplates a small Czechoslovakian rump state surviving like Luxemburg. Very earnest, very conceited but a good man, I should say.

H. saw Ellen Wilkinson today and was much impressed by her. She told him how much the Labour Party hated the P.M. He spoke of the need for National Government on a wider basis than at present. After consideration of this she sent him a message to say that Labour would be prepared to co-operate provided the P.M. went and A.E. came in!

May 13th

Another bad day for the League. Appeal of Spanish Government for support against foreign intervention was turned down flat. There is in fact nothing that can be done but it is tragic that the League should have to confess to so many failures at once.

May 15th

Left Geneva last night and home this afternoon. Cabinet crisis has been developing fast since we left over Air Ministry and complete failure of Winterton[1] in debate in House of Commons last Thursday. Necessity for Cabinet changes has also arisen over death of Lord Harlech,[2] there being too many Ministers in Lords. We were much amused to read in train that Halifax intended to retire and was to be replaced by Malcolm MacDonald.

Rex Leeper dined. He had seen W. Tyrrell again. Latter had now given up his idea that A.E. should join N.C.'s Cabinet and thought he should keep out of it altogether. He wished A.E. to see T.U.C. leaders and also certain industrialists. Tyrrell also said he knew P.M. was in direct touch with Mussolini and he believed (but could

1. Lord Winterton, M.P., Chancellor of Duchy of Lancaster 1937–1939, with responsibility for Air Defence.
2. Father of Colonial Secretary, Mr Ormsby-Gore.

not prove) he was in touch with Hitler too. H. was summoned to see P.M. at 7 p.m.

May 16th

Jim Thomas dined. We had just heard Cabinet changes. Kingsley Wood to be Air Minister in place of Swinton who has resigned; Ormsby-Gore to go too. No Ministry of Supply as there should have been. A poor reconstruction, which we are sure will go badly in House of Commons and Press. P.M. laid up with gout. Jim thinks the rot will go very fast now. No approach was made to A.E. by Number 10. A.E. returns to London tomorrow: he has been visiting armament factories in his constituency. He has not been back to House of Commons yet: we both thought he ought to begin again this week but are not so sure whether he should speak in further air debate on Thursday.

May 19th

Reception of Government changes is pretty unenthusiastic. I gather Ormsby-Gore was most reluctant to go, and was in fact pushed out by P.M. who hates him and the whole Cecil connection. *Times* today has a curious reference to the present changes being only provisional and pending a larger reconstruction which might include even A.E. I hear from Charles Peake that his journalist friends have told him that this article was from Dawson himself. It looks as if certain elements (not, I feel sure, the P.M.) realise that the Government's basis is now too narrow to carry through the drastic re-armament campaign which is needed if we are to catch up the dictators and they are accordingly preparing opinion. I wonder if H. is privy to this: Dawson eats out of his hand and I doubt of his putting it in (for he is no friend of A.E.'s policies) without some very high authority. The "Shiver Sisters"[1] are also now rather scared of the P.M.'s methods. H., from our talks, is aware of the harm which the P.M. is doing by hitting up the opposition and in his speech in the House of Lords purposely inserted an appeal to the opposition for co-operation, etc.

Debate in House of Lords last night lasted till 11 p.m., most

1. Label applied in political and journalistic circles to Lady Astor and the Cliveden set – Lothian, Dawson, Garvin, etc.

unusual. A very fine speech from the Bishop of Durham[1] controverting what that old Caiaphas, the Archbishop of Canterbury, had just said. H.'s speech in conclusion was impressive, and the best I've heard from him: the conclusion with its reference to the support the Labour Government had given him when he was Viceroy of India went extremely well. I think he wants to set himself as free as possible to correct the partisanship of the P.M. H. is well qualified to do this, as he is a reconciliator by nature and has a large fund of good will on the left to draw on from his Indian record.

May 20th

Lunched with Nigel Law. City very pessimistic and bewildered. Saw A.E. before dinner. He has already been back to H. of C. and said he was much interested to see how those people who may be regarded as barometers did not at all seek to avoid him. On the contrary. He means to attend regularly now, but not to speak yet. I think this is wise because, as I told him, events seem to be moving fast in his favour and it is better that he should not appear to seek to precipitate them. He can afford to sit back. He has been visiting Shadow Factories[2] and his constituency. He learns that the Government are feeling that they are in an awful stew and that the greatest pressure will be put on him before long to return to the Cabinet. He has no intention of accepting. He told me very confidentially that S.B. when he saw the P.M. last week told him that it was no use his asking A.E. to return at present. We agreed that two things were necessary – a Ministry of Supply and an All-Party Government. The P.M. has as yet no intention of having either but his hand may be forced as it was over Swinton's resignation. If A.E. is asked to return, he should base his refusal on the need for an All-Party Government. Only an All-Party Government will be able to put across the drastic regimentation of industry and labour which is essential if we are to equal the Totalitarians without ceasing to be a Democracy. Anything less would be playing with the problem. He heard however that the Government are completely defeatist and hold that a Democracy can never compete with the Dictators – which, as A.E. said, is all rot: we won the War without ceasing to be a Democracy. A.E. is

1. Dr Hensley Henson, Bishop of Durham 1920–1939.
2. Set up for occupation in time of war as part of the Re-armament programme.

writing his £800 article for the American press on this theme. The fact remains however that the P.M. is the great obstacle to an All-Party Government as Labour would never serve under him; A.E. is now the only possible leader.

May 21st

Czechoslovakia is blowing up for the week-end. Municipal elections are to be held on Sunday in the Sudeten areas and the usual electioneering incidents are occurring and being exploited by the German press. Last night there were reports that the Germans were concentrating troops on the frontiers and that the Czechs were considering mobilising, but that the French were seeking to restrain them. In answer to his inquiries Henderson was told that there were no unusual troop movements (but this is what the Germans told us on the eve of the Anschluss). This morning a stiffish telegram was sent to Berlin conveying a warning of the consequences of any rash action.

Meanwhile Henlein has announced his refusal to meet the Czechoslovak Government until law and order is restored and assured in the Sudeten areas, and this in spite of the very reasonable attitude he adopted while over in London last week when he met various M.P.s (Winston Churchill and Harold Nicolson) and Van. What he then told them of his claims made it appear quite possible to reach a compromise on a federal basis within the Czechoslovak state; but it looks as if it was all too good to be true and that he is a different man on his return after passing through Germany and meeting his followers.

H. while at Geneva derived the very definite impression from Bonnet and Co., that they would welcome *any* pressure we put on Benes to reach agreement and so avoid a head-on collision which would place France in the dilemma of fighting or dishonouring her signature. But if a clash occurs, all French Ministers assure us that France will have to mobilise. I wonder! I'm always a little doubtful of Daladier's decision if he was in a tight corner, remembering his complete collapse in the February 4th riots. Anyway so far as we can, we are pressing Benes to make a really courageous offer to Henlein. Newton has seen both him and Hodza, but the former still seems inclined to prevaricate. Equally we are saying all we can to get Berlin to damp down. But the German press is deliberately magnifying incidents and discounting in advance the value of any Czechoslovak concessions.

Margerie has just rung me up to say that Poncet[1] has telephoned to Paris from Berlin that the position there is distinctly dangerous owing to news of shootings in certain Sudeten areas. Henderson has warned us that if there is serious bloodshed, nothing will restrain Hitler from marching in.

I went back to Foreign Office at 6 p.m. because of a further telegram from Berlin reporting a most disturbing interview Nevile Henderson had just had with Ribbentrop who was very pugnacious and truculent and declared that as Henderson had repeated to Reuters the assurances which Ribbentrop had given him that no military movement had taken place, he must refuse to give any further assurances. He further threatened that Germany could not stand aside if there were bloodshed. We telephoned to H. who had gone down to Eton, to return and a messenger is being sent to the P.M. who was in Winchester. H. got back at 9.45 and came to the F.O. He telephoned to the P.M. who is returning tomorrow afternoon when there is to be a meeting of Ministers. Further telegrams were sent off to Newton at Prague urging the need of utmost moderation and to Henderson at Berlin to inform him of the *démarche* at Prague and to convey a personal message from the Secretary of State to Ribbentrop again urging moderation and patience.

Phipps also reported a conversation with Bonnet who had also spoken very severely to the Czechs about the unwisdom of having called up two classes of reservists. He told Phipps however that if Germany did attack Czechoslovakia, France would have to intervene. The French certainly do not want to do so and will use every pressure on Czechoslovakia to avoid it. No news of the Soviets (their alliance with the Czechs does not come into operation unless the French come in).

All information tonight makes it look certain that Germany intends either to conrront Benes with an ultimatum or to march in – in any case that Czechoslovakia is for it.

May 22nd

No further telegrams this morning but H. sent for the German Ambassador at 12.30 to tell him what we were doing. Latter definitely

1. André François-Poncet, French Ambassador to Germany.

denied troop movements and said German press today were much calmer having been damped down. We heard from Berlin that all the women and children of the Embassy were to leave for England to-night – a special coach! H. was horrified at such alarmist action and we have telephoned to stop them.

H. saw the P.M. at 2.30 as a result of which a telegram is being sent to Phipps to warn the French Government to be under no illusion about H.M.G.'s position. We would of course stand by France if she were attacked but she must not assume that we would join her in action to save Czechoslovakia. In view of weakness of our military situation and doubtful outcome of a European war we strongly urged her to consult us before taking any drastic action. H. saw Corbin at 4.30 and went to the Minister's meeting at five.

At the latter it was decided to send further telegrams to Newton at Prague to urge Benes to make a most generous offer to Sudeten, and to Berlin suggesting to the Germans that we might propose to Czechoslovakia that we should send an observer to Sudeten area if Germany thought it a good thing to do. H. saw the Press at 6.30 and urged them to adopt moderate tone and not espouse either side whatever their sympathies might be. We telephoned to Prague and heard that they had had a better day, no incidents and pouring rain.

May 23rd

Better news. No further incidents, and elections have passed off with relative calm.

May 24th

Our sources tend to show that Hitler had really intended to go for Czechoslovakia but that he has shied off in face of our warnings. Strang is to pay a quick visit to Prague and Berlin in the next few days.

May 26th

German press is now violently attacking us for interfering in Central Europe and for claiming the credit for stopping a German offensive which had never existed. Discussion in Secretary of State's room with Alec C. and Van, which Sam Hoare joined. H. is turning over in his mind what we can do supposing that Henlein and Benes fail to reach terms within the Czechoslovak constitution. Would a plebiscite be possible and or neutralisation under some guarantee? The French have made it absolutely clear that they will support any course which will avoid for them the dreadful dilemma of fighting or dishonouring their signature: but that if there is a head-on collision, then they must fight. They have spoken most severely both in Prague and to Osusky[1]. The Germans, on the other hand, are stiffening Henlein in putting forward pretexts for avoiding conversations with the Czechoslovak Government (now it is a demand that the one class mobilised by the Czechs should be demobilised – which the Czechs say is impossible until the elections are over as it is needed to preserve order). They are also making continual complaints of violation of the frontier by Czech aircraft, etc. The Soviets, it must be admitted, have behaved with exemplary discretion and have made no move to encourage the Czechs or make matters more difficult. Henlein himself seems a reasonable man but not a strong one, and he is harassed both by his own extremists and by Berlin. Benes is a doubtful factor – does he yet realise or believe in the necessity of doing his utmost to reach a settlement with the Sudeten if Czechoslovakia is to survive, or does he still think he can rest on French and British protection?

In debate in House of Commons yesterday on Air Armament, P.M. flatly refused either an inquiry or a Ministry of Supply. Demand for latter is now being pushed persistently in many Government quarters including *Times* and *Daily Telegraph* and I am sure P.M. will have to give way in the end. I am convinced however, that his opposition is due to belief that Minister of Supply will require special powers, that these will bring to a head relations with Labour and that Labour is not prepared to trust him – in fact that it will only be workable with an All-Party Government. Labour is perfectly ready to co-operate but will not do so with the present P.M.

P.M. had talk with T.U.C. leaders today, with what result I do not know.

May 31st

A.E. came to Foreign Office to see H. who had asked him to come. He discussed the Czechoslovak situation and H.'s ideas for neutralisation. A.E. told me afterwards he had seen S.B. that day and that he

1. Stefan Osusky, Czech Minister in Paris.

was very worried over internal situation and the narrow basis of the Government.

I lunched with Liddell Hart, the Military Correspondent of *The Times*. His theory is that the defence is stronger than the attack, and that even a relatively modest defence may be adequate. Here the aircraft defence force was much more satisfactory than the anti-air defences. He thought that we exaggerated the efficiency and strength of the German forces – large numbers of the total air strength would be necessarily required for attachment to the field armies and to frontier defence so that the actual striking force would be much reduced. The German army was not ready, *cf*. the mess it made of the march into Austria – the standard of officers was not very high either. He agreed with the view of the need for a wider basis for the Government and said that Dawson had no contacts with the Left. He is a strong advocate of "collective security" and of our getting as many states into our system as possible.

Strang gave an account of his trip to Prague and Berlin this evening. He said that Czechoslovak foreign relations were as important an aspect of the problem as the Sudeten: in fact if the Sudeten had not existed, the problem would have still been as acute. Both Henderson and Newton were opposed to a plebiscite being suggested, at any rate at this stage. Whilst the danger of a serious incident leading to German intervention still existed Germany was now convinced that a "limited operation" for the absorption or disruption of Czechoslovakia was not possible. On the whole he thought German opinion did not favour a surgical operation for the amputation of the Sudeten but wished to secure autonomy for the Sudeten plus neutralisation (i.e. dissolution of the Soviet and French alliances). The German army was not yet ready. H.M.G.'s warning to Germany had convinced Europe that Great Britain would intervene if there were a row in Central Europe.

H. now intends to tell Benes that we regard a settlement of the Sudeten question "on London Lines" (i.e. on what Henlein told us in London) as possible provided it is swiftly made, and that if he does not go forward on these lines, our own attitude towards his country will be adversely affected. He hopes to get the French to say the same thing only more firmly since they are allies.

146

June 1st

I saw Jim Thomas this morning. He said he had the firm impression that the Government was beginning to break up. The P.M. had lost a lot of caste over Swinton's resignation.[1] Paul Emrys Evans, with whom I lunched later, said the same thing and the feeling in the House of Commons was one of uneasiness. Swinton and Billy Gore are both very bitter over their departure. Paul told us he had heard that the P.M. had turned over the idea of offering A.E. the Dominions Office but that he had funked it. I am trying to track down the idea which Rex Leeper is now fervently advocating that H. should be the next P.M. with A.E. as Leader of the House of Commons. I am convinced that this would not work (a) because you cannot nowadays have a P.M. removed from daily contact in the Commons, and (b) because I fear a clash between A.E. and H. who is not to be regarded as King Log and whose ideas on foreign affairs are definite and different from A.E.'s. H. works well with the P.M. now because their ideas approximate or rather he is about half-way between A.E. and the P.M. He ran the F.O. during the recent crisis because being nearer the P.M. than A.E. he could get him to agree more easily whereas A.E. antagonised the P.M. But if a real divergence occurred between the P.M. and H., the latter would resign as A.E. did. The P.M. cannot afford to lose another Foreign Secretary so that H. is in a stronger position than A.E. In any case why should not A.E. be P.M.? He is the one man the country knows and recognises and who commands the sympathy of the Left and could lead an All-Party team. The idea of H. as P.M. while A.E. is trained up was mentioned first to Paul by T. Dugdale[2] so it looks as if it had some blessing from the party headquarters. It apparently does not emanate from W. Tyrrell as I thought. The only way such an arrangement could work would be if S.B. became P.M. again. The difficulty of course that all see is how A.E. is to succeed N.C.? It is impossible to foresee how circumstances will fall out but I feel sure S.B. will play a vital part in securing the succession. A.E. will have difficulty with his own party unless S.B. weighs in.

Jim and I discussed when he should speak in the House of

1. He resigned on May 16th 1938, and was succeeded as Air Minister by Sir Kingsley Wood.
2. Later Lord Crathorne; Minister of Agriculture 1951–1954.

Commons. I thought he should certainly make one big speech before the end of July on broad national issues, not foreign affairs. He agreed. Meanwhile he should go about the country and study industrial conditions at first hand.

Inskip has got into trouble with the Amalgamated Engineers Union over situation.

Lindsay has written asking to be allowed to resign from Washington in November or December. Alec Cadogan has spoken to H. who has spoken to the P.M. who has been good enough to say that as the Americans are so rotten and as it does not therefore matter who we send there he is content to leave the post to the Service. What a man! This at least is good news for us. Our only obvious choice is Lampson who is not perfect and whose wife is an Italian. It would have been better if we could to leave him in Egypt till the end of his career. Who else can we send? Not Snatch[1] – nor Ronnie Campbell[2] (who should be kept for Paris). Snatch and Seymour[3] should be sent to Cairo and Ankara (Loraine is now approved for Rome). Of course Van ought to go. I spoke to H. about this some time ago and said it afforded a last opportunity of liquidating his anomalous position gracefully. His activity made Alec's position almost intolerable and only someone with Alec's temperament would bear it. To which H. said he thought very few Secretaries of State would bear it either! He felt however he was in a weak position to insist on it as he (H.) was still new and could not yet honestly say the arrangement which he had inherited had broken down. He would speak to P.M. about it. The feeling of our Promotion Board also strongly favoured Van going. But it is evident that no one has the courage to tell him to go where he is told.

June 5th

We seem to be drifting more and more into the position of allowing Russia to champion the Democracies while we seek to placate the Dictators. An impossible position for this country which is getting visibly restive. In Spain the Government are praying for Franco's victory and bringing all the influence they can bear on France to stop

1. Sir Hugh Knatchbull-Hugessen, severely wounded in an air attack on his car when Ambassador to China the previous year.
2. Sir R. H. Campbell became Ambassador to France in November 1939.
3. Sir Horace Seymour, Ambassador to Persia.

the inflow of munitions to Barcelona. Yet Franco is sinking our ships and Italian airmen are bombing defenceless villages while Mussolini goes on extolling his volunteers – to the growing rage of public opinion here. The French Government would like to help us – or rather Bonnet would – but with a *Front Populaire* majority it is necessary for them to go very warily. That snake Flandin has sent to the P.M. a sneaking letter about his own Government's attitude over this! Although I believe Russia now has very little influence and very few men in Spain, she proclaims her sympathy from the house-tops and exposes the farce of the Non-Intervention Committee. Again, in the Far East, Russia alone is affording substantial aid to China in munitions. Here also British public opinion is outraged at Japanese bombing and atrocities. We are trying to make up our minds to lend China a little money under cover of a deal over Wolfram and Antimony. H. is very keen on getting this through but the Cabinet is defeatist and obstructive and can only see the ill-effects on the future of Anglo-Japanese relations. And then in the Balkans, H. prompted by Maurice Ingram has put a plan for the Balkan Committee to examine and agree its financial, commercial and cultural assistance to Balkan countries so as to afford some alternative for them to complete capitulation to Germany and Italy, but here again, the Foreign Policy Committee in the Cabinet can see nothing but difficulties. There is no spirit in them. Their one success – and that I grant a notable one – has been over Czechoslovakia but they are now so frightened of it that I fear they may yet spoil their success by apologising to the Germans and by compelling Benes to commit suicide in order to forestall murder. We continue to suck up to Mussolini who treats us and our friends to abuse every time he makes a speech. He has not done a single thing to make appeasement easier since we signed our agreement. England cannot afford to be on the side of the Dictators for we shall then soon find we are left alone with them.

The Government cold water policy towards the League of Nations is already having its effect in the gradual withdrawal of the lesser members into neutrality or isolationism. We shall soon have the Scandinavians, etc., abandoning it – for it is a dangerous ship to be found in if the Great Western powers are going to run away.

It should not have been left to Mr Hull alone to make the speech he did this week on the decay of respect for law and the increasing spirit of militarism and tyranny. The natural result of this at home is going to be a violent swing away from the Government to Labour (West Derby election shows this) together with Labour difficulties over re-armament; consequence, further weakness in our foreign policy necessitated by bitter party strife; tendency for pacifism and fascism and communism all to develop simultaneously. Only A.E. can stop the rot by coming out as the leader of the middle section.

O.H. to Secretary of State – June 7th 1938

I cannot help expressing my feeling that it would be unwise for His Majesty's Government at the present time to take any overt action which would appear to public opinion here as indicating a decline of interest in the League. His Majesty's Government are already under suspicion of cold-shouldering the League in favour of direct bilateral methods of diplomacy. A drift from the League has also set in among the minor Powers. Whilst it is all to the good to seek to re-define the obligations of Members in the sense that Article 16 should not be obligatory but facultative, a reform which all intelligent opinion here is prepared to accept, any decision which implied that the Secretary of State, or at least the Under-Secretary, would not in future attend the Council himself in person would, I am convinced, be fraught with grave political danger here. Rightly or wrongly, public opinion here will judge His Majesty's Government by their League record. If His Majesty's Government appear to disinterest themselves in the League, a general movement away from the League will set in, and British opinion will hold His Majesty's Government responsible for having killed the League.

June 7th

The Edens dined tonight. He told me that Horace Wilson had been to see S.B. to ask him to make a speech in support of the P.M. as he was having such a difficulty. S.B. had refused, adding that he could hardly believe any speech from him was necessary for the Government in view of the powerful support they were getting from Lord Beaverbrook! I told him that I knew that Wilson had also been specially to see Tyrrell during the week-end in order to discuss Germany with him: he won't get much comfort from that quarter. A.E. had been staying in the same house as Rumbold[1] who was most outspoken in his criticism of the Government's handling of Spain and Germany. Bobbety has apparently written a letter on how Mussolini was bombing his way in Spain and the Anglo-Italian

1. Sir H. Rumbold, Ambassador to Germany 1928–1933.

agreement which he hopes to get his father to sign and send to *The Times.* A.E. is speaking himself at Leamington again on Saturday and has decided to hit out, taking up his text that the Tory Party must be progressive or succumb. He is horrified at the reactionary views of the back-benchers.

June 8th

I saw Victor Mallet back from Washington today. He said the Americans could not understand the P.M. and disliked him: the man they admired was A.E. and we had lost much there by his departure. We spoke of the Roosevelt plan; he was inclined to think that although we ought to have accepted it at once, it would probably not have led us anywhere. It might have created a violent revulsion of feeling in U.S. if it had gone wrong, although it would have committed Roosevelt personally.

H. back in London for the day. Discussion on Czechoslovak foreign relations. H. feels that we must be prepared for deadlock over Sudeten negotiations and should be ready to weigh in with a solution of the foreign treaties aspect which Strang says is just as important in German eyes as the former. He is always seeking to deal with the French dilemma of war or dishonour arising from the Franco-Czech guarantee treaty: he feels that Germany will probably not allow a settlement of the Sudeten question to be reached alone and in fact we must be prepared to deal with the *whole* problem. Our idea is to reduce Czechoslovakia to the position of Belgium, viz., to take out of the Czech-Soviet and Czech-French treaties Czechoslovakia's guarantee of Soviets and France (as needlessly irritating to Germany) leaving only the latter's guarantee of Czechoslovakia, and to arrange a Czechoslovak non-aggression pact with Germany coupled with an undertaking not to allow Czechoslovak territory to be used as a passage for others. But this would still leave the French and Soviet guarantee of Czechoslovakia against Germany and would probably still be unacceptable. Another idea is to copy the status of Luxemburg, i.e., no foreign policy at all and a joint guarantee by all the Big Powers. But a joint guarantee means it cannot operate at all unless all signatories are ready to act, and would give Czechoslovakia no real protection. The question is to be discussed by the Foreign Policy Committee of Cabinet, and then we would approach the French. In the meanwhile we continue to press Benes to meet the

Sudeten as quickly and generously as possible. Henlein is in a difficult position between Berlin and his own extremists.

William Strang tells me that there is nothing Machiavellian in the story of the special coach ordered by the Embassy at Berlin to evacuate the women and children of the staff. What happened was that several were going home about then in the normal course and as there were not places, it was decided to beat up a few more so that they could get an extra coach put on the train. The story got about that it was a tremendous stroke of diplomacy designed to show the Germans how much in earnest we were.

June 9th

Discussion in H.'s room today about bombing in Spain[1] to discover what we can do to stop it. Admiralty (James[2] and Dankwerts[3]) Board of Trade (Foley[4]), Air Ministry all represented. Admiralty as usual defeatist. They are determined to do nothing which might injure Franco. They hated Nyon. Board of Trade were most anxious to help but there seem no weapons we can use which won't recoil on our own trade and interests, e.g. withdrawing Hodgson, seizing Franco ships, whilst direct action such as shelling a naval base is repugnant to us and posting warships in harbours to shoot at aeroplanes amounts practically to intervention. The truth is we are being deliberately bombed in Spain by Italian and German airmen (more or less in spite of Franco who can't control them) because of our weakness in other directions. But the Government is going to have a bad time in the House of Commons after the recess next week.

June 12th

A.E. spoke at Leamington last night – a good speech, pretty stiff for the Government, dispelling optimism and calling for national unity and a robuster policy. I wonder what effect it will have. The incredible thing is that the Government has won the Staffs by-election in a straight fight.

1. Attacks on British ships in Republican harbours.
2. Admiral Sir W. James, Deputy Chief of Naval Staff 1935–1938.
3. Rear-Admiral V. H. Dankwerts, Director of Plans, Admiralty, 1938–1940.
4. Sir J. Foley, Under-Secretary at Board of Trade 1929–1939.

O.H. to Secretary of State – June 13th 1938

There is one point, which is really covered by paragraph 20 of your speech, which you might think worthwhile emphasising – namely, the limitations imposed on the Government's foreign policy by the strength of public opinion. It may be worth emphasising this at the present time when we are being pressed by Mussolini to implement the Anglo-Italian Agreement. Dictators have no difficulties with their public opinion and can bring about sudden changes of front without any risk of being overthrown. A British Government can only move forward very slowly, and any act of policy which may be wise in itself is liable to be defeated if it is not acceptable to the bulk of the country. The Hoare-Laval case is a classic example. It is all very well for Mussolini and Hitler to rate the British Government for not doing this or that, but unless the British public can be brought along too, the Government is materially unable to deliver the goods.

I attach a few sentences to express this in case you think it worthwhile.

June 13th

Conservative Central Office in their current notes for speakers hold up (i) France, (ii) Spain and (iii) Soviet Russia as examples of how badly Socialism works! What a gift for the Opposition who say the Government are pro-Dictators.

June 14th

I hear that Dawson, disturbed at the internal situation, has been to see S.B. from whom he got cold comfort. This has resulted in a leading article in *The Times* about the floating vote and the need for a wider appeal. I learn also that Londonderry is off shortly to Berlin to see Hitler and Goering and it is strongly rumoured that he will bear some sort of "appeal" from the P.M. to Hitler. H. has asked him to come and see him before he goes, as I hope, to stiffen him up a bit. Great interest has been aroused in Conservative circles by A.E.'s speech, especially the younger circles where already there is talk of a split in the Party in the Autumn. There is relief and satisfaction that A.E. has hoisted the Conservative flag and not that of the Left.

The Government's extremely negative statement on bombing in

Spain went badly in the House of Commons today. It is a pity that they did not at least agree to the gesture of recalling Hodgson from Burgos to report, as R. A. Butler wanted them to do.

June 18th

As a result of Foreign Policy Committee of Cabinet on Thursday, a telegram has been sent off to Perth to see Ciano (who has been pressing him regarding bringing Anglo-Italian Agreement into force) to explain that there can be no question of recognition of Abyssinia until some settlement of the Spanish question has been reached in accordance with the P.M.'s pledge, that the agreement is not universally popular over here, and British opinion is difficult, whilst on the other hand an early victory for Franco is unlikely and no speedy result can be expected from the Non-Intervention Committee's scheme even when it is finally adopted. In these circumstances we propose that an effort should be made to bring about an armistice; Mussolini to call off Franco while the French answer for Barcelona. If this could be obtained, then withdrawal of volunteers could be speeded up and H.M.G. could then implement Anglo-Italian Agreement. Would Mussolini agree to this procedure? Bonnet has told us that France would.

Such are Perth's instructions. He won't like having to deliver them. But I do not believe there is any chance of Italian or, for that matter, Franco's acceptance. The truth is we are in a jam over Spain, exactly as A.E. said we would be.

A telegram has also gone to Paris proposing that France should consider the possibility of modifying Czech foreign relations in the sense of the Belgian solution.

June 19th

Lunch with Thelma Cazalet[1] in the country. Gwilym Lloyd George[2] and Osbert Peake[3] there. Supper with Harry Crookshank. He is very annoyed over refusal of P.M. to allow distribution of F.O. tele-

1. Miss Thelma Cazalet (later Mrs Cazalet-Keir), M.P. for East Islington 1931–1945, and P.P.S. to the Minister of Education.
2. Later Lord Tenby. Home Secretary in post-war Conservative Government.
3. Later Lord Ingleby. M.P. for North Leeds 1929–1955.

grams to Junior Ministers and may even make it a reason for resigning later.

June 20th

Jim Barnes[1] to lunch. As he is very close to the Italians, I sought to impress on him how powerless Government here were to bring about cordial relations with Italy unless and until British public opinion were persuaded. To achieve this Mussolini must give up insulting references to democracies and get on better terms with France. Present French Government were now most anxious to help us over Spain but this was made impossible for them if Mussolini did not help them by restarting the Franco-Italian negotiations.

A.E. asked me to look in on my way home. He told me he had decided not to speak in tomorrow's debate on Spain although pressed to do so by various people including Lord Salisbury. I said I was sure he was right: events were panning out so exactly as he foresaw that it was more dignified to be silent. He is convinced that Mussolini is seeking deliberately to drive a wedge between us and France by pressing us to recognise while refusing to continue his talks with the French. If he spoke, he would make a point of this. He thought we should make a Franco-Italian agreement a condition of ratification of our Anglo-Italian agreement. So do I. He does not believe our latest armistice proposals have a chance of acceptance from either Mussolini or Franco. I urged him, as I always do now, to make a speech purely on internal affairs, e.g. the need for democracy here to revise its methods if it is to compete with the output of totalitarian states whether in peace or war.

June 20th

We received at midday Perth's replies to our instructions *re* our wish for renewal of Franco-Italian conversations and armistice in Spain. Completely negative. Ciano turned down flat any idea of early resumption of talks with France, and was almost as discouraging over armistice idea, although he said he must refer to Mussolini.

1. Author, and admirer of Italian Fascism.

June 21st

I hear from all sides that in debate in House of Commons P.M.'s speech was deplorable, even his own supporters being discouraged at his negative attitude towards bombing of our ships in Spain and his refusal to do more than send further futile protests. Lloyd George and Philip Baker were both very good. Quite unnecessary for A.E. to speak.

Jim, Liddell Hart and Virginia Cowles[1] lunched. Liddell Hart spoke about the extremely bad show the German Army had made of their entry into Austria. I asked him what he thought the French Army would do if it had to send help to Czechoslovakia. He said he feared they intended to launch an attack into German territory. If they once left the security of the Maginot line, they would expose themselves to an overwhelming German counter-attack. In fact in the Anglo-French staff talks we ought to stipulate that if we sent any expeditionary force, the French should agree not to launch a land offensive. The armies should adopt a strictly defensive role and remain in the Maginot line, while the air forces bombed German targets. But the military mind could not see this.

June 23rd

Another debate on Spain on adjournment. P.M. spoke again and yielded to pressure to extent of sending for Hodgson from Burgos to report.

June 24th

Telegram sent to Perth asking his view as to possibility of appealing to Mussolini to use his influence on Franco to stop bombing in view of increasing difficulty in which it is placing H.M.G.

I hear that Van is much depressed at lack of contact with Secretary of State and omission to consult him. He is even talking of resigning. Van has only himself to blame for accepting this ridiculous position instead of going to an Embassy.

1. American journalist, now married to Aidan Crawley.

June 27th

Alec Cadogan told me that there is now an idea of sending Oliver Stanley to Washington as Ambassador when Lindsay goes as his health is not up to Cabinet work. I daresay he would make a good Ambassador but it would be a serious thing for the Service to lose this post just now. Cadogan is going to urge strongly the claims of Lampson or alternatively of Ronnie Campbell.

Perth has now been instructed to speak to Ciano about the bombing in Spain on the lines suggested above but as coming from himself not from H.M.G.

July 2nd

The excitement of the week has been the Sandys case.[1] The P.M. and Belisha between them have been extraordinarily unwise in immediately turning the Attorney-General on to Sandys. The latter can be relied on to extract the maximum nuisance value from the case of breach of privilege – which anyway will make the House very touchy and will be money for jam to those who accuse the Government of pro-Fascist tendencies. I hear Winston is in the brightest spirits over it. All that can be said for it is that it has driven Spain off the front pages of the newspapers. I hear the Chairman of the Select Committee is likely to be Gilmour[2] who can be relied on to take a stiff line against arbitrary authority.

Meanwhile bombing has in fact temporarily stopped as a result of orders from Franco. Ciano gave Perth the reply to be expected, namely that Italy had no control over Franco or the volunteers, etc., but that he would do what he could. The French are getting increasingly restive over having closed *their* frontier as a result of our urging, whilst the Portuguese frontier is still open, and large supplies of men and material, as they allege, are pouring into Franco Spain from Italy. Daladier and Herriot[3] are both anxious to call Italian bluff by denouncing Non-Intervention. Bonnet is anxious to work in with us and wishes us to strengthen his hand against his colleagues.

1. Mr Duncan Sandys, M.P. for Norwood Division of Lambeth, was supposed to have contravened the Official Secrets Act.
2. Sir John Gilmour, former Minister for Agriculture.
3. Edouard Herriot. President of the Chamber of Deputies.

Mussolini refuses, in spite of our pressure, to renew the conversation with the French Chargé d'Affaires, thereby making the position increasingly humiliating in France. Hodgson returned on Thursday with Franco's reply to our protest. It is a friendly but woolly document, denies that there has been any *deliberate* bombing (which is untrue) and offers a neutral port for foodstuffs and medical supplies. We discussed the position with Hodgson on Friday: he does not see what action we can take which would effectively screw Franco's tail. To bomb aerodromes or capture a warship of his would, he thinks, only make the Spanish character more obstinate and possibly precipitate a war. To withdraw Hodgson himself would only leave the field clear to Italy and Germany. There is to be a further meeting next week to consider possibility of developing idea of a neutral port safe from bombing for ships not carrying contraband.

H. is worried, I think, at the impasse and would genuinely like to take effective action to stop the bombing if it could be found. There seems no alternative between paper protests and some positive action tantamount to intervention which might lead to general denunciation of Non-Intervention and war. The question is, would the mere threat of such action be sufficient to stop the bombing (as I believe) or should we have to go through with it? Nyon worked because Mussolini withdrew his submarines at once. We know that the deliberate bombings are the work of Italian and German airmen.

I have had a long talk with Fitzroy Maclean[1] back from Moscow. He said the Soviet Government under Stalin was now firmly opportunist – Stalin with his purges was merely concerned with securing his own position. The purges, amounting to 75% of the higher command in the army for instance and as high or higher a percentage in all other walks of life, had gravely shaken efficiency. During the Czech crisis the Soviet Government had remained absolutely silent and were terrified of being drawn in. Nobody's life was safe.

A.E. asked me to dine on Thursday night. He is becoming more impatient at Government drift and now inclined to speaking in next House of Commons debate on Foreign Affairs. Bobbety whom I also saw, favoured this too. A.E.'s speech to the Brotherhood had gone very well. He proposes to make each speech of his rather hotter.

---

1. Sir Fitzroy Maclean, M.P., was then 2nd Secretary at the British Embassy in Moscow.

July 4th

Secretary of State had further discussions with Hodgson about bombing. Sargent put forward strongly the prestige argument, viz., that we cannot afford to be kicked about in Spain without disastrous consequences to ourselves in other parts of the world. (I also hold this view and wrote to Secretary of State a note about it some days ago.[1]) H. fully agreed with importance of this and said whole question turned on whether we could be sure a threat of retaliation would be enough to stop it; if he was certain of this, he would do it; but if it became necessary actually to take retaliatory action, then the risks of other nations intervening in Spain, the break-up of Non-Intervention and of a direct Franco-Italian clash were too great to justify it. It has been decided that Hodgson should return to Burgos with instructions to draw a sharp distinction between bombing in territorial and non-territorial waters – the latter being absolutely unacceptable – and again between deliberate and non-deliberate bombing in territorial waters, the former to be stigmatised as much as possible. He is to endeavour to get Franco to agree to procedure to establish facts and to provide compensation. Finally, he is to explore idea of neutral bomb-free port in Republican Territory for certain kinds of cargoes – food and medical supplies.

Meanwhile we have received a blackmailing telegram from Mussolini. There can be no other word for it – complaining that whereas he, Mussolini, had done everything on his side of the bargain, H.M.G. had done nothing, had failed to give recognition of Abyssinia, etc., and so he must resume freedom of action, including return of troops to Libya, etc., unless Anglo-Italian agreement were brought into force. He also threatened to publish this communication which was in the form of a memorandum.

I have rarely seen such an offensive communication and it is safe to say that if it became known it would be held to be the most complete justification for A.E.'s resignation. What can have prompted Mussolini to send it at this moment we cannot conceive except the fact that we know he is again in serious internal difficulty over the bad harvest and it is to be supposed he expected the Spanish War to be over by now, and the Anglo-Italian Agreement consequently implemented, which would have given him a little triumph to set

1. See Appendix L.

against the general Italian belief that Hitler *rouled* him over Austria. Now he is turning nasty and hopes to blackmail the P.M. whose foreign policy has been so dangerously based on improvement in Italo-British relations, failing which he will hold us up again as Public Enemy No. 1 and distract attention from his internal difficulties on to us.

July 5th

Non-Intervention Committee met today with H. in the chair. British Plan was at last adopted *in toto* and it was decided to despatch it to the two parties in Spain. A step forward at least but the prospects of any speedy result are remote. The Plan offers endless opportunity for the Spaniards of either side, while accepting in principle, to raise objections of detail.

July 6th

H. told me that the P.M. had a talk with Kennedy, the U.S. Ambassador, on his return from America. Latter had said there had been a remarkable change of opinion there since last he was over. Whereas when A.E. resigned he was regarded as "second cousin of Jesus Christ", now opinion had adjusted itself and thought much of the P.M. He had also said that Roosevelt was very anxious to help us whenever he could: he intended to send the fleet into the Atlantic and if there were a war, he meant to operate the Neutrality Act in such a way that it would not hurt us.

I am inclined to doubt what Kennedy says about U.S. opinion and P.M. It was not borne out by a deputation of Americans representing the American Institute of Foreign Affairs (though this of course is a Specialist body) who made it quite clear to the Secretary of State when he received them that they had the greatest misgivings about the P.M.'s attitude. A.E. himself made a short speech as guest of Americans in London on Independence Day which had, I hear, a most enthusiastic reception in America.

July 7th

Cabinet yesterday again boggled over idea of a currency loan to China in spite of H.'s efforts to persuade them. Simon as usual full of fears. H. is very keen on this and is determined, I think, to push it through somehow or other but wishes to meet his colleagues by giving it a commercial rather than a political façade. But the spirit of the Cabinet is defeatist and timorous to the extreme: they cannot see that Japan is up to the neck in the Chinese bog and in no case to do anything to us more than bluster.

We had meeting today with Phipps and Van, Cadogan, etc., to discuss with Secretary of State our attitude to France over Spain and Italy. S. of S. was impressed with importance of allowing no encouragement to Mussolini's game of driving wedge between us and France. Phipps was also told that the Italians were, we knew, sending stuff into Spain continually although mainly replacements: France, on the other hand, was now allowing nothing to go through. Bonnet was most anxious to improve relations with Italy and to send an Ambassador but if Mussolini went on as he did, insulting France by word and deed, French opinion – even Right opinion, would oblige the Government to reopen the frontier.

Van is now as violently anti-Mussolini as formerly he was pro. He now says he is convinced that he is our inveterate foe. What a pity he did not hold these views when he was doing his utmost to defeat the Sanction Campaign.

July 8th

Reply to Mussolini has gone off – firm, unruffled and reasoned. I wonder what effect it will have!

July 11th–16th

Secretary of State has received two mysterious approaches from Germany, one through Oliver Hoare, Sam's brother, and one through Lady Snowden – neither exactly the go-betweens one would choose – to effect that Hitler is anxious to send an important personage, i.e. Goering, secretly or anyway unofficially to London, to hold conversations with us. Ribbentrop is said to know nothing about this but Neurath is aware of it. It is desired to know whether H.M.G. would be ready to receive such a personage. H. sees how odd this procedure is but feels none the less that it is not for us to take the responsibility of turning it down. After much thought a reply was drafted, saying that it would obviously be much easier to hold conversations if the Czech question had been satisfactorily settled, but if the Germans were able to give an assurance that they would continue to co-operate with us in working for such a settlement it still might be possible to hold conversations. If the Germans also thought this could be done, H.M.G. would require a formal approach to be made through regular official channels but they held out no hope that conversations could be held without publicity and whilst taking all precautions, they could not guarantee that the presence of the "personage" might not give rise to undesirable demonstrations. Oliver Hoare brought Princess Hohenlohe,[1] who is one of the links in the chain, to see H. (not at the F.O.). (She is of course a well-known adventuress, not to say a blackmailer.) She undertook to bring Wiedemann (Hitler's A.D.C. who comes over here a good deal in order to nose about) to see H. next Monday at 88 Eaton Square, where he proposes to speak on the lines of the draft reply mentioned above. Alex Cadogan will also be there as a witness.

Meanwhile Van is very excited again as his own mysterious sources tell him that things are going from bad to worse in the Czechoslovakian question: that Benes is holding back again, that Henlein is fed up and has been to see Hitler to tell him that Benes's negotiations are nothing but a swindle, that the Nazi party bosses are pressing for an *Einmarsch*, whilst Ribbentrop and the moderates are losing ground. H. does not take all this too tragically. H. does not see what more can be done. We are pressing Benes very hard. We are also hoping to secure Runciman's services as an arbitrator to be produced if the negotiations reach an impasse. R. should be very good if he will accept but at present he is jibbing rather.

Much excitement has also been caused by an alleged lecture by General Reichenau, the German G.O.C. at Leipzig, given to Nazi party chiefs there on the subject of Spain. He explained in the lecture the valuable lessons which Germany had drawn from the warfare in Spain, the training for her air and tank experts, the economic concessions which she was obtaining, her intention to use Spain as a base for future warfare against Great Britain.

Altogether about as bad a document as could be imagined. A copy was first sent off by Ellen Wilkinson, M.P. and H. sent it to the Service Ministers and Inskip who asked for it to be circulated to the Cabinet. The C.I.D. studied it – were much impressed by what it

1. Arrested by U.S. Authorities on entry of America into the war as an active Nazi propagandist.

said. Next it appeared in the *News Chronicle*. This caused, naturally enough, intense annoyance in the German Press and the German Government issued a prompt denial of its truth. Is it true or not? We do not know but it is certainly not improbable.

Cabinet on Wednesday finally turned down any idea of a currency or other loan to China. What a pity! All because of nervousness of what Japan might do and of what Mussolini might do if Japan did anything. So the Russians are to have the field to themselves as the only champions of China. I fear we shall pay for this. It all goes back to our weakness in Spain.

H. talked to me about the Washington Embassy. He said he was not quite convinced about Lampson being the right man – anyway he favoured his staying in Cairo. He wanted something more striking and original of the Bryce type. We went over a number of names. I said that I thought the Service ought to have it unless there really was an outstanding outsider. There was no modern equivalent of Bryce.

July 18*th*

H. and Alec Cadogan saw Wiedemann, Hitler's A.D.C., this morning at 88 Eaton Square. He made a good impression and appeared serious and straightforward. He said he had come on Hitler's authority to discuss the possibility of a visit here by Goering to carry further the conversations initiated during H.'s visit to Germany. Hitler had been disappointed that these had not been followed up: he was still anxious to bring about Anglo-German friendship and had great admiration and respect for Great Britain. H. said the times were not very favourable to such conversations but if the Czechoslovak question were once settled satisfactorily it would be easier. Wiedemann said that he could say on the highest authority and as a message from Hitler that no forcible measures were contemplated by Germany: she had no present intention of intervening by force in Czechoslovakia and would never do so in present circumstances unless something occurred such as a massacre of Sudeten which she could not as a Great Power ignore. He suggested that Germany might give an assurance that she would observe the peace for a definite period if that would help. H. spoke of all H.M.G. had done to help in Czechoslovakia: W. said it was felt that we had not yet done enough. H. asked what G. would do if negotiations broke down.

W. said they would endeavour to get them started again. W. said that besides Hitler, only Neurath and Goering were privy to his mission but not Ribbentrop nor Dirksen.[1] H. asked whether it would not be resented by Ribbentrop if such talks were held behind his back. W. said that Ribbentrop's position with Hitler was no longer what it used to be and that he would be brought in only when it was necessary. He promised however to tell Dirksen before he left London. It was finally agreed that W. should return to Germany and say that H.M.G. favoured conversations in principle but that they needed careful preparation beforehand and the times must be favourable also if they were to be successful and fruitful: that to hold conversations and for them to fail would be worse than not holding them at all – that the present moment with Czechoslovakian question unsettled seemed hardly favourable but might be made more favourable by exchange of assurances as regards Germany's peaceful intentions or by some overt act by Germany having the same effect. The next step, if these views commended themselves to Hitler and Goering, should be formal proposals through the German Ambassador here or from Neurath to Nevile Henderson in Berlin.

Meanwhile Runciman has finally agreed to act as mediator or arbitrator if accepted by both sides. Our news from Prague about the state of negotiations is distinctly bad: Benes appears to be adopting a take-it-or-leave-it attitude, having got agreement among the Czech Government parties on proposals which indeed go far but yet not far enough, he seems to intend to throw them at the heads of the Sudeten and pass them through Parliament whether they like them or not. We now intend to weigh in with an offer of an arbitrator and threaten to make it public if he does not accept.

July 19th–24th

I returned from the Royal visit to Paris late on Friday night. We started off in a fog from Dover in the *Enchantress* and at first it appeared as if we should scarcely get across. The fog lifted and we found our destroyer escort outside the harbour. Halfway across the Channel the escort was taken over by French destroyers and we passed down a line of French warships off Boulogne. From Boulogne to Paris what impressed us most were the number of people who had

1. Herbert von Dirksen succeeded Ribbentrop as German Ambassador in 1938.

164

gathered in the fields and villages to wave as the train went by. It was clear that the whole of France had turned out to do us honour. We all lunched together with the King and Queen at one long table in the train. We reached the Bois de Boulogne Station about 4.30 and were there met by M. Lebrun.[1] The station – in which we cannot have spent ten minutes – had been specially built for the occasion, and decorated with Union Jacks and Beauvais tapestry. Outside troops were massed and we all got into cars preceded and surrounded by escorts of *Spahis* and *Cuirassiers*. The crowds down the Champs Élysées were kept well back on the pavements and there were double rows of troops and police but the crowds were quite dense and vociferous. Finally we got to the Quai d'Orsay but set out again almost at once to pay our official call on the President at the Élysée. That night we dined at the Élysée and the King and the President made their speeches. The King spoke well and clearly in French with practically no hesitation. To bed, dog tired, about twelve. The next morning, Wednesday, we went with Their Majesties by boat from the Quai d'Orsay to the Hotel de Ville, a perfectly arranged excursion, crowds and crowds on the banks and fountains specially constructed playing in the water. At the Hotel de Ville we proceeded through room after room until we finally reached the principal hall where the King again made a short speech in reply to Prévost de Launay's address of welcome.

Halifax had a talk with Bonnet and Daladier at 12.30 and Ronnie Campbell and I joined them at luncheon when Herriot, Blum and Chautemps also came. Herriot in great form, showing himself, as I thought, a much bigger man than any of the others. He told us a killing story of how the King of Montenegro had mistaken him at Lyons for the Prefect's valet and had given him his umbrella to carry. We talked about Spain but, contrary to what we expected, Herriot did not press for the opening of the French frontier but only urged us to try and attempt mediation. Halifax had previously told Daladier and Bonnet of the Wiedemann visit (news of which had leaked out in the *Daily Herald* on the Tuesday morning) but they showed no annoyance and were interested, if slightly sceptical, at the assurances he had brought from Hitler about Czechoslovakia. Halifax also told them of the Runciman idea under the strictest secrecy. They fully approved the plan and promised to support it at Prague.

1. French President 1932–1940.

On Thursday morning we all went off by train to Versailles and saw a review of 30,000 troops, horse, foot, artillery and tanks, a most impressive parade which our War Office will, I hope, please note. From the review we drove into the Château to a marvellous luncheon of 250 covers in the *Salle des Glaces*. All the waiters were in eighteenth-century costume with powdered hair and indeed the guests in their black tail coats were the only discordant note. A magnificent luncheon of eight or ten courses and a different wine to each course perfectly served. After that we saw an entertainment in the gardens and finally got back to Paris about five in time to rest and dress for the dinner and reception at the Quai d'Orsay itself. We discussed before dinner the possibility of the King and Queen appearing on the balcony after dinner so that the crowds could see them. Hardinge had thought of their going for an impromptu drive but the French authorities thought it too risky. Halifax suggested their appearing at a window of the Ministry of Marine on the Place de la Concorde but here again the French authorities were obviously unwilling to take any risks. Sarraut told us he had no anxiety as regards any Frenchman of any party but that Paris was full of foreigners, Spanish, Italian, Russian, and they were the danger. In the end it was decided that they should appear on the balcony of the Quai itself where the number of the crowds was limited by the width of the roadway. They did this after the reception and were loudly cheered and had in the end to appear a second time.

The next day, Friday, we left Paris at 10.30 for the Villers-Brettoneux War Memorial and thence home via Calais. Again the same crowds in the fields and villages as we passed. Altogether a most memorable visit – most striking for the perfection and precision of all the arrangements, the wealth and taste of the decorations and the obviously spontaneous enthusiasm of the crowds. The King and Queen by their simplicity and dignity could not have made a more fortunate impression. The French had obviously split themselves to make the visit a success and had more than succeeded. It should go far to convince people abroad of the fundamental ability of the French to make a success of anything they have a mind to – and also to convince the French themselves of this fact, which some of them had seemed to have forgotten in the recent wave of defeatism which has swept over them, particularly the Right. Altogether the success of the visit should make the dictators think.

After our return we heard that the P.M. had received Dirksen on

Friday 22nd, the day of our return, and spoken to him about the Wiedemann visit. P.M. welcomed the German assurances about Czechoslovakia but took up the point that it had been said that if a number of Sudeten were massacred Hitler would march in and observed that Germany must not regard us as accepting the inevitability of forceful action even in this case. Dirksen reiterated that Berlin did not desire any conflict and added naïvely that a certain amount of propaganda was essential to keep up the interest of the German people though this should not be taken as an intention to use violence! (It is curious that this talk should have been arranged to take place the day of our return. Why not wait for the Foreign Secretary? Is this No. 10 up to its old tricks of stealing our thunder when the Foreign Secretary is out of the country? I do not think Halifax was pleased when he learnt of it.)

The Czechoslovak Government have now asked us to appoint a mediator.

Barcelona has intimated that they will accept the British plan.

There is a lot of intrigue going on apparently between Poliakoff,[1] Tyrrell and Horace Wilson but I cannot make out who is using which. Van says Poliakoff is now in German pay.

September 6th

I came back to work yesterday after a month's leave in France. During that time I saw no one except W. Tyrrell when we stayed a night at Bièvres with the Crawshays[2] on our way South and one or two people in Paris on my way back.

W.T. told me that he had seen Runciman before he left and had recommended him to take Gwatkin[3] with him. He highly approved of his mission,[4] not least because it committed H.M.G. up to the hilt. He had also seen Osusky and warned him that the Czechs must lay all their cards on the table and not try to nobble him. He was very anti-Benes. W.T. had seen S.B. and found him ten years younger. He was worried about internal affairs (as I already knew from A.E.) and

1. V. Poliakoff, Russian émigré journalist who acted as a contact between Ciano and Chamberlain.
2. Captain J. W. L. Crawshay, Hon. Attaché at Paris Embassy.
3. Mr F. Ashton Gwatkin of the Foreign Office.
4. The Runciman Mission was to mediate between the Czechs and the Sudetens.

W.T. had begged him to help Chamberlain over this because of the dangers of the foreign situation. I was surprised how violently anti-Van he was: he said Van should take a year's leave to recover his sanity; he ought to have gone abroad when he was offered Paris and the present arrangement would break down through Van himself. Van had got himself into a position which was unconstitutional for a civil servant.

Halifax has been at work practically the whole of August dealing with the Czech crisis. A pretty gloomy situation! Runciman seems to be preserving the peace precariously by his presence but he seems to have moved very near to the Henlein point of view. The German press and German speakers could not be less helpful by their attitude of exaggerating every drunken brawl into a major incident, and belittling every Czech concession. Benes is inclined to backslide and requires continual stoking from Newton, from Runciman and from the French. Henlein himself seems a moderate sensible man who wants to remain in Czechoslovakia provided he can get reasonable terms but he is pushed by his own extremists and frightened by the German Nazis and Hitler. In Germany itself we are now confronted with a gradual mobilisation of all the armed forces, including considerable concentration on the French frontier and German naval manœuvres in the North Sea! All this is represented to us as perfectly legitimate autumn "manœuvres". The French are outwardly uncannily calm, though they are taking certain counter-measures such as calling back reservists to complete the occupation of the Maginot Lines. We are announcing our own naval manœuvres in the North Sea at the same time as the German. Everything points to the fact that Hitler is determined to have everything ready for war at a moment's notice if required. Whether he intends to go to war and invade Czechoslovakia, or whether he only intends to use his force as blackmail to impose a settlement of the Sudeten question nobody, not even his entourage, can say. Probably he does not know himself yet. Certain elements are urging immediate direct action, notably Nazi leaders such as Himmler, Goebbels, and now it seems Ribbentrop. Goering is a doubtful factor. The Army are inclined to hang back but after the Anschluss are in a weak position. Ribbentrop is a public danger because we know he is continually assuring Hitler that Great Britain will never move, and that in consequence France will not move either, and he stops as far as he can any information to the contrary effect from reaching Hitler. To ensure that Hitler and

Germany should realise that once war started it is extremely likely that France and we would be unable to stand aside, Simon spoke at Lanark in this sense, and Halifax sent a personal message to Hitler calling attention to the disturbing effect of the announced German manœuvres. Simon's speech was greeted with indignation in Germany, whilst Halifax's memo has produced no reply whatever from Hitler but only a furious outburst from Ribbentrop at being successfully short-circuited.

Meanwhile under pressure of all these things Benes has now come forward with a further offer to the Sudeten including territorial autonomy. What its reception will be we do not yet know. Henlein saw Hitler a few days ago when the latter professed "that he wanted peace" and did not otherwise adopt any menacing attitude. Runciman has also drawn up a scheme himself for production in an emergency in case of a breakdown between Benes and Henlein: he is also ready to announce his intention of producing a scheme of sorts by September 15th. The important thing is to convince Hitler that *actual progress* is being made so that he shall not commit himself to some irrevocable action when he speaks at the Nuremberg *Parteitag* next Monday. Henderson in Berlin sends streams of telegrams to emphasise the urgency of settlement and the necessity of it being 100% of Henlein's Karlsbad demands if it is to be worth the paper it is written on.

There was a meeting of Ministers last week when the prospects were examined. It was agreed to make no declaration to German Government that if they had recourse to war over Sudeten, H.M.G. would declare war, but to try and keep Germany guessing and to press on French Government the need to consult us before taking action likely to lead to war. Question of British attitude if France became involved in war with Germany over Czechoslovakia was reserved for consideration if and when it arose. The younger Ministers, especially Duff Cooper, De La Warr, Elliot and Stanley favoured a firmer attitude; the older generation – who carried the day – opposed this – especially of course, Simon, and, most inept of all, the Lord Chancellor. The latter section emphasised the view that the country would not stand for any more definite attitude over Czechoslovakia, and drew attention to the inadequacy of our defences. Yesterday Halifax again considered in the Office the possibility of a further warning to Hitler but after very careful consideration he decided against it. Cadogan would have preferred another warning to be sent – Strang, however, thinks that H. is right and that a further warning would merely irritate unless it could be made a good deal stronger than before. We have however, authorised Henderson, if Hitler should ask to see him while he is at Nuremberg, to repeat as his personal opinion what he had already said to Weiszacker[1] in Berlin on his return from his visit to London last week, namely that he, Henderson, had been astonished at the change of opinion in England since his last visit and at the unanimity with which German action was disapproved and of the great likelihood that Great Britain would join in if a war began. It is thought unlikely that Hitler will ask to see Henderson and he is not to ask for an interview.

Great help has been given by the Americans. Roosevelt is fully with us, and he authorised the United States Ambassador in Paris, Bullitt, to make some strong remarks in a speech at a war memorial last week. But of course this is only moral support; it would take a very great deal to move the U.S.A. out of benevolent neutrality. Even so this is a great deal, and a very great deal more than we had in 1914.

Today H. discussed the question of his going to Geneva. We were due to start on Friday next, and decided to give it up or at least postpone it. I said that I did not think he ought to be out of London this weekend, at any rate not unless the P.M. (who is in Scotland) returned to London to take charge, and even so, I thought that he, as Foreign Secretary, should remain at the helm. He was rather concerned at the idea that he would be represented as letting the League down. I said I did not think any serious body of opinion would think this at this juncture. Alec was much against his going, so was Rex and Strang. Stevenson[2] and Mounsey wanted him to go because of the League's prestige and because of the importance of his meeting the other Foreign Ministers, especially Beck[3] (who will now probably leave the Council) and Litvinoff. Horace Wilson whom H. also saw was strongly opposed to his going and that I think clinched it. We urged however that Malcolm MacDonald be sent if possible for two or three days to take his place as otherwise the U.K. delegation (De La Warr, Butler and Wallace[4]) are such a painfully light team.

1. Ernst von Weiszacker, State Secretary at German Foreign Ministry.
2. Sir Ralph Stevenson, then Counsellor at Foreign Office.
3. Colonel Beck, Polish Foreign Minister.
4. Euan Wallace, M.P.

September 8th

News last night bad. Fresh incident had caused Sudeten leaders to suspend negotiations with Czechs on new plan. The British observers had been sent to investigate. Bonnet asked if Henderson could not be instructed to make a personal appeal to Hitler at Nuremberg. We have asked Runciman for his views on this. If the last Czech offer really substantially meets the Sudeten demands as seems to be the case, and if Germany is honest and wants a peaceful settlement, she will allow the Sudeten to accept. If she is dishonest and only playing with us, then now is the time to force the issue by exploiting an incident because if she refuses the offer public opinion will put Germany in the wrong. Moreover there is always the danger that Nazi extremists may deliberately stage an incident in order to drive Hitler off the deep end if they think he is wavering.

Times leader yesterday referring to the possibility of the cession of the Sudeten areas to Germany has had calamitous effect in spite of *démenti* from Foreign Office that it represented views of H.M.G. It was broadcast in Germany and it has been interpreted everywhere as a *ballon d'essai* and as foreshadowing a fresh surrender by H.M.G., especially in U.S.A. This is all due to that little defeatist Geoffrey Dawson – Halifax lunched with him yesterday – and spoke to him about its untimely and unfortunate nature; yet, today, *The Times* repeats the offence!

Our Geneva visit is definitely cancelled and this is being announced today.

P.M. returned last night and he, H. and Simon with Alec and Van had a meeting today at 11 which lasted till 1.30 and was resumed at 5 to consider the advisability of sending a further warning to Hitler in view of persistence of reports that Ribbentrop and others of his entourage are assuring him that Great Britain would *in no circumstances* intervene. Runciman has telegraphed to say that he does not favour a further warning as it appears probable that negotiations between the Sudeten and Czechs will be resumed in a day or so as the incident is being promptly and satisfactorily liquidated by the Czech authorities. The meeting at No. 10 however felt strongly that some further warning was necessary in view of the information in our possession which is not known to Runciman. The possibility of a statement by the P.M. to journalists as an alternative to a personal message to Hitler is also being considered.

We dined with A.E. last night just back from Ireland. He was very worried at situation and felt strongly that a much more definite warning should be given to Hitler. The Lanark speech was not nearly enough and coming from Simon was immediately discounted. He thought we should publicly endorse next Czech offer. He is wondering whether he ought to say something going rather further than the Government. He had been much struck by the remarkable reception he had had everywhere he had been – at Glasgow when he visited the Exhibition, in Dublin and on the Tyneside. S.B. had written to say he too was very worried and urged A.E. "to go about as much as possible but not to say anything on internal affairs until he had seen S.B." A.E. full of impressions of industrial conditions and need for revival of Disraeli Tory democracy.

September 9th

Local news from Czechoslovakia rather better – calm in Prague – incident found to be (as usual) grossly exaggerated and in course of settlement. Hitler still the enigma but from secret sources we hear further concentrations of troops are being made towards Czechoslovakian frontiers which look exactly as if war had been decided upon.

Soviet Government is proposing a joint *démarche* at Berlin by Great Britain, France and Soviets, whilst the French Government is pressing for a more definite warning to Hitler from us.

A.E. came to see H. at 2.45 and strongly advocated a further and more definite warning being sent to Hitler, viz., that H.M.G. should say the Czech offer was a good one and ask Hitler to urge the Sudeten to accept it as a basis, that if conflict arose, it was impossible to conceive that it would be localised, and finally that if as a result France were in, we were in too up to the neck. He told me afterwards he found H. very depressed and he is very much afraid H.M.G. may yet run away and let the Czechs down.

At 3.30 the meeting of Ministers begun this morning was resumed (P.M., Simon with Alec, Van and H. Wilson) in order to discuss the warning to Hitler. As a result a draft telegram to Henderson was approved instructing him to see Ribbentrop and repeat the warning, saying that H.M.G. regarded the last Czech offer as a reasonable basis for negotiations, that if war began France would almost certainly come in and we might then well be unable to stand aside. Reference was also made as proof of British opinion to the T.U.C. manifesto. As the meeting was ending, however, we received a press telegram saying that N.H. had seen both Hitler and Ribbentrop that afternoon. It was thereupon decided to send the instructions to Nevile Henderson at Nuremberg but to tell him not to act upon them until we had heard whether or not he had seen Hitler, and, if so, what he had said.

This however was not the only decision reached during the day. In the morning, whether at a meeting or whether only by the P.M. and H. I do not know, it was decided to ask Henderson's views on a proposal that the P.M. himself should visit Hitler. This was sent in a letter from Wilson to Henderson by special messenger by air.

The French Ambassador called at 7.30 with a further message from Bonnet to say that according to very reliable information reaching the French Government (which is corroborated by our own) Hitler is determined to use force against Czechoslovakia, being convinced of the irresolution of Great Britain and of the consequent weakness of France: he therefore begged H.M.G. to consider what action we could take to open Hitler's eyes.

September 10th

Telephone message from Gwatkin came late last night to say the incident had been satisfactorily settled and negotiations between Czechs and Sudeten were to begin again today. Runciman in a letter to H. yesterday seemed quite hopeful that agreement could be reached by the end of next week. He said that he and Newton had really shaken Benes who had now gone forward manfully. Thus from the local point of view there is no reason now why a settlement should not be reached. All the danger now lies in Hitler and in incidents – faked or genuine. There are for instance ominous reports that a framed-up assassination of Henlein may be attempted.

Henderson rang up Cadogan early this morning to acknowledge receipt of Wilson's letter and to say that he had not seen Hitler but only Ribbentrop; his report was being sent back by air and he begged that it should be read before we instructed him to act on the warning which he evidently did not like. He was told therefore to await further instructions.

173

P.M. much annoyed this morning, I hear, at categoric reports in *Daily Mail* and other papers that definite instructions had been sent to Henderson yesterday to give a stern warning to Hitler or Ribbentrop. A *démenti* was issued from No. 10.

Kennedy, the U.S. Ambassador, called to ask for any information. He said he thought it essential to take every possible step to clear Hitler's mind and only overwhelming evidence should prevent us from sending the proposed message. He approved the fleet moves announced this morning. (Calling out of certain minesweepers and minelayers decided on yesterday and announced intentionally in press today.) He even suggested the Soviets might do something in the way of military measures.

Owing to delay of aeroplane Henderson's report only reached us about 4 p.m. It was at once considered by meeting of Ministers (P.M., H. and Simon plus S. Hoare who has now joined them, with Cadogan, Van and Wilson). Its purport was a most earnest plea that he should not deliver any further warning because he, Henderson, was satisfied that all the important people round Hitler now understood our position and that Hitler did not contemplate any immediate action or any irrevocable threat in his speech on Monday: that Hitler was waiting to see if Benes really meant business, and provided this was the case and no incident occurred, all should be well. A fresh warning, however, especially, as would be inevitable, one that would be reported in the Press, would place Hitler in the dilemma of choosing between war or resounding diplomatic defeat, and he might well choose the former and risk it. As for the idea of a visit by the P.M. he evidently rather liked it although saying that it would need careful staging in advance. The meeting finally decided to accept Henderson's advice at the present stage and to withold the further warning.

Such is the position at the moment. I cannot say I feel easy about it. By not telling Hitler again and more definitely of the likelihood of our coming in we are taking a very great risk in view of what we know of German military concentrations and of the persistence of reports that responsible Germans, especially Hitler, do not believe we would ever move. This would be the view of A.E. and Winston, let alone Labour and Liberals. Again, it is also the view of the French and the U.S.A. On the other hand, I see the risk of Hitler going off the deep end if confronted with the alternative of a diplomatic defeat which his regime – none too strong – might not survive. We know that the

Sudeten are now themselves urging Hitler to allow them to accept Benes's offer as a basis and want a settlement. Hitler can claim, if he wishes to, that it is he who has won a bloodless victory for the Sudeten. There is no reason now because of any Czech backwardness why Hitler should not in fact gracefully approve and so preserve peace. I have a feeling that A.E. is right when he says that the present Government will run away if it comes to a show-down – a fresh Hoare-Laval – rather than go to war if they possibly can and that Hitler senses this. If so, it is extremely dangerous. I do not believe they realise that the independence of Czechoslovakia, if allowed to be overthrown without any counter-action by the Western Powers, would spell the end of British prestige for a very long time. We should suffer for it in every quarter of the globe. As it is, Japan is watching and waiting. We should lose every friend we have, and so would France. Also I am not reassured by the nature of the Cabinet Committee – especially Simon and Hoare – which is taking all the decisions. None of the younger generation there. A Cabinet is announced for Monday and then they may make their influence felt – particularly Duff Cooper, for it must be confessed that the remainder are a poor lot – Oliver Stanley flabby, Elliot a windbag, De La Warr sound but a very light weight, Morrison now quite *dégonflé*, it seems.

September 11th

No fresh news except that the German Naval Attaché is most upset at the movement of minesweepers and minelayers which we have announced and called at the Admiralty to ask for explanations: he said he for one at last now realised Great Britain was in earnest. This had evidently seriously shaken the German experts anyway. We for our part are telling our Military Attaché in Berlin to ask for explanations of the alleged concentrations on the Czechoslovak frontiers.

A.E. telephoned to me from the country last night that he was very worried at the decision not to send a further warning: he wondered whether he could help by making a speech. I advised him to come and see H. Winston also rang up H. himself last night and urged need for an immediate ultimatum to Germany.

A.E. came to see H. at three today and suggested that he should write a stiff letter to *The Times*. H. rather liked the idea and said he would show A.E.'s draft to the P.M. (I hear P.M. also approved the idea and the letter will go forward). A.E. said he saw the point of not sending warning in view of Henderson's advice but he mistrusted the man's judgment: he urged that the Government should announce further naval movements.

Kennedy rang up to say that he had telephoned to Roosevelt who had agreed to divert two U.S. cruisers here: *Nashville* arriving at Portland tomorrow, and *Honolulu* at Gravesend on 22nd.

H.'s mind is turning over possibility of a plebiscite. He does not believe any settlement reached between the Czechs and Sudeten will last and a separation is the only hope of avoiding war. If a plebiscite could be held under agreed conditions, he would try by means of a loan to secure some transfer of populations out of the respective areas. In order to enforce such a plebiscite the idea would be to summon a Four-Power Conference – Great Britain, France, Germany and Italy.

September 12th

A very anxious day. Cabinet met this morning – with what result I do not know yet. A.E.'s letter appeared in *Times* today and will I hope do some good. H. has been studying all the afternoon his idea of a Four-Power Conference and plebiscite. Lord Lloyd[1] came to see him to urge strongly the need for drastic and courageous action and to beg that H.M.G. would not consider any surrender in Czechoslovakia which would in fact spell the end of the democracies. Van says Ministers yesterday were lamentably weak and indecisive and turned down the idea put forward tentatively by H. that we should announce further fleet moves. I cannot help feeling myself that in their anxiety for non-provocation and peace they overlook the real issues now at stake – not Czechoslovakia but the position of democracies as a whole and all they represent, let alone the interests of the British Empire which every jackal in Europe and Asia is watching. I am certain that there can be no assured peace for us so long as the Hitler and Mussolini systems last.

I forgot to mention that Masaryk has left an official note to say the Czech Government can in no circumstances accept a plebiscite.

I listened to Hitler's speech[2] on the wireless at the Jebbs. It was like a madman, or rather an African chieftain haranguing his tribe.

1. Lord Lloyd of Dolobran, High Commissioner in Egypt, 1925-1929.
2. At Nuremberg.

The general impression is that it leaves things much as they were – the reference to self-determination is obviously near a demand for a plebiscite.

Ministers met afterwards and then adjourned.

September 13th

News of incidents following on Hitler's speech which has worked as an incitement to violence among the Sudeten. The Czechoslovak Government have announced a state of emergency in certain districts to enable them to deal with this.

French Government have asked that Runciman should be told to produce his own plan. Runciman has been consulted already on this and was opposed to it.

At Cabinet yesterday no further decisions were taken. Duff Cooper pressed for more naval measures but this was held up for further consideration later. The Cabinet is to meet again tomorrow.

Nevile Henderson telegraphs that he is convinced Hitler means to march unless Sudeten get "autonomy" very shortly; he says Hitler has weighed up risk of Great Britain and France going to war and is prepared to risk it. The only chance is for Benes at once to grant autonomy or for Runciman to announce plan and for us to back it, and to tell Czechoslovakia that if she will not have it, we wash our hands. He adds that if now after warnings he has given, we do not march in event of aggression, we should be regarded with complete contempt in Germany.

Report came this evening that Sudeten had sent an ultimatum to Czechoslovak Government demanding removal of special police measures within four hours. Ministers met on and off all day. It was decided this evening to instruct Henderson to inform Hitler through Ribbentrop of P.M.'s wish to come and see Hitler personally as soon as possible in view of gravity of situation.

Position as I see it at 11 p.m. tonight is as follows:

In Czechoslovakia, thanks to Runciman, Benes has come forward with an offer which the Sudeten regard or did regard as a basis for negotiation. The speech of Hitler has acted there as an incitement to violence just when negotiations looked promising. Czechoslovak Government thereupon imposed special police measures: the Sudeten have again broken off negotiations and demand revocation of these measures in six hours. There are also ugly rumours of Sudeten demand for a plebiscite. Czechoslovak Government have told us they cannot accept a plebiscite.

In Germany Hitler's speech is interpreted as a determination to see Sudeten get autonomy very shortly – either peacefully or by war if necessary. The German forces are on war footing and there would be no opposition in spite of much internal discontent and the misgivings of German soldiers, etc. Henderson assures that nothing will stop him now except immediate grant of autonomy and that if France and Great Britain do not actually fight if Czechoslovakia is oppressed, we shall be despised for ever. At any moment Hitler may support Sudeten demands for calling off police measures or call for a plebiscite with threat of force or march in because of incidents.

It is for France who has special treaty relation unlike us to decide if and when a *casus belli* arises. She need not ask our advice nor can she justifiably make us responsible for any action she may take. We have asked her to consult us before she takes action likely to lead to war: we are entitled to ask this as we have a treaty obligation to defend France in certain circumstances. H. however has been markedly discouraging to French Ambassador and Phipps in Paris. Phipps reports that Bonnet (who has lost his nerve) now says he would accept Karlsbad points if Runciman would back them and suggested a Four-Power Conference to be called by Great Britain or France. Phipps also saw Daladier tonight; latter also showed signs of weakening and Phipps thought French Government were bluffing over alleged determination to fight. D. proposed in a message to P.M. (i) that, in order to avoid French Government being faced by their obligations, Runciman should produce his own plan, (ii) Runciman should bring two sides together in his presence and (iii) failing that, a Three-Power Conference – Great Britain, France and Germany should be summoned to deal with Czechoslovakia.

The British Cabinet are painfully anxious to avoid war at any price. As a last resort they contemplate sending the P.M. to Hitler personally to prepare an all-round scheme including Anglo-German settlement. British public on the other hand is very worked up and anti-German.

Whole question now is how situation develops. If a firm demand is made by Sudeten or Hitler for a plebiscite, however much Czechoslovakia dislikes it and however false such a situation would be, it would be impossible to get British public to regard it as worth a war. French would be in much the same position. If Czechoslovakia

178

nonetheless resisted by force, situation resulting would be very obscure. Would even France fight to stop a plebiscite? The Chamberlain visit plan is a hazardous gamble and not well thought out.

September 14th

No fresh news except that Nevile Henderson telephoned to say that he had given message to Weiszacker for transmission to Ribbentrop and Hitler.

Cabinet Meeting.

N.H. telephoned at 3 to say that Hitler was at Prime Minister's disposal. He will therefore start at 8.30 by air tomorrow with William Strang.

Meanwhile further appeals come to us from Bonnet to save them at any price from war. He told Phipps French Government would prefer a federated or neutralised Czechoslovakia with autonomous Sudeten area inside but in last resort and to avoid German aggression they would agree to plebiscite on whole question whether or not Sudeten should remain inside. "We are not ready to fight and must recognise fact" is what he says. Outstanding factor is now this peace at any price French attitude which of course lets H.M.G. out and should facilitate a settlement – at the expense of Czechoslovakia. Not very pretty!

Van is extremely agitated over failure of H.M.G. to give Hitler a final warning and maintains that all moderate opinion in Germany was wanting us to do this so as to give them something to enable them to stop Hitler with. Conwall-Evans[1] who was at Nuremberg, has come back with passionate pleas from moderate German leaders begging H.M.G. to take some step to stop their mad Chancellor!

September 15th

P.M., Horace Wilson and W. Strang started at 8.30 today and got to Munich at 1: they went on to Berchtesgaden by train.

We received Runciman's and Newton's views on a plebiscite. They both thought the Czechoslovak Government would reject it, as they have told us they would, but they might possibly be induced to accept it if both France and Great Britain pressed it very strongly upon them. They said it would be extremely difficult to arrange

1. T. Conwall-Evans, an English Professor teaching in Germany.

proper conditions unless overwhelming force were available and doubt whether it would solve the real problem of Czech relations with Germany.

Daladier, Phipps says, was not very pleased when told of the P.M.'s proposed visit to Hitler – he was told only just before it was publicly announced in order to prevent leakage – and said he had been pressed to go to Germany himself but had always replied that a British Representative should go too: he preferred his idea of a Three-Power Conference. Nonetheless in official communiqué today he takes first credit for having suggested idea himself and whole French press praises it. Lindbergh[1] has just returned from Germany and gave French Government most alarming accounts of superiority of German air force over French, and this is largely responsible for the present pusillanimity.

At Cabinet yesterday P.M. unfolded his plan. He had already proposed himself to Hitler and received the *ex post facto* approval of his colleagues. Duff Cooper said he had been going to propose mobilisation of the fleet, but must now postpone this in view of P.M.'s action. P.M. said he intended, if Hitler was amenable, to call in Runciman and propose his becoming arbitrator between Czechs and Sudeten. If Hitler insisted on plebiscite, he felt it would be impossible for a democracy to resist such a demand but he should then seek to establish reasonable conditions, possibly a delay for passions to cool before plebiscite was held. As regards rest of Czechoslovakia, he felt it might be necessary to neutralise it under guarantee of Great Britain, Russia, France and Germany. Parliament is to be called as soon as P.M. returns.

King returned to London today and H. had long talk with him this afternoon.

British press receives news of P.M.'s visit with marked approval. City is much relieved. Reaction in Germany also one of relief. In America it looks as if it were regarded as a surrender. Winston says it is the stupidest thing that has ever been done.

According to the news tonight the Sudeten have now declared a general strike. What if Germany should march in while the P.M. is actually at Berchtesgaden? It looks certain now that a plebiscite is the utmost that we can possibly hope for – it will have to be forced on the Czechs who may however be compensated by a guarantee. In any

1. Colonel Lindbergh, U.S. Airman who flew solo from New York to Paris in 1927.

event, as William Strang thinks, the Sudeten after the encouragement they have received are never going to settle down again as peaceful and loyal citizens of Czechoslovakia and the latter would probably be better rid of them in spite of the strategic and economic arguments about the unity of the country.

September 16th

Strang telephoned last night that P.M. was returning to London today and that Runciman was to come back too. No other news of results of the visit were to be gathered except that in communiqué issued from Berchtesgaden this morning it was said that P.M. would probably be returning there.

General impression is of *détente* and probability of Four-Power Conference. On other hand, rumours of possible *coup d'état* in Prague and very ugly press in Berlin over alleged incidents in Sudeten areas even to extent of crowding news of P.M.'s visit off front pages.

Meeting of Ministers is called for six and Cabinet summoned for tomorrow.

Mussolini has now come out with heavy backing of secession of Sudeten – this is believed to be intended to show Hitler that he will not stand for absorption of Czechoslovakia as a whole. We believe Hitler has been applying very strong pressure to Mussolini ever since May visit and we know he is in great difficulties in Spain – wastage of 500 men a week – very unpopular in Italy. He recently sent us a mysterious message through King Boris of Bulgaria (who is over here) that he was contemplating withdrawing his infantry. We had a meeting in H.'s room today with Perth to discuss how far H.M.G. should take up this and make it an occasion for implementing the Anglo-Italian agreement. Department are anxious to do this (Moley and Maurice Ingram) so as to enable him to wriggle a bit freer of Hitler's embrace. It is to be considered by Cabinet but H. felt we could not accept withdrawal of infantry alone and should also receive assurances at least that he would not send more pilots and aircraft. (We know he is doing this as well as sending more material.)

Frank Gwatkin arrived about six. He said Benes offer had been "too good" as it had compelled Hitler to act quickly. Latter had never believed Benes would ever make such a reasonable offer. He said there was a distinct possibility that if a plebiscite was proposed the

Czech army would fight anyway. In the Sudeten areas the Czecho-slovak writ still ran and incidents were all grossly exaggerated. The Sudeten leaders wanted to accept the Benes plan, but received their orders from Berlin.

Gladwyn Jebb came in with a first hurried impression of what had passed. It is this: Hitler demands the Sudeten areas delivered to him by the end of the month or he will go to war to get them. He does not want the Czech areas. So there we are – at least we know now what he wants and what we are up against.

P.M. who got to No. 10 at 6.15 went straight into his meeting which lasted till eight. Nothing is being given out tonight and nothing said to the French (who would leak) till after the Cabinet has considered it tomorrow.

My first impressions are of disgust that we should be reduced to treating with Hitler under a threat. What a change since A.E.'s time! It is a very astute move by Hitler as we can scarcely be expected to fight – any more than in Austria – to keep Germans out of Germany. But what at least we must secure if we are to save our faces is a plebiscite under some sort of decent international conditions plus guarantees for the rest of Czechoslovakia. But shall we be able to get this in our present state of surrender? Our one hope now is to take stand on principle of self-determination and see it is applied tolerably. Poor Czechoslovakia! Poor Benes! But I cannot comment more till I've seen what was actually said. How will the country take it?

An odd message reached me from the Resident Clerk who had been rung up by Lady Van to say she had had a message from Paris that if Daladier was being invited over here it was most important that "his second man" (presumably Bonnet) should not come too – and would we hold up any telegram to Paris on this subject until Van – who was on the way out to Denham – had arrived and could explain. As a matter of fact no telegram is being sent to Paris tonight but I wonder what this is. A message to Van from Léger to short-circuit his chief, the wretched Bonnet, and get the stiffer Daladier invited alone?

September 17th

Poles and Hungarians have now both put in their claims to receive equal treatment with the Sudeten.

Cabinet met this morning and went on again this afternoon. At lunchtime we telegraphed to Paris to invite Daladier and Bonnet to come here as soon as possible. They accepted and arrive tomorrow at 9 a.m.

Strang told me that he had been greatly impressed by the spontaneous welcome of the German crowds to the P.M. as though he were the man who could save them from war. The P.M. and Hitler had talked entirely alone with only Schmidt the interpreter. The others had no idea what passed until after dinner when the P.M. dictated his record. Hitler did not strike W.S. as looking particularly mad – nor did he see any great change since he last saw him when A.E. went to Berlin.

This is what passed between the P.M. and Hitler:

The P.M. meant to start with generalities and proceed to Czechoslovakia question next day; but Hitler insisted on plunging straight in. Hitler said that according to today's information 300 Sudeten had been killed and the question could not wait. (We have checked up that this report was perfectly untrue though maybe Hitler did not know that it was.) There followed a long account of what Hitler had done – the Polish agreement, the Saar, the renunciation of Alsace-Lorraine, the Anglo-German Naval Treaty[1] (which Hitler threatened to denounce unless there was an understanding between the two peoples). He said he was obsessed with the racial theory – wherever there were Germans on the frontiers: he was concerned with ten million Germans of whom three million were in Czechoslovakia. The latter should come into the Reich: they wanted to and he was determined that they should come in. Apart from that there were no other frontiers presenting territorial difficulties, not even Memel, so long as the Sudeten observed the statute. But it was impossible for Czechoslovakia to remain a spearhead in Germany's side.

P.M. said he wished to be clear. Would Hitler be satisfied with the inclusion of three million Sudeten or did he wish, as many asserted, to dismantle Czechoslovakia? Hitler replied that he did not want a lot of Czechs but he must also have abolition of the treaty with Russia. P.M. asked whether, supposing it were modified so that Czechoslovakia no longer undertook to assist Soviet Russia and latter could no longer put aerodromes in Czechoslovakia, Hitler would be satisfied. Hitler said that if the Sudeten were included in Germany, then the Hungarians and Poles would also secede – what was left would be so small that he would not bother about it. P.M. replied

1. Signed in 1935.

that as a practical man he foresaw difficulties in secession – what about the inevitable minorities and the question of transfer of populations? Hitler said that where Germans were in a majority the territory ought to go to Germany: the Czechs in Sudeten areas could pass out and vice versa. But all this was academic and they must get down to realities. Three hundred Sudetens had been killed and it could not go on. "It must be settled at once. I am determined to settle it. I do not care if there is a world war or not. I am determined to settle it soon and am prepared to risk a world war rather than allow it to drag on."

P.M. said that if Hitler had determined to settle it by force, why did he let him come? If he was prepared to discuss the question as to whether a peaceful solution was possible, why not make a joint appeal for quiet while they talked? Hitler retorted that he could not appeal to victims but if H.M.G. would accept the idea of secession in principle and say so, there might be a chance for talks.

P.M. replied that he could not give such an assurance on behalf of H.M.G., nor without consulting French Government and Runciman: but he could give his personal opinion that he, in principle, had nothing against separation of the Sudeten provided practical difficulties were overcome. He suggested returning to London to consult his colleagues and a further meeting later.

Hitler agreed. P.M. asked if in meanwhile the situation could be kept as it is now. Hitler said the German military machine once put in operation could not be stopped but he was willing to give an assurance that he would not give the order to begin to operate it if he could help it. If further incidents occurred it might be impossible to refrain.

Hitler suggested that Czechoslovakia should recall the State police from Sudeten areas, confine soldiers to barracks and withdraw mobilisation. P.M. said it was unreasonable to ask for the last but he would do his best to influence the Czechoslovak Government regarding the other two if Hitler would do his best to keep his people quiet.

After Cabinet P.M. and H. saw T.U.C. leaders and had a rough time with them. Later they were to see American Ambassador. Anglo-French talks all tomorrow.

Harry Crookshank dined with me. He is very unhappy about his position. He was amazed to hear that H.M.G. had not told Germany that Great Britain would march on the same day as France. I explained that we had only said that we might march if France became

184

involved and were in difficulties. He said he is convinced British public has been misled by press on this and will be furious on learning the truth. He has seen A.E. I'm glad to say. He is all in favour of the Winston policy of organising all states who will be against aggression and of so confronting the gangsters with a ring of force. I am sure he is right. We shall only defeat the dictators if we show courage and resolution. He is disgusted at our pusillanimity and at our wish for 150% superiority before we attempt anything. He refuses to accept German estimates of their own strength at their face value.

September 18th

Meeting with French Ministers at 11. P.M., H., Simon, Hoare and Alec, Van and Horace Wilson on our side. It went on till lunch and then again from 3.30 on and off up till midnight.

No more news from Czechoslovakia except that it looks as if situation in Sudeten areas was more and more threatening. Sudeten are declaring themselves in open revolt and Czechoslovak Government say they are obliged to consider general mobilisation but are prepared to hear what we have to say. This is now being considered by the Anglo-French meetings.

Our Embassy in Berlin who were to have forwarded us Schmidt's record of the P.M.'s talk with Hitler telephoned that Germans say that they do not intend to send us any record in view of the misunderstanding which had occurred over Ribbentrop's record of conversation with H. last March. Hitler thought that the P.M. had understood what he had to say but that if he had not, he was ready to repeat it.

Possibility of holding a plebiscite is now being feverishly examined in the Foreign Office under instructions from No. 10 "in order to bamboozle the British public"! The least study however shows that it is impossible to hold a plebiscite in existing conditions without a vast army to control the whole area and without it degenerating into a complete farce. There is also danger that mere announcement of plebiscite would lead to a massacre of Sudeten or a coup by the Czech army giving Hitler his excuse for immediately marching in and thereby ruining the beautiful plan of bringing about a peaceful amputation and hiding the ugly fact that it is surrender to Hitler's armed threat.

I hear the conversations have passed off in quite a friendly atmosphere – no mudslinging! Daladier defined the problem as how to preserve European peace whilst preserving as much as possible of Czech independence. The French were opposed to a plebiscite as of too dangerous consequences to other parts of Europe, but were ready to consider some form of cession in which Czechoslovakia must agree. They would like to see all Germans moved out of rest of Czechoslovakia. They would agree to neutralisation of Czechoslovakia, remodelling of Czech treaties – but insist on our joining them in a fresh guarantee of remainder of Czechoslovakia. As regards Czech threat to mobilise it was decided to send telegrams to Prague from both parties urging Czech Government to hold up mobilisation in view of London efforts for peace, to inform Berlin of this and to ask Berlin to moderate German press.

P.M. in talks made great point of Runciman's opinion that in view of recent events he did not think mediation between Czechs and Sudeten was now possible – the only solution being some form of self-determination. "Sudeten and Czechs could not live together any more."

At about midnight agreement was reached on joint appeal to Benes to accept a "cut" on basis of areas with Sudeten majority in interests of appeasement *plus* a guarantee by Great Britain and France of remainder. The appeal however is not to be fired off until the French Ministers have got back and P.M. has seen his Cabinet.

I saw Runciman this evening. I was horrified at his appearance. He looks ten years older and ashen and very anxious to keep out of any row over Czechoslovakia at any cost!

I had a quick dinner with A.E. who is miserable. He had just heard all about the meetings from Philip Sassoon who had had Sam Hoare dining with him. Sam had been in his smuggest and most complacent mood! A.E. is determined to go for the Government over this when House of Commons meets.

September 19th

I saw French Ministers off at Croydon at 8.15. I must say they looked wretched. Nevertheless at 12.30 we heard from Paris that the French Cabinet had agreed to action being taken on the telegram to Prague – we then acted too (our own Cabinet does not need to be consulted – it is merely informed). P.M. also sent a message to Hitler proposing to return to Germany on Wednesday – which Hitler has now accepted. Meanwhile every pressure is being applied to Benes to accept and to accept quickly. Poor Masaryk has taken to his bed with grief, and is unable or unwilling to come and see H. The German press continues its foul attacks on the Czechs, and Hitler himself in an interview with Ward Price in the *Daily Mail* goes out of his way to insult them *à la* Goering as a third-rate nation. These are the people the P.M. is hurrying to visit and to "appease". Henderson continues to urge the need for speed and instant surrender at every point if war is to be averted. All now depends on whether Benes accepts and if so, whether he can carry it through.

I spoke to Hardinge this morning for the information of the King about what had been decided yesterday. He was horrified at the whole course of events and the Government's defeatist attitude.

Runciman is being brought into action to help the Government in the dirty work. He said in our room, "I feel I must do everything to make the P.M.'s position easier." The idea is that he should write a long letter to the P.M. giving his views on the problem and that the P.M. should show this to Hitler and it should then be published. Unfortunately the old man says one thing to the Cabinet and another to Gwatkin who is drawing up his letter. According to the letter Runciman advocates a cut of regions containing 80% Sudeten and application of the Karlsbad-Benes plan to the other Sudeten areas remaining in Czechoslovakia. This is what Gwatkin himself regards as an ideal solution which would give Germany $1\frac{1}{2}$ million more Germans and would preserve to some extent the strategic and economic unity of Czechoslovakia. But Runciman when confronted with the Cabinet says quite a different story, viz., that all areas with 50% must go "as Czechs and Sudeten after recent events cannot ever live in peace again together." Runciman is quite broken down and is now rather pathetic. I am afraid we were mistaken as to his sticking powers; in spite of all, he now has nothing good to say of the Czechs and adds his influential voice to the chorus of blame and abuse which is now their lot.

H. had rather an academic discussion in his room this afternoon with Malkin, Sargent, Alec, Van, Gwatkin to discuss what it is hoped the P.M. might try to secure out of Hitler, viz., a joint German-Czech Commission with a British Chairman to supervise the transfer of territory. He is very anxious to have British troops sent to show the flag. He believes naïvely that a few British regimental bands marching up and down the Sudeten areas would suffice to keep order.

I must record my view that Phipps in Paris has done his utmost to discourage the French from anything resembling positive action in fulfilment of their treaty with Czechoslovakia. He has skilfully worked on Bonnet's fears and weakness and he has consistently reported his views without seeking or encouraging the views of other more important Frenchmen such as Blum, Herriot, Paul Reynaud[1] or Mandel[2] who stand for firmer policies. He has given the definite impression that H.M.G. wish to hold France back (which of course is true). Again over Spain he has consistently supported the Franco side and done his utmost to stop the French Government from helping Barcelona. In all this of course he has faithfully interpreted and anticipated the views of the present Cabinet. But I do not think it is wise to blanket other opinion to the extent he has. H.M.G. are entitled to know all sides and not only what they want to hear. Whilst it is true that the French Government now are just as anxious as H.M.G. to avoid war at any price, it is also true that the French with the sensitiveness of the Latins caught their defeatist note from us. Had we been robust, the French would have been robust too.

September 20th

I learn that when P.M. saw T.U.C. leaders what shook them was the account he gave of the French army and of the Soviet intention not to go at once to the help of Czechoslovakia but to take up the issue at Geneva.

The proposed guarantee to Czechoslovakia is not intended to commit us to guaranteeing the existing frontiers of Czechoslovakia (including remaining Polish and Hungarian minorities which are already being claimed by Warsaw and Budapest) but only related to unprovoked aggression.

We received Newton's account of his and French Minister's meeting with Benes – very painful but it looks as if Czechoslovakia would give way. We also heard a reassuring report that Czech army would remain loyal and obey its Government whatever was decided. Meanwhile German military machine is being cranked up more and more, and we receive disturbing accounts of further moves towards Czech frontiers, so much so that a further telegram was sent to Berlin

1. Minister of Finance. 2. Georges Mandel, Minister for Colonies.

urging that these should stop. Czech cabinet sat all day and it was not till 6 p.m. that Newton received the reply which had not reached the Office owing to deciphering, etc., till late tonight. According to a telegram giving the gist, the Czech Government are asking for arbitration under the Czech-German Arbitration Treaty – which is regarded as a last despairing wriggle before final submission.

Meanwhile P.M. has sent word to Hitler that he will come on Thursday morning to Godesberg. The meeting had been provisionally fixed for tomorrow but owing to the delay in Czechoslovak reply – without which P.M. could make no plans – Ribbentrop proposed a postponement till Thursday and this has been accepted although we have grave doubts lest this delay may not be used to provoke an incident and precipitate events.

According to all accounts, the German army is to march in the next few days. Hardinge, to whom I spoke this evening, said he thought in the long run this would really be the best solution because it would force us to fight. He is absolutely disgusted at our attitude.

I hear Winston has left for France presumably to ascertain the real state of opinion there. He too is in absolute despair at H.M.G.'s policy.

September 21st

Newton finally received reply from Czech Ministry of Foreign Affairs at 8 p.m. last night. It amounted to a proposal for arbitration under the Czech-German Treaty of 1926. Czech Government were convinced the Anglo-French proposals would not bring peace. They had not been consulted – the minorities problem would still arise. Newton made a further appeal for definite acceptance to which only alternative was war. Impression he received was that Czech Government was resigned to the worst but that solution would have to be imposed on Government because of internal opposition. He suggested therefore a sort of ultimatum being given saying that, if Czechoslovakia did not accept, H.M.G. would take no further action.

Meanwhile a telegram from Paris said that Phipps had asked Bonnet if it were true that French Left elements were putting pressure on Benes to refuse – Bonnet replied that he thought it likely and admitted that Benes's reply was likely to be evasive. Phipps then suggested that moment seemed to have come when we should inform Benes that unless he gave a simple acceptance, France and Great Britain would wash their hands in event of aggression. Bonnet did not demur but asked Phipps to ask H.'s views. This caused consternation at Foreign Office where it was feared that it would be used as evidence against us that we had pressed French Government to evade their treaty obligations. H. was got back from his house (at 11 p.m.), when it was considered in conjunction with the Czech reply. It was then decided at one a.m. to send a further telegram to Newton to join with his French colleague in pointing out to Czech Government that their reply in no way met critical situation and would lead to immediate German invasion. He was to urge Czech Government to withdraw it and to say we regarded Anglo-French proposals the only chance of avoiding immediate German attack. No hope in such circumstances of any useful result from Godesberg and P.M. might decide to cancel it. We would have been willing to put up arbitration proposal if we thought it had any chance of acceptance but we could not believe this. "If on reconsideration the Czech Government feel bound to reject our advice, they must of course be free to take any action they think appropriate to meet the situation which may then develop." This last sentence was designed to meet the danger of Phipps's suggestion – we do not say in so many words that we will wash our hands of them.

At 6.30 a.m. (September 21st) Hodza telephoned to Newton that the Czech Government accepted the proposals.

Cabinet met at 3.00 p.m.

A further hitch occurred because Benes was reported to be having difficulties with his political parties. British and French Ministers applied further pressure. Newton told Czech Government that he anticipated H.M.G. would not accept any further responsibility if there were delay. The delay was due, it seems, to Osusky, Czech Minister in Paris, who had reported that there was no need to hurry. Benes then asked for a written declaration by British and French Governments that if Czechoslovakia accepted and if Germany then attacked her, the two Governments would come to her assistance.

Phipps spoke to Bonnet and suggested he should speak severely to Osusky: he reports that Winston and Spears[1] are giving bad advice to Osusky and to French politicians.

Finally at 5 p.m. we received the official reply that Czechoslovakia "sadly" accepted the proposals under pressure of British communica-

1. Major-General Sir E. L. Spears, M.P. for Carlisle 1931–1945.

tion on supposition that two Governments would do everything to safeguard vital interests of Czechoslovakia and that they would not tolerate German invasion of Czech territory which would remain Czech until transfer had been effected by international court.

Meanwhile there is a marked and increasing degree of pessimism and disgust in both British and French press.

September 22nd

Cabinet yesterday discussed what line P.M. should take in his talk with Hitler. If Hitler were to demand equal treatment for the other minorities, P.M., it was agreed, should say he could not deal with that and must return to consult his colleagues. It was thought that this was really a test of Hitler's good faith, whether he was really only interested in Germans or whether he was out for world domination. About the proposed guarantees it was agreed that it should be joint and not several, and that France, Great Britain and Russia should sign, whilst Germany (as the most likely aggressor) should sign a separate non-aggression pact with Czechoslovakia. If Hitler objected to Russia being in it, P.M. should refer home. It was agreed that neither Germany nor Italy should be in the guarantee (since they might prevent the operation of a joint guarantee) and none of the small neighbours. As regards maintenance of order, it was thought that Hitler might demand immediate withdrawal of Czech forces from predominantly German districts. Benes might prefer presence of German soldiers to *Freikorps*[1] in undoubted German areas as being more disciplined.

P.M. hoped he might secure joint appeal by Hitler and Benes for maintenance of order, and possibility was considered of British troops being used in intermediate areas between those predominantly German and those predominantly Czech. It was thought that Hitler should demobilise the *Freikorps*, and that British observers should be increased. It was agreed that no German troops could be allowed on Czech soil without Czech consent. P.M. would start by urging despatch of additional observers plus withdrawal of Czech state police and troops from Sudeten areas. His next line would be to propose an international force: if it was not possible to agree on this, he would consult Cabinet.

In view of movement of Italian troops back to Libya (in spite of

1. Sudeten Nazi gang.

the Anglo-Italian agreement) it was also decided to send the Mediterranean fleet to Egyptian waters at once.

P.M. arrived today at Godesberg at 2 p.m. and talks were to begin at four.

Both Stanley and Duff Cooper have written to H. to protest at terms of telegram to Prague as foreshadowing our possibly tolerating German occupation of Czech territory without Czech consent. This, I think, was a misreading but it shows that both are restive. So too is Walter Elliot who rang me up to express his misgivings and feeling that it cannot go on and it would be better to get it over now. A message came from Bonnet that the *Freikorps* had occupied Asch, according to information received from Benes, but that Czech Government had offered no resistance. Benes also sent word to us through Bonnet that a new Czech Government was being formed on a large national basis, acceptance of Anglo-French plan was maintained and if soldier was head of new Government it did not mean a military dictatorship – he wished P.M. to know this at Godesberg in case Hitler tried to claim there was no Government in Czechoslovakia. Both these messages were repeated to Godesberg.

Meanwhile German press gets more and more violent and the official *Volkischer Beobachter* says, "Away with the Benes State!"

French Government now asks us for advice about their taking more military measures on Maginot Lines. (We reply that we cannot advise.) There is also unconfirmed report from Prague that German *Freikorps* as well as *Reichsgerman* S.S.[1] and S.A.[2] have taken over Ezer. We therefore telegraph to Paris to say we think we ought to rescind advice to Czech Government to hold up mobilisation and to ask their views. Paris agrees that such action should be taken. It is to be considered by Ministers tonight. It was finally decided at 7.30 on this to authorise Newton to tell Czech Government at 8 p.m. that we withdraw our advice not to mobilise.

At 8.15 Horace Wilson telephoned from Godesberg to say they had had a pretty difficult time and were all exhausted. They had spent much time poring over large-scale map produced by Hitler. The P.M. was issuing an appeal to ensure that local conditions were such as not to interfere with the conversations. He had also sent a personal message through Newton to the Czech Government informing them of this and adding that he trusted the Czech Govern-

1. *Corps d'Élite* of Nazi party created originally to curb ambitions of S.A.
2. Nazi para-military organisation auxiliary to Army and Police.

ment to do all in their power to help. Nothing was to be given to the Press that night. P.M. had also spoken to Newton for his own information that Hitler had agreed to issue orders "in this respect" – which was taken to mean not to advance for the time being.

The next question was whether in view of this message Newton should still act on his instructions regarding Czech mobilisation at 9 p.m. When Ministry met at Foreign Office just before nine it was decided to instruct Newton to suspend action. We telephoned at once accordingly.

At 11 p.m. a further message came from P.M. saying that conversations had been very sticky indeed. Hitler rejected the Anglo-French plan as too slow and was insisting on marching into Sudeten areas and occupying them up to 50% line. When that was done, Hitler would agree to an international commission to demarcate the frontier. P.M. had said this would not do but feared that he had not made Hitler understand British and French opinion would not accept this. He was considering whether to write a letter to Hitler.

Still later we learned that the P.M. was sending a letter to Hitler giving cogent reasons against this course and asking him to consider alternative methods of maintaining order with a view to their discussion at talks next morning. Meanwhile suspension of advice regarding Czech mobilisation was to be maintained pending the next day's talks. Hitler had given his word not to cross the frontier and P.M. thought he could rely on it.

September 23rd

French opinion like ours seems to be getting more and more restive and takes line that P.M. must get as minimum full acceptance of Anglo-French plan. Meanwhile German press howls for complete disintegration of Czechoslovakia. Poles and Hungarians are now in close touch with Hitler over their claims.

At 11.30 a.m. Horace Wilson telephoned that Hitler was going to reply in writing to P.M.'s letter and talks were postponed. A later telegram from Godesberg reported that Hitler was still insisting on immediate occupation of line based on language map giving most favourable results to Germany: he would agree to a plebiscite after. Failing acceptance he would take "a military solution" and then draw "not a national but a military and strategic frontier".

Grave doubts felt here now at wisdom of continued suspension of further advice to Czech Government about Czech mobilisation. We telephoned to Godesberg that we are instructing Newton to act on his instructions at 3 p.m. H. said to me: "I think we are in the soup over this!"

At 2 p.m. we heard again from Godesberg that Hitler's letter was expected at any moment. They thought we should wait a little longer before acting in Prague. In any event communication should point out that such action by them would probably precipitate action by others.

Ministers met at three and finally agreed to telegraph to Prague removing our request that Czechs should not mobilise but pointing out that in view of possible consequences the Czech Government might prefer to avoid publicity.

French are taking certain further military measures. Mandel and Reynaud in French Cabinet reported to be very restive. Text of P.M.'s letter to Hitler was received at 3.30. He was ready to put to the Czech Government the suggested areas; no need for a plebiscite in predominantly German areas; no doubt Czech Government would accept plebiscite proposal to determine any further adjustment of the areas; but impossible to put forward proposal for immediate occupation, Czechoslovakia would have to resist and whole basis of agreement would fall: the only question therefore was how to preserve order and surely there were alternatives to immediate occupation, e.g., the Sudeten themselves might maintain order in certain areas under neutral observers: he was prepared to ask the Czech views on above and if accepted to urge them to withdraw troops but not otherwise.

About 5 p.m. we had a further obscure message from Horace Wilson that Hitler's reply had been received but he apparently maintained his original point of view. P.M. was asking for a memorandum. Finally, we learnt that Horace Wilson and Henderson had talked to Ribbentrop and that the P.M. was to see Hitler again tonight and would be returning home tomorrow.

Meeting of Ministers at Foreign Office after dinner developed qualms for internal political reasons lest P.M. should not have been sufficiently firm in talking to Hitler and might have lost sight of strength of public opinion over here. A stiff telegram which was drafted by H. after talking to Van but was strongly endorsed by Sam Hoare was therefore sent to him by telephone *en clair* just before he left to see Hitler.

Hitler's letter which was telegraphed to us, was nothing but torrent of abuse of the Czechs. At last we heard the P.M. was passing on to the Czech Government Hitler's memo of terms together with a map and was returning home.

September 24th

Press reports that some final offer was made as a result of the P.M.'s talk with Hitler at 11 p.m. last night but we have no information as yet at Foreign Office. P.M. is arriving at 1 p.m. and Minister's meeting is called for three and Cabinet at 5.30.

Russia has warned Poland that if she attacks Czechoslovakia, Russia will denounce Polish-Soviet Russian Treaty whilst Litvinoff at Geneva has stated that Soviet Republic will fulfil terms of her treaty with Czechoslovakia and would like a conference with Great Britain, France and any others to discuss military measures.

I have never seen anything like the defeatist stuff which Phipps is now sending us. He is either not reporting honestly feeling in France or else is taking no trouble to find out opinions which may be unpalatable to H.M.G. It is tragic that at such a time we have three such wretched Ambassadors (Rome, Berlin and Paris).

Hitler's memo which P.M. finally elicited in order to obtain precise definition of his terms is couched in the terms of an ultimatum. All German areas on map attached are to be occupied forthwith and a plebiscite is to be held in certain other areas. There is to be a total withdrawal of Czech forces, police and officials, and all material, etc., is to be handed over intact.

P.M. has now sent this to the Czechs and has declared to the Press here "It is now up to the Czechs". Meanwhile the Czechs have now begun to mobilise and the French have undertaken a partial mobilisation. I learn from Strang that the only concession which the P.M. got out of Hitler at his midnight meeting was to hold up military operations for six days.

Ministers met at three and whole Cabinet at 5.30. The only decision which emerged was an invitation to Daladier and Bonnet to come over and hear P.M.'s report tomorrow.

September 25th

Cabinet continued this morning and again this afternoon. I hear they are divided. P.M. very pleased with himself and thinks Hitler's offer not too bad and should be recommended to the Czechs. Winston, A.E. and Amery[1] are horrified at the possibility of our urging Czechoslovakia to accept. No news yet about Parliament.

I hear that Benes is thinking of publishing Hitler's memo and that Masaryk has been instructed to make an appeal to British and French Ministers when they are here.

A.E. sent H. a message this morning urging Cabinet to reject proposals. I hear Alec Hardinge has asked A.E. to go to see him.

At yesterday's Cabinet P.M. described his second talk with Hitler. Latter said at once our proposals were unacceptable to him. He showed intense dislike of Czechoslovakia and then produced map. He said he could not enter into a guarantee unless certain other Powers were included, e.g., Italy. P.M. then spoke of non-aggression pact. H. said he could not conclude such unless other minorities were settled. He wanted immediate occupation of the transferred areas by German troops but would withdraw them from disputed areas during plebiscite. P.M. said this was impossible proposal. Conversation was continually interrupted by messages reporting fresh outrages. P.M. suggested to Hitler that he should appeal to Sudeten and P.M. to Czechoslovakia. Hitler agreed to appeal to his own people. At this point talk was adjourned and P.M. decided to send Hitler a letter asking for a definite statement of claims. On receipt of the reply P.M. sent a further letter (a) in order to get details and (b) to secure extension of assurance not to attack Czechoslovakia during talks. Hitler had given his word not to attack Czechoslovakia till reply had been received. No particular date had been mentioned.

Horace Wilson and Ribbentrop had then discussed possibility of partial transfer at once. Ribbentrop had said this was "of no value"! P.M. then went to say goodbye and asked if he could see memo. This was produced and found to be exactly the same proposals as before and demanded evacuation by September 26th. P.M. then reproached Hitler for having made no contribution. Hitler said he had, by now agreeing to a nationalist frontier instead of a strategic one. Hitler eventually conceded that evacuation should be complete by

1. L. S. Amery, M.P., Colonial Secretary 1924–1929.

October 1st and renewed assurance not to attack Czechoslovakia while negotiations continued. P.M. said he would send memo to Czechoslovakia and report to H.M.G. and French Government.

P.M. told the Cabinet he was sure Hitler was anxious for friendship of Great Britain. He had said that after this he had no more territorial ambitions. P.M. thought he had established an influence over him and that H. trusted him. If so, this was an opportunity to put an end to an armaments race. No chance of peaceful solution, otherwise. Was it worth a war? Not much difference between H.'s proposals and ours as regards areas. Inadequate protection in United Kingdom against bombing.

Duff Cooper did not put any confidence in H.'s promises. He thought we ought to mobilise. Belisha likewise as well as Elliot. P.M. said this should be considered next day. P.M. and H. wanted decision on general policy first. (Cabinet then adjourned till Sunday.)

This afternoon Masaryk delivered formal note rejecting Hitler's memo. "The nation of St Wenceslas, John Hus and Thomas Masaryk will not be a nation of slaves . . . we rely on two great Western Democracies to stand by us."

Alec Cadogan feels as I do that events are now taking charge. He cannot see how French or we can possibly recommend last proposals to Czechoslovakia. He says feeling in Cabinet is very strong that P.M. went far too far beyond his Cabinet instructions in even considering the last terms. He believes that if Czechoslovakia can hold up Germans for a little while, public opinion will force Great Britain to take action.

French Ministers who had had a Council of Ministers at 2.30 arrived at Croydon at seven and started talks at 8 p.m. These adjourned at 11 p.m. for a Cabinet meeting which lasted till one a.m. Our Cabinet had reached no decision before they saw French. The latter were very stiff and said the proposals must be rejected and they would honour their obligations. Our Ministers pressed them to say how they would fulfil them but they refused to be drawn. Finally it was agreed to send for Gamelin[1] who is arriving tomorrow.

I talked to Hore-Belisha in an interval at Number 10. He was very stiff and bellicose. He felt the proposals must be rejected and now was the time to fight Hitler. He was sickened at the slowness of the Cabinet in reaching decisions and complained of "these old men" and how it would be impossible to let them run the war. He ridiculed

1. French C.-in-C.

P.M.'s view that he could influence Hitler. He complained bitterly of our Ambassadors (Phipps and Henderson). He said C.I.G.S.[1] thought the present moment was of great strategic advantage to us as Germans had only seven (?) divisions on Western front.

Last night's Cabinet finally decided to send Horace Wilson to Berlin with a further letter to Hitler reporting Czech refusal, pointing to consequences of solution by force, saying solution by negotiation still possible and suggesting a German-Czech Conference under British auspices. Hitler was also to be told that if Czechoslovakia refused and Germany attacked, French would fulfil their obligations, and if France were in active hostilities against Germany we would support her. French were informed of this and agreed on understanding that no further concession by Czechoslovakia was involved.

September 26th

Roosevelt today addressed appeals to Hitler, Benes and P.M. to keep negotiations going. Anglo-French talks resumed at 10.30 and Cabinet at twelve. Gamelin arrived and had talks. Hitler is to speak tonight on wireless.

Only bright feature is report that Benes has offered to give Poles Teschen if they keep out. French and ourselves have urged Beck to accept this and told him we could not tolerate aggression. French finally left about midday after "complete accord" had been established.

At Cabinet yesterday H. for first time said he was not sure whether he and P.M. were quite together now. He wanted destruction of Nazism. Hailsham said he did not trust Hitler. Stanhope[2] favoured advising acceptance of proposals. Inskip thought it not in our interest to go to war. Kingsley Wood also favoured acceptance. Duff Cooper was firm. MacDonald for acceptance.

Preparations are being made for a broadcast in German of our point of view.

Telegram received from Wilson in Berlin that he had "a very violent hour" with Hitler and had in the end not delivered the warning about our fighting with France and Russia if Czechoslovakia were invaded. He is to do this at a final meeting tomorrow. Hitler's speech at eight violent as ever. P.M. issued a communiqué after hearing it.

1. General Sir Edmund Ironside.
2. First Lord of the Admiralty.

September 27th

P.M. issued a statement last night after listening to Hitler's speech. H.M.G. and the French Government were ready, he said, to undertake that Czechoslovak promises were fulfilled in a reasonable time provided the German Government agreed not to use force. We heard that Wilson had at last issued warning to Hitler in his final interview this morning.

Precautionary period has been introduced. Gangs of men digging trenches in the parks. Queues lining up for gas-mask fittings.

Roosevelt has sent a personal letter to the King. P.M. and H. are considering a final appeal to Hitler and Prague to agree to immediate occupation of Egger and fulfilment of rest of plan. Question of P.M. broadcasting too. Parliament is called for tomorrow.

In the late afternoon, a telegram was despatched to Prague informing Benes that H.M.G. were convinced Germany would attack Czechoslovakia almost immediately unless by 2 p.m. tomorrow Czech Government had accepted, with the result that the country would be over-run and nothing could stop it. We could not take responsibility of advising Czech Government.

Shortly after, telegrams were sent to Prague and Berlin making a further offer based on a time-table. If Hitler could not accept Benes's word we undertook to see goods were delivered by certain dates. On October 1st Germans should occupy Egger and Asch.[1] On October 3rd Czech and German plenipotentiaries should meet with a British representative in Sudeten area to arrange for evacuation of Czech troops and police and lay down broad lines for minorities and frontier. On same day International Boundary Commission of Czechoslovakia, French and British Representatives should meet. On same day neutral observers and four British battalions plus British Legion should arrive. On October 10th German troops should enter zones indicated by International Commission. Whole frontier should be delimited by October 31st and all Czech authorities over that line and German authorities in by then. Negotiations to begin as soon as possible between G.B., Germany, France and Czechoslovakia regarding demobilisation and treaty relationships.

Gamelin in his talks with C.I.D. made it clear that he contemplated offensives on land in West over Maginot Line. He attached

1. Frontier towns in the Sudetenland.

great importance to Poland remaining at least neutral, which he counted on in virtue of a letter from Smygly-Rydz[1] to himself. He gave an impression of calm confidence. We subsequently asked French Government however not to confront us with a *fait accompli* but to consult us before taking any offensive action.

Attitude of Dominions is definitely lukewarm. They see the issue as purely a Czecho-Sudeten question. S. Africa is the worst. French attitude however is now much stiffer. In order to check up Phipps's defeatist telegrams which we cannot credit, we have been obliged to instruct him to call for reports from all Consuls in France on French reactions to possibilities of war and to request them to report by telegram direct to Foreign Office (to prevent the Embassy doctoring them!) Almost all these reports are unanimous in saying the French are resolute and resigned to the necessity of making a stand now. We also told Phipps, who only quotes us the opinions of Caillaux[2] and Flandin, to go and find out the views of Blum, Herriot, Reynaud, Cardinal Verdier[3] and Jeanneney.[4]. These reports are also coming in – nearly all in an anti-defeatist sense.

William Strang and I discussed the situation tonight. He has great misgivings that war now is not to our advantage. We are disarmed and Czechoslovakia is not a British interest. Yet we must admit war is being forced on us by Hitler who seems determined not to have a peaceful settlement. Hitler blew up Runciman and he blew up the Anglo-French plan and will now probably blow up the new plan. Yet war may mean great surprises for us. Effect of bombing is unknown factor. German internal régime may crash. Czechoslovakia may resist longer than we expect. I said I felt something of the crusading spirit: we cannot have peace while regimes such as Hitler's and Mussolini's exist. Cabinet after dinner.

September 28th

Roosevelt addressed a 4 a.m. appeal to Hitler to accept a conference. P.M. sent a further appeal saying in effect "You can get all essentials without war" – offering to go out again to Germany and discuss with

1. Marshal Smygly-Rydz, Polish C.-in-C.
2. Joseph Caillaux, former French Premier, had been convicted of corresponding with Germany in the 1914–1918 war.
3. Archbishop of Paris.
4. Jules Jeanneney, President of the French Senate.

Hitler as well as with Czechoslovakia and France and Italian representatives if desired the means of transfer. (The French Government last night proposed to offer Hitler a further extension of the proposed occupation contemplated under the P.M.'s plan which they did not regard as radical enough.) P.M. sent also a personal message to Mussolini to ask him to support us.

Today we mobilised the Fleet.

At 1 p.m. we received Mussolini's reply that at his suggestion Hitler had agreed to postpone mobilisation for 24 hours. At 3.20 we received a message from Berlin that Hitler had invited the P.M., Daladier, Mussolini to meet him at Munich tomorrow. The message was passed to the P.M. while he was actually speaking in the House of Commons and it brought his speech to a dramatic close. He said at once that he accepted and the debate was adjourned. Is this a climbdown by Hitler?

September 29th

P.M. and Co. were off at 7.30. We hear the Czech Government have accepted the last plan with certain reservations and a message has come from Benes to P.M. begging that Czechoslovakia be not put in a worse position at Munich.

Prague reports that the Poles are now adopting a threatening attitude and demanding evacuation by a certain date *à la* Hitler of the areas proposed to be ceded plus some more. Czech Government ask us to tell Poles we guarantee execution of their promises.

I cannot help thinking this new move is a climb-down by Hitler brought about by a variety of causes perhaps – our naval mobilisation and the various other military preparations of France and ourselves, pressure by the moderates at home, the generals and diplomats encouraged by our firmness: Roosevelt's appeals, discontent in Germany among the working classes. For why otherwise should he have consented now to stop? But we shall have a great deal of bluster and sabre rattling and I am only afraid that the P.M., Wilson and Henderson – those weaklings – will not give even more away and seek to impose further sacrifices on Czechoslovakia. Mussolini has evidently been immensely flattered to find himself in the news again and he has at last got his Four-Power Conference which he always wanted; he certainly did not want a world war and his influence on Hitler was undoubtedly for peace. The whole question now is will P.M. and

Daladier stand up to Hitler and Mussolini? I doubt it. I believe the P.M. will side with the dictators and they will *roulé* him. He has cut loose from his Cabinet. He has no proper official advisers and it has never entered his head to take Halifax with him. If he goes too far. we may have a Hoare-Laval again when he returns.

At the last Cabinet on Tuesday, P.M. gave the most gloomy assessment of the situation – the Dominions unhappy, all the High Commissioners having recommended further pressure on Czecho-slovakia, Czech military morale bad and finally on the basis of Wilson's report he actually suggested asking Czechoslovakia to agree to withdraw her troops from the whole of the predominantly German areas at once. Halifax stood out and said he could not agree to this which would mean "complete capitulation". Duff Cooper was also stout as always. This however shows the P.M.'s frame of mind which is coupled with his self-complacent conviction that he can trust Hitler and that he has established an influence over him.

I lunched with Jim Thomas. He said S.B. whom he had just seen, was completely with the P.M. over this question "Peace at any price."

H. is by no means persuaded that we are going to get out of the wood. "I wonder," is what he says. He has lost all his delusions about Hitler and now regards him as a criminal lunatic. He loathes Nazism.

September 30th

Midnight agreement reached at Munich was announced in Press this morning. It provides for immediate occupation by Germany of series of predominantly German zones beginning on October 1st. The areas to be handed over by an International Commission com-posed of British, French and Italian Ambassadors and Czech representative; plebiscite for other areas. At least it is an agreement and my first reaction is one of relief. It remains to be seen what the areas are on the map. The wretched Czech Government have been told brutally to agree at once. But I fear it looks only too much as if we had presented Germany's ultimatum for her.

A.E. and Sinclair both rang up H. to protest against this aspect of it.

We heard at lunch-time that Czechoslovakia had accepted this decision taken "without and against them". Poor Czechs! Meanwhile

P.M. has had further talk with Hitler this morning as a result of which he has issued a declaration and is flying back this afternoon.

Vast crowds in the streets – hysterical cheers and enthusiasm. P.M. on balcony at Buckingham Palace. But many feel it to be a great humiliation.

Part Four
October 1st 1938 - December 24th 1939

October 1st

P.M. at Cabinet at 7.30 last night immediately after his arrival described the results of Munich. Whereas the Karlsburg memo was an ultimatum of six days, Munich amounted to a reversion to the Anglo-French proposals – the period for occupation was extended from one to ten days. In various other respects improvements had been introduced and it amounted in the end to an orderly carrying out of the Anglo-French proposals. P.M.'s further talk with Hitler touched on armaments, Spain and South East Europe, but he did not then disclose to his colleagues what was said.

What is causing the greatest misgiving is the P.M.'s declaration which he signed with Hitler saying that Great Britain and Germany will never go to war with one another, which is being waved in the face of the British public. What does it mean? Are we on the basis of it to give up re-armament? I fear only too much that this will be the P.M.'s and Simon's inclination. The P.M. is infatuated with Hitler and believes he can trust him. There is talk even of a general election immediately. It is also reported that the P.M. is next going off to Rome.

I saw Paul Emrys-Evans on Friday and he was absolutely horrified at it all. He thinks the fact that the debate will take place on Monday and not on Saturday will make a great difference as during the week-end people will get over their first sensations of relief and look more closely at what has been done.

The Poles today sent their ultimatum to the Czechs demanding acceptance of cession of Teschen by October 1st and the remainder in six days. The French have proposed that the P.M. should call a conference. The latter has sent a personal appeal to Beck.

The evening papers announced Duff Cooper's resignation. This is certainly courageous. I wonder if any of the others will have the courage to follow his lead. De La Warr certainly ought to from what I know of his feelings. So ought Walter Elliot and even Stanley. But

I much doubt their moving. If several went it would make a tremendous effect. If poor Duff goes alone, it will make no immediate effect except that he will be a valuable addition to A.E.'s little band. I dined with Harry Crookshank, who is very uncomfortable indeed. I think he may resign.

Meanwhile the paeans of hysterical praise are almost nauseating. Not a word about the Czechs and poor Benes, at whose expense and by whose consent peace has been achieved. I want H. to say something for Benes in his speech on Monday. I am sure he will want to and I have drafted him a passage. He told me he thought it was a horrid business and humiliating, no use blinking the fact, but yet better than a European war. I do admire the great dignity and restraint which H. has shown over all this. His position has been most difficult, P.M. taking all the limelight and scarcely doing the Foreign Secretary, let alone the other colleagues, the civility of consulting them. Yet he has shown no annoyance (which he would not be human if he did not feel); he can certainly claim a large share in preventing the P.M. going even further in his concessions.

October 2nd

We heard today that the Czechs had yielded to the Polish ultimatum.

October 3rd

Debates began in House of Commons and House of Lords. Fine speech by Snell; Archbishop of Canterbury spoke like Caiaphas as usual; Cecil said there had been nothing like it since Naboth's Vineyard. H.'s speech was certainly the best possible defence of a bad business – "disgustingly good" as Cecil said.

October 4th

H. told me today that there had been only one night when he did not sleep, and that was when the question had arisen of putting further pressure on the Czech Government to accept the memo. Alec Cadogan had said they could not; the High Commissioners had all said they should. H. had woken at one a.m. and did not sleep again. He said that once he had made his decision, he did not worry again.

We spoke of his speech, which I told him I thought was the best defence that could be made of a very nasty business. H. said he did not believe in not facing up to facts and criticism: it was a very horrid business. I said the real test now was our determination to re-arm.

Ciano has announced to Perth the intention of Mussolini to withdraw 10,000 men from Spain: the Italian Government now considered H.M.G. should bring the Anglo-Italian agreement into force. P.M. at Munich had suggested to Mussolini that a Four-Power Conference should take place first, but Mussolini could not participate in any further conferences with Powers which had not recognised the Italian Empire. There was to be a meeting of Fascist Grand Council on October 6th, when decisions would be taken on foreign affairs. If Agreement were not brought into force, "Italy would have to take certain action which up to now she had definitely refused". In other words, the usual blackmail. Italy will throw herself into the arms of Germany unless we do what she wants. She has not taken long to claim her price for Munich! Perth says this is the parting of the ways and if we do not respond, Mussolini will think we are still bent on chloroforming him and will adopt a definite military alliance with Germany.

Meanwhile the French Government have just told us they intend to go ahead at once and accredit an Ambassador to Rome (involving recognition[1]). So we shall be left alone. Of course Italy is not withdrawing men from Spain because of us: it is because she is in a fix in Spain: she has heavy casualties there and cannot maintain her forces without great cost, while the war is very unpopular in Italy.

October 5th

H. discussed Italian demand with P.M. and draft telegram has been prepared and sent off. H. says that H.M.G. cannot implement treaty at present without Parliamentary consent: that Mussolini should make position easier by including airmen in withdrawals and that Cabinet would then consider it with a view to action being taken after Parliament returns in November.

---

1. Of Italian conquest of Abyssinia.

October 8th

Mussolini has replied agreeing more or less to above procedure but not making any promises about airmen.

P.M. has gone back to Scotland after his "triumph". Meanwhile Germany is completing the occupation of her new areas, she has been hustling the International Commission and now her new line is to be practically the same as what she originally demanded at Godesberg. There will probably be no plebiscite areas at all – everything being handed over on the give-and-take method – mostly "take" by Germany – but this is probably a good thing. We are all agreed that a plebiscite in present conditions would be fantastic. Czechoslovakia has lost her best coal and her railway communications. She is broken strategically and economically. Nothing remains for her except to throw herself on the mercy of Germany and beg her to exploit her resources in return for peace and some sort of independence. Benes's resignation will facilitate this, and already now that he has gone there is a notable increase in forthcomingness by Germany in the negotiations. Such, then, is the result of all this; Czechoslovakia blotted out as a factor of any independence in Central Europe. Indeed, after the Poles and the Hungarians – the jackals – have finished with her there will be scarcely anything left at all. Shameful. The Western democracies have bought "peace" by sacrificing a small nation to the dictators because they were afraid or unprepared to fight.

In the debate in the House of Commons all the good speeches were against the Government (A.E., Bobbety, Harold Nicolson, Law,[1] Sidney Herbert[2]). Duff has been the only resignation. One cannot admire the courage of the wobblers. What should A.E. do? Should he break away from the Party and lead a crusade in the country? Or should he stay just inside the Party, pressing re-armament? Too firm a stand now might force the P.M. to have an immediate election which he might win. There must be an election within a year – a policy of attrition from within, damaging speeches from the backbenchers, may be more effective in breaking the hold of the Party machine and securing a more easy change-over from the P.M.'s regime to a wider Government. I gather balance of opinion

1. Richard Law, now Lord Coleraine, Conservative M.P. Minister of State in Churchill's Government.
2. Captain Sir Sidney Herbert, Conservative M.P.

of A.E.'s supporters in the House of Commons is in favour of less heroic course. I feel myself the country is ready for a Gladstonian crusade and would respond to it. But it would be very dangerous. It might not come off and A.E. would have shot his bolt in vain. It would be a direct challenge to the dictators and might precipitate war. I still think this would be the right cause. I have an uneasy feeling that the present Party system is effete and cannot rid itself of its own waste and that unless we go outside and straight back to the country, somebody else quite fresh, a sort of English Mussolini, may arise and kick over the old parties and sweep in. Who knows what such a Boanerges might stand for?

October 10th

Hitler's speech at Saarbrucken mentioned Duff and A.E. as war-mongers: no bouquet for the P.M. who was only lumped in with Daladier as "the other statesmen", after full honours had been given to Mussolini. The whole burden of the speech was "Hands off Europe".

I lunched with A.E. He is very unhappy at future and what we have all lost. He is to speak at Cardiff on Friday and at Southampton on Saturday – very important speeches. I feel that he must speak very strongly or he will lose support in the country. At the same time I no longer think he ought to burn his boats as regards the Government. After all, what is the aim? A broad National Government, including Liberals and Labour, such as alone can undertake re-armament and social reforms necessitated by a drastic overhaul of our system in face of the Nazi challenge. If A.E. goes out on a lone crusade, he must break with his party and every party machine besides his own will be against him. It is too dangerous to split the country now with Hitler at the gate. If he advocates national union, it is very difficult for any party to oppose him. The idea of national union is in the air. Even the *Daily Mail* has caught it. A.E. agreed but said it must not look as if he was only out for office himself. I said this would be covered by a demand for All-Party Government. He said he had been sounded by Stanley Baldwin, who told him he spoke without any authority but wished to know for his own infor-mation whether A.E. would come back as First Lord. A.E. had said no. I said I thought it would be a fatal mistake for him to rejoin the old Cabinet. They would give him impossible job, withhold support and saddle him with responsibility. He agreed. It appears that Stanley Baldwin attached great importance to reuniting the Government, but he has not got as far as to advocate going beyond the parties of the present majority. I said what seemed to me a vital need today was a real wide National Government for re-armament and social re-organisation on a wide scale. He should decline any offers to come into the Government again except as part of a wide reconstruction. In his speeches till November he should demand National Government as the only means of meeting the national emergency. He could refer to his own record over re-armament, continually pressing, etc., and say he was now convinced only a National Government could achieve it.

A.E. and all his friends are having difficulties with their local executives. The party machine is being screwed up. Of course the P.M. will resist widening the Government to the uttermost as it will spell the end of his own dictatorship. He likes his present Cabinet of yes-men. The last thing he wants is to have A.E. and any others like him back. He must now anyway find a fresh First Lord in Duff's place and will soon have the Dominions Office too as poor Stanley[1] is dying.

October 11th

A.E. came to see H. this afternoon. He told me afterwards that H. was strongly in favour of enlarging basis of the Government "including Labour", which is what A.E. wants. H. was probably going to write to P.M. to propose it. A.E. thinks P.M. will certainly resist.

I had written to A.E. earlier in the day about his speech at Cardiff urging need for very frank speaking in regard to the results of the crisis. He need not attack the Government but he should be "brutally frank" in describing what has been the price of this peace or respite – destruction of Czechoslovakia, the sufferings of refugees, the pre-dominance of Germany in Central and S.E. Europe, the loss of markets. Unless these ugly facts are rubbed in, the British public will soon be lulled into a false security again and the Government will do nothing for reconstruction or re-armament. Also A.E. owes it to his friends who, whatever the House of Commons may have thought, were disappointed, not to say shocked, at his House of

1. Lord Stanley, Secretary of State for Dominions.

Commons speech. He must raise the wind in the country if he is to induce the Government to face a real widening of its basis. For without such a widening it will not be possible to carry through the drastic measures of social and economic reorganisation necessary to put us on our feet again.

October 12th

Miss Maxse dined here. We discussed frankly the P.M.'s dictatorship in the Cabinet and his very odd behaviour *vis-à-vis* H. She also believes he has a sort of infatuation for Hitler and has no serious intention of drastic re-armament. She denied that Party Headquarters were in any way responsible for making things difficult for A.E.'s friends in their constituencies – on the contrary, she said she had been to talk to the St George's Hanover Square[1] people to induce them to make their peace with Duff Cooper. I asked her about A.E. She said she felt he had lost ground but should be more positive, use shorter sentences and crisper words, and say exactly what he wanted, with plenty of punch. She sees as well as I do the need for a wide National Government but feels that the P.M. and Co. will resist to the last ditch. She is horrified at the loss of prestige of Great Britain and the potential consequences of this surrender.

October 13th

I saw A.E. this evening and he showed me his speech. It contains all the essentials – need for re-armament, need for National Government, challenge of dictatorships to democracies, need for greater efficiency and greater output. "We are on a peace basis – they are on a war basis" – likelihood of vast social and economic changes in this country as a result. I hope it will go well. A.E. said he had spoken to Stanley Baldwin about a National Government including Labour. S.B. was now in favour of it but had said that he did not think the P.M. could do it, adding "I might be able to do it". S.B. was going to see the P.M. on his return from Scotland before he filled up the Cabinet post.

1. The St George's Westminster Conservative Association.

October 16th

A.E. dined here. He had had an immense reception at Cardiff and the other places and was much heartened at evident strength of his own position in the country which he had thought might have diminished. He felt the country was really worried and perplexed, and also that it was fed-up with both Parliament and the Government. He has got two more speeches this week and will crack away on the same lines. He does not believe the P.M. will agree to a widening of the Cabinet except if it is forced upon him. I agreed. We discussed what he should do if he were invited to join the Government again as it is. He quite sees that this would be both impossible and futile. I said that he should hold out for an All-Party Government, and if Labour refused then he could consent to come in provided he could bring two or three friends with him, e.g. Bobbety and Harry Crookshank, into the Cabinet. He owed it to his followers in the country, to whom he was the symbol for a certain attitude of mind, not to return unless and until he was in a position to see that policy carried out. His loyalty to his supporters must be greater than his loyalty to his former Cabinet colleagues.

We discussed the Italian position. A.E. said definitely he could not agree to recognition on the basis of 10,000 infantry only – this was another point on which he would have to be clear before rejoining the Government. He thought the country would still feel very strongly about this. I said I really wondered. I felt the country had lost interest in Spain. He said all the best traditional elements in the Conservative Party – except H. – were now opposed to the P.M. who had reduced the Government to the businessman.

Stanley died today so there is a second Cabinet post to fill.

October 20th

Cabinet on Wednesday postponed consideration of the Italian question till next week, but the general idea now is to have a debate in the first week or two of Parliament on the bringing of the Anglo-Italian agreement into force forthwith on the basis of 10,000 volunteers. It is hoped to push this through at once and then recognise. The Liberals and Labour are already on the warpath and A.E. told me he would have to oppose it himself. Mussolini refuses to take away more infantry at present or any airmen. British ships are still being bombed from Majorca and no assurance against this can be obtained either. Mussolini is in a truculent mood, although he is in a very difficult position himself – with this unpopular campaign on his hands, with Abyssinia costing a fortune and still untidy, and with Hitler getting much too big to be a comfortable bed-fellow. However, he is taking a stiff line with H.M.G. – threatening with vague threats – and H.M.G. will certainly give way.

No decisions have yet been taken about the vacant Cabinet posts. P.M., however, in reply to H.'s letter, said he would allow the idea of enlarging the Government to simmer in his mind but that he could say at once he saw great difficulties in it. Meanwhile A.E.'s speeches in favour of National Government are getting a very good press.

October 22nd

The Polish-Czech and Hungarian-Czech disputes are still unsettled. Beck, the villain, has been trying to enlist Rumanian support for his idea of a common Polish-Hungarian frontier across Slovakia and Ruthenia, but so far he has met with no support, indeed the reverse, definite disapproval from Bucharest, where the King has been playing an admirable part. It is worth noting that Rumania alone has behaved decently in all this towards Czechoslovakia. But Germany is believed to be opposed to the Beck plan as she is anxious to keep open the Ruthenian corridor towards the Ukraine for future eventualities. If that is so, Beck and the Hungarians will get their knuckles rapped. Czechoslovakia from having been a dagger pointed to the heart of Germany is now rapidly being organised as a dagger into Russian vitals. Czechoslovak economic *gleichschaltung*[1] with Germany proceeds apace. The Czechoslovak-Soviet Pact has just been revoked by Czechoslovakia.

October 27th

Cabinet yesterday agreed to announce to Parliament next week their intention to bring Anglo-Italian Agreement into force at once on basis of withdrawal of 10,000 volunteers only from Spain.

Great excitement over Oxford election and chances of Lindsay,

1. A classic Nazi expression: connecting, coupling up.

Master of Balliol, who is standing as Independent. It looks about 50:50. A.E. was tempted on Sunday to intervene on his behalf. He says he represents entirely his own point of view. Only Harold Macmillan[1] of the Conservatives has done so actually.

Two new Cabinet appointments out tonight. Stanhope is to be First Lord, and De La Warr Minister of Education. Lord Privy Seal and Dominions Office still left vacant, but I gather Runciman has accepted one of these, "making way for older men"[2] with a vengeance. These will not be popular. With De La Warr's attitude of mind it is unbelievable that he can find it in his conscience to be in the Government at all. No move up for Harry Crookshank.

O.H. to Mr Anthony Eden – November 6th 1938

Thinking over our talk yesterday morning, I do hope you will make a big speech in the debate this week on the lines you suggested. I know how much you must be chafing at being out of things and at the slow way things are moving, but I do feel you must go pegging away, it is the only course open at present and in the long run – I hope it won't be too long a run – the tide will turn.

I think it is vitally important that you should always make bigger and bolder speeches than the Government. These needn't be in the form of direct attacks on them, but indirect by way of implication and comparison. Personally I would like to see direct attacks on specific issues such as A.R.P. muddles, the Air Ministry, etc., but you must judge how far you feel you should go. My own very definite feeling is that you should hit hard and mercilessly and that you are more likely to consolidate your position in the country and so to get a move on by hard-hitting than by damning with faint praise. You must beat a drum rather than play a piano.

I think you should always speak very gravely and always emphasising the national effort needed for the national emergency. It is important that you should become more and more identified in the public mind with this grave view of the situation and with the programme of the sort of fundamental changes you would advocate to deal with it. You spoke of the three problems, re-armament, trade and unemployment, in regard to which our present methods are leading us nowhere. You could develop these and indicate the fundamental changes which are demanded.

The Government's attitude of shallow optimism and improvisation is not enough and its specious nature should be shown up by your own more far-reaching diagnosis of the real nature of the challenge. You should make

1. Conservative M.P. for Stockton-on-Tees.
2. Runciman was born in 1870.

it quite clear that you have studied the problem deeply and that you understand the nature of the drastic state socialism of the totalitarian states against which we need something more than the half-hearted and faltering social experiments which the democracies have so far achieved. In fact, what we need here now is a new deal, just as has been seen in the U.S.A.

Here I would certainly rub in the hard fact that there is no half-way house for this country between remaining an absolutely first-class power and the status of a Portugal or a Belgium. We hold what we have – colonies, protectorates, dominions, goodwill of other great states – because we are strong and for no other reason. Then one might well rub in how vast those resources are, strategic, raw materials, money power, moral power – we have all the cards in our hand – and if we are unable to readjust ourselves to the new realities and to the new sacrifices required of us, we shall fail miserably and that because of ourselves not because of our enemies. And if we do fail, let us make no mistake, the lights will really go out in Europe. In short, "great empires and little minds go ill together". We must be ready to try new methods, as in the past, and show courage and vision.

That, I feel, is the sort of thing which wants saying, again and again, in the House and in the country and without mincing words. But this week's speech must be a very big one indeed, the opening of your campaign and the nailing of your flag to the mast. I feel you must fairly eclipse the Government speakers by a really statesmanlike note so different from the "appeasement in our time" patter of the Government. I know you have the ear of the country, but the country doesn't yet see how the change is to be worked and, above all, it is crying out for leadership. It wants to be told what it has got to do. Nor does it merely want to be soothed. It is quite ready for sacrifice. No leader of modern times has arrived by soothing words; one and all, they have won support by constructive programmes of hard work and sacrifice.

November 13th

Outstanding events of last fortnight are P.M.'s soporific speech at Mansion House, "We can all look forward to a Happy Christmas"; A.E.'s speech in House of Commons on 10th appealing for far profounder reforms than H.M.G. have yet contemplated, and last, the most ghastly anti-Jewish riots in Germany since the Middle Ages.

A.E.'s speech to all accounts was the best effort he has ever made and has got the House and the Press guessing as to whether he intends to found a Centre Party. The Jewish pogroms have shaken up world opinion – even the City – as to the character of the criminal regime we are up against in Germany. Every scrap of information, secret and public, we get from Germany now shows that the German Government are laughing at us, despising us and intending to dispossess us morally and materially from our world position. There is a deliberate German campaign to represent A.E., Winston, etc., as warmongers so as to debar their return to power as it is felt in Germany that they are the only people who understand the danger and would be able to rouse this country to take appropriate action. The German people, or the better part, on the other hand, are probably in their heart of hearts opposed to the Nazi regime, particularly its worst excesses, and want peace – but they are passive, they will not oppose Hitler and they will march – though without great heart, if required to do so.

What is the policy of H.M.G.? To re-arm as quickly as possible *on existing peace basis* (which means that the German lead over us gets always greater) (a) because they fear we cannot afford more drastic methods and (b) because they fear, if we could, they would only antagonise Hitler; secondly, to use as many fair words and fair offers as possible, treating him like a gentleman as if he was one; thirdly, to trust to vague hope that as Germany sees she has got Austria and Sudeten and Balkan trade, etc., etc., without war, the people will get more passive still and even drift away from Nazi sympathy to such an extent that the party bosses will find themselves high and dry with no support in their own country; and lastly, when that stage is reached, to weigh in with fresh disarmament proposals and after that the millennium.

Meanwhile King-Hall's newsletter[1] hammers away week after week on exactly the right lines, bringing home the real nature of the totalitarian challenge. Is the country beginning to stir? It is frightfully difficult to say. On all sides you hear of uneasiness and dissatisfaction, especially among the people in the provinces – working classes, etc., also among all the intelligent classes in London, journalists, writers, artists, civil servants, professionals generally. The smug ones are the rich, the industrialists, the landowners, the idle, the party hacks – these still do not see that the Nazis will not save their dividends and their estates.

Changes in France look imminent. Paul Reynaud as Finance Minister may prove a cuckoo in the nest. I hope so! He seems to

1. Sent weekly to subscribers. It had a wide and influential circulation.

understand the nature of the threat and the need for real action. He is something of a French Winston. I go to Paris next week with Halifax and P.M. on a two-day visit and must try and find out what is really happening there.[1]

There is also the possibility of a visit to Rome in January. We are trying to cadge an invitation out of Mussolini, but what Ciano wants is to come here. The Anglo-Italian Agreement is to be implemented this week – a poor piece of work unhonoured and unsung by anybody except the Government. However, if we can weaken the axis by making much of Mussolini I am all for it, but I do not believe it is possible to have a real entente between the two countries so long as Mussolini's regime lives. Anyway, his show is getting pretty decrepit now.

I feel A.E. must develop a programme. Everybody is now asking what exactly he would propose to do. I would like to see him come out with a big plan for increased social services – lower school age – earlier age pensions – (all of which help unemployment); proposals for helping the export trade (so as to pay for the social services) by greater Government support – amalgamation of competing firms, bigger units, subsidies, besides re-armament, a Ministry of Supply and a National Register with compulsory service for A.R.P. Then for the Jews, why should he not come out with an offer to take, say, 100,000 Jews and put them in Palestine in return for undertaking to Arabs that the Jews should never have a majority and that we should not give up the mandate? We must have the courage to make bold proposals.

November 15th

U.S. Ambassador came today to see H. He said the effect in the United States of the German Jewish policy was a violent reaction against "appeasement", and opinion in America was definitely less sympathetic to Great Britain.

A.E. spoke in Oxford yesterday – another good speech with a little more programme in it. The political world is now agog to know what he means to do – found a new party or capture the Conservative Party. The Party and Cabinet (though not the P.M.) are greatly worried at A.E.'s success, much helped by the Nazis, in arousing

1. See Appendix M for memorandum of October 27th on French situation, occasioned by a dispatch from Phipps.

the country against "appeasement". The City is also losing faith in the P.M. A.E.'s supporters in the House of Commons have put down an amendment to the Address and mustered some 30–40 signatures.

November 16th

At Cabinet Committee on Monday it was decided, I learn, that owing to the Jewish persecutions it was no good trying to attempt further progress with Munich settlement and any question of making an offer of colonies must be set aside. H. acquainted the Committee of our recent secret reports which all go to show that the Nazi hotheads are in the ascendant, that Hitler himself attaches less importance to an agreement with Great Britain – which he regards as hopelessly weak and defeatist – although the German people were genuinely thankful to P.M. for saving them from war – indeed, Hitler was angry with Great Britain because P.M. was getting the credit and not himself. It was agreed that there was nothing more to be done at present except to try and get on to better terms with Mussolini and so weaken the Axis from that end. It has now been agreed in principle that P.M. and H. should go to Rome in second week in January.

H. spoke up strongly in favour of a National Register if only because of its psychological effect at home and abroad, but the P.M. is dead against it – as also against the Ministry of Supply.

As regards the Jews, it was decided to try and produce a large-scale and impressive plan for settlement. British Guiana is now suggested as possibly able to take 10,000, and the rest of the Colonies and Dominions are being approached.

It is intended to try and intensify broadcasting in German.

King of Rumania[1] is here – very anxious to screw economic and financial concessions out of us so as to afford Rumania some freedom from German monopoly.

November 17th

I am very anxious to get Phipps' retirement settled on before we go to Paris. Promotions Board last week recommended against any prolongation after next April (when his two years terminates) owing to block in promotion. Alec Cadogan and I both feel strongly that he

1. King Carol.

did not show up well during the crisis and that Ronnie Campbell would be far better. Phipps is well over age now. H. had agreed to this when he received a letter from Hankey (now on the Suez Canal Company) praising Phipps to the skies as the greatest Ambassador ever! I think Phipps must have got him to do this – anyway, it shook H. and we are now trying to get him to agree on a compromise extension till the autumn only.

On the other hand, we have been able to secure the prolongation of Lindsay's appointment over the Royal Visit to America next May. Lothian, who was to have gone out in January, would hardly know anything of the ropes then, and it would have been a fatal mistake to let Lindsay go. Fortunately the King himself and Hardinge had very strong views on the subject and these overruled H., who wants to get Lothian out quickly as he thinks he will be able to explain the P.M.'s policy there better than Lindsay.

Party at Buckingham Palace for the Rumanians. The Queen came up and spoke to me about the Paris visit.

November 18th

Bridgnorth election result – Vernon Bartlett wins as Independent.[1] Amazing victory – as he puts it – "for the Eden policy" – if only this had come yesterday P.M. would not have been able to stone-wall over National Register and Ministry of Supply. *Daily Telegraph* on Camrose's orders is now demanding the latter daily and fiercely. A.E. and his friends voted for the Government on Thursday over Ministry of Supply instead of abstaining – wrongly, as I think.

A.E. inclines to think that with defeat of Munich policy and dropping of any further offers to Germany through Jewish persecutions gap between him and Government is narrowing. I do not think so, because Government are going to try now to win Mussolini by making concessions to him (i.e. over Spain), and because they still are not arming fast enough or undertaking the social reorganisation which we need. A.E. continues to get evidence of desire to get him back as they think they cannot fight an election without him, but these feelers do not come from P.M. Sam Hoare, however, is on the prowl again and wants to meet A.E. A.E. says he is only going to see H. He wants if possible to avoid splitting the Party so as to lead a Right Coalition (Conservatives and Liberals) rather than a Left

1. By a majority of over 2,000 against the Conservative candidate.

Coalition (Left-wing Tories-Labour). I think this is right provided it does not take too long. "Tory democracy" is his line and a younger Cabinet.

I had a long talk with W. Strang today about Munich and after. He is quite certain that Hitler would have fought and that we were in no condition to fight. He also sees the P.M.'s arguments about trying to temporise with Germany, because there is a chance that Germany may be much weaker than we expect and may want to, or be obliged to, come to terms; because the risks of war are greater for us by far than for her – if we lose, the whole Empire goes, if Germany loses, she can recover, vide 1914–19 and after; we should therefore only fight for a vital interest when we must take the risks. Again, we do not know yet the effects of air warfare on our position in war: we have not in any case overwhelming air strength. Finally, any war will bring vast and unknown social changes – win or lose – and no war is a solution – vide 1914. Therefore play for time and avoid fighting at all costs except on a first-class vital British interest. On the other hand, while accepting this reasoning as tenable, W. Strang says the corollary is that we should at the same time re-arm as hard as possible, and that is what the Government and P.M. are not doing. Strang and I agree that the real opposition to re-arming comes from the rich classes in the Party who fear taxation and believe Nazis on the whole are more conservative than Communists and Socialists: any war, whether we win or not, would destroy the rich idle classes and so they are for peace at any price. P.M. is a man of iron will, obstinate, unimaginative, with intense narrow vision, a man of prewar outlook who sees no reason for drastic social changes. Yet we are on the verge of a social revolution.

November 23rd

We set off on our Paris visit today. P.M. and H. (and wives), Alec C., W. Strang, Charles Peake and I. Just as we were starting, we heard from Paris that French Government had concluded their agreement with German Government on lines of P.M.'s Munich Declaration and wished to announce it that morning and the arrival of Ribbentrop in Paris next week to sign it. Although Bonnet has kept us informed of these negotiations which we have in fact encouraged, it seems a bit hot to announce the agreement on the day of our arrival. We have asked them to hold it up until we arrive.

A frightful crossing.

At Paris we were met by Daladier and Bonnet, plus a guard of honour. Crowds in the streets – very drastic *service d'ordre* – cheers, but some boos near the Gare du Nord. *"Vive Eden!"* and *"À bas Munich"*. P.M. had wanted to drive about Paris in an open car so that people could see him. Fortunately this idea was squashed by Phipps and the French or he might have had things thrown at him.

November 24th

P.M. annoyed with the papers this morning – all of which speak of boos in the streets yesterday.

Talks began at ten and went on all morning and afternoon, with interval for luncheon at the Élysée. There was then a reception at Hotel de Ville, a cocktail party for journalists at Quai and finally dinner at Embassy.

I did not go to conversations but went to see Palewski,[1] Paul Reynaud's *chef de Cabinet*, to try and find out a little about the situation. He thinks that his chief's "plan", though drastic, will be accepted as the Chamber will not dare to overthrow the Government. The strikes in the North are tiresome, but they would be put down firmly. Reynaud and Blum are very close friends. He urged the need for financial support and encouragement from London. I also spoke to a number of journalist friends, but none of them could see very far ahead. They regard the situation as distinctly disquieting – the strikes spreading, the mistrust of Daladier and Bonnet. There is a minority, it appears, going all through the country from Right to Left, which is defeatist and pacifist and favours "contracting out" of world politics. This is our danger. Dislike of the Munich business, distrust of the Government, reluctance therefore to give them further confidence. There is talk in France of a Nogués'[2] Government with Reynaud in it. Daladier, who is said to be drinking heavily and certainly looks it, has much deteriorated, and Bonnet was never anything more than a little intriguer. France is in a bad way, I'm afraid, and the people are in a thoroughly non-co-operative mood. The truth is democratic governments must watch their step and be

1. Gaston Palewski, *Chef de Cabinet* to M. Reynaud, and then to de Gaulle when he came to England in 1940.
2. General Nogués, C.-in-C. French North Africa.

frank and honest with the people and not as both in England and France first deceive them (over our defensive strength) and then falsify their wishes (to stand up to the dictators).

I also had a visit from Riesser who used to be Head of the Chancery in the German Embassy in Paris in Wigram's[1] and my time, now *ausgeschaltet*[2] and living in Paris in business. He had just returned from Berlin and said he had never seen such a change in opinion there – discontent far more outspoken against the Nazi bosses who were ruining his country. As usual, like all the moderates and exiles, he saw the only hope in our standing up to Hitler.

The official conversations went well as far as they went. The Franco-German Declaration is on similar lines to our own, and we must bless it for the same reasons. A thoroughly dishonest declaration intended to chloroform public opinion, it does not, however, in any way affect France's obligations to third parties. Daladier expressly reaffirmed Delbos' undertaking to come to our defence if attacked – this reaffirmation is important. There was a good deal of discussion of defence – the French wanted us to undertake to send more men to France because now Czechoslovakia had gone Germany could concentrate more forces on the West against her. We said that we thought it might well be Great Britain which would be singled out for attack and we must concentrate on air defence. We explained our air programme (which really now looks very impressive on paper – the fruits of past two years now coming in) and urged them to speed up theirs – they produced some impressive figures for production by next spring and for purchase from abroad, but we were sceptical of their fulfilment. It was agreed to continue and extend staff and technical contacts.

As regards colonies, both sides said they had no proposals to offer and the subject was not further discussed.

About Spain we agreed situation was pretty hopeless and depended on Mussolini who was showing no helpfulness. We said we did not intend to give Franco belligerent rights in advance of the Non-Intervention Plan – which greatly relieved the French. They asked us to urge Mussolini to help by pressing Franco to accept plan: they thought, too, we should try and work for an armistice.

Czechoslovak guarantee: French pressed us to give it at once and make it individual. We were unwilling unless it were several and

1. R. F. Wigram of the Foreign Office. He died in 1936.
2. Another Nazi phrase meaning "purged".

included Germany and Italy. The French are anxious to make an Embassy at Bucharest, which we deprecate. If we make one there, we must make all Balkan posts Embassies and also Holland, Persia and Scandinavia – all or none. Soon the post of Legation will cease to exist.

P.M. went to see the Duke of Windsor at the Hotel Meurice before dinner. It was arranged beforehand with the Palace that his and H.'s name should be written in the Duke's book soon after our arrival in Paris and that if, as now anticipated, the Duke asked to see the P.M., he should arrange to do so. The Press naturally have taken this up as something startling, but it had no particular significance.

November 27th

I hear A.E. is now thinking again of going to America next week for his address to the Association of Manufacturers. He would be back by Christmas. He is evidently keen to go and thinks it would help this country's position there where our stocks are very low and he would meet Roosevelt. Kennedy is anxious for him to go. I don't like it much. He is needed to watch the situation here: if he goes to America he goes either as the adversary or the supporter of the P.M.'s policy. But he ought not to appear as either there. No doubt the Government would like him to go because they think he would play up there, help them with American opinion and weaken himself with British opinion.

December 4th

A.E. left for U.S.A. yesterday. He is to see Roosevelt and will be back again before Christmas. I think the talk with Roosevelt is the chief justification of the visit. He should have a really heart-to-heart talk, going all over the ground from the days of the Roosevelt Plan up to the present and the future. Our stocks there are getting lower and lower owing to the P.M.'s pro-dictator policy, and it is now reacting on sterling.

It is now decided that the P.M. and H. visit Mussolini in Rome on January 10th and that H. pays a visit to Geneva on the way back. The arrangement has not been badly received. But the Italians are now raking up claims against France and clamouring in the Press for Tunisia, Corsica and Nice. We have supported French representatives

D.D.O.H.—P

in Rome against this propaganda, and all this may well affect the atmosphere of the visit, if it does not make it impossible. Just as Germany is making up to France (Ribbentrop goes there this week) and attacks us, so Italy attacks France and smarms over us.

Government have brought out their plan for voluntary National Register which on the whole has gone well. I think myself, if time permits, it is good from the point of view of organisation to begin with a voluntary system, but from a psychological point of view they ought to have started off at once with compulsion.

Daladier has broken his general strike and his shares are going up a bit. Franco has collared two ships carrying the Rumanian wheat H.M.G. had purchased to the U.K. After strong representations they have been released, but there are still a number more British ships or British cargoes in his hands, which we have not got out.

There is a plan of Schacht's to come over and see Norman[1] with some new proposals. We are letting him come.

A further effort is being made to get the Cabinet to agree to a currency loan for China – but they will not unless America comes in too.

December 11th

Uneventful week. H. in Yorkshire. A.E. in U.S.A.

Italy still grinding at France over Tunis. Franco still hanging on to our ships. Cabinet still unable to make up their mind to risk a currency loan to China unless assured of U.S. participation.

The voluntary National Register has gone badly in the House of Commons, where I hear there is much discontent, not only among A.E.'s friends but among the Under-Secretaries and Government supporters. A spontaneous movement has also begun in the City for more resolute and more "national" Government.

The Ribbentrop visit to Paris has gone off without incident. R. seems to have disavowed to Bonnet any intention of supporting Mussolini's claims against France. I do not trust Bonnet a yard! The French strikes have collapsed and the Government got a majority in the Chamber, albeit one of the Right and Centre Socialists joining Communists in opposition.

Gwatkin has produced in triumph a half-baked scheme of

1. Montague Norman (later Lord Norman), Governor of the Bank of England 1920–1944.

Goerdler's[1] (he is a crypto-enemy of Nazism who is in with the moderates who are supposed to be only waiting to overthrow the regime). Goerdler wants assurances from us that H.M.G. will not take advantage of an internal revolt to impose fresh sanctions on Germany, that they will provide a large interest-free loan, that they will return colonies and give a free hand in the East – in return for which the Goerdler Germany, if and when successful, would agree to limit arms. A mad scheme which we cannot possibly have anything to do with. But what a commentary on Gwatkin's qualifications that he should think we should take it up! Both P.M. and H., of course, turned it down and declined to agree to any message being returned.

On the P.M.'s instructions a letter has gone to Perth from Alec Cadogan saying that Mussolini's anti-French campaign is increasing the P.M.'s difficulties in following up Munich, etc., and arming his critics and that unless it is dropped he and H. may have to give up their journey to Rome.

December 13th

I hear the discontent of the Under-Secretaries in the Government has now culminated in a draft letter of resignation being prepared. The malcontents are Hudson,[2] Strathcona,[3] Dufferin,[4] Kenneth Lindsay[5] and Harry Crookshank. They wish to resign because of their dissatisfaction with re-armament, failure of Munich policy and agricultural policy. They are hesitant because of the risk that the P.M. will spring an election on them and that the dictators may precipitate a war.

Meanwhile the P.M. is to speak tonight at the Foreign Press Association dinner. An Empire and world broadcast hook-up has been arranged. To show how these speeches are prepared Alec C., after much telephoning to No. 10, succeeded in getting a draft text late last night. The Secretary of State only returned this morning to the Foreign Office (though he has been taking papers in Yorkshire and could have been sent a draft). Alec was horrified at the speech which was extremely weak, and showed it to the Secretary of State

1. Karl Goerdler, Mayor of Leipzig. Executed by Hitler in 1944.
2. R. S. Hudson, M.P., Under-Secretary for Overseas Trade.
3. Lord Strathcona, Under-Secretary for War.
4. Marquess of Dufferin and Ava, Under-Secretary for Colonies.
5. Parliamentary Secretary, Board of Education.

this morning. They were then told by No. 10 that copies had all been Roneoed and distributed and it would be extremely difficult and most annoying if it had to be altered. H. replied to No. 10 that he thought it a very bad speech but as he had had no time to go over it he could only leave it.

A.E. in Washington is seeing Roosevelt today – one bright spot.

December 14th

P.M.'s speech was a flop – the audience applauded loudly the references to the Anglo-American Trade Agreement and to France, but received the Munich part in stony silence. The Germans, headed by the Ambassador, stayed away at the last moment because of the remonstrances to the German press for its attacks on Baldwin. (An advance copy of the speech had been circulated to the news agencies beforehand.)

December 17th

A curious thing has happened about the P.M.'s speech. Alec C. received a message for Rex Leeper from the P.M. to say that he was sorry he had not used the text which Rex had prepared for his use at the dinner, which he thought would have been a better one than that prepared by his own people (? Horace Wilson) which he actually had used: he would be very glad if Rex would prepare him a fresh text for his speech in the debate on Monday (foreign affairs). Rex duly set to and he has produced an admirable draft of a kind that A.E. himself could almost have made; this has been approved by Alec C. (who stiffened it up still further) and by H. and it has been sent across to No. 10. Will the P.M. use it? If so, does it mean that the old man is going to exercise a *volte-face* and try to lead his troops in the opposite direction?

Kirkpatrick[1] has returned from Berlin and brought such alarming news that the C.I.D. met this morning most secretly to consider it. It is, in short, that he had been told by a German official friend that Hitler was fed up with us and intended to attack us in March.

Meanwhile the rebellious Under-Secretaries have been calmed down again after personal interviews with the P.M.

1. Sir Ivone Kirkpatrick, then 1st Secretary at Berlin Embassy.

December 25th

The revolt of the Under-Secretaries has not been allowed to die down. First of all, I gather, the draft letter was never sent but some of the rebels went to see the P.M. in person. Then last Tuesday (December 20) the whole thing leaked out in the *Evening Standard* (given away by Randolph Churchill) – giving their names, Hudson, Strathcona, Dufferin, and their demands that Belisha, Inskip and Winterton should go. On Wednesday there was a great to-do and *The Times* itself foreshadowed a reshuffle during the vacation. The Under-Secretaries are now said to be refusing to resign but waiting to be sacked. I gather Harry Crookshank is in touch with the rebels and supporting them.

Anyway, the general idea now seems that reconstruction is inevitable since without it the Government dare not face elections. There is renewed gossip about A.E. being brought back as the only possible successor. Meanwhile the fact that the P.M. is making stiffer speeches about the dictators is held to have lessened the gap between them. Certainly the P.M.'s speech in the House last week – which included a good deal of Rex's draft – was much stiffer than his wont and he was even more outspoken at the (private) luncheon to the lobby correspondents. The old man seems definitely to have given up hope of Germany but clings to the hope of detaching Mussolini. He is certainly pressing on with re-armament, but not as fundamentally as the situation demands, and the C.I.D. machine with Inskip in command goes slower and slower, the Committee for Impeding Defence as Strang calls it. Inskip must certainly go. A much more vigorous and imaginative personality should be there. Winston is the obvious man, but I believe the P.M. would die rather than have him.

I saw A.E. on Wednesday night on his return from U.S.A. He was most enthusiastic about his reception and most encouraged by all he had seen and heard. Our stocks could not have been lower there as a consequence of the P.M.'s policy regarded as pro-dictator and pro-Nazi, and he felt he had really been able to put before American opinion a bigger view of us. He had emphasised at the start that he had not come to America "to get them to pull our chestnuts out of the fire for us" – a remark which brought the house down. He had seen Roosevelt who was very worried at the European situation and

229

particularly at our air defences which he urged should be pressed on with at once. Roosevelt was also very worried at our Jewish policy in Palestine. R. was also very anxious about Barcelona, Spain, and food ships are now going there from U.S.A. A.E. was much struck by the greater freedom and frankness of the Press about Germany and Italy as compared with our damped-down organs. A.E. saw H. and was also bidden to see the P.M. – to whom Kennedy, the Ambassador, had telegraphed that A.E.'s visit had done more for Anglo-American relations than any other visit within memory.

I told A.E. a bit about the situation here and warned him of the likelihood of approaches being made to him soon. I said the whole question would be whether the P.M. was only trying to prop up his tumbling Government or whether he intended a really big reconstruction. A.E. could have nothing to do with the former but must insist on a clear understanding of what the foreign policy was to be and must also insist on his own friends – Bobbety, Harry, for instance, going into the Cabinet with him so that he could not again be isolated there. He quite agreed. We both wondered and doubted whether the P.M. really yet wanted him back. A.E. said he would also have to insist that no financial impediments be put in the way of re-armament. He wondered whether he might be offered Co-ordination of Defence and rather fancied the idea, I think.

And what about the situation? To begin with China, I see a faint ray of hope. The U.S.A. have decided to offer commercial credit up to £10 million, which is causing intense annoyance to Japs, who have always represented us as the bad boys of the piece in their anxiety to keep on the right side of the Americans who through their trade hold the Japs in the palm of their hands. If the Americans went further and cut off commercial relations, the Japs would be sunk. Anyway, this will bring immense encouragement to China and will, I hope, strengthen our wavering determination to help China a little. We have already agreed to grant £500,000 credit for motor lorries, but are boggling, especially Simon, over a currency loan for which we want U.S. participation before we budge. Locally, the situation seems worse for the Japs, whose armies are coming to a standstill and have increasing difficulties behind the lines.

The situation is therefore slightly better – but not thanks to H.M.G., whose battle in the Far East is being fought for them by America and Russia. A less pusillanimous spirit here – a little more heart and courage – and we could expedite and consolidate the stalemate in China, and stalemate means defeat for Japan. However, America at least is now moving in the right direction. What a pity she could not have done so earlier after the Brussels Conference, when A.E. would have been able to help her!

In Italy we have Mussolini getting into economic difficulties again – an unpopular war in Spain, nothing yet out of Abyssinia, more and more subservience to Germany, the Ciano clique more and more pro-Axis and unpopular. We go there on January 10th determined (at least H. is) to give "nothing for nothing", that good Fascist principle, and I only hope the P.M. will stick to it. We shall ask Mussolini to clear out of Spain and he will ask for belligerent rights for Franco first – to which we shall say "no". We shall ask if he will join in an armistice appeal. Of course nothing has come of the Anglo-Italian Agreement – even the troops in Libya have gone back. The only justification of the visit is to strengthen the likelihood that the Italians, *more suo*, will betray the Germans if and when there is a war. An immense programme of banquets and fiestas has been arranged to flatter the P.M. I hear the Italian people are likely to use the occasion as an anti-Axis demonstration by cheering P.M. wildly as opposed to the comparative lack of enthusiasm when Hitler went. That, too, would be a good thing. But we cannot win Italy at the expense of France. (We had a meeting last week in H.'s room to discuss our line in Rome and it was decided "to give nothing for nothing", that we must make clear that we could not support any territorial claims on France, that the Anglo-Italian Agreement referring to the *status quo* in the Mediterranean covered French possessions, that if Italy wanted to discuss non-territorial matters she must first improve her relations with France. As regards belligerent rights in Spain, we could not do anything in advance of the British Plan, but we would propose a joint appeal for an armistice.) I hate this running after Mussolini as his system is only less hateful because less efficient than that of Hitler. It is hostile to our interests everywhere. His is moreover a weakening force and we are again going to strengthen him (as we did by our ineffective use of sanctions). By doing so, we annoy France and make America suspicious. It is the old policy of running after the dictators which has never paid. Mussolini is too much in German hands now to come out openly on our side in peace time, and if there is a war he would almost certainly betray the Germans anyway, as Giolitti[1] did in 1914. There will

1. Giovanni Giolitti, Italian Statesman, 1842–1928. Several times Premier.

never be assured and civilised peace as long as either Hitler or Mussolini is alive.

Then in Spain we have the same stalemate continuing with this difference, that the Barcelona morale is now much higher and the army by all accounts much improved. The food situation is bad but not catastrophic, all the foreigners are being evacuated with complete loyalty through the League of Nations Commission. In Burgos, on the other hand, discussion is rife between the *Requetes* (Conservatives) and the *Falangists* (Fascists), and the former want to get rid of Franco who is regarded as the prisoner of the Germans and Italians. An immense spy plot has been discovered by which news was smuggled out, in all innocence, by the British consular bag from Burgos! It seems to be admitted that Franco can do nothing by land now (even the air-raids cause only civilian damage and much less of that now). He dare not dispense with his foreign troops and accept the British Plan; his only chance is to get belligerent rights soon and so be able to blockade the food-ships for Barcelona. Food is now going to that side from America – which would make in any case the operation of belligerent rights much more difficult for Franco.

Nonetheless, a fresh offensive on the Catalonia front has just been launched – doubtless as the only way of keeping Franco's dissident forces together. One thing is certain, I think, that opinion here is also getting more and more pro-Barcelona and would not now tolerate any grant of belligerent rights in advance of evacuation of the Italians and Germans. Yet here again, as in China, we have democracy fighting for itself and receiving no positive help from us – only a frigid impartiality. Those who have helped are France and Russia – and now, too, the U.S.A.

Finally, we come to Germany, where even the P.M. now realises his policy is bankrupt. He is despised when A.E. is hated. The whole question is whether Hitler is going East to the Ukraine, or whether before going East he feels he must deal with the West first, but once involved in the Eastern marshes with Russia and possibly Poland, France and ourselves should fall on him. Here we are Public Enemy No. 1 as it is felt, probably rightly, that France will not move without us and can be placated so far as her Eastern obligations are concerned. Bonnet and Flandin are certainly working for a loosening of bonds with Poland and Soviet Russia: Daladier is less certain, and the best of France is certainly against any such loosening of that sheet anchor. The French Air Force in any case is in a wretched state and at least two years behind even us. The army is good and so is the navy. But the C.I.D. are being very sticky about staff conversations in spite of great pressure from the F.O. Bonnet is a public danger to his own country and to ours, and the first healthy sign there will be his dismissal. But I doubt any real change for the better there until we put our own house in order. From Germany itself little comfort can be derived from the growing discontent among the middle classes – those worms will never turn – or from the economic difficulties. This discontent might break Hitler once a war had started and was not going well, but I doubt if it would ever break out before. It is just possible that one Nazi faction, however, might shoot up another Nazi faction – or the generals take on the Nazis, but I doubt it.

The chief assets that I see are: (1) the increasing interest and concern with which Roosevelt and U.S.A. are following world affairs, especially in China and Germany. American-German relations have never been more outspokenly hostile – this must give Germany (and Japan) to think unless she seriously believes she can knock France and ourselves out by a lightning blow; (2) the slowing up of the Japanese advance in China and the stalemate in Spain (accompanied by increasing self-respect of Barcelona). Against this are: (1) Hitler's increasing "hubris" and outward armed strength, far worse than a year ago; (2) our still delayed Government reconstruction and persistence with old men and old methods which are antediluvian compared with the men and the systems we are opposed to.

December 29th

I lunched with Lady Oxford[1] today. She is all out for the P.M. but not so Elizabeth[2] or Puffin.[3] Lady O. did say that she had told Mrs C.[4] that the P.M. ought to bring in some younger men: she said he was very loyal to his colleagues and, unlike Austen, not at all conceited. I wonder! She also deplores the fact that he had no friends, "he knows nobody" and had no one to talk things over with.

I dined with Maurice Ingram last night. He is much concerned over the prospects of the Italian visit. He thinks it has all got on to the wrong foot from the moment when we did not wait to be invited but cadged an invitation. He is much alarmed lest the P.M. should in any way acquiesce in Italian claims against France and we both

1. Widow of H. H. Asquith.   2. Princess Bibesco, her daughter.
3. Anthony Asquith, her son.   4. Mrs Neville Chamberlain.

233

fear the effects on him of Italian flattery and hospitality. On the other hand, he does think that it is our interest to keep Mussolini going as, if he fell, there would be a weak and divided Italy instead which would greatly facilitate Hitler intervening.

January 2nd 1939

Vernon Bartlett lunched today. He agrees with me that this is going to be the critical year: he told me about his election and how all the country people are passionately interested in foreign affairs and frankly bored by the agricultural part of his speeches: he is intensely worried at the future because of our failure to re-arm fast enough, and finds that even the House of Commons is ahead of the Government in this respect. He is coming to Rome with us for the *News Chronicle*. About A.E. he feels that he has missed the bus by not coming out definitely against the Government – a Midlothian Campaign – and says he is now regarded by the Left with great suspicion: he thinks he should still come out against the P.M. and split the Party and take the risk.

I am certain that A.E. should be extremely careful about any approaches which are made to him. It would be fatal for him to accept to come back without a clear understanding with the P.M. of what the foreign policy is to be and he must insist on coming back with his friends. (I have written to him to tell him this.) Vernon said that it was essential that he should return to the Foreign Office itself if the bad effects of his returning were to be mitigated.

We heard tonight that that mountebank Montague Norman is off to Berlin. The alleged facts are that he is due at Basle on Friday and that as he is Schacht's grandson's godfather he intends to pay a long-deferred visit to Berlin for the christening: that he does not intend to see anyone beyond the Reichsbank people and that he mentioned it to the P.M. and Nevile Henderson, both of whom thought it a good thing. No word of this reached H., no attempt to ask his opinion either by Norman or by the P.M. We only heard of it tonight by a side-wind from Germany itself, which came to Van. After hearing Van's news, I told Alec C. who authorised me to ring up Leith-Ross at the Treasury to ascertain what he knew. He knew nothing at the time but eventually found out as above. Such a visit can only do harm – by encouraging the pro-German proclivities of the City, by making American and foreign opinion think we are doing another deal with Germany behind their backs – another example of the P.M.'s pro-Nazi tendencies – and finally in Germany itself where it will be regarded as proof of our anxiety to run after Hitler.

January 4th

Further meetings yesterday and today with H. (who came back from Yorkshire on Wednesday) to discuss Rome visit agenda.

On Spanish question H. considered that it would be most undesirable and dangerous if belligerent rights were ever granted as Franco would then borrow German and Italian ships to exercise them – or might have German ships thus operating in the Channel. We must insist on evacuation of all foreigners first.

As regards Suez Canal, all agreed presence of Italians on Board would be most undesirable, especially because of access to secret defence plans; on merits of case, Italians could point to increase of shipping. It was decided that this again was a case where Italy must first restore her relations with France. It was a French company with majority of Frenchmen on Board and as shareholders; unless Italy was once again on good terms with France she would get blackballed. As to Abyssinian frontiers, idea of reciprocal transfer of territory to include tribal grazing areas did not appeal to H. who preferred idea of arrangements for grazing on different sides of frontier without transfer. H. said that he had asked P.M. to make a point of making records after every talk with Mussolini and to send Mussolini a copy for verification, so as to avoid risk of misrepresentation.

I must record further development of Norman's visit to Berlin. On Tuesday Press came out, as was to be expected, with announcement of the visit as front-page news, it being added that he was going to follow up Schacht's recent visit here and to discuss plan for helping German credit and imports in connection with Jewish expatriation. A.C. spoke to H. in Yorkshire about it and was authorised to write to Norman to say that he had not been consulted about the visit, but he hoped that in any conversations he (N.) might have he would be completely non-committal. This brought Norman down to F.O. in a rage, saying that he was not going "for pleasure" and that he had talked it over with P.M. and Horace Wilson! We thus see a further use of P.M.'s policy of working behind his Foreign Secretary's back and keeping a side line out to the dictators.

Roosevelt's splendid message to Congress today was the best news we have yet had. He has said what we ought to say and is at present the real spokesman of democracy. I wish A.E. could speak out as bluntly as that.

The Honours List has two Privy Councillors – R. A. Butler and Harry Crookshank. I am sorry about the latter: it is much more difficult for him to resign now and it will be regarded as a reward for silence.

January 6th

Victor Gordon-Lennox lunched. He said his editor thought Rome visit "inopportune". Speaking of A.E., he said people were saying that he was thinking now more of political tactics than of strategy and that he was lying pretty for the leadership of the Party. He should hit out more and seek to consolidate the discontent lying behind the Sandys movement (which has proved a complete flop). He does not wish him to found a new party but to be much more brutal and out-spoken in the old.

I saw A.E. himself this evening, just back from Yorkshire. He told me H. had asked him whether he would return, from which A.E. thought H. must have some sort of authority for asking, but he was very non-committal. H. had intimated that he thought Inskip ought to go and from this A.E. concluded they might be contemplating offering it to him. A.E. had said that he could not return alone. He is obviously very anxious to get back, not for any careerist motive but simply because he itches to be back at work and pushing things along in view of what he knows to be the country's danger. I begged him to be as stiff and difficult as possible. I said I was sure there was no change of heart in the P.M. whose outlook and methods were still the same as a year ago; it would be fatal for him to return and find himself again a prisoner. He could not resign a second time without looking ridiculous: moreover, his return would be fraught with the utmost danger to his personal position unless it was clearly shown that he returned on his own terms and with his own friends: any suggestion that he was just going back again without any clear change of policy and tempo would be interpreted as meaning that he was no better than the rest of the politicians and he himself would have lost all power to effect anything for what he held important because of this failure of popular support without which he would be powerless. The ideal would be for him to refuse to come back at all except as part of a real National All-Party Government: if that was impossible, then the least should be a clear understanding about foreign policy and Cabinet posts for his friends – especially Harry Crookshank and Bobbety – he should insist on the latter coming in as a minimum *sine qua non*. In any case, he should consult Bobbety himself and S.B. very carefully before making any move. I told him that Rex Leeper in his anxiety to get A.E. back, underestimated, I thought, the gap which still remained and did not realise the danger to A.E.'s personal position by too easy reunion.

A.E. was very worried at the international situation. He has heard now that the financial situation is also extremely black. (This led me to say he must really also insist on the removal of Simon.) The present Government is awful, no redeeming feature except H. Even among his own friends there are very few of Cabinet calibre. A.E. was horrified at the lack of progress with A.R.P. – vide the trenches in the parks. He would like to see Winston back – so would I.

January 7th

I saw Tyrrell today. We lunched alone – and I have written a note of what he said for H.[1] His chief point was that we should tackle the dictators on the moral issue of the use of force versus discussion and refuse to be drawn into discussing the merits of any question at this stage. The country would respond to a moral issue, c.f. Gladstone who fought Disraeli because of his dealings with Abdul the Damned. He thought the Germans would go East and we should let them, as because of years of neglected defences we were in no position to do otherwise. He said S.B. now realised his own responsibility for our present weakness. He spoke highly of Sir J. Anderson[2] and said he was the ablest civil servant he had ever met and he would see to it that by March the voluntary registration would have failed and compulsion would have to be introduced. He spoke bitterly of the Norman visit to Berlin because it deceived the German people into believing erroneously that we approved of their masters. The P.M. was totally ignorant of foreign affairs but, on the other hand, he was interested in electioneering and for this reason he did seem to have come to

1. See Appendix N.
2. Sir John Anderson (later Lord Waverley) had become Lord Privy Seal in October 1938.

realise that British public opinion was now violently anti-dictator and he would take account of it – a hopeful development. The shame of Munich was due to past policy over years: at the time itself there was no alternative. (W.T. let out that the P.M. had sent for him to consult him before he went to Munich.) Where the P.M. went wrong was in signing the Anglo-German Declaration and that was because the applause had gone to his head. Hence the danger of a similar folly in Rome.

Franco's offensive is making disturbing and unexpected progress, thanks to the arms and stiffening of officers and N.C.O.s which Mussolini continues all the time to send in.

Roosevelt's message has roused the Nazis to a pitch of fury.

January 10th

We started off for Rome today. P.M., H., Alec Cadogan, M. Ingram, C. Peake, Dunglass, Cleverly[1] and myself; from Victoria Station amid the boos of a Communist and unemployed demonstration. Bonnet and Daladier met us at the Gare du Nord and took off the P.M. and H. to tea at the Quai d'Orsay, while the rest of us went to the Embassy. I saw T. Cadett of *The Times* and heard of Phipps's intrigues against him. The general view seems to be that Bonnet's shares are declining and that it is not safe to rely too much on the present French Government. Paul Reynaud's shares are rising, thanks to the success of his financial plan, and Bonnet has become the most vulnerable member of the Cabinet. What a pity there is no strong Frenchman now, a Clemenceau, a Poincaré or a Barthou: the French should never ask our advice, they ought to go resolutely ahead, confident in the knowledge that we must come to their rescue if they get in a mess.

January 11th

We were met at Genoa by a guard of honour and high officials and bands playing. There was some consternation when it was thought that Mussolini might not be going to meet us at Rome, but in the end, sure enough, he was there. Apparently he never announces his

1. Sir Osmund Cleverly, Principal Private Secretary to Prime Minister 1936–1939.

238

movements in advance for fear of assassination. At the station were large crowds, including the British colony who cheered wildly when the P.M. and Mussolini walked down in front of them. We then all got into cars and drove in procession through the streets to the Villa Madama – crowds and crowds all most enthusiastic. P.M. went first with Ciano (Mussolini went straight home from the station), H. with Bastianini[1] and Alec and I with Anfuso,[2] Ciano's chef de Cabinet, in fourth car.

The villa, which is well outside Rome on Monte Mario, was quite lovely; we had tea there and then set out again at 5.45 for the Palazzo Venezia to see Mussolini. There we were ushered through room after room lined with blackguards with drawn daggers till we reached Mussolini's anteroom: the P.M. and H. then went in alone and we stayed outside. There were crowds and crowds on the piazza cheering and shouting for *Il Duce*.

The interview lasted about an hour and a half and then we drove back to the villa where the P.M. and H. went over their talk. He said Musso had made a good impression and one of frankness. M. had said he wanted peace for internal reasons as well as for external: he did not want a multiple Mediterranean Pact but was well satisfied with the present pact which he intended to keep. The trouble with France was due to Spain: France was helping Barcelona with flour (!) and Russian agents had power to interfere: it was ridiculous that Franco had not been given belligerent rights when he held three-quarters of Spain. He thought the Jews ought to be settled in a state of their own: this was a world problem and required a big solution: he undertook to use his influence with Hitler to allow them to take out money. He did not think general disarmament was possible, but qualitative possible now and quantitative later. P.M. agreed to this but said what about Russia? Mussolini replied that Russia would not matter if the four other Powers agreed.

Perth made a bad impression: he did not seem able even to talk Italian. That evening we had a dinner of 180 at the Venezia, and here the P.M. made his speech to which Mussolini replied in a most off-hand and perfunctory manner. After that there was a reception of what seemed like thousands. Our party were shown through rooms which have wonderful art collections.

---

1. Giuseppe Bastianini, later Italian Ambassador to Great Britain 1939–1940.
2. Filippo Anfuso, Ciano's Private Secretary.

January 12th

H. went to see Ciano. I went with him and waited outside with Anfuso and Vitetti[1] – who are supposed to be his principal admirers. The latter booted and spurred like a cavalry officer as all Fascist officials and members of the hierarchy. From there we went to the Pantheon, where we joined up with the P.M. and laid wreaths and then on to do the same at the "Unknown Soldier". We lunched at the Quirinal with King[2] – looking to me quite unchanged since we were in Rome before, fourteen years ago. The Crown Prince, a tall good-looking young man, was there too. After that H. paid a visit to the English college where he had a tremendous welcome from the budding priests. On our way back to the Villa we looked into St Peter's. Wherever we go we are recognised, crowds collect and clap and wave to us.

We next went to the Foro Mussolini, where our whole party stood on a sort of rostrum with the P.M. and Mussolini in front like on the prow of a ship while a gymnastic display took place before us. The display was by youths and girls of 14–18 and a few small boys of eight upwards. The drill was very good, but we all found the *passo romano* quite ridiculous. It is all very militaristic, and the sight of the little boys with their miniature rifles was rather revolting. Grandi, who was next to me, surprised me by saying its real purpose was to counteract the influence of the Pope! Mussolini was evidently immensely proud of himself, taking the salute and squaring his shoulders: he stood there like a bull – not fat or unhealthy-looking, but very fit.

After the display there were further talks between the P.M., H. and Mussolini: then we dined at the Embassy and went on to the Gala at the Opera (Falstaff and Boutique Fantasque), after that a supper party given by Ciano and to bed about three.

January 13th

H. to Embassy to see French and United States Ambassadors to tell them of what had passed at the conversations. Then we went to the Vatican Legation where we were transferred into Papal cars which

1. Count Leonardo Vitetti of Italian Foreign Office.
2. Victor Emmanuel III.

240

conveyed us to the Vatican. Cleverly, Maurice Ingram, Peake and I went with the P.M. and H. We were received by Monsignori on the steps and led through room after room lined with papal and noble guards, including a roomful of students from the British, Scottish, Bede and Canadian colleges who let out loud cheers till we reached the ante-room of the Pope[1] himself. The P.M. and H. then went in alone and the rest of us waited. After about half an hour the door was flung open and we were all ushered in as well. The Pope, who was dressed in white, was sitting on a sort of throne at the top of a table at which the P.M., H. and D'Arcy Osborne[2] were sitting. He rose as we came in and came towards us, a most impressive figure, very small, very frail and fragile-looking, skin transparent like parchment as if he were only alive by willpower. The P.M. presented us in turn as we fell on one knee and took his hand. I believe the strict protocol for Protestant diplomats is to *bow* only and take his hand as to the King or any other sovereign: but we were too overcome to remember this. He then moved to the side of the room where stood a triptych of Sir Thomas More and Bishop Fisher which he said had been given to him by the English College and he always kept with him "to remind him of England". He spoke Italian very slowly as if with some effort and Osborne translated. He said that "England is always with us", saying this in English. He then again gave his hand to each of us as before and we all bowed ourselves out. In the private interview he asked the P.M. to help over the plight of the Roman Catholics in Germany and expressed his deep concern over the fate of all minorities everywhere. We afterwards paid a short call on Cardinal Pacelli and then left again for the Vatican Legation where Osborne had Cardinals Pacelli and Pizzardi to lunch.

After a short visit to the British school in the Valle Giulia we went to the Mostra Metallurgica, a Fascist exhibition of which the Duce is very proud, very well arranged, machinery, metallurgy, armaments, but very exhausting. After that we were rushed to the Campidoglio for a concert and then I went to dine with Arthur Yencken,[3] while H. and P.M. dined at the Embassy. I sat next to one of Mussolini's private secretaries who told me M. lived an absolutely regular life, began work at 8 a.m., worked till 8 p.m., seeing people, etc., at the same hours every day – after eight he shut down and was never ever to be disturbed. He certainly knows how to keep fit.

1. Pius XI.   2. Sir D'Arcy Osborne, Minister to the Holy See.
3. First Secretary at Rome Embassy.

After dinner there was a reception at the Embassy and a vast concourse of people came.

H. and I left the Embassy about twelve for the railway station, where the Italians gave us a special sleeping car for the night to save us from getting up to catch the early train for Genoa. The P.M. and party are to catch the Paris express at midday tomorrow.

January 14th

H. and I went on to Genoa, where we were not due to arrive till 11.30 p.m., and the P.M. and Co. started back later by the ordinary Paris express. H. and I got out at Milan, where we had an hour's wait, to see the Cathedral and go for a walk. H. was at once recognised and had a spontaneous ovation – large crowds quickly gathering.

We talked over our impressions in the train. Had we weakened the Axis? We had certainly proved that the Italian people were on our side; there could be no doubt of our spontaneous welcome; when Hitler came we were told they could not drive the people into the streets. Mussolini said to the P.M., "You are a very popular man here!" H. said his definite impression was that Mussolini did not want war; he found him calm, unaggressive and different from what he had expected him to be. Edda,[1] he thought, was a neurotic, talking about her health and how she could not stand Rome climate. She is thin, large eyes, dyed yellow hair, not unattractive: we doubted her being so dangerous a political schemer as she is supposed to be. H. was amused to hear her express very anti-Bolshevik sentiments. Ciano, obviously a lightweight enjoying the sweets of life to the full, did not make an unpleasant impression. We both felt that Mussolini remained himself in complete control in spite of reports that he was losing his grip. He has recently changed mistresses. He had an Italian woman who was supposed to be exhausting him and he now has a German or Czech one who is said to be calmer!

H. and P.M. were both much impressed by the social services, *Dopolavoro*, which the Fascist regime had achieved. P.M. was anxious to copy some of the physical training which he saw at the Foro Mussolini.

I was much struck by the extent to which the Army and Navy and regular forces were kept out of the picture, only party and militia

1. Ciano's wife.

seemed to appear at the functions. None of our people, for instance, seemed to have been introduced or talked to the Chiefs of Staff or any real Admirals or Generals. Yet I have never seen so many uniforms – everyone wears a uniform, the civil service clerks, the diplomats (all day and not like us only on state occasions), the schoolmasters, the men who take photographs at shows, Grandi, the Ambassador, dressed as a Fascist general: Vitetti and Co. like cavalry officers, boots and spurs, for work in their offices!

Though I asked various people I sat next, none could recommend the name of a good new Italian book – that is the reverse of the medal. The anti-Jewish legislation is also unpopular and there have been several suicides. Nor is there any good reason for it: there never has been a Jewish problem in Italy (only about 60,000 altogether), quite different from Germany: it has upset Fascist relations with the Vatican: the Jews are not particularly rich. The poor famed Italian air force is now very different from what it was two years ago: all its reserves have been used up in Spain. The impression remains that Mussolini himself is the one outstanding man and that when he goes there will be a dog-fight between his lieutenants for the succession: none of them would willingly recognise any other. Ciano hates Grandi; Balbo[1] is in some sort of exile. These are all men of forty and under: Mussolini is fifty-five: there is no one between those ages who is close to Mussolini; he is like a father among his sons. But there is no sign yet of Mussolini cracking up physically or of his hold over the country weakening, though he is certainly less popular. He has done immense things for the country, public works, stiffening the morale, youth movements, increasing or creating self-confidence and national pride. But the country remains what it has always been, a lightweight outfit, no raw materials, no real stamina to face a modern war. Mussolini will use every opportunity to blackmail us, the French and the Germans, but *not* to fight.

H. and I also had a talk about our own internal problems; the P.M.'s character – H. said he was shy and bottled: he talked a good deal to Kingsley Wood and took the advice of Horace Wilson about such things as Norman's visit to Berlin. He said he did not think, as I suggested, that he was jealous of Austen's career. (He certainly has none of Austen's charm, and even in a small party like when we were going to Rome he was quite incapable of making any pleasant personal impression; he is a sort of robot.) H. is very loyal to him and I have a

1. Marshal Balbo had been Chief of the Italian Air Force.

hunch that he is finding him more trying than he admits. H. said that if the P.M. died tomorrow he did not really see who could succeed. He did not think Simon or Sam Hoare or Inskip could. I suggested H. himself, but he said that would be impossible because of his being in the Lords. He then spoke of A.E. and wondered whether he was not perhaps too sensitive to criticism, not tough enough to be P.M. We agreed he read too many newspapers and paid too much attention to them. H. emphasised the great value of being unconcerned and unaffected by public opinion; he quoted instances of his own experience of opinion at home over his Indian reforms and how that had taught him how quickly it changed.

He said he thought it very necessary that Cabinet colleagues should always speak very frankly to each other so as to avoid misunderstandings which were easily fomented by gossip. Had A.E. always done that with P.M.? I said I thought he had. We in Foreign Office had been longing for the day when N.C. became P.M., because during the S.B. period (when he got no support from the P.M.) it was always N.C. who helped him and whom he always consulted; we thought now at last A.E. will be able to get on with his foreign policy with the full support of the P.M. Hence our great surprise and disappointment when the rift began. H. said he wondered whether it was not that A.E. not having been controlled by S.B. resented any control by N.C. I said I thought not but that it arose from P.M.'s well-known method of doing things on his own without consulting the F.O., like the letters to Mussolini. H. said he was not conscious of either Sam Hoare or Simon being out to trip A.E. up as the latter always thought. He thought, however, great forbearance was necessary to make the present system work with the Foreign Secretary in the House of Lords. I heartily agreed.

We spoke of the need for a real big reconstruction. H. said he had told P.M. that it was no good just changing a few faces. The difficulty was to know who to bring in; the P.M. despised the Labour leaders. As between the P.M. and A.E., I said I thought it was a real clash of personalities and totally different temperaments.

We touched on the reform of the House of Lords and I was interested to find that his plan was the same as mine, the creation of life peers whilst leaving the Parliament Act untouched.

January 15th and 16th

Geneva. Two very busy days during which H. made it his business to see all the more important members of the Council.

Charles Peake and I had lunch with Masdyk, the Berlin correspondent of the *Niewe Rotterdamsche Gourant,* who gave us the most definite forecast of Hitler taking offensive action in the spring. He is convinced that Hitler means to occupy Holland in order to hold us up to surrender; the extremists, notably Ribbentrop, are in control, the economic situation is worse and worse, bad food, lack of coal; a determined drive will be made to seize and monopolise the resources of S.E. Europe; he did not think the Ukraine plan was yet ripe. I introduced him to H.

H. talked to Bonnet in the train from Geneva to Paris on Monday night and the latter spoke of his great difficulty in resisting pressure to do something for Barcelona and suggested that we urge Mussolini to make a gesture by withdrawing another 5,000 men in view of the withdrawals from the other side.

January 17th

We were met in Paris by a telegram from Perth to say that Ciano had sent for him and used the most threatening language about France. Mussolini had made up his mind that he would not tolerate any intervention by France on behalf of Barcelona and that if France did intervene he would send divisions in spite of the risks of a general conflagration. So much for Mussolini's policy of peace which he spoke to the P.M. about!

We got to London at four and went straight to Foreign Office. We found then that Alec Cadogan has put together a mass of evidence which has reached the Foreign Office from secret and other sources all pointing to some German offensive action in the spring, either against the East or against the West (i.e. us) there is too much to ignore. H. went to see the P.M. about it tonight. It is to be brought before a Foreign Policy Committee on Monday.

A.E. rang me up in the evening and I urged him to come and see H. next week and meanwhile to take a stiff line in his speeches. Rex is so horrified at the weakness of the P.M.'s attitude in Rome that he is now quite convinced that the old man has not changed and therefore that his hopes that he and A.E. can now work together are vain.

January 18th

Cabinet. H. left for Yorkshire in the afternoon till Monday.

O.H. to Secretary of State – January 19th 1939

There are, I think, three points which require to be brought up and rubbed in more and more in public speeches at the present time.

The first is that the totalitarian systems have probably come to stay, or at all events a great part of them. Their methods are applicable to peace work as well as to war. They are the response to conditions demanding socialism at home, coupled with military and economic nationalism abroad. It is not enough for us to turn out a few more machine-guns and aeroplanes than they are doing and to suppose that, having beaten them in the armaments race, we can settle down to old ways and business as usual. This is a necessary warning to certain Conservative and business circles in this country who do not begin to realise what we are up against. The position, as I see it, is this. If there is a war of any length, those classes will almost certainly be ruined; if there is not a war, though they will not be ruined, their standard of life will nonetheless be greatly reduced by the cost of defensive re-armament and by the change over to more totalitarian methods of production and industry. What there is no chance of is to win or avoid war on the cheap and then revert to pre-war.

The second point – and this is one for the Left – is that, in pressing on with our armament programme, we must never allow ourselves to let up on social legislation. The Nazis and Communists get the workers on their side by looking after their bodies, while killing their souls. The worker in democratic countries is inclined to feel that the State, while leaving him free to think and read and preach, is not organised enough or determined enough to deal with the needs of his body. There is a danger of the democracies being regarded as safe places for the upper and middle classes but not nearly so good for the working classes, and this is where Nazi and Communist propaganda join up with one another. If, as is essential, we are to keep the Labour movement in line and keen over re-armament and resistance, we must convince them that we will never re-arm at the expense of their housing, etc. There is no danger of the British workman becoming either Nazi or Communist, but he is prone to the non-co-operative and defeatist pacifism of George Lansbury's section of the Labour Party. We cannot carry through the drastic re-armament and the changes of method in industry as a whole, which are necessary to enable us to stand up to

246

the totalitarian system in peace or war, unless we have a confident and keen Labour movement behind us.

Lastly – a point for the foreigner – we must continue to emphasise that there *are* things for which we will fight, that our democratic system needs no apologies (the French and English democracies went victoriously through the last war and the three great continental autocracies collapsed) and that it can and will be adapted and expanded, as it has in the past, to cover the new stresses and strains. We should cry out our wares a little more and seek to fire the imagination of youth, not so much by our achievements in the past but by what we intend to do in the future by way of making life more liveable, more secure and more interesting for the masses. In our natural British way we are apt to be apologetic and self-deprecatory.

I think these points are all covered in your Hull speech, but they can be repeated again and again.

January 20th

I had a talk to Jim Thomas who said he had learned that the P.M. contemplated no startling changes in the Cabinet reconstruction – certainly not an invitation to A.E. I said I agreed and that I did not now see A.E. returning except as a result of a war this spring or of an election in the autumn. He should remain stiff and bring as much pressure as he could in favour of more vigorous foreign policy, quicker re-armament and A.R.P. The future lay before him: he must face unpopularity if necessary so long as he spoke out what he honestly felt and did not give the impression of waiting for office.

H. and the F.O. were very anxious to send an early reply to Ciano, upbraiding him for using such language and speaking so lightly of risking a European war; in fact, a vigorous riposte. The P.M., however, refuses to do so. H. also wanted to make an appeal to Mussolini to withdraw 5,000 to help Bonnet – this the P.M. also does not want to do, but it is to be discussed at the Foreign Policy Committee on Monday.

January 24th

Foreign Policy Committee yesterday when the disquieting information from Germany was considered. As one result it was decided to send a telegram to Washington laying before Roosevelt what we heard and feared, viz. the possibility of a coup against the West; and

247

adding that in event of a crisis we might propose appointment of three neutral arbitrators. It was also decided to set Chiefs of Staff Committee on to study strategic importance of Holland to us and what we could do to protect her.

When we left Villa Madama we asked the Embassy to find out from the *cerimoniale* what tips we ought to pay the servants and chauffeurs there for our three days' stay. The Embassy telegraphed today to say that all previous M.F.A.s who had stayed there had given 10,000 lire and they thought that as P.M. had gone we should give 15,000 lire or about £170! Expensive business accepting Italian hospitality. It would have been cheaper to have taken a floor for ourselves at the Excelsior.

January 26th

Cabinet met yesterday: very flabby about our German information. Chiefs of Staff have reported on Holland that there is no hope of our being able to prevent Holland from being overrun, that an attack by Germany on Holland would be a first step to attack on us and must be regarded as a direct challenge.

We hear P.M.'s speech next Saturday is to be "conciliatory". Alec C. wants H. to try and stiffen P.M. up, but I fear he won't. Meanwhile a stiff speech of De La Warr is being toned down. Hitler is to speak on Sunday.

Barcelona fell today.

January 29th – Sunday

Foreign Policy Committee of Cabinet met again on Thursday to consider possibility of attack by Germany on Holland. For a wonder it showed more sense of reality, P.M. giving a strong lead in view of all information F.O. are receiving. It was decided to recommend approach to France and Belgium to ascertain their views on attitude to be taken if Holland were attacked, and extension of staff talks on basis of war in which both Germany and Italy were hostile and of either Holland or Switzerland being invaded. It was also decided not to allow the *Repulse* to take the King to Canada but to keep her in commission in home waters.

P.M.'s speech on Saturday, as was feared, and in spite of H. having urged him to put some stiffening in, again very weak.

248

A.E. came and dined on Saturday, quite clear and rather relieved, I think, that P.M. had no intention of inviting him back into the Cabinet. He had learnt this from S.B. who had just lunched with the P.M. A.E. had been having very successful meetings in all parts of his constituency, all in favour of more vigorous attitude towards dictators. A.E. disquieted at Cabinet changes and astonished at weakness of Winterton, Morrison, Hudson and Strathcona in accepting to be kicked about by P.M.

I think Chatfield's[1] appointment as Minister of Co-ordination a disaster. In the last three years he has been the great defeatist, besides being very reactionary in sympathies – pro-Italian, pro-Franco. He is certainly able and clever. In any case, it is wrong in a democracy and against our custom to have experts at the top. Professionals do not make good Cabinet Ministers. They are apt to be too specialised and too unpolitical – intolerant in their own sphere and uncritical in others. Now we have Chatfield, Anderson (a civil servant) and a farmer as Minister of Agriculture.

I have heard a queer story that I am not disposed to believe without further confirmation that R. A. Butler,[2] in unburdening himself to a friend the other day, said his views were those of the P.M. rather than those of H., furthermore that Horace Wilson was "the real P.M.". I also hear that while H. has been giving Dawson a stiffish line for *The Times*, the P.M. has been giving him a different one.

February 6th

I came back today from Paris where we went for a little holiday.

Hitler's speech on Monday last was interesting. It looked like marking time. I cannot help feeling that the American attitude (Roosevelt is reported to have said "the frontiers of America are in France") in conjunction with our re-armament may be making their weight felt. He makes therefore a vague speech including a sort of forecast of peace in the future, whilst complaining a lot about economic necessities, to see the effect – in the hope that we may at once relax our efforts or allow ourselves to be divided from France.

1. He had been First Sea Lord. The post was Minister for Co-ordination of Defence, previously held by Sir Thomas Inskip.
2. R. A. Butler, M.P., had become Under-Secretary for Foreign Affairs when Halifax became Foreign Secretary.

It is a speech at which the City, the London and French salons and our Cabinet defeatists will clutch. The P.M., speaking in the House of Commons on Tuesday, took it up but with commendable firmness insisted that there must be confidence, and acts before confidence could be born.

I found opinion in France far more optimistic and far less impressed by the German menace than we are. The French are only thinking about Mussolini; and against him they are absolutely raging. They are faced by a terrible problem in the arrival of floods of refugees from Spain, being driven on by the battlefront behind. They have sent Léon Bérard[1] to Burgos to try and negotiate for their peaceful return. Bonnet seems to be universally unpopular, but Daladier is generally respected. On the whole, the Government seem to have weathered their storm, and the general impression I received was of greater self-confidence than a few months ago, less defeatism, less self-criticism, better economic outlook. Though most people I met agreed that it was very necessary to be on the lookout and to go on re-arming, none took the view that there would be a war with Germany. Whenever, however, the need for more solid re-armament was pressed, the immediate reply was an inquiry as to when we were going to introduce conscription! This demand is now heard on all sides in France and it figures in the reply sent to our note regarding the threat to Holland and the need for closer co-operation. There is considerable mistrust of the P.M. on the Left, and the hope was unmistakably expressed that he would not go on any more visits.

I had a long talk with Ciecanowski,[2] who takes the view, judging by the accommodating way in which Hitler is dealing with Poland, that he really is in difficulties. The Ukraine problem is not ripe,[3] and Beck apparently gave the Germans clearly to understand that his alliance with France held good if the latter were attacked. Then, again, the references in Hitler's speech to future support for Italy are decidedly ambiguous.

I also talked to Bassée (of Havas)[4] at the Embassy dinner we went to on Saturday night and was interested to hear him express anxiety

---

1. Later French Ambassador to the Vatican 1940–1944.
2. Polish diplomatist at this time in retirement and living in Paris.
3. A reference to the Ukrainian separatist movement which the Nazis believed could be stirred up to their advantage.
4. The official French Press Agency.

lest Germany and Russia should get together. A wholesome anxiety! I urged the need for our two Governments to warm up their relations with Russia a bit – regardless of ideologies. He quite agreed.

February 12th

On Monday last, in view of increasing Italian press attacks on France and information about calling up Italians and military concentration in North Africa, P.M. made a statement in House of Commons that as all the forces of France would be at our disposal in event of war in which both were involved, "any threat to vital interests of France" from whatever quarter must evoke immediate co-operation out of this country. This was indeed a mouthful from the P.M. and was prompted, as I hear, by H. It has had a marked and sobering effect though the dictators try to ignore it.

Evidence increases of malaise in Germany, economic difficulties (confessed by Hitler himself in his speech) and military preparations. In Italy there is a steady concentration of troops in North Africa. Italy has gone back, of course, on the undertaking in the Anglo-Italian Agreement to reduce the Libya garrison, and when Ciano was remonstrated with, he calmly replied that it was because of France's attitude and another 100,000 were to be sent! It looks unpleasantly like the pre-war period in Abyssinia. Is Italy contemplating war with France or only bluff? And what is Germany's attitude? I doubt if Hitler has given Mussolini a blank cheque, but he is obviously glad to see Franco-Italian relations bad. How else can he be sure of keeping Italy on his side? Mussolini, for his part, certainly does not want a war, but he has seen what can be accomplished by bluff – Czechoslovakia. He hopes to use our reluctance to fight and Germany's backing to blackmail France into another Munich. The danger is that he will bluff too far and France will fight, and then Germany may or may not come in but will in any case "help" Italy. Hence the importance of the P.M.'s statement.

What are Italy's claims? Minimum a free zone in Jibuti and a seat on Suez Canal Board: these are reasonable and France would grant them if Italy behaved and asked properly. Maximum – Tunis, Jibuti itself, French (and British) Somaliland, base in Majorca: France would fight rather than grant these.

We have further evidence of Italian iniquity from Belgrade, where we learn from Prince Paul that Ciano on his recent visit secretly proposed to Stoyadinovitch[1] the partition of Albania on the ground that the Zog[2] regime was very unpopular and that oil wells in the South were necessary to Italy! As a matter of fact, Albania has never been quieter. Prince Paul is in a quandary because the last thing the Yugoslavs want is Italy in Albania, but rather than see her there alone they feel they must agree to partition or fight to keep her out. Immediately after this Stoyadinovitch fell over an internal Croat question and there is a new Government, probably more loyal to the Balkan Entente and less pro-Italian than the shifty Stoyadinovitch. It remains to be seen if Ciano revives his evil design. Stoyadinovitch's fall was a rebuff for him as he had only just reported how solid S.'s position was.

In Spain we are doing rather well. Barcelona having fallen and Franco's advance up to the French frontier being complete, a descent on Minorca was being planned. We received word that the garrison might surrender if an opportunity for parley were provided, and so we agreed to allow a Spaniard from Majorca to go in H.M.S. *Devonshire* to speak to the Governor. The two discussed on board the ship in Mahon harbour and terms were arranged. In the midst of this came an air-raid by Italian bombers, furious at seeing their influence eliminated, and the surrender nearly broken down. The Majorcan Spaniard was just as indignant as anybody else at this unauthorised raid. However, matters were finally fixed up and a peaceful change-over took place – the *Devonshire* removing those whose lives would have been forfeit.

It is now generally felt that the sooner we recognise Franco and get in the better. The French agree and it is clearly useless, now that the Spanish Government has ceased to exist, to leave the Germans and Italians in undisputed possession any longer. The dictators are already furious at our success over Minorca. On the other hand, as we suspected, Franco's side is full of rifts. The Generals are beginning to fall out, as well as the Carlists and the supporters of Alfonso and the Falangists. We had a meeting on Friday to choose an Ambassador and it was agreed to recommend Peterson[3] as our most energetic man: we hope to organise a regular drive – commercial missions, propaganda, etc. – to get Franco over to our side, or at least back to real neutrality. After all, we have no Spanish blood on our hands.

1. Yugoslav Prime Minister. 2. King Zog of Albania.
3. Sir Maurice Peterson, Ambassador to Spain 1939–1940.

The Pope died on Friday – exactly four weeks since we saw him. I am sad and fear he has died too soon. No other Pope can at once acquire his prestige or wield the influence he did from the edge of the grave. It is doubtful whether any other Pope would be so courageous in standing up to the dictators, and Hitler and Mussolini must be rejoicing. We shall probably have some saintly peasant in his place and the Vatican will fade out again from the moral leadership it had won in the last year or two. If he had lived longer, I believe he would have filled up the College with his own men and prepared his succession. I wonder if this seals the fate of the Catholics in Germany.

In response to our inquiry the French agree to extension of Staff talks to cover possibility of attack via Holland, Belgium or Switzerland (while suggesting we should now have conscription) – the Belgians say they think absolute neutrality their best defence and want no talks. There is division in Belgian ranks between the King and his entourage (who are absolute neutralists) and his own General Staff (who would like talks), but clearly there is nothing to be done with them at present. We are to have talks with the French alone therefore (they are to cover the case of Italy also being hostile), and I hope they will begin soon.

Japan has occupied Hainan, off French Indo-China and South of Hong Kong. The French are very agitated and we are mildly so. More protests.

O.H. to Secretary of State – February 14th 1939

I believe that as a result of the Prime Minister's statement of last week the gulf between the Government and the Eden group has been much reduced.

Indeed, as regards Germany, the two points of view are now very near. This is attributed to your influence and, as I said in another note, the firmness and frankness of your Focus speech caused the greatest satisfaction among the Edenites there. Their only fear is lest the Prime Minister should not keep steadily on this course.

Nor do I believe that Spain will be a serious difficulty now that Franco has won and become the master of the country. The question of recognition will be regarded as a severely practical issue to be decided on its merits from the point of view of British interests. On the other hand, the more generous any references which can be made to the beaten Republicans, the better it will go. The Prime Minister's taunt in the House of Commons

253

yesterday implying that he could not find the Spanish Government has had a deplorable effect and was regarded as in the worst taste.

Only as regards Mussolini do doubts linger. It is felt that though the Prime Minister may have seen the light as regards Hitler, he still harbours illusions about Mussolini and may be prepared to agree to another "Munich" for Italy at France's expense. If the dissidents can be satisfied that there can be no question of this, their opposition will virtually cease.

February 16th

Discussions have continued all week about recognition of Franco. H. is in favour of acting quickly and this is general view of meetings in F.O. – even Van. It was decided on Monday after H. had seen P.M. to prepare a paper for Cabinet on Wednesday advocating this course in conjunction with France. Van sprung a surprise on us by suggesting that Chetwode[1] should go as Ambassador – an idea which rather appealed to H. as a temporary appointment to stage a big drive. H., who is rather anxious as to effect of immediate recognition on opinion here, however, was interested to hear that Bobbety, in a letter to me, said he thought the sooner we recognised Franco the better in order to wean him from his undesirable friends. He also learned through Rex that A.E. was not opposed to it. I also saw Vernon Bartlett, who said that it would be criminal to encourage Negrin[2] to resist further and that he saw need for early recognition but that it would make all the difference to him if we could secure some sort of assurance or amnesty from Franco for the Government side beforehand.

This latter view appealed strongly to H. We have had an offer from Negrin to cease hostilities if Franco agrees to withdrawal of volunteers, no reprisals and freedom of Spanish people to decide future regime, and it was decided on Thursday (14th) to telegraph this to Burgos, suggesting that from what Franco himself had said he might be willing to consider it and emphasising great advantage of earliest cessation of hostilities. H.'s view is that while he does not want to bargain over recognition or attack conditions, he would like to get Franco to do something which would ease both his position and ours.

1. Field-Marshal Lord Chetwode.
2. Juan Negrin was Finance Minister in the Spanish Republican Government.

Cabinet yesterday also did not like idea of immediate recognition and wished to pursue idea of getting some assurances and if possible surrender of Madrid first. A further telegram was sent to Burgos saying H.M.G. were giving earnest consideration to recognition which will be based on facts and any delay would be due to necessity for public opinion to rally itself; position in U.K., Dominions and U.S.A. would be greatly assisted if Franco could make "some restatement of policy already in mind", i.e. that when fighting was over he would not allow unauthorised or general reprisals.

Today we had a further message through Azcarate,[1] offering surrender if only assurance against reprisals and permission to escape to leaders were given. It was decided to draft a further telegram to Burgos in this sense, but before sending it we asked Azcarate to get authority of his people. He went off to Paris, where there is evidently a row going on between Azana[2] (who wants surrender) and Negrin and Del Vayo (who want resistance); he is to return on Saturday with a reply. In meanwhile, Mounsey is seeing Alba[3] and urging strongly the need for a statement by Franco.

February 17th

I hear from Paul Emrys-Evans and Jim Thomas that H.'s speech at the Foreign Affairs Committee of the House of Commons yesterday made an admirable impression on the Edenites, as well as on the orthodox. They liked his firm tone, and his reference to Spain and the line he was taking of trying to secure assurances before recognition went very well. He also spoke of our intention of warming up to Russia and sending a Minister there: this pleased the Edenites but was rather strong meat for the rest.

I feel H. now sees his way much more clearly: he has mastered his subject and speaks and acts with greater confidence and boldness. We may have trouble with the P.M. before long! H. has a speech in the House of Lords next Thursday; he is carrying out his own line more and more – it is very close to A.E.'s. He is almost unrecognisable from the H. of a year ago. He says bluntly "no more Munich for me"; and I am sure he is convinced that now we are stronger we

1. Spanish Republican Ambassador in London.
2. Manuel Azana, Spanish President at start of Civil War.
3. Duke of Alba, on Franco's side. Became Spanish Ambassador to Britain, August 1939.

must stand firm. He felt in September that we were not strong enough to risk fighting unless it was absolutely vital to us and that the Czech issue was not vital, but he always spoke of our being "between two horrible alternatives" and never saw anything to be proud of in the result. He won't allow us to get caught again like that.

February 19th

Azcarate came to see Mounsey yesterday but he said he had been unable to get a clear answer as Negrin was in Madrid in the midst of difficult negotiations with his various sections of opinion – some for resistance, some for surrender, etc. Azcarate hopes to be able to get a reply today in which case our telegram will be sent to Burgos containing the offer of surrender provided there are no reprisals.

I saw Virginia Cowles today back from Soviet Russia – very disappointed and horrified at what she saw – great inefficiency, complete ignorance of outside world, no foreigners hardly there, almost complete seclusion. I asked her about the chances of Russia joining up with Germany: she said that the German Embassy there were always urging the advantages of this, pointing out the resemblance between the two systems now, but that Hitler was obstinately opposed – thank goodness! She said our new Ambassador – Seeds[1] – had astonished them by talking Russian.

February 22nd

Still no reply from Azcarate and he has now been told that we cannot wait indefinitely and if we do not receive a reply shortly we must go ahead and recognise. We have telegraphed to Paris proposing that we should, in fact, recognise at earliest moment, not later than February 24th, basing ourselves on a statement by Franco that he will not accept foreign domination and that reprisals are alien to his Government although he must insist on unconditional surrender.

It has also been decided that Peterson is to be Ambassador and the Chetwode idea has been dropped.

A.E. dined. He is anxious about the future and the question of his rejoining the Government. Halifax and Stanley have both told him that they want him back, but there has been no sign from P.M.

1. Sir William Seeds, Ambassador to U.S.S.R., January 1939–April 1940.

Stanley[1] wants A.E. back with a view to a future combination by A.E. and H., the latter as P.M. and the former as Leader of House of Commons. A.E. would like to work with H. in such circumstances, and as a preliminary and in order to ensure H.'s succession he would like to return soon after Spain has been cleared up. But he feels that by Whitsun at latest either P.M. must ask him back or he, A.E., must be free to take independent line at elections; he will not give P.M. a blank cheque to fight elections (if he is not a member of Government) as he does not trust him. Baldwin, A.E. said, thought an H. *cum* A.E. combination might be possible but was not sure yet in his own mind: he thought P.M. – like Austen and old Joe – might suddenly have a stroke without any warning. I said I was sure he and H. could work together as on foreign affairs they saw eye-to-eye, but I did not believe the P.M. wanted him back and I feared if he did come back that he and P.M. would fall out over latter's foreign policy.

February 28th

In agreement with the French, we are both going to recognise Franco on Monday.

H. made a little speech in the House of Lords on Thursday on our relations with France which, following on the Forces and Foreign Affairs Committee speeches, has made a great impression for firmness. He quoted extracts from *Mein Kampf* to the effect that it was always a mistake to regard the English as decadent! Even the *Yorkshire Post* was delighted.

March 2nd

A.E. spoke in the debate on Spain on Tuesday and supported the Government's action in recognition. All his supporters favoured this. Recognition has not, in fact, gone at all badly for the Government.

We dined at the Birkenheads'[2] and met Winston and Seymour Berry.[3] Winston in great form although it was his first day up after

1. Oliver Stanley, M.P., President of Board of Trade.
2. Second Lord Birkenhead, Halifax's Parliamentary Private Secretary.
3. Elder son of Lord Camrose, proprietor of *Daily Telegraph*. Succeeded his father in 1954.

flu – very concerned over what he regards as inadequacy of A.R.P. – too much dispersion of effort – not enough concentration on vital targets which he believes would be continuously attacked. However, he is more satisfied with our armaments. He fears, as I do, that Mussolini may precipitate a crisis and that Bonnet may run away as in September. Nonetheless, he says H.M.G. can never accept responsibility for advising French Government to resist if our advice is asked, especially as we have no army to offer but only two divisions. He is well pleased with H. but does not trust P.M. He thinks Mussolini is near to breaking point.

I was very impressed with Berry, who runs *Daily Telegraph* more and more, favours very firm attitude and was infuriated by Sam Hoare's recent "jitter-bug" speech since it was Sam who in the recent crisis spoke to the newspaper proprietors and was then the complete jitter-bug himself. He favours H. as P.M.

All delighted to hear the news of Pacelli's election as Pope.[1] A bad knock for the dictators. He used to be Nuncio at Berlin and knows of all their iniquities.

March 3rd

Lunch with Cleverly. He also favours H. as P.M. and believes it would go. He says Sam is no good and hated by everybody: Inskip will go to Woolsack after election.

H. still away with flu.

One amusing thing. Lothian, whose appointment as Ambassador to Washington when Lindsay goes has been approved but is actually held in abeyance, recently passed through America and went to see Roosevelt. George Trevelyan[2] wrote to H. the other day and sent him a copy of a letter he had received from Merriman of Harvard, enclosing a copy of a letter he had had from Roosevelt himself. In this the President described the conversation with Lothian, who had taken the completely defeatist line that we could not possibly stand up to Germany and Italy, that our day was done and it was now for America to step forward and take up the torch of civilisation from our drooping fingers. Roosevelt was furious with Lothian and went for him: as R. told Merriman, if Great Britain took that line and not one of robust self-help, American opinion would never consent to help. This is, of course, just typical of the line that conceited ass

1. Pope Pius XII.　2. Professor of Modern History at Cambridge.

258

(and the whole Cliveden set) takes. If any man had his hands dripping with guilt for the Versailles settlement it was Lothian, who was then Lloyd George's Private Secretary. Yet, according to himself, he knows America well and expects "to swing public opinion there!" However, I hope and pray this fortunate letter will kill the appointment. H. has sent it across to the P.M. who is much concerned at it. Alec Cadogan does not think L. can possibly be sent there now.

But who to send? Our only possible candidate is Lampson, but he is better left where he is. Stanley would be better than Lothian. I have now suggested Lytton[1] – if he would consent to serve with this Government – but he would not be a bad Ambassador and his views on foreign affairs are both robust and idealistic.

March 9th

I saw Jim T. and Hinchingbrooke[2] on Wednesday. We discussed A.E.'s prospects and agreed that there was extremely little likelihood of P.M. asking him back and that A.E. should prepare to be out for a year or two. I said I thought he should devote himself to study of internal questions and generally constitute his group on the basis of a New Deal, acting as a ginger group to the present Government and preparing to be the next Government. He should inspire the Conservative Party to renew itself and to seek to catch the imagination of the people and of the youth – much as Disraeli had done last century. They agreed, but admitted that A.E. was really only or much more interested in foreign affairs. There is no doubt that A.E. wants to be back dreadfully, but it would be tragic if he went back except on terms. They both agreed that H. should be the next P.M.

We have now got Ashton Gwatkin's report of his visit to Berlin. All he saw there were anxious for more commercial and economic concessions but took the line that these must precede political concessions such as arms limitation, etc., and not vice versa. All admitted the economic difficulties of Germany, albeit they are as yet far from desperate.

We lunched today with R. A. Butler. Shakes Morrison and Maisky there. Maisky said Moscow thought Hudson Mission[3] too good to be

1. 2nd Lord Lytton (1876–1947).
2. Lord Hinchingbrooke, M.P., now Mr Victor Montagu.
3. To Moscow of Robert Hudson, Secretary of Department of Overseas Trade.

true and were very mistrustful of us since Munich. There was a strong movement towards isolation now.

March 10th

Times and other papers today all contained identical and rosy accounts of present position in foreign affairs which were obviously inspired. It was said that the Spanish affair would soon be over and after that Franco-Italian difficulties would remain to be tackled. But they did not warrant any undue pessimism. Then the next step would be a halt in the armaments race. It was felt that if in the course of the present year we could achieve some agreement, it would do much to restore confidence: much depended on Anglo-German relations, but here, too, the position was more promising.

When H. came to the Office he asked where this had come from, believing it was the News Department. It was then found on inquiry that the P.M. yesterday had received all the lobby correspondents and given them a discourse on foreign affairs. He had never even told H. that he intended to do so or discussed what he should say. No. 10 had not even warned the News Department that it was being done – so that they could at least pretend that the F.O. were in on it; and Horace Wilson had not even mentioned it to Cadogan, though he saw him at four yesterday.

H., though he did not show it, was annoyed and asked to see the P.M. We then heard that he had left for Chequers last evening! H. therefore wrote to him and had it sent down by the pouch.

Alec Cadogan feels it particularly unwise to speak now of arms limitation, anyway a very difficult subject which needs most careful preparation and mention of it will only make Germany think we are feeling the strain. Similarly, to speak glibly of settling Franco-Italian relations will cause suspicion in France, where it will be thought we are preparing to do a deal, and make Italy think so too and encourage her to stiffen her demands.

The P.M. said practically the same as what he said to the lobby correspondents in a private letter to Nevile Henderson a month or so ago. H. then followed it up with a letter of his own, saying he thought the P.M. took an over-optimistic view.

But what is one to think of the P.M.'s behaviour in not even speaking to H. before he gave such an important interview? Is it mere obtuseness to decent behaviour; is it jealousy again and determination to do everything himself? Is it a reply to H.'s recent "Halt, Major Road Ahead" speech which No. 10 thought too stiff?

Of course the rumour has started that H. and the P.M. no longer see eye-to-eye.

March 12th

Franco is not being kind to the Government for having recognised him. After declaring a blockade of the Spanish coasts (submarines to sink at sight within three-mile limit) and introducing a special penal law to deal with those who fought against him (in spite of our pleas for assurances against reprisals), though, it is fair to say, it does not contain a death penalty, he is now, we learn, about to join the anti-Comintern Pact.[1] Quinones[2] is much disturbed at the strength of German and Italian influence and is most anxious for the democracies to get in with Franco.

March 13th

P.M. has written a contrite letter to H. about the interview with lobby correspondents, saying it was entirely his fault, he had never thought the Press would take it so literally, he had been under the impression that the F.O. had been consulted and he would not do it again!

H. amused and (?) half-convinced.

March 14th

Fresh Czech crisis – a nice comment on P.M.'s interview. Slovakia declares herself independent with German support, Czechs reported to have acquiesced before German threats (we know German troops are on the march towards the Czech frontiers), Czech Minister of Foreign Affairs on the way to see Hitler, reports that Germany is appointing two *Staathalters* for Prague and Bratislava, and troops move in tonight.

We had a meeting in H.'s room to discuss the position. It was agreed we must make no empty threats since we were not going to fight for Czechoslovakia any more than for Danzig, although we

---

1. Originally between Germany and Japan in November 1936, it had been merged with the Rome-Berlin Axis when Italy joined in November 1937.
2. Chargé d'Affaires of the Spanish Embassy.

would fight for Switzerland, Belgium, Holland or Tunis. We should stop Stanley's visit to Berlin (due to start tomorrow) and perhaps recall Henderson to report. P.M. might also make a statement deploring this departure from Munich spirit. We should not, however, regard ourselves as in any way guaranteeing Czechoslovakia.

H. saw P.M. this evening and there is to be further discussion tomorrow about Stanley visit. H. thinks he ought certainly not now to go.

March 16th

Meeting in H.'s room to discuss his speech in House of Lords on Monday. P.M. is speaking in Birmingham tomorrow and H. had previously talked to him about it.

March 17th

Rumanian Minister (Tilea[1]) called to see Secretary of State and said that Germany was demanding in the form of an ultimatum a monopoly of Rumanian exports in return for restriction of industrial output in Germany's favour: in return for this, Germany would guarantee Rumania's frontiers, the Rumanian Minister asked whether H.M.G. would support Rumania if she were attacked: he also asked if it would make any difference to our attitude if Poland and Rumania agreed to a treaty provision applying against German aggression, and if the Balkan Entente proclaimed joint determination to guarantee each other's frontiers.

As a result of this visit telegrams were sent off to Warsaw, Ankara, Athens, Belgrade and Moscow informing them of the demands and instructing our representatives to ascertain what would be the attitude of the Governments. Also to the French Government informing them of what we were doing and saying that before H.M.G. took a decision they would wish to consult the French Government.

March 18th

No fresh news until midday when we received a telegram from Hoare at Bucharest asking for suspension of action on our telegrams pending

1. I. M. Tilea, Rumanian Minister 1938, started Free Rumanian Movement when the Germans invaded his country.

a further telegram from him. Cabinet had meanwhile been summoned for 5 p.m. and by that time a further telegram had come from Hoare to say he thought our information so improbable that he had seen the Foreign Minister – Gafencu – who had said "there was not a word of truth in the reported German ultimatum". The Foreign Minister was bewildered at what the Rumanian Minister here had said, adding that the commercial negotiations between Rumania and Germany were proceeding normally as between equals and "*for the moment*" no threat to Rumanian economic or territorial independence had been made.

This mysterious affair was not made clearer by the return of the Rumanian Minister to the Foreign Office today, when he told Cadogan that he still maintained a threat was being made. The Cabinet, I gather, favours an inquiry being pursued in the various capitals as originally intended: they took the view that if Rumania were attacked and defended herself, we must support her. (In support of the Minister, I must say that just before his original visit to H. on Friday I was rung up by Walter Elliot who said that Bernays[1] had just telephoned to him saying that Marthe Bibesco[2] had sent him a message to the effect that she had just been speaking to Bucharest to the President of the Council who had told her that Germany had presented an economic ultimatum to Rumania. I told this to H. immediately before showing the Minister into his room when he came to say exactly the same thing.)

A.E. came to see H. yesterday and today mainly in connection with his idea of enlarging the Government to one of real national union, which he launched in his speech in the House of Commons on Tuesday. H. was sympathetic, I gather, and said he would press it on the P.M.

P.M. spoke at Birmingham last night – half the speech devoted to justifying Munich, the other half to reproaching Hitler for broken promises.

Dirksen came to complain about Duff Cooper's attack on Hitler. H. fairly let him have it, referring to Hitler's own attacks on Benes. We hear that Dirksen has now been recalled in reply to our recall of N. Henderson.

French Government are asking for full powers from the Chamber.

1. Mr R. Bernays, M.P.
2. Princess Marthe Bibesco, a Rumanian writer who lived in Paris.

March 19th

Cabinet last night approved the line proposed by the P.M., viz. that approaches should be made to Soviet Russia, Poland, Yugoslavia, Greece, Turkey and Rumania to ascertain if they would join us in resisting German aggression in Europe. It was agreed that if these assurances were forthcoming, a public announcement should be made of our intention to resist any such action by Germany.

P.M., H., Chancellor of the Exchequer and President of the Board of Trade met this morning to draft the telegrams – and again at 4.30 in the afternoon.

Maisky called on H. with a proposal for a conference at Bucharest to discuss joint action.

I lunched with A.E. He said that the idea of enlarging the Government was being pressed by H. and Stanley: that a National Government with Labour in was thought possible owing to Labour's attitude towards P.M.; but that he thought he and Winston might be asked to join. A.E. asked me what I thought he should do. I said I thought he ought to get in some more of his own followers too (e.g. Bobbety) or at least insist on, say, Crookshank being brought into Cabinet – otherwise he risked finding himself again, as last year, unable to enforce his views. I think he is over-optimistic of likelihood of P.M. doing this, and told him so, saying that I was sure P.M. would not do so unless his hand were forced by a revolt in the Cabinet or the majority or by the Central Office.

Henderson returned yesterday and looked very shattered. He said Hitler was now quite unpredictable: he thought his action against Czechoslovakia was taken simply and solely out of fury aroused by broadcast accounts of alleged Czech atrocities against Germans – all of which had been either invented or magnified by Goebbels. He did not know what Hitler might do now as a result of P.M.'s speech and Duff Cooper's remarks.

March 20th

Cabinet met at 10.30 to consider telegrams. No fresh news. Debate in Lords today. H. made a great speech – very impressive. House and galleries packed. After he sat down, Archbishop of Canterbury got up – and everybody rushed away until the House assumed its ordinary afternoon appearance. Served the old sheep right – nobody wishes to listen to his mouthing nowadays.

Meanwhile the telegrams, after being revised and approved by Cabinet and due to go off, were held by Cadogan after a visit from Corbin this afternoon as he expressed strongly the view that the French Government would not think them strong enough and that unless he said more definitely that we would fight for Rumania, then Poland, etc., would not play at all. H., A.C., P.M. and H. Wilson discussed this later at 7.30, and finally agreed on a slightly amended text which was then despatched. (I must say telegrams as first drafted after Cabinet amounted to no more than reaffirmation of our existing League of Nations obligation to consult together – we were all to declare that in event of aggression we would at once consult; of course, what is now wanted is the League of Nations, but the P.M. has so derided that body that he cannot any longer make use of it. Yet there at Geneva is all the machinery necessary for consultation *and* action if once the will is there.)

A letter is to be sent by the P.M. to Mussolini recalling the Rome visit and what Mussolini had then said of Hitler's peaceful intentions and asking him to use his influence in sense of peace.

We are also inviting U.S. Government to resume the naval exchanges of information begun last year, adding that we may not now be able to reinforce fleet in Far East on a larger scale.

Situation is fairly satisfactory. H.M.G. seem to be taking position seriously at last. Public opinion undoubtedly stirred. Still doubtful how far we will commit ourselves to *action*. Uncertain what Hitler will do next. I doubt of his climbing down and feel he can only be stopped by violent means – war or internal revolt. Very possible that we shall get it in the neck to begin with. Mussolini very uncertain factor – undoubtedly sore at Hitler taking everything and not even consulting him – may either make him go for France in hope of forcing Hitler in on his behalf, or make him readier to listen to reason from our side and prepare to betray Hitler. One thing certain, that Italy ought to be dealt with drastically if she shows signs of moving against us. If we knock out Italy, the Mediterranean and the Balkans are relieved and we shall be free to deal with Japan and Germany in North and West and help the Balkans. So long as Italy is actively hostile or doubtful, we cannot send ships off to Far East or be sure of Canal or Egypt, valuable forces being pinned down for defence in Mediterranean.

French Government have got their full powers and are very resolute, Phipps says.

March 21st

The telegram as finally sent off to Soviet Russia, Poland and France last night proposes a formal declaration that in the event of any action which constitutes a threat to the political independence of any State in Europe, the respective Governments undertake to consult immediately as to the steps to be taken to offer joint resistance to any such actions.

(Note: attacks not only by Germany – "amateur collective security" – as it is described by Roger Makins.[1])

Hoare has now seen the King who confirms that no actual ultimatum has been yet addressed to Rumania. The Rumanian Government, however, are now much disturbed at Hungarian mobilisation and concentration in Ruthenia. They are concentrated in turn towards that quarter.

Aras[2] came to see H. today and said that Turkey would do what Great Britain did – regardless of the replies of the others. If Great Britain were at war, Turkey would join – whether the war began in the East, South East or West, but Turkey must know the British attitude.

The French President arrived today.

We hear Germany will probably walk into Memel tonight.

We learn (but not from the French Government) that Daladier and Bonnet are negotiating secretly with Mussolini.

March 22nd

Roosevelt has replied about the resumption of the naval talks. He agrees but wants it done inconspicuously through the Naval Attaché in Washington.

The Poles are in a dilemma because they fear that any public declaration in which they were included would only bring down upon them the wrath of the Germans.

Bonnet gave us the impression that we were too bellicose. The

1. Sir Roger Makins (now Lord Sherfield), Ambassador to U.S.A. 1953–1956.
2. Turkish Ambassador.

P.M. and H. told him the issue now was nothing less than an attempt by Germany to dominate Europe.

March 23rd

As a result of the talks with Bonnet, a fresh telegram has gone to Poland – proposing that there should be no declaration but that we should develop the Rumanian position. If Rumania were attacked, we would fight for her – would Poland do likewise? And the same thing vice-versa as regards an attack on Poland. It was also proposed that Soviet Russia should not appear in the forefront with Poland but that we should reach a separate agreement with Soviet Russia providing for support in the event of war arising.

Rumanian Government told Hoare yesterday that Hungary's mobilisation was reaching threatening proportions and that twenty-five German divisions were on the Hungarian frontier. They considered general mobilisation essential but would do it with all secrecy in next ten days. We replied that Polish Ambassador and our representative in Budapest were seeking a *détente*.

We hear that Beck is now going to propose a secret agreement of consultation with Great Britain.

March 24th

We heard last night that Rumania had signed her trade agreement with Germany – giving away, as it appears, almost all her economic freedom.

P.M. reproached Bonnet the other day with slow progress of French air armament. He retorted to H. yesterday by urging us to adopt conscription.

March 25th

Polish Ambassador came yesterday with Beck's proposal for a secret understanding with Great Britain to consult as to action in event of aggression. Poland cannot agree to a public declaration in which Soviet Russia figures, as being too provocative to Hitler. She is also terrified of any publicity.

Soviets meanwhile have accepted our declaration plan and suggest

Balkans, Baltics and Scandinavians should all be asked to accede after. The French Government also agree.

Poles still working hard on Rumanians and Hungarians to make them sensible.

Long meeting in H.'s room about our future policy in view of Polish attitude and of Rumania's signature of her trade agreement with Germany.

H. feels adherence of Poland is essential to any effective scheme to hold up Germany in event of aggression. He also feels we should not make it too difficult for Italy to betray her Ally. He therefore thinks we cannot have Russia in the forefront of the picture, although both for internal reasons and because of her ultimate military value, if only as our arsenal, we must keep her with us. He proposes to discuss all this very frankly with Beck when he comes. He is equally sure that we cannot possibly agree to any secret understanding with Poland because of our Geneva pledge and because of Parliament. What we want to secure is the certainty for Germany of a war on two fronts – East and West – in the event of any aggression by her. The line of approach he proposes is this: to ask Poland if she will herself resist aggression by Germany upon her, and to say, if so, Great Britain and France will fight for her too: then to go a step further and ask if she will fight for Rumania if attacked as, if so, we and France would do so too. He would then put the same questions, *mutatis mutandis*, to Rumania. As regards Russia, his idea at present is to suggest that she and France should simplify the Franco-Soviet Pact which is at present surrounded with exceptions and turn it into a straight defensive alliance.

Referring to the difficulty of conducting delicate and swift diplomacy with a parliamentary government, he said it all really now pointed to the need for an All-Party Government.

O.H. to Secretary of State – March 26th 1939

You mentioned on Saturday how it had become nearly impossible to carry on diplomacy now without a non-party government. The need is really a crying one. A non-party, or rather an all-party, government would have the following obvious advantages:

a. foreign policy – easier to conduct swiftly and confidentially,
b. home policy – conscription or national compulsory register, labour restrictions, diluting of labour, overtime, pooling of trade secrets, "mobilisation of industry" all become possible,

c. psychological effect at home and abroad.

The difficulty lies in the personal position of the Prime Minister *vis-à-vis* Labour. It is very doubtful, indeed I believe impossible, that Labour would consent to serve under the present Prime Minister, who in the past has never taken the least trouble to reconcile them but has only embittered party divisions and gone out of his way to taunt them. Labour does not trust the Prime Minister. Lord Baldwin never allowed himself to get into this position.

A less good alternative would be the widening of the existing National Government by bringing back Anthony Eden and one or two of his friends, say Cranborne and Duff Cooper, promoting some of the good younger ones to the Cabinet, say Crookshank and Hudson, and introducing Winston Churchill. This would go some way towards placating Labour, but it would not avoid debates and I doubt if it would cover compulsory service or register or any serious modification of labour restrictions. It is also doubtful to my mind how far Winston Churchill and Anthony Eden would work with the Prime Minister, having regard to his methods and egocentric mentality. To bring back Anthony without Winston and merely to change one or two faces in the Cabinet would not be enough. It would antagonise the dictators without frightening them.

On the other hand, the country apart from the politicians would welcome an all-party government as an earnest that we were really getting down to the job, and it cannot understand the present impasse. Such a government would be the natural response at a time of national danger when every good man available is needed. It would be our counterpart to the French full powers.

If an all-party government could be formed under your leadership it would be acceptable to all. You are now regarded in all quarters as the most obvious successor to the present Prime Minister in spite of the House of Lords difficulty. What is required is a very drastic remodelling of the Government, many old ministers retiring to make way for new blood and for those representing the other parties in the new administration.

But, as I said at the beginning, the Prime Minister himself remains the great difficulty and obstacle. I do not believe that he would consent to bringing back Anthony and Co., still less Winston, except across his dead body. He believes they would be tiresome to him (and I am bound to say I think they would), and unless he is confronted by refusal of his present ministers to go on or by a serious party revolt in the House, I do not think that he would agree to enlarge his government; and even then he would probably prefer to resign himself.

I am afraid the Prime Minister honestly believes he can best handle the situation, with whatever far-reaching decisions including going to war may be involved, with the existing Cabinet. But I am equally afraid that it is not possible for this Government on a party basis to put across the measures which the national emergency requires.

March 27th

Foreign Policy Committee of Cabinet met to consider draft telegrams to Warsaw, Bucharest and Paris based on above considerations which P.M. had approved after talk with H. at No. 10 last night. The telegrams were approved by the Committee and were then despatched to our representatives at Warsaw and Bucharest, who were told to take no action in presenting proposals to Governments concerned until we had secured French Government's approval and latter had instructed their representatives to act too. Instructions also sent to Phipps to get French to agree.

I saw Jim Thomas late last night and I lunched with P. V. Emrys-Evans today – both spoke of rising indignation in country against Government's inaction on home front. They both agreed with me that P.M. would be most reluctant to enlarge Government. There are also reports of discussions in Cabinet over conscription. But I have no evidence of this and am sceptical. The usual wobblers are doubtless wobbling again. Stanley, De La Warr, Elliot – but when they have wept and confessed their *crise de conscience* and flagellated themselves, they will settle down again as usual. They have not the courage to resign or the loyalty to be silent.

No more news except that it is clear nothing can be done till we get Beck over here next week.

Mussolini's speech yesterday (I listened in) full of bluster and self-importance. I was horrified at the groans and catcalls at mention of Great Britain and France. The usual apotheosis of war and bloodshed – greeted with hysterical cries. "Those who live by the sword . . ." He does not make it any easier for France to make any approach.

Georges de Castellane[1] brought to dine a most interesting man, a Mr Archdeacon of the American Banker's Trust in Berlin, a British subject with a German mother. He said it was essential if we were to stop a war to show Hitler now unmistakably that we and France would fight if he attacked Poland. He would not face war on two fronts. Czechoslovakia was a try-on, and if we let it pass without further ado it was certain he would go for Poland. Germans were as

1. Marquis de Castellane, Counsellor at French Embassy.

much surprised as British at Czech invasion and were shocked at Hitler's treatment of P.M. after Munich: if we did not react vigorously, German people would never understand and would acquiesce in despair. There was still a pathetic belief in Germany in British power.

March 29th

I was in bed with a cold yesterday.

Cabinet this morning decided to announce doubling of the Territorial Army today – as a first gesture. Meanwhile demand for conscription or at least national compulsory register growing.

Colvin, Berlin correspondent of *News Chronicle*, called on H. today and made great impression. He said he was convinced Hitler would attack Poland very shortly unless it was made quite certain that we would then attack him. There would then be a good chance that German generals would stop him or revolt. Generals had been prepared to revolt in September if we had stood up to Hitler. H. took him over to P.M. and as a result it may be decided to announce at once, i.e. tomorrow, our decision to fight for Poland without awaiting Beck's reply.

March 30th

We sat up till one a.m. last night. H. came back after dinner to draft a statement for P.M. to make announcing an immediate guarantee to Poland by Great Britain and France pending the conclusion of the negotiations with the other Powers. This draft was considered by Cabinet Committee and then by Cabinet today. Telegrams were sent off to Warsaw and Paris proposing to make this announcement if Paris agreed. To Warsaw we merely said "we presumed it would be in accordance with their wishes".

March 31st

French and Polish Governments having agreed, Cabinet met today at twelve and finally approved statement which P.M. made in House of Commons at 2.45.

H. saw Maisky just before to tell him what we had decided.

We dined last night with the Birkenheads and met Camrose. Latter was very critical of P.M. and said he could never lead a really All-Party Government or carry compulsory powers as Labour did not trust him.

I saw Ewer today who was pleased at what was being done. He said compulsory powers could only be carried with approval of T.U.C. leaders – the parliamentary Labour leaders did not count. T.U.C. were very mistrustful of compulsory powers in capitalist hands and would take a lot of persuading.

April 3rd

P.M. is speaking in House of Commons today and H. has been preparing his brief over the weekend. Will he use it, I wonder, or put in some disastrous stuff of his own or Horace Wilson's? *The Times* and Beaverbrook began already on Saturday to imply that our guarantee was not so definite as all that and did not cover "every inch" of Polish territory. The Poles at once took fright and the P.M. had to issue a *démenti*. Beck arrives today, bringing with him, we hope, his reply to our wider proposals. Rumania is rather shy and says she must consult her partners of the Balkan Entente. Meanwhile I am afraid we have got on the wrong side of Russia: Seeds had a very bad interview with Litvinoff who professed to be outraged at having been left out in the end in spite of his proposal for a conference and his acceptance of a Four-Power Declaration and talked about isolating themselves. All the same, if we want to keep the Poles in, we cannot have the Russians in too. And the Poles are better military material immediately than the Russians in spite of their numbers and their arsenals.

Lunch with Rennie Smith[1] – very pro-Halifax since the Focus lunch: wants the Winston plan of a league of peace-loving states: mistrusts P.M. profoundly: despairs of Labour Party: says H. could talk over T.U.C. to agree either to join a National Government or to accept compulsory powers – convinced we are not going fast enough in "mobilising" the resources of the nation – a realist.

April 4th

Rumour reached us of an Italian coup against Albania.

Talks with Beck began – fairly satisfactory. He agreed at once

1. Labour M.P. 1924–1931. Lecturer and journalist.

that Poland and Great Britain should give a reciprocal guarantee. As regards Soviets, he made quite clear that Poland could not be party to an agreement with Soviet Russia which would only increase risk to Poland without compensating advantage. If we reached an agreement with Soviet Russia, Poland would have to make clear that it did not affect her own position. Beck said he wanted correct relations and he already had a non-aggression pact, but closer relations would mean a breaking point with Germany. The point was to get maximum collaboration from Soviet Russia without antagonising Germany, and suggested this might be done by France simplifying her pact with Soviet Russia.

As to Rumania, Beck was reluctant to commit himself further for fear of throwing Hungary into Germany's arms: he thought both Hungary and Italy were perturbed at Germany. He had an alliance with Rumania but it only applied against Russia. He wished to discuss with Rumanian Government before going further. He thought we should all give Rumania some backing – economic and military assistance – but not bring her into a rigid political system which would react on Hungary. He was also sticky about idea of regarding attack on Netherlands, Belgium, Switzerland and Denmark as *casus belli*.

April 5th

A ridiculous affair occurred today through Stanhope. Yesterday we had a report from Berlin that the Germans, in their rage, might just possibly deal a lightning blow at the fleet in harbour while the men were on Easter leave. We did not seriously believe it but felt that some precautions should be taken. H. talked to Stanhope with Alec and Van and suggested that S. should make it clear in some way (e.g. in a speech) that the Navy was always ready and was not to be caught out. Stanhope happened to be attending a concert on an aircraft carrier that night and in a speech to be broadcast said that just before leaving London some information had come in which had necessitated issuing orders for manning the A.A. guns! In the meanwhile the B.B.C. and the Admiralty had been in touch with No. 10, where Horace Wilson was horrified at what he regarded as the provocative character of this, referred to the P.M. in the country and got it cancelled on the wireless. The papers had, of course, already got it and the attempt at suppression as well, and there was a fine row in the House of Commons and the P.M. had to make a statement. All due to Stanhope being heavy-footed.

April 6th

One of our minor problems is to know what to do with Henderson, who is now here having been ordered back "to report" after the annexation of Czechoslovakia. H. asked me and I said I would not send him back on personal grounds as I thought his reports were bad and had a bad effect here, whilst his attitude in Berlin had the effect of convincing the Germans we were flabby. On the main question of whether there was any advantage or disadvantage in not having an Ambassador there, I rather agreed with him that it was better in principle to have an Ambassador. H. has also talked to Alec and it is under consideration whether he should not now be replaced. But it is complicated. No Ambassador can do any good in Berlin at present. It is going to be announced that Nevile Henderson has been given a short period of leave. I discussed with A.C. whom we could send there – the favourites are Archie Clark-Kerr[1] and Horace Seymour.

April 7th

Rumours and reports of Italian landing in Albania. Crolla (Italian Chargé d'Affaires) came to see H. at twelve with a personal message from Mussolini saying that he had read with great interest the P.M.'s statement in the House of Commons and he gave his formal assurance that the solution of the Italo-Albanian question would take place in such a form as not to provoke a crisis in Anglo-Italian relations or in the international situation in general.

At the same moment we learned that Italian warships are bombarding the coast and landing troops!

H. off to lunch from twelve to three and not to be found.

I saw Beck off at two.

(H. saw Lothian this week and after showing him a telegram from Lindsay describing a talk with Roosevelt in which he had asked him about L. as Ambassador, and the latter gave a grudging and contemptuous acquiescence, Lothian decided that he would like to go and H. has agreed – what a bad appointment!)

1. Just appointed Ambassador to China.

274

Maurice Ingram dined with me and when we were discussing the day's doings there was a knock at the front door. I went to open it and saw a strange-looking man who said he was Mr Solomon and wanted to see Lord Halifax's secretary. I asked him what he wanted and he said he wished to send Lord Halifax a message that we had just 36 hours to unite Christendom and the Moslems against Italy if we acted at once – as they were both so enraged at Mussolini's behaviour in Albania!

A further telegram was sent to Rome last night saying we were gravely concerned: we found it difficult to believe that the difficulty could not have been solved by negotiation: if reports of landings were true, it would appear that independence and frontiers of Albania were threatened in spite of the Anglo-Italian New Agreement. We asked, therefore, for further explanation.

April 8th

There was little fresh news this morning. It is still not clear whether Tirana has yet been occupied, but heavy fighting seems to have been in progress. No news from our Minister in Durazzo about whose safety we have telegraphed to Rome.

The meeting of Ministers who were near London proposed by H. yesterday has developed into a gathering of ten – including Simon and Sam Hoare, who will not be left out.

P.M. still in Scotland fishing does not intend to return for the moment.

Both Winston and Attlee are pressing for meeting of Parliament next week. H. quite disposed to agree to this so as to allow public opinion to express itself.

Van very anxious about British ships in Mediterranean, certain of which are in Italian ports at the moment. They will probably be ordered away today.

This is certainly Italy's counterpart to absorption of Czechoslovakia – and equally futile because Albania was already under Italian control and exploitation. Why offend world opinion – and on Good Friday? And Queen Zog escaping with her two-day baby? Is it a concerted measure with Hitler – or has it been taken independently just as Hitler moved into Czechoslovakia without consulting Mussolini? Because of a desperate need to show some results? In any case, the presence of Italian garrisons in Albania will have a festering effect

275

in the Balkans where relations to date had been getting healthier and healthier, even Bulgaria getting on to better terms with her neighbours. Zog himself had both kept the country quiet and satisfied his neighbours. There is not a shred of truth in Italian allegations that the country was in disorder, that Italians were being maltreated or – most fantastic of all – that Zog was about to attack Yugoslavia.

It will help to open the eyes of world opinion (and especially British opinion) to the fact that Mussolini is just as evil as Hitler and that is to the good. But it is impossible for us to do anything to stop it: it also makes it impossible for us to do anything for Yugoslavia (who seems to have reluctantly acquiesced in Italian coup). Our only reply can be to organise an alliance with Greece and Turkey. With Poland at one end and Turkey at the other, we can build up our anti-axis front, fitting in Rumania and Greece in between.

Bad for the P.M. His other line of appeasement is now shown to be bankrupt.

Meanwhile Franco has joined the anti-Comintern Pact.

Perth reported that he had seen Ciano yesterday, just back from a flight over Durazzo. Ciano said he fully intended to respect Albanian independence. A large number of chiefs had asked Mussolini to intervene and save them from Zog. Italian troops had been sent to restore order. Italy would require a new treaty giving her certain rights. He had told the Yugoslav Minister of Zog's request for Italian troops to launch attack on Nish!

Meeting of Ministers this morning decided to move ships from Italian ports, to suggest to P.M. that Parliament should meet on Thursday and to press on with Greek and Turkish arrangements.

P.M. returns tonight.

The Albanian Minister came today to appeal for help for his country.

April 9th

Crolla went to see H. last night after dinner to express concern at tone of press messages and probable effect on Mussolini. The Italian Government had acted in accordance with wishes of Albania – proof of good intentions was shown by calm of neighbours. Crolla referred to reports that we might occupy Corfu. H. denied this at once and said it was not our way but that we would take a very grave view if

276

anybody else did so. C. referred to report that we might denounce Anglo-Italian agreement and bad effect this would have on Mussolini and on withdrawal from Spain. H. said no decision to this effect had been taken but great good would be done if Mussolini did withdraw from Spain.

Greek Minister came at 11.15 this morning in great agitation at reports read by Greek Government that Mussolini was in fact going to occupy Corfu. (We had already had reports of this from press correspondents in Paris, Rome and Berlin independently last night.) H. went over to see P.M. at once and came out again to see Crolla. The latter came again with a message from Mussolini at twelve.

Chiefs of Staff met at three. A further stiff telegram was sent to Perth instructing him to go at once to Ciano and repeat Crolla's assurances and say that if what he had said about respect for Greek territory was true the Italian representative should inform the Greek Government, adding a clear warning of grave view we should take if Corfu were attacked. Phipps is also being told to see Daladier and Bonnet and inform them and to add that if Greece is attacked we should feel bound to assist her and to ask if the French Government concur.

Crolla came again at 5.30 to say all Italians would be out of Spain after the Madrid Review; Duce was giving assurances to Greece to respect her integrity on land and islands.

Late last night came reply from Phipps who had seen both Daladier and Bonnet – very satisfactory. Daladier did all the talking. Bonnet quite silent. Daladier said French Government would declare war on Italy. He did not believe any Italian assurances. He thought Albanian coup was the prelude to a big Italian-German offensive from North Sea to Egypt. French Government were bringing Atlantic fleet into Mediterranean, concentrating air force against Italy and reinforcing Tunis and Somaliland. French Ministers feared a Fascist coup against Gibraltar or Egypt. Mediterranean was vital for both France and Great Britain.

April 10th

Cabinet met this morning and Foreign Political Committee this evening. Parliament on Thursday. Rumanian Minister came to see H. to ask for an immediate guarantee: they do not want a Four-Power Agreement as implying encirclement of Germany.

277

Crolla came to say Mussolini agreed to our making use of his assurances in debate.

O.H. to Secretary of State – April 11th 1939

You said the other day that you wanted to gain time because every month gave us 600 more aeroplanes.

While I don't wish to emulate Van, I do find it very difficult to decide in my own mind whether delay really does benefit us.

By delay we gain 600 aeroplanes, etc., a month,

we also perhaps consolidate British opinion and certainly protect ourselves from any charge of precipitancy or warmongering.

On the other hand,

we encourage the view of the forward school in Germany and Italy that we don't really mean business,

we make our potential friends and protégées despair of us (the small nations must be on the side of the big battalions and unless we can convince them that we do mean business, they must perforce make their peace with the Totalitarians, i.e. Greece, Turkey, Rumania).

Therefore, unless we can really tie up the small nations, delay means that we have more aeroplanes but fewer allies.

Then there is the moral aspect. We shall only get the British public to give their best and to fight on a moral issue. The British public as I see it believes we now have such an issue both as regards Germany and as regards Italy. American opinion, which has always been much more outspoken than our own, thinks the same. I am very much afraid that delay may mean loss of ground at home in America, as well as among our small would-be allies in Europe.

But what, it may be asked, can we do more than we are doing? We are getting on with Poland, Rumania, Turkey and Greece. I believe we ought to wave much more the banner of moral indignation and righteousness, and line up more publicly with the Pope and President Roosevelt. I doubt if we can maintain the Anglo-Italian Agreement without loss of face out of all proportion to its intrinsic value to us. After all, what Mussolini has done in Albania is quite as bad as anything which Hitler has done and we should be very careful not to condone it. I believe we should gain by a firm stand on a moral issue more than by delay on strategical grounds.

I am absolutely convinced that nothing will convert Mussolini into a friend of ours or of peace. (I was in Rome during the first three years of Fascism and have studied it from the beginning.) In this respect his system is exactly like Hitler's. They are forces of evil and there can be no peace until they are overthrown. We may succeed in overthrowing them without a war by internal revolution if we look ugly enough or they may break down from lack of popular support after a war has begun, but the more we seem to compound with them, e.g. by maintaining the Anglo-Italian Agreement and talking about future collaboration, the more I feel we get the worst of both worlds. We discourage the sensible moderate people in Germany and Italy, we antagonise the Opposition at home and the latent discontent with the Government's foreign policy (which is still thought not to be moving fast or vigorously enough), and we lose the goodwill of America.

April 12th

Telegram has gone off to Turks asking if they will support Greeks if attacked and if we support them and the French do so too. (The French have agreed to this.) In addition, a further telegram is being sent to say Great Britain will help Turkey if Turkey will help Great Britain in a war with Italy.

April 13th

Cabinet agreed to terms of statement and to include Rumania in the immediate guarantee. This latter point was decided at last moment in view of French pressure. We had intended not to give a guarantee at any rate until after we had had Polish reply.

The news today points to the probability of King of Italy becoming King of Albania with Ciano as Viceroy!

H. is anxious to find a way round Russian difficulty and is now working on the idea of proposing to Stalin that he should make a unilateral declaration of support against aggression on much the same lines as we have.

Debate in House of Lords this afternoon. H., dead tired, had only scraps of time to prepare his speech. We worked all through luncheon at the Foreign Office, piecing it together. He hopes to get away tomorrow to Yorkshire – so do I.

A.E. spoke in debate in House of Commons last night – against H.'s advice. He came to see him before the debate. H. said to me afterwards he feared A.E. had not the virtues of restraint and if it had been him he would have remained away in Yorkshire. I think H. is right.

April 14th

Office meeting to discuss Russia. It was decided to send a telegram to Seeds to see Litvinoff and put to him idea of a unilateral declaration and for H. to tell Maisky this afternoon. When Maisky came, he was unexpectedly reasonable and said Soviet Russia was thinking of giving Rumania (*not* Poland) some such declaration.

H. and I escaped at 4.30 to catch our train – he to Garrowby – me to the Edens at Kirkdale.

April 16th

Kirkdale Manor – Yorks.

The news today was Roosevelt's message to the dictators – great enthusiasm.

We have had long talks with A.E. about his position. Noel Coward is also here and very vehement in his feelings about P.M.'s treatment of A.E. We discussed whether he should have attacked last April and all rather agreed that he should have done so, but more doubtful whether he should do so now (though Noel Coward thought he should). A.E. had some reason for thinking Government were now thinking of enlarging basis and asking him and Winston back. A.E. said he would not go back without Winston and he did not think Winston would go in without him. I said A.E. should certainly refuse to go back alone: he quite agreed. Winston had had an unwonted and prolonged talk with Chief Whip. I said I was sure P.M. would not bring him back unless forced to do so: this might happen through a press campaign or by a revolt in the Cabinet or by pressure from the Central Office. H. and Stanley certainly wanted it. Sam Hoare too, they say. *Daily Telegraph* wants it but has not yet come out into open. A.E. does not believe P.M. can last out physically much longer as he already shows signs of failing. A.E. had spoken to H. about need for looking to future but does not know if anything is happening. I doubt it. H. would be a good P.M. we all agree. Would H. like it? We think "yes". A.E. said again he himself would much rather be at Foreign Office than at No. 10.

A.E. is itching to be back at work again and cannot bear to be out of things at this critical time. But I am afraid he much overestimates likelihood of his coming back soon. P.M. does not want him back, as I am sure he thinks A.E. would cause him trouble. I tried to urge him to be patient and said I thought the outside limit of this enforced idleness would be the general elections which must almost certainly take place in the autumn. He really feels sorry for the P.M., not understanding why he should not welcome his help. P.M. had been much touched at his speech in the last debate (which H. and I had advised him against making) and sent him a most grateful note.

April 18th

Poles agree to include attacks on our small Western neighbours being included in their guarantee – but are still sticky about Rumanians and resent our unilateral guarantee to latter.

Soviets have now weighed in with a comprehensive plan for a mutual guarantee between Great Britain, France and Soviet Russia with various frills to cover neighbours.

April 19th

The movement of the German fleet to the South of Spain is causing much speculation. Is it bluff? Or is it a real threat? The Admiralty say the former. In any case, it is being successful in agitating the Portuguese and the French.

Another theory is that Hitler means to stage a coup in Danzig for his birthday.

The Turkish reply to our proposals is not very satisfactory. They want a vague public declaration and a secret understanding with us to cover wide assurances and staff talks. They are also trying to promote the entry of Bulgaria into the Balkan entente. They want to form a United Balkan States against Germany. They are working on the Bulgars and the Rumanians in this sense.

The truth is no one believes we can fulfil our new commitments – hence absolute need for compulsory service. French are pressing us strongly and we hear that even Roosevelt is dismayed that we haven't yet taken this step. No foreigners can understand it, and without this weapon our diplomacy is deprived of half its force as a deterrent to the dictators and as an encouragement to our friends.

April 20th

The new Ministry of Supply was announced with Burgin at its head. The effect can be imagined on a public which owing to rumours had been led to expect that it would be Winston. A ghastly selection which has gone very badly. What, however, is far more important, the Government have decided on a measure of compulsory service which is to be announced next week. Henderson is to be sent back to his post as a counter-weight to the effect of this decision. We can only be thankful that it has been taken at last.

Trouble has arisen over Loraine's credentials which were signed some time ago and contain naturally enough no reference to the "King of Albania". Perth was told to sound Ciano and explain that we could not at present recognise but that we hoped in time to be able to do so – in the meanwhile we counted on Mussolini not to make unnecessary difficulties over Loraine's credentials being in the old form. Ciano was very tiresome about it and implied that they must be torn up and fresh ones issued. Perth, who is to have his farewell with Mussolini too on Saturday, is to take it up with him personally. Thank God, however, Perth is to leave next Monday anyway and it is too late now to prolong him again (though H. inclined to doing so). I cannot say how relieved I shall be when he is finally away.

April 21st

One cannot tell from day to day what may happen. We are now past Hitler's birthday and the next date is April 28th, when he gives his reply to Roosevelt before the Reichstag. It is generally agreed that Hitler is in explosive state because of fury at our guarantee to Poland against whom he was preparing a frame-up. He may still have a go at Danzig on the assumption that we should not fight for what is not a part of Poland. Or he may go South East and, working through Hungary, go for Yugoslavia or Rumania. The encirclement argument is being used in Germany to considerable effect in order to rally opinion round the Nazi Government as the Germans with their claustrophobia take it readily. Or, finally, there is never to be excluded the possibility, however improbable, of an attempt at a sudden knock-out blow against us. Here the development of A.R.P. is our best deterrent. Again, Mussolini may move once more. There are reports of German soldiers going through Italy to Libya, and the presence of the German fleet in the South may mean pressure on Italy. Italy is certainly heaping up troops in North Africa and she has now a very large force in Albania, which is being turned into a military base. We gather Mussolini did not tell or consult Hitler before he went into Albania, which was a counter-demonstration by the south end of the Axis to Czechoslovakia. We are getting the usual influences from Italy in favour of buying her off, and we have gone so far as to urge France to open negotiations with her. (I think this a mistake: we ought to ignore Italy now and go ahead with our new policy and treat her as part of Germany: we know she is not part of Germany and that the Axis is unpopular, but I am sure that is the right way to handle blackmailers.)

I can see the encirclement argument. The faults of the past have produced Hitler, and now in our necessity we are forced to start a new encirclement to stop him. It ought and would never have got to this if we had faced our responsibilities earlier and entered into firm mutual guarantees of collective European security. But there it is, and there is nothing, I am convinced, to be done with Hitler except to ring him in. But we must always be on the look-out to convert the present system into a generalised one and not to slop back into isolationism. In the meantime, while ringing Hitler in, we are not aggressive, non-expansionist, and always ready to talk. But the German people being what they are it is difficult to put across.

April 23rd

Went with H. to meet Gafencu at Victoria. He looks very young and pleasant – much better than the last Rumanian Minister of Foreign Affairs.

Our decision to introduce conscription has been imparted most secretly to the French as a lever to get them going with Italy. Mussolini tells Perth that the ball is on their side of the net as Bonnet had already made certain indirect approaches to which Mussolini had responded favourably, since when nothing more has occurred. (Mussolini has played up, incidentally, over Loraine's credentials and says he will accept them as they stand, i.e. having been signed by the King before the addition of Albania.)

April 25th

Gafencu thinks Hitler's next push will be against Poland over Danzig, and also for colonies. His attitude towards Soviet Russia is much the same as Beck's. He does not trust her and believes her real objective still to be world revolution. He does not want open association with Russia any more than Poland does. He is very doubtful of the ability of the Yugoslavs and Prince Paul to resist German and Italian pressure. He is strongly opposed to any territorial concession to Bulgaria. Gafencu himself makes an excellent impression and H. likes him very much.

April 26th

When H. and I were driving in a taxi to say goodbye to Gafencu at Victoria, he told me how very badly the P.M.'s talk with the T.U.C. leaders this morning about conscription had gone. They had apparently been shocked that all this machinery was being applied for only some 180,000 men, implying, as H. thought, that a bolder measure would not have been objected to so much. Yet the measure had been whittled down and hedged about on purpose to placate Labour. I said that the trouble was the P.M. was not trusted by the Opposition whatever he did and they still did not trust his foreign policy. Moreover, although the foreign policy was now very largely that of the Opposition, so long as no attempt was made to broaden the Government, one could hardly be surprised that the Opposition should continue to mistrust and oppose. But ever since the P.M. had been in power, he had pursued a policy the Left did not approve, especially up to Munich. H. caught me up at this and said *he* was as much responsible for foreign policy as P.M. I said that was so but that the Left did trust H. and they believed that the recent change of our policy and its stiffening was due to his influence. The Left would take anything from him. H. said, "Oh, that is only what Anthony tells you!" I said, "No, it was based on all sorts of opinion – journalists and people generally." H. said that they only like you while you do the things they like. I said I did not think so, but I thought that once you had built up a fund of confidence you could do what you liked with people. I reminded him of India and said what he did in India would never be forgotten. He said he was attacked by half the

284

Conservative Party. I replied that nonetheless he had gone on with that policy which happened to be the policy of which the Left approved and his attitude over that had put him on a pedestal from which he would never be knocked off. At that point we had reached Victoria.

P.M.'s announcement about conscription went badly in House of Commons too: failure to consult T.U.C. and Labour earlier and the fact that a pledge against it had been given as lately as end of March being chief causes of bitterness.[1] Yet Cabinet themselves only decided on it a week ago, and even then, not as a broad measure so much as one of immediate necessity in order to enable them to keep the Anti-Aircraft Defences permanently manned. The usual hand-to-mouth methods.

There is to be a debate tomorrow.

April 27th

Reply to Russia is still under discussion between us and French.
Daladier is still opposed to any approach to Italy.

April 29th

Further telegram to Paris about Russia. We wish to revert to our original idea of a unilateral declaration that Soviets would afford assistance if desired and in way most convenient if Great Britain and France are involved in hostilities as a result of their obligations. H.'s object is not to lose Soviet, not to jeopardise the common front and not to give too much handle to Hitler's anti-Comintern propaganda.

Hitler's speech yesterday leaves us fairly calm. It seems to leave matters much where they were, but William Strang thinks it ominous.

Meanwhile conscription appears to be going down better than seemed likely at first. Labour is divided about it, and if only the P.M. were trusted, I doubt if there would be any trouble at all. But so long as he will not have back even those on his own side, A.E. and Winston, etc. – who always advocated the present policy – how can Labour be blamed for doubting its sincerity?

We learn that Ciano and François-Poncet[2] have had a conversation

1. The Labour and Liberal parties opposed the Bill.
2. Now French Ambassador in Rome.

285

in which the former actually defined Italy's claims as a free-zone at Jibuti, two seats on the Suez Canal Company and reversion to 1896 Convention for Tunis. We are urging Bonnet and Daladier to go ahead. Bonnet is working as usual behind Daladier's back and through Phipps to bring the necessary pressure on Daladier, who is very sticky. Anyway, it looks as if Mussolini were in a bad way; though it is obvious that he cannot openly break off the Axis, he may be seeking to prepare the ground for its betrayal in the hour of need; his manœuvres to form a Hungarian-Yugoslav-Italian bloc look to be aimed as much against German penetration into the Adriatic as against anything else.

Meanwhile German propaganda is taking two forms – the old encirclement story – to which the only reply is that "the peace front" is non-aggressive and if it came to that would be prepared to guarantee Germany against aggression – and the preposterous suggestion that the Eastern States are confronted with a choice between Soviet domination and that of Nazi Germany – to which we can only say that nobody is going to be dominated by anyone in our world.

May 3rd

"Appeasement" is raising its ugly head again. I keep hearing indirect reports that No. 10 is at it again behind our backs. There is the usual *Times* leader striking the defeatist note – "Danzig is not worth a war" and a letter from Lord Rushcliffe[1] whom nobody supposes could have written a letter himself and the paternity of which is attributed to Horace Wilson. I have written a note for the Secretary of State expressing my fears.[2] The return of Henderson to Berlin, the refusal to invite A.E. and Winston to join the Government, both are causing mistrust in the Government's sincerity in its present policy. H. told me he was fully conscious of the points I raised. I am nervous of our bringing excessive pressure to bear on the Poles to compromise over Danzig and on the French to treat with Mussolini. Phipps continues to intrigue against Daladier through Bonnet and to send us patently one-sided accounts of French opinion. Henderson sends us streams of hysterical telegrams and letters from Berlin.

1. See Appendix O for this classic statement of appeasement.
2. See Appendix P.

May 4th

The German fleet, which recently left German waters, is now assembling in Spanish and Portuguese ports on the flank of the route to be taken by the *Empress of Australia* with the King to Canada. The *Repulse* (which can deal with any of the German ships) is therefore being sent as escort. The German fleet, the Admiralty now say, is fully equipped for three months' war, store ships and everything, and is in position and absolutely ready, if required, to scatter and raid commerce. In fact, what the Admiralty say now is the exact reverse of what their views were when we first had the news of the fleet going out, when they said it was a sign that the Germans were *not* going to war and the ships could not be in a better place from *our* point of view. I continue to have my doubts of the Admiralty.

We had a meeting this morning about Danzig with Roger Makins, just back from seeing Burckhardt at Geneva, and Clifford Norton,[1] very definite that Danzig could not be ceded to Germany without Poland losing her independence through resultant economic pressure by Germany. A telegram has already been sent to Beck asking him to keep us informed and to go steady when he speaks in reply to Hitler on Friday.

News of Litvinoff's[2] resignation came as a complete surprise not only to Foreign Office but also to Seeds and Maisky (who has only just returned from Moscow and first heard of it by a Reuter message during a public dinner last night). Does it mean Russia will turn from the West towards isolation? And if so, won't she inevitably wobble into Germany's arms?

This evening came Monsignor Godfrey, the Apostolic Delegate, who brought a message to say the Pope proposed to invite Great Britain, France, Italy, Germany and Poland to a conference to discuss the causes likely to lead to war. H. very interested, says we cannot possibly refuse. Van full of mistrust and wants to insist on Russia being invited. H. is discussing it with P.M. tonight.

---

1. Counsellor at Embassy in Warsaw 1937–1939.
2. Replaced on May 3rd as Foreign Minister by Molotov.

May 5th

Telegram from Osborne at the Vatican today reports the proposed peace move of the Pope, but according to him, and contrary to what we supposed from Godfrey, the Pope does not intend to convene the Conference himself but only to urge the Powers concerned to get together themselves. If this is true, it is a very different thing – much more dangerous. It is one thing to participate in a conference with the Pope in the Chair, so to speak, but quite another to have a Five-Power Conference, which would be much too like Munich over again. This must be cleared up and we must consult the French and Poles.

H. saw Camrose yesterday at the instigation of R. A. Butler, who wished him to urge Camrose not to allow such "provocative" leaders in the *Daily Telegraph*! When I heard of it I warned H. of the disastrous effect Sam Hoare had had on Camrose when he tried to swing him during the crisis in the autumn and impressed on him how sound Camrose really was, pro-H. though anti-P.M., robust and not defeatist.

May 7th

A provisional reply has been sent to the Pope that we must consult our friends and suggesting that, as France may not care to have Germany intervening in her dispute with Italy, the Pope might prefer to offer his good offices to France and Italy, and separately to Germany and Poland over Danzig. We think it possible that Mussolini may have got the Pope to make the move to get him out of his own difficulties.

Meanwhile Beck's speech on Friday was firm, non-provocative and calm – just what was wanted. All German propaganda is now making out Danzig as a special and isolated claim, while we know after Czechoslovakia that it is only the first step to the weakening and partition of Poland. If it were a particular case, we could settle it, but it is a symptom of a general disease.

I hear Perth has wangled the job of Director-General for the Ministry of Information which Sam Hoare is industriously organising for himself to lead if war comes.

Still great obscurity about Russia though Maisky assures – as he

288

must – that there is to be no change – Potemkin[1] says the same to the Turks. But I do not like it and there are hints here and there that it may mean a Russo-German rapprochement.

May 8th

A.E. dined with us last night. He notices a change for the worse in opinion in the House of Commons towards the P.M.: he thinks even Winston is fast becoming a possibility as P.M. He said the P.M. "looked like a turkey who has missed his Christmas". A.E. is very disturbed about our Soviet negotiations which he thinks lack boldness and imagination: we ought to agree to tripartite alliance with France and Soviet Russia. He saw H. today and talked about Soviet Russia.

May 10th

We have suggested that either Potemkin or Molotov should go to Geneva.

There is a hitch in the Turkish negotiations owing to objection raised by the Yugoslavs that the proposed pact is contrary to the spirit of the Balkan Entente.

May 13th

Geneva has now been postponed a week at the request of the Soviet Government. We have gladly agreed, hoping that it means Potemkin himself is coming.

Meanwhile the Anglo-Turkish agreement has been tied up and the announcement of our guarantee has been made.

May 16th

Meeting in Secretary of State's room about Soviet negotiations. Soviet reply just received turns down our proposals and presses again for a tripartite alliance on the ground that our proposals leave Soviet Russia exposed to a direct attack by Germany via the Baltic States without any guarantee. It is a case of mutual trust. It is difficult for a British Conservative Government to negotiate an

1. Soviet Vice-Minister of Foreign Affairs.

agreement with a Russian Communist one. I saw A.E. at luncheon. He was very anxious at failure to conclude agreement and had heard that H. took the view that Soviet Russia was anti-Christ. I assured him that this was not the case, though he did mistrust them. The Foreign Policy Committee met this evening to consider a draft reply which meets some of the Soviet points. Tonight we heard disturbing rumours that Potemkin cannot after all go to Geneva and that Maisky is to represent the Soviet Government – and this after the meeting had been postponed a week at great inconvenience at Soviet request to allow Potemkin to be there!

May 20th

On our way to Geneva H. discussed on the train and in the boat ways of getting round Soviet difficulties. He said P.M. was very reluctant to agree to full tripartite alliance, although many in the Cabinet favoured it. He himself took the view that we had gone so far that the little more would not make much difference in its effect on Hitler, whereas the P.M. feared that it would finally tip the balance over to war. Malkin tried to draft a further guarantee to get nearer to Soviet requirements without being an alliance – not very convincing and very legalistic. William Strang and I agree that we ought to go the whole hog as Soviet Russia will now take nothing less and we are slowly being dragged along. Strang thinks that what is in the back of P.M.'s mind, and especially of Horace Wilson's, is that appeasement will be dead after this. He says that all at No. 10 are anti-Soviet.

Talks took place in Paris with Daladier and Bonnet. French were strongly in favour of our accepting Soviet Russia tripartite pact plan. Daladier was very firm that France could not negotiate with Italy in her present truculence, but only if Italy made some counterpart. As to Danzig, Daladier was insistent on necessity in any eventual solution of preventing its being fortified. H. suggested the possibility of its being neutralised with the Reich under the guarantee of the Powers.

I hear much annoyance has been caused to Phipps by the announcement of A.E.'s lecture for June 15th at the Ambassadeurs without his pre-knowledge and because he had tried to prevent his coming! What happened was that A.E. wrote about another invitation which he had received to lecture in Paris and which he had turned down as not being suitable: he had then asked me to ask the Embassy as to when and where he could lecture as he was anxious to do so, having received so many invitations that it had become almost rude to turn any more down. I wrote to the Embassy to put this to Phipps and received reply that "June was a bad month for lectures and it would be better to reconsider it in the autumn"! This was obviously nonsense and intended as sabotage. Charles Peake and I therefore arranged the whole thing ourselves through the *Figaro* correspondent in London who fixed it with A.E. and the Ambassadeurs people. Phipps and Charles Mendl are furious, especially as the whole French Cabinet propose to give A.E. a banquet first!

Propaganda for prolonging Phipps is beginning to work heavily and obviously from all sides.

Riesser came to see me in Paris to warn me of the importance of clinching matters with Soviet Russia "as there already were contacts between the Soviets and Germany".

May 21st

We arrived at Geneva early. Maisky came and had a further talk with H. He made quite clear that what was worrying Soviets was the possibility of direct attack on them by Germany, through a Poland or a Rumania which had collapsed or gone over to the Nazis, in which circumstances our proposed guarantee would not operate.

Report came from London of a German commercial mission to Moscow, exactly confirming what my friend Riesser told me yesterday.

May 23rd

In answer to our inquiry both Poland and Rumania have now intimated that they do not wish to stand in our way as regards negotiation of a tripartite pact with Soviet Russia. There is little doubt now that Soviet Russia will take nothing less. H. is still doubtful whether the P.M. will agree at Cabinet tomorrow.

May 24th

We flew from Le Bourget and were in London by 10 a.m. in time for the Cabinet at eleven. At Le Bourget we had a letter from Alec Cadogan saying that the P.M. was finally disposed to swallow the

Soviet *desiderata* but wished it to be covered up as much as possible by introducing it into the League machinery, if possible as part of Article 16. Really the wheel has come full circle when we have the P.M., who has done more than any responsible statesman to side-track Geneva, trying to cover himself with Geneva clothes in order to hide the shame of direct agreement with Soviet Russia.

At the Cabinet agreement was reached for the despatch of a further telegram to Moscow with a new text, with a fine League of Nations preamble, offering Soviet Russia practically what they want.

A real scandal has been perpetrated in the appointment of Perth as Director-General of the new Ministry of Information which is to come into existence in the event of war: in the meanwhile he is to sit in the Foreign Office as a special Under-Secretary for publicity with £2,900 a year (i.e. his pension plus £1,000) and do or try to do the work which Rex Leeper has built up and has been doing to universal satisfaction and which by rights he should continue to do as an Under-Secretary. It is a ramp of Sam Hoare and Horace Wilson, with the tacit and really unforgivable acquiescence of H.

May 27th

We are to have a quiet Whitsun apparently. The telegram to Moscow, after being approved by the French Government, has gone off and awaits Stalin's reply. For the moment there is no more to be done. The Turkish negotiations for the second and more permanent stages of our agreement are about to be taken up, and meanwhile the provisional guarantee against aggression in the Mediterranean area still holds. I heard from Douglas Colyer, Air Attaché in Paris, that the French air production has at last turned the corner and is really at last going ahead. Our own air re-armament is going ahead by leaps and bounds. Conscription is on the statute book and the first militiamen are to be called up next month. The Army still seriously lacks equipment. On the other hand, staff conversations are going ahead with France and Poland very satisfactorily. We have had a snub from the Belgians: it had been arranged (through the Belgian Prime Minister) that Beaumont-Nesbitt[1] should go over from the War Office to have informal talks there, but when he arrived the door was

1. Major-General F. G. Beaumont-Nesbitt, Director of Military Intelligence, War Office, 1939–1940.

closed and the Minister of War and Chief of Staff had gone off for the day! This, of course, is the influence of the King and the Palace clique who are scared of any derogation from the present neutrality.

Faced by this situation, Hitler seems to be piping down for the moment. Quite a serious incident at Danzig has been passed over in comparative silence. Danzig, it is said, has now only an incidental importance for him as part of the general anti-Polish campaign which may be launched in two months or so after the harvest is in. The much vaunted German-Italian alliance[1] has been signed, but nobody thinks it means anything at all – nothing can bind the Italians except their own view of their own interests. But Italy is getting more and more into German toils through the natural operation of the Axis, and Mussolini and Ciano are getting more and more unpopular because of this. But Mussolini cannot betray the Axis in peace-time or the Germans would be in Trieste in half-an-hour: he can only betray them in an hour of need when Germany might be occupied with war in the East and in the West. Germany knows this, of course, and will try to push Mussolini into a war first, but Mussolini ought to be too clever to fall into that trap and can be counted on, I think, to exercise a moderating influence on Berlin. I doubt whether it makes much difference in the long run whether France can be induced to negotiate with Italy now, as we are always trying to make her; Italy will always side with the stronger side or what she thinks to be the stronger side.

I hear it is intended to get rid of Henderson at last. A.C. and I want to send Horace Seymour there, who can be counted on to report faithfully what is going on without *parti pris* and to carry out his instructions loyally. No Ambassador is going to swing Hitler or German opinion. German policy is governed by British policy in London.

Alec proposes that I should go to Paris in December as Minister in place of Ronnie Campbell, who will have to go when the other Ronnie Campbell goes there in November. It is very flattering and in some ways very tempting, but I don't want to go! I hate moving again and again: I hate the idea of leaving London. On the other hand, it looks as if I could not stay on much longer as Private Secretary. I might linger another six months and then be offered something far less attractive. As Private Secretary my position is very different from

1. The "Pact of Steel".

what it was in A.E.'s time. H.'s method of work is quite different. He does not expect much more than fetch and carry from his Private Secretary, certainly not a confidential political adviser. He does all his work through A. Cadogan. The only alternative to going would seem to be a new lease of life in the Foreign Office, say as an Under-Secretary. Anyway, all is still very uncertain and it is not by any means sure that we shall get Phipps out in October. Alec is anticipating a campaign for his renewal, but he hopes to be able to resist it.

May 29th

Seeds has seen Molotov about our latest Soviet proposals, and the latter's first reaction was most unfavourable. He fastened on to the P.M.'s precious references to the League of Nations which aroused all his mistrust – did it not mean that we intended to hold up our guarantee until the cumbrous machinery of Geneva could be put in motion? All Seeds' efforts to persuade him of the contrary were in vain.

H. is away and L. Oliphant[1] has spoken to him on the telephone. He is to see Maisky and explain that the references to the League mean no more than adherence to its principles, not to its procedure.

Moley is filled with the deepest misgivings at Perth's appointment and says he is to be Horace Wilson's spy and will end by ousting Alec himself. I feel too we shall be nursing a snake in our bosom. The treatment of Rex Leeper is disgraceful and I feel we are now for a whole series of ramps of this sort.

Percy Loraine has had his first interview with Mussolini. The latter took H.M.G. seriously to task for damaging the *status quo* by our Anglo-Soviet and Anglo-Turkish negotiations and generally encircling policies, and finally ended by asking whether we still thought Anglo-Italian agreement served any useful purpose. Loraine stood up to him like the stout fellow he is and answered point for point by referring to the absorption of Albania and the signature of the German-Italian alliance. A very good first round which must have been a surprise to Mussolini after years of the miserable Perth.

1. Sir L. Oliphant, Deputy Under-Secretary at Foreign Office. Later Ambassador to Belgium.

May 31st

We hear tonight on the tape that Molotov has said in his speech that our proposals are so confused that he cannot make out whether we really want an agreement or not; and that in any case he is about to negotiate a Soviet-German commercial agreement.

The P.M. is fishing in Wales and H. in Yorkshire.

June 5th

Submarine disaster[1] seems likely to react unfavourably on Government's position. Stanhope did not go to the scene and obvious precautions appear to have been neglected – no proper guardship, etc.

Russian negotiations have reached a further stage with receipt of Molotov's reply – not so bad as at first feared. Soviet Russia insist on inclusion of Baltic States and also our agreement not coming into force until military agreement has also been concluded. They also want an undertaking not to conclude separate peace. Our counterdraft which had been prepared in anticipation goes some way to meet former case but not last two. The difficulties of negotiation between London and Moscow are obvious – no plenipotentiaries. A.E. feels that a Minister should go and has offered H. (whom he saw on Saturday) to go himself.

A.E. said H., when he saw him, brought up on his own the unsatisfactory state of the internal position. H. is to see S.B. who is also worried at failure to prepare for future by bringing fresh blood into the Government.

Lord Tyrrell, whom I saw on Saturday, spoke of the tiredness of the present Cabinet and of the provincial character of the P.M., "a man without a spark of imagination"! He, like me, did not think it would make much difference whether or not France made an agreement with Italy. In fact, he thought it would be wrong to press Daladier any more as he did not think that with his present majority it would be possible for him to make any further move. The important thing was that Mussolini knew that if he wanted it, he could have an agreement tomorrow.

Lord Tyrrell had heard Van was to go to Paris in succession to

1. The *Thetis* sank in shallow water and remained for two days with its stern held above water before a cable parted and it was finally lost.

Phipps. He begged me to warn H. of fell consequence of such a step and said both Piétri[1] and Bérard had expatiated about the danger it would involve as Van was so much involved with French party politics. I told him I did not think there was any question of it.

June 8th

It was decided not to send a Cabinet Minister (and certainly not A.E.) to Moscow but to get Seeds back here and indoctrinate him for further negotiations with Molotov. It now appears that Seeds is ill with flu and so W. Strang is to go to Moscow instead. This has not gone too well with Moscow who, of course, regard it as a *dénigrément*.

The Russians are so suspicious that it is essential if we are to get our agreement to take the most extraordinary precautions that our procedure or approach does not arouse mistrust. But the P.M. cannot see this, and even H. is not very imaginative where the Bolsheviks are concerned.

I hear that the proposal to set up a Ministry of Information and to appoint Perth as Secretary-General was badly received in Cabinet this morning and it was referred back for further consideration. Both Belisha and Kingsley Wood did not think it went far enough. Whether objections are to Perth personally I do not know, but the view was expressed that the scheme would be much criticised – yes, criticised indeed.

I told H. I thought it would be a mistake to go on pushing Daladier to start negotiations with Mussolini. I doubted whether it was possible for him to do so on account of the united opposition of all parties to this course. H. said, as he always does, he did not think such opposition mattered: if you were determined to do it, opposition died down. The great thing was that we were now strong, but he favours deferring any further approaches, anyway to Germany, unless we have the Russian agreement.

June 9th

Paul told me that when Lindley[2] spoke at the Foreign Affairs Committee of the Conservative Party he violently attacked the policy of agreement with Russia. This, of course, has leaked out and Lindley

1. French politician. Minister of Marine in Flandin's Government.
2. Sir Francis Lindley, former Ambassador to Japan, Portugal, etc.

having been the P.M.'s host at Whitsun, it is taken as a further proof here and in Russia that the P.M. is not genuine in his desire for the agreement.

H. made a great speech in the Lords yesterday – nicely balanced between firmness and conciliation – emphasising that H.M.G. would not tolerate any further aggression but that they were ready to discuss reasonably at a table. The Press and public, however, have taken it up as further appeasement and weakness. This was not H.'s intention: he was really only trying to counter Hitler's encirclement propaganda.

June 13th

We had a meeting on Danzig to discuss Roger Makins's report of his meeting with Burckhardt at Basle. The latter had just returned from a round trip to Warsaw, Danzig and Berlin. He did not see any possibility of any permanent solution at present, but he also did not think the Germans were likely to make any move for another two months anyway.

June 17th

Tientsin[1] has suddenly swum into our ken. As a result of the refusal of the concession authorities to hand over four Chinese alleged to be terrorists to the Japanese military, the latter have declared and imposed a blockade. H.M.G. have now to make up their mind either to give way or to apply reprisals. The actual issue is not a very sound one in law as the four men are *a priori* under strong suspicion: on the other hand, the Japs are apparently determined to challenge our position and we must take up the challenge. Consideration is being given to various economic sanctions – with a good deal of misgiving owing to the precarious position in Europe.

Adrian Holman,[2] on leave from Berlin, dined. He is convinced that a Russian agreement would impress the Germans and nothing less than firmness may stop a war – no wobbling or appeasing, and he feared H.'s speech had had a bad effect.

1. A Chinese port south of Peking with a large foreign concession, the rest of the town being occupied by the Japanese. A specially tempting area for Japanese harassment of Europeans as no American interests were involved.
2. First Secretary in Berlin.

June 19th

Poor Weizmann and Mrs W. dined last night. It was most moving to listen to him. I have never seen him so unhappy. He is convinced that his cause[1] will win through in the end, but he is more than doubtful of ours. "For years I have been trying to make something out of nothing, and you are now trying to make nothing of something." I fear he is only too right. He described the twisty arguments of Malcolm MacDonald. I feel thoroughly ashamed over the part of H.M.G. and particularly of the Foreign Office, which only sees the problem through Arab spectacles, in all this.[2]

Weizmann said that French scientists (Joliot-Curie) were on the point of splitting the atom in such a way that its energy might be canalised and utilised. (Hitherto the splitting of the atom as at Cambridge has involved more energy than it released.) An experiment is to be conducted shortly in the Sahara to see if it is safe. American scientists are also close on the same solution in New York. If the experiment is successful, then all question of power, light, transport, etc., will be revolutionised. What will be the effect of this? For the benefit or the destruction of mankind? We discussed it without any satisfactory conclusion for mankind.

Chiefs of Staff have produced their report on Tientsin – make it clear that we cannot take on the Japs with sufficient ships unless we denude the Mediterranean, and if we do that we cannot fulfil our commitments to Greece, Turkey and Rumania.

The question was discussed by the Foreign Policy Committee today when it was decided to stage as graceful a climbdown as possible by means of Craigie and the Americans – if the latter will play.

Lord Lloyd called on Saturday and asked me to tell H. (who was away) in strict confidence that he had again received a message from a German intermediary (as, I think he said, in last September) to the effect that General Brauchitsch, the German C.-in-C., had told him that zero hour for the attack on Poland had been fixed by Hitler for

1. The Zionist cause.
2. The Palestine Round Table Conference of February 1939 had come to no agreement. In May the Government White Paper had laid down that Jewish Immigration should cease after they had reached one-third of the population.

July 31st and that Brauchitsch said he would be able "to deal with the Nazi regime" on the first day of mobilisation.

June 24th

Russian negotiations still hanging fire owing to the insurmountable suspicions of the Russians. We really do want to meet them over the Baltic States but we cannot convince them. I doubt if we shall ever convince them with this Government. There seems still little doubt that the Soviets want agreement, although there are reports to indicate that our attitude in Tientsin and the forthcomingness of the Germans (who are working in Moscow very hard) are having their effect, and they are losing interest. After all, we are already committed to guarantee Poland and Rumania and so Soviet Russia is already well covered herself. On the other hand, if we lost the agreement, in spite of the doubtful quality of the Russian forces, it will work as a direct incentive to war by the totalitarians and as discouragement to our small allies.

Foreign policy is a unity – we cannot be weak in China and strong in Europe. It is all or nothing. We were weak with Franco, and as a direct consequence Japan is now bullying us. If we are weak again with Japan, we shall have Hitler and Mussolini beating us up. And, above all, if we are weak in helping China, who is fighting our battle, we shall find our own little allies ratting on us. Why shouldn't they? We missed our first and great chance: not facing up to Mussolini over Abyssinia and forcing him to his knees by immediate drastic military sanctions. Hitler was not yet ready and was watching – so was Japan. We could have overthrown Mussolini and freed the Mediterranean from menace. Hitler would have been isolated and Spain would never have been an international complication. We should have defeated our enemies in detail. As it was, we showed ourselves to be so scared by the cowardice of the old men in the Government and the fear of the Chiefs of Staff that Italy might beat us, that we faltered and ended by merely antagonising her, whilst we convinced all our other enemies by our conduct that we were funks.

I hear from A.E. that S.B. is extremely worried over the Rome situation and is saying that after Munich the P.M. should have had an All-Party Government at any cost with A.E. back.

June 30th

P. V. Emrys-Evans came to see me today to say that there was great activity in the A.E. group. Harold Macmillan, it appears, has drafted a letter which he is to send to the *Daily Telegraph* expressing the urgent need for national reconstruction. It is hoped that Camrose will take it up and start a campaign for immediate inclusion of A.E., Winston and Labour.

I happened to be lunching with Tom Martin, *Daily Telegraph* lobby correspondent, today, and he told me much the same thing and added that he was urging Camrose to take up this line and to press it strongly. Martin expressed some doubts about A.E.'s "toughness" and said his line in the past had been too influenced by the old-school tie. He seemed to prefer Churchill as a leader – and this may be Camrose's opinion too.

July 1st

Fresh scare about Danzig from France arising out of reports of infiltration of Nazi stormtroopers, etc., with a view to internal coup following on a visit by Hitler. French Government much concerned and anxious that we should *prendre les devants*[1] by issuing some immediate warning to Berlin. Kennard[2] (British Ambassador in Warsaw) who arrived back last night, on short leave, is also anxious for some declaration being made at once. We have, as a matter of fact, telegraphed to Warsaw to ask Beck what he has in mind to do in the event of a "spontaneous" declaration by Danzig of inclusion in the Reich and proposing concerting of plans with us and French.

A.E. asked me to go and see him before lunch to look at his speech which he is to make at Ealing tonight at a National Service Rally. It seemed to me excellent – brief and to the point, emphasising that unchecked aggression was at an end – and including some passages I suggested saying that there can be no return to the selfish ways of the past and that we must "organise, plan and finance on a scale not yet attempted".

Late at night he rang me up to say his meeting had been a howling

1. i.e. get in first.
2. Sir Howard Kennard, Ambassador to Poland since 1935.

success – 30,000 people and an immense personal ovation to himself. He told me about the *Daily Telegraph* plan and it is intended to open the campaign on Monday with a leader. He had seen Camrose on Friday. Astor's group is also to meet on Monday to discuss the same question of the need for a widening of the Government, always with the same object of emphasising the oneness and determination of this country *vis-à-vis* any further aggression. Astor had not wanted to call his group back but Balniel had insisted. Amery has also been tackling the Whips.

Meanwhile H.'s speech at Chatham House on Thursday night has created a great impression here and abroad for its firmness. All at home approve it, including Labour. H. was appreciably stiffened at the last minute owing to the rumours of an early coup in Danzig and to further reports that Ribbentrop was still telling Hitler that we would not fight.

Nothing fresh from Russia – negotiations still hanging fire. We are now offering Molotov almost any amendment he wants and he persists in making fresh demands. The Dutch have just protested officially against their being made the object of any negotiations or guarantee by us – just as the Baltic States, Poland and Rumania have done against guarantee by Russia. This is really an intolerable attitude for them to adopt, though when it was the Poles and Rumanians in respect of Soviet Russia we took their objection seriously enough. Their negotiations are now in a proper mess – chiefly owing to slowness and reluctance with which we first tackled the Soviet Russia. This Government will never get anything done.

Tientsin affairs in suspense pending opening of negotiations at Tokyo – more or less on Japanese terms.

July 4th

Polish Finance Mission has left in state bordering on despair at attitude of H.M.G. and Treasury towards financial assistance for Poland. They were told we did not regard it "as of great urgency" and we wished to attach all sorts of conditions.

Kennard over here and went to see P.M. with H. yesterday in order to advocate issue of a firm declaration and warning against any internal coup in Danzig. Both H. and P.M. incline to water it down so as to leave a door open for need. But negotiations not possible now and Poles would not even agree to negotiate in present conditions as Kennard insists. Latter is also insistent on absolute need for really large loans to enable Poland to pay and equip her forces. The men are there and even the factories are there, but money is required at once and permission to spend it in Poland, and not as Treasury insist, only after long delay – then on condition that it is spent here.

Daily Telegraph campaign opened yesterday with strong article in favour of Churchill being brought into Government – no specific mention of A.E. It is followed today by articles in *Yorkshire Post* and *News Chronicle*. The Astor group met last night and sense of meeting was that Government should be enlarged to include Churchill and A.E. I hear *Daily Mail* is to follow it up tomorrow.

Roosevelt has offered to maintain a neutral patrol on Western side of Atlantic and asks for use of British bases for it.

Further meetings about Soviet negotiations. Soviet Russia now say they cannot agree to cover Holland and Switzerland as that would increase their commitments even though we cover Baltic! H. favours reversion to plain tripartite agreement against direct aggression on any of three signatories, leaving out other states for later agreement if possible.

A warning message is being sent to Mussolini that we mean to fight over Danzig and that it is up to him to get busy if he wants to avoid it.

July 9th

Henderson came over to see his doctor. Position is that Halifax and No. 10 would be very glad if he found he was no longer fit to return to Berlin, but they did not want to retire him themselves. The doctor says, however, he is quite fit. He does not look at all fit and is obviously in a very nervous and overwrought state – quite unfit to be in such a post at such a time. He ought, of course, to be withdrawn at once – if only because the policy he was chosen to represent, appeasement, in which he passionately believes, has been reversed, and so long as he is there Germany and everybody else will never believe we may not have more appeasement.[1]

P.M. is to make his statement on Danzig tomorrow.

Russian negotiations still hanging fire – H.M.G. getting more ready for agreement at any price for political reasons and Soviet Russia getting more and more difficult and elusive. Tokyo negotiations not

1. See O.H.'s memo to Secretary of State at Appendix Q.

yet started, Japs represented that when they do start they must cover our whole attitude towards China and Chiang Kai-Shek and not only Tientsin.

Pro-Churchill campaign dying down – no sign whatever of a move in No. 10.

July 23rd

I have written nothing in my Diary for days, but there is little to report. Russian negotiations still held up. Tokyo talks only just begun. There is some evidence that Hitler is soft-pedalling over Danzig – the result, I believe, of increasing evidence of our firmness. This, however, is now again threatened by publication in the Press of amazing story of a peace offer to Germany, alleged to have been made by Horace Wilson and Rob Hudson to Wohltat,[1] German economic adviser. The offer was that Germany should disarm under some international supervision and in return H.M.G. would give a loan of a thousand million to buy raw materials and to finance turning over of Germany to peace work. Story leaked into the Press and the *Daily Telegraph* and *News Chronicle* both published it on Saturday. All we know is that Horace Wilson did see Wohltat, but he denies having talked about anything except the Czech loan. The story is calculated to do infinite harm to Soviet negotiations and to U.S. opinion, where our *bona fides* are not so above suspicion as not to be easily called in doubt. Whether the story is true or not – I can hardly believe it to be true – it is a very silly proposal and linked up with pre-election propaganda.

I hope Halifax will tackle the P.M. about it, but he has not yet.

August 22nd

Returned from leave today. News of German-Soviet Russian non-aggression pact announced today came as a complete shock to H.M.G., although one warning received from Washington a few days ago but telegram held up in general congestion. My first impression is that it is a very severe blow to Peace Front, though too early to form definite view yet. How can the German Government go on with anti-Comintern Pact and what about effect in Japan and Spain? Is it a terrific bluff?

1. Helmut Wohltat, German Trade Official sent by Goering.

Cabinet meeting this afternoon to consider position. Meanwhile Polish attitude unchanged and firm. General belief that Germany means to walk into Poland on the 25th.

August 23rd

Letter from P.M. to Hitler sent last night emphasising Great Britain would fight, but peaceful settlement still possible if with international guarantees.

The King returns tomorrow when Parliament meets.

No doubt of reluctance of Italians to fight.

Meanwhile Molotov told Seeds in the most cynical manner possible that German-Soviet rapprochement is due entirely to lack of good faith shown by Great Britain and France and would not say when negotiations could be resumed. Russians had asked for authority to pass troops into Poland in North and South. Poles had refused anyway until war began!

Distinct signs of wobble in Italy. We have asked Muss to use influence with Hitler, whilst assuring him of our determination to fight.

August 24th

Hitler's reply to Nevile Henderson quite uncompromising. He says if we take any further military measures he will mobilise. Soviet-German non-aggression pact signed and published today seems to leave no loop-hole for any agreement with us.

Poles very firm and determined. So, too, the French. Much depends now on Italy.

Halifax made statement in House of Lords. Very crowded House. Snell's reply most impressive and moving. Broadcast later at No. 10.

Meeting with Dominion High Commissioners and Ter Water's[1] idea of some final attempt at conference. Halifax turning this over in mind and wonders if Roosevelt could be induced to do so. Is consulting P.M. (Rather late?)

1. South African High Commissioner.

304

August 25th

News of President Roosevelt's appeal to Hitler and Poland last night urging direct negotiation or arbitration or conciliation. This will anticipate the Secretary of State's idea of last night.

Otherwise no more news yet.

Hitler summoned Nevile Henderson to see him at 1.20 and he telephoned that he had one and a half hours with him. He has made certain proposals and the Ambassador is coming to London to-morrow.

Meanwhile telegram sent to Percy Loraine to authorise him to assure Muss that if he is fearful of consequences of ratting from Germany we would allow him support.

Idea of mission to Turkey with A.E. at its head proposed by latter in order to make sure of Turks.

Return to F.O. after dinner when Nevile Henderson's report of interview ready: the most impudent document I have ever seen, in that it is the old story, "You leave us free in the East to deal with Poland and we will then guarantee you, but you must return our colonies."

Hitler very calm but absolutely immovable. Repeated again and again his intention to deal with Poles for their intolerable persecution of Germans!

Returned to F.O. at nine. Halifax with P.M. till eleven, then dictated draft reply, thinks something can be made of it. R. A. Butler very favourable of course.

August 26th

Nevile Henderson arriving at twelve.

Idea of A.E. leading mission to Turkey turned down "because of effect on Muss" who is very wobbly now. Halifax put idea to P.M. who welcomed it. Maurice Ingram, Van and A. Cadogan thought, however, that effect on Muss would be disastrous, though favoured sending mission, but not with A.E. at head. Halifax asked me to convey this to A.E. as he had to go over to the P.M. A.E. bitterly disappointed, feels this excuse will be used to debar him from any return to public life.

Nevile Henderson arrived at one and lunched with P.M. and

Halifax at No. 10. All closeted together rest of afternoon. Cabinet fixed for 6.30.

Draft *very* flabby, prepared by Horace Wilson and R. A. Butler. What a pair! This, however, rejected by Cabinet, and a drafting committee of P.M., H., Simon, Butler and A.C. met at 10 p.m. to try again. They adjourned without success at one a.m.

O.H. to Secretary of State – 26th August, 1939

I gave Anthony your message. He thanked you for it and said he hoped that the mission would be sent nonetheless as soon as possible.

I felt he was very disappointed. He feels passionately anxious to serve his country at this juncture and I think he felt that the Mussolini argument was one which would be used to debar him from any return to political life at present. He also felt that it was the wrong way to deal with Musso, who would come over to us if he felt we were strong and determined and likely to win, regardless of other considerations.

I must say I feel myself that his view is right as regards Musso. He will be won over by a display of great strength, not by any sign of weakening. It is also essential to clinch the Turks. And no one would have greater influence with them than A.E.

But what is far more important than his going on a mission to Turkey is his inclusion in the Government as soon as it is enlarged. If the Musso argument were used to deter this, it would be really a crime. The gangsters are not affected by such niceties, and we should be losing the services of one who more than any other stands, both at home and abroad, for vigour and national unity.

August 27th

Halifax at Office at ten working with Alec Cadogan on last night's draft. Roger Makins and William Strang both came in and helped to stiffen it up. Strang now reasonably satisfied with it. Cabinet to meet at three to consider it.

Meanwhile the Swedish emissary Dahlerus,[1] who is a friend of Goering and went to see latter last week with a message for Hitler, is returning to London today. He had seen Goering, who was much reassured by message, and also Hitler (this emissary is an industrialist and a friend both of Goering and of certain British industrialists and offered himself some time ago as intermediary).

It looks to us here as if Hitler was wobbling. The German-Soviet

1. Birger Dahlerus of Stockholm, a Swedish businessman.

Pact (which was a measure of desperation) has not had the effect expected. We are still firm and have since signed the Anglo-Italian Treaty. But Spain has gone neutral, Japan is reconsidering her position and Musso is very wobbly. If only we remain firm! I am terrified of another attempt at a Munich and selling out on the Poles. Horace Wilson and R. A. Butler are working like beavers for this.

Dahlerus arrived and gave a rather woolly message on much the same lines as Nevile Henderson's (the point being that Hitler wanted to negotiate with Great Britain, not with the Poles). Whilst he was telling this to Halifax, Ciano rang up H. He begged that we should not turn Hitler's offer down flat, but should allow time for others' to work! He added that Mussolini was very pleased at collaborating with us, to which H. reciprocated!

Cabinet has adjourned again till tomorrow without reaching agreement on text of reply to Hitler.

7 p.m.

Dahlerus has now been sent back to Berlin where he is to see Goering tonight. He will give an account of the atmosphere here and say roughly:

(i) That we are as anxious as Germany for peace;
(ii) that we have definite obligations to Poland, and therefore;
(iii) that any solution between Germany and Poland must take account of that.

General feeling of some relaxation in the tension tonight. Hitler evidently hesitating. Musso working on him: we have urged Beck to consider offering exchange of population and neutral observers in respect of minority and frontier problems. He is willing that this should be put forward by a third party.

We learn that the Jap Government are about to fall and we shall probably get a much more Anglophile one in exchange, thanks to German-Soviet Pact.

Halifax has gone home and hopes to have a quiet night. I'm still nervous about text of reply to Hitler. The draft as it left the hands of Halifax and Alec C. this morning was fairly good. Afterwards the Cabinet was turned loose on it, while H. and the P.M. were engaged on their prolonged talk with Dahlerus. The result was that each and all had bright ideas for improvement and are to submit their amended views in writing. These are to be collated by John Simon: the Cabinet is to see it again tomorrow at twelve, N. Henderson to return with it tomorrow night. N.H.'s very presence here is a danger as he infects the Cabinet with his gibber. I expressed my anxieties about the Cabinet reply to H. today and showed him a note of mine[1] and one of Kirkpatrick's about the need for firmness in view of Hitler's difficulties. But he said we needn't worry – he had it all in his mind and we mustn't be suspicious of any attempt to rat on the Poles. I assured him we had no doubt of *him*.

August 28th

I was rung up at 2 a.m. this morning by the resident clerk who said telegram had come from Warsaw that Polish Government had ordered general mobilisation in view of Hitler's reply to Nevile Henderson.

Great curiosity in Press at visit of emissary whose identity has not been disclosed. He is thought to be a Dr Schmidt from Ribbentrop's office.

Meanwhile reply received this morning of interview Dahlerus had with Goering last night on his return from London to Berlin.

Goering had referred to Hitler the three points mentioned here, viz. Great Britain's desire for settlement with Germany – Hitler asked if this meant alliance or treaty – Great Britain must honour her obligations to Poland (Hitler agreed), Great Britain considered it essential that there should be direct negotiations between Germany and Poland and that any agreement should be guaranteed by the great powers of Europe. Hitler said Great Britain must persuade Poland to negotiate with Germany immediately. Dahlerus had the impression that Hitler agreed to the guarantee idea. Hitler was impatient over colonies and felt Great Britain insincere.

Cabinet agreed on text and message and Nevile Henderson left for Berlin by air at five. Message includes statement authorised by Beck that Poland is ready at once to enter direct discussions with Germany.

Further message from Dahlerus that German troops are in position to attack Poland on August 30th, advancing from East Prussia and Slovakia on Warsaw. Therefore, Dahlerus says, it is very urgent to start negotiations.

Goering said that minimum German demand would be whole corridor for Germany with corridor for Poland to Gdynia. Goering also said a neutral Italy would suit Germany just as well, as an allied Italy would have to be supplied with material, etc. (This is a pretty good confession of German-Italian position.)

1. See Appendix R.

308

August 29th

N. Henderson saw Hitler at 10.30 last night and account of conversation was received this morning. Hitler is to send a written reply later. In conversation N.H. insisted that Hitler had to choose between moderation towards Poland and war with us. Hitler insisted that he must have Danzig and the corridor back and rectifications in Silesia. Hitler was willing to negotiate if the Polish Government were reasonable and really controlled the country. He said Poland never could be reasonable with Great Britain and France at her back and harped on ill-treatment of Germans in Poland. N.H. asked if he was ready to contemplate exchange of populations – Hitler said yes – and if he would negotiate direct with the Poles – Hitler couldn't answer till he gave considered reply. Hitler finally asked if Great Britain were ready to accept alliance with Germany.

Meanwhile all German troops are in position for attack on Poland, and the Poles have practically completed mobilisation. All stories of incidents and atrocities are either grossly exaggerated or pure inventions.

Evidence of Musso wanting to keep out continues. Halifax is going to ring up Ciano at lunch-time to keep him sweet.

Halifax walking across to the House of Lords to make his statement, said the moral issues were now clear. He agreed with me that Hitler was now in a fix. His new deal of Russia in place of Japan, Musso and Spain was a very poor exchange and made things better for us. He thought it significant that Frick[1] had been called into council on the reply. Halifax thought it very important to get into negotiation and then be very stiff and then Hitler would be beat.

A further message from Dahlerus, who had seen Goering, and said that the reply would be moderate and reasonable. Nothing about Silesia, only Danzig and part of the corridor; Hitler very anxious to meet Great Britain and therefore to negotiate with Poles, but feared Poles might be destructive; Hitler now prepared for international guarantee, all proof of strong desire for friendship with Great Britain.

6 p.m.

We hear Poles have ordered general mobilisation. The Hungarian Government, we learn, are most anxious to remain neutral.

1. Nazi Minister of Interior 1933–1943.

7 p.m.

Hitler's reply not yet ready. We can now not get it till late tonight and it cannot be considered before tomorrow morning.

August 30th

Hitler's reply arrived during the night. The upshot is that he hates the Poles but wants British friendship. Therefore, although German-Polish relations must be liquidated, corridor and Danzig back and minorities settled, he is prepared to negotiate and to receive a Polish plenipotentiary in Berlin today and to accept International Guarantee which must include Soviet Russia.

We replied at once that it would be impossible for any plenipotentiary to arrive today but that we were studying the document. Beck during the night said he must proceed to general mobilisation in spite of appeals of British and French Ambassadors. We have since told him that we cannot take responsibility for stopping him. Beck also declared that the Polish Government must not be regarded as prepared to accept the March offer.

Cabinet meeting at 11.30. Dahlerus has returned again from Berlin. Reply to Berlin sent off and also to Warsaw. The former notes agreement to negotiate and to accept guarantee but reserves our position as to nature of proposals; it proposes a military standstill and a *modus vivendi* in Danzig. The letter urges the Polish Government to agree to negotiate, said we believed the territorial demands are not the minimum and urges the Polish Government to enter negotiations but to be reassured that we will back them up.

August 31st

Reply delivered by N.H. to Ribbentrop for Hitler at midnight. Ribbentrop said all provocation came from the side of Poland. When N.H. said H.M.G. were using moderating influence, Ribbentrop said it had damned little effect.

Report received from source in Berlin of bad morale, 70% against Hitler, party divided and soldiers, etc., only hoping Great Britain would be firm and then regime would crack. Other reports from other sources confirm. We also hear that Hitler had forced the General Staff to change plans against Poland at last minute. Fear of General Staff of war on West and East.

310

Telegram from N.H. at 9 a.m. to say he learns from best possible authority that if nothing happens by midday German Government will declare war on Poland.

Ciano rang up Halifax at ten to say Musso wanted us to get Poles to agree at once to give up Danzig and then enter negotiations. H. said this could not be expected of Poles, but German Government should communicate their terms to Poles and these should then be considered as a whole. Would Musso urge Hitler to agree to this and we would urge Poles to send Lipsky[1] to receive proposals. (A bit of pure blackmail by Musso.)

H. feels, I think, that Hitler is in a difficulty, and as he said, "he must hold on to him" and not yield to blackmail. I know he wants negotiations to start and then to be very firm.

H. rang up Ciano at twelve to repeat that Poles could not be expected to give up Danzig and that Hitler must give Poles his proposals. Would Ciano urge this at Berlin? Ciano said he had already done so through Attolico.[2]

A telegram from N.H. sent off very early this morning (which has only just been deciphered) describes N.H.'s talk with Ribbentrop when former urged that when German proposals were ready, German Government should invite Polish Ambassador to come and take them and that H.M.G. could be counted on, if proposals were reasonable, to help in Warsaw.

Rib replied by reading a lengthy document proposing restoration of Danzig to Germany, plebiscite in Corridor on 1919 figures under International Commission, Gdynia reserved for Poland, Danzig a commercial and demilitarised city. Rib said, however, it was now too late to hand these over as the Polish Ambassador had not arrived by midnight. N.H. urged that they should now be given to the Ambassador and Ribbentrop said he would refer this to Hitler.

We have now urged Polish Government to instruct Polish Ambassador in Berlin to transmit any proposals to his Government.

Meanwhile Musso has suggested a conference on September 5th to revise the Treaty of Versailles and hopes we would support it with Hitler. Daladier has replied at once to say he would rather resign than agree to this.

Late tonight the German wireless broadcast the German proposals in sixteen points which they said the Poles had had before them for

1. Joseph Lipsky, Polish Ambassador in Berlin.
2. Bernardo Attolico, Italian Ambassador in Berlin.

311

two days! Sixteen points are on lines of what Rib read to N.H. yesterday and which, of course, were then revealed for the first time but even then weren't communicated to us.

Navy being mobilised and children evacuated from London at last.

September 1st

Poles reply to us that they are ready to exchange views with the German Government on the basis we proposed, to give formal reciprocal guarantee and accept *modus vivendi* in Danzig.

Telegram from Percy Loraine that Ciano had sent for him last night and said Italian Government would not fight against either Great Britain or France.

10.30 a.m. Polish Ambassador saw Halifax and told him of violations of German-Polish frontier and bombings. He said it seemed a clear case as provided by Treaty. H. said no doubt we should take the same view and spoke of the extraordinary performance of Germany over the peace procedure.

Hitler wirelessing announcement of his attack on Poland.

I learn Chiefs of Staff want to declare war tonight and get at Germany as soon as possible. By 6 p.m. the children will have been evacuated.

Cabinet at 11.30 and Parliament to meet at 6.30.

2 p.m. Idea now, I understand, is to declare war at midnight. French Government have ordered general mobilisation and their Parliament is to meet tomorrow; they can't declare war today without Parliament.

Warning telegram being sent to Berlin (5.45 p.m.) to say if reports are true we shall fulfil our obligations to Poland.

Proclamation by Italian Government that they mean to stay neutral. Halifax busy preparing statement for House of Lords at 6.30. I walked over with H. and Lady H. to Lords – H. said, "How can a man be so wicked as to launch this?"

Great crowd, cheers, House of Lords very impressive, tall bent figure of H., sorrowful tones, Snell, Crewe and Archbishop.

Embassy in Berlin having great difficulty in getting interview. They can get no reply till 9.30 when Ribbentrop receives N.H. Rib told the latter he would refer the note to the Führer, "but it was not Germany who had aggressed the Poles but the Poles Germany".

We now learn the French Government can't declare war till 5 p.m.

tomorrow afternoon. H. says if German reply unsatisfactory we can't wait till then. He feels Germany may put forward peace feeler now to which our only possible reply is that Germany must evacuate all Polish territory before we can consider anything. No further information of German invasion of Poland. Perhaps not pressing attack yet? Complete blackout in London tonight.

At 11.30 H., after seeing P.M., decided to go to bed. P.M. had said he would do nothing before 9.30 in the morning.

September 2nd

No more news this morning. Nothing further from Berlin. Phipps reports the French are anxious that we should not declare war before them, which for constitutional reasons cannot be till this evening.

Parliament meeting again this afternoon. Cabinet likely to be reconstructed, I hear, with Winston in War Cabinet.

We are beginning to feel a good deal of anxiety over French attitude and their apparently delaying tactics. Bonnet is attempting another intrigue for a Five-Power Conference and has instructed French Ambassador in Warsaw to sound Beck about it. Latter naturally repudiated any such idea. We now hear rumours are current in Paris that Musso's mediation has been accepted by Germany. I can't believe French are going to rat, but nobody trusts Bonnet. We have asked the French to agree by 3 p.m. to terms of statement to be made in Parliament today. This they have done, but French Government are urging 48 hours' delay after presentation of ultimatum!

Halifax at 2.30 just about to go to House of Lords when Ciano rang up to say he believed Berlin might still agree to a conference of Great Britain, France and Poland on Duce's proposals on the understanding of an immediate Armistice. He had put this to Hitler who had been prepared to consider it and would not meanwhile reply to our note but must first know whether our notes of yesterday were ultimate and whether he could have till noon tomorrow to consider. Ciano said the Italian Government understood that there should be an immediate armistice with the conference on the following day. Halifax said he was sure H.M.G. wouldn't contemplate a conference with German troops on Polish soil and withdrawal must be the first condition. According to Ciano (who had also telephoned to Bonnet) latter had replied yes to both points but he was still awaiting reply of Daladier.

313

H. and I rushed over to the House of Commons just in time to catch Simon who himself was about to make a statement. Halifax and Simon decided they must postpone statement and consult P.M. H. said to Simon and me he didn't see how we could contemplate a conference with Germany on Polish soil. Simon said he agreed and believed it to be a plant to gain time and allow more ships out, etc. We then went to No. 10 where I read over my record of the conversation to the P.M.

Halifax subsequently rang up Bonnet who said he had hedged with Ciano and told him he must discuss with Daladier and us. He wants to know our view on (a) idea of conference with German troops on Polish soil with armistice only, (b) idea of giving Hitler till noon to consider, and (c) idea of 48 hours' delay as desired by French General Staff. The P.M. said the Cabinet must meet at once. Statements in Parliament have been postponed.

Meanwhile the Turks are getting restive at our inaction. *Bremen*[1] getting nearer home and more German ships getting out. Essential we should act swiftly and send ultimatum to Germany before Polish morale breaks.

Cabinet decided in favour of ultimatum at midnight unless Hitler evacuated Polish territory, and of a conference (but with this precondition) if Poland agrees. This was then put to Bonnet by telephone. Latter put forward every wriggle in favour of delay – "evacuation of women and children not yet ready", "Army not yet ready". He said H.M.G. would undertake grave responsibility *vis-à-vis* France if the ultimatum expired tonight. We are now ringing up Phipps (Bonnet is side-tracking everybody) to communicate the draft of the statement to Daladier. The statement says we cannot be party to negotiations while German troops are on Polish soil and if they are not out by a certain time (to be agreed with French Government) we shall act.

We have rung up Ciano 6.30 p.m. to tell him that we cannot agree to a conference unless Germany withdraws and Mussolini is to impress this on Hitler.

Statement finally approved by Daladier and made by Secretary of State in House of Lords and by P.M. in House of Commons to the effect that we could not agree to a conference unless Germany first evacuated Polish soil and that we were in communication with the French Government regarding time limit to be accorded to German

1. The German Liner which was at sea.

Government. This went very badly in House of Commons, who were horrified at no time limit having been fixed. Later De La Warr told me Simon, he, De La Warr, Morrison, Elliot, etc., had held an indignation meeting and said that unless the French Government agreed to midday tomorrow for zero hour they must insist on midnight tonight.

Hasty dinner and then back to F.O. at 9.30 to learn that Halifax already at No. 10 seeing Corbin and Polish Ambassador.

Moley very worried at French delaying tactics, which he attributes not only to Bonnet but to General Staff.

We hear from Military Attaché in Berlin that German army came up against unexpected opposition in Poland and morale of troops generally very bad. Time is of the utmost importance therefore. German ships are stealing out all the time and the *Bremen* is getting nearer.

Hardinge came in late for the news. He also spoke of the importance of urgent action, without necessarily waiting for the French Government. He said what a pity it was that the Government had not been widened before; as they were, nobody trusted them *vis-à-vis* Germany. If only they had had some non-Municher in, the country would have trusted them.

I heard from De La Warr that there was almost a revolt in the Cabinet after the statement over the failure to put in a definite ultimatum. This was led by John Simon, Morrison, Elliot and De La Warr.

11 p.m. Halifax still at No. 10 seeing the Polish Ambassador, while the Prime Minister is seeing Corbin. Daladier is being very stiff and insisting on 48 hours' limit.

At 11.30 word came from No. 10 that a message was to be sent to Berlin warning Nevile Henderson that he might have to make a very urgent communication to the German Government during the night – (? presumably ultimatum to expire at midnight even without the French Government) – and the Cabinet to meet now at midnight. By a later message he was told to ask for an appointment at 9 a.m.

Finally, about 1.30 a.m., Malkin, who had been sent for earlier, brought back the telegrams to be sent to Berlin saying that Nevile Henderson should notify the German Government at 9 a.m. that unless the German Government by 11 a.m. announced that they agreed to withdraw, we would regard ourselves as at war with

315

Germany. The French Ambassador would do the same but with a different time limit, probably of six hours.

And then exhausted to bed.

September 3rd

F.O. again by 10.30. All awaiting 11 a.m. and any reply from Berlin. Dahlerus, ringing up from Berlin, says he is doing "his damnedest"; German reply being prepared but condition about withdrawal impossible. He said if we thought it any good he would ask Goering to come over here. Halifax sent reply, "No good, we have made our position clear and must have definite reply."

At 11 a.m. we hear reply on telephone from Berlin. But this turns out incorrect and at 11.10 we get through to our Embassy and hear no reply received. Authority to do this was given at 11.15 a.m.

11.30 a.m. air raid warning went as I was at No. 10. We all went at once to war rooms, but after 20 minutes all clear went. Halifax and I then walked across to House of Lords, where Halifax announced state of war with Germany. Chatfield told me air raid was false alarm owing to our planes being mistaken for German.

Strange silence in F.O. after this. Office to be closed this afternoon. I went home exhausted to bed.

I heard tonight that Anthony had been made Dominions Secretary and Winston First Lord of the Admiralty. Best news I could have had! Anthony is not in War Cabinet but is to have access to it.

September 4th

Another air raid alarm at 2.45 last night.

War Cabinet met at 11.30 today and are to do so each day.

Germans have sunk *Athenia* by torpedo, 300 U.S. citizens aboard. Fortunately all saved.

Our aircraft over North Germany last night dropping leaflets and reconnoitring.

September 5th

British air raid on German ships off Kiel last night. We lost five machines out of fifty. Unfortunately one machine in course of fighting with German dropped bombs over Esjberg and others flew across Holland. Dutch are furious!

September 6th

Position of Italy now of capital importance. Does she mean to be neutral or benevolent to Germany with ultimate intention of coming in against us? Halifax's view is we should go very gently to start with with our blockade measures and try to get her to agree to blockade in exchange for supply of coal and possibly purchase of Italian war material.

September 8th

General view seems to be that Germans intend to finish off Poland as quickly as possible whilst remaining strictly on the defensive on the West and then to make a peace offer supported by Mussolini. If, as is certain, we reject this offer, then Hitler will turn all his guns on us unless he decides to go south-east. He no doubt hopes the French Government, especially Bonnet and Co., will fall for the peace trap; he may hope to divide us.

Here, as in France, there are two schools of thought, one which favours going slow with Italy and keeping Rumania and the Balkans neutral, the other which wants to have a grand offensive up from Salonika, with Greeks, Turks, Rumanians and Yugoslavs, and to force Italy into acquiescence or hostility. At present the former have had their way in the Cabinet here and we are trying to secure French agreement.

I met Nevile Henderson and Embassy staff on arrival from Holland at Victoria last night. They all testify to calm in Berlin and lack of any hostile demonstrations. They were well treated in the train, etc. Population in Germany quite numbed and dazed by events and incapable of reaction.

I hear Perth was sacked this morning from his new post as Director-General of the Ministry of Information. He only survived four days of war. Horace Wilson did the deed and he is being replaced by Findlater Stewart from the India Office. Perth is being given some other, but purely decorative, appointment.

317

September 11th

A quiet weekend for us. German advance in Poland still going forward but slower. French operations on Western Front developing. More paper-dropping by the R.A.F. over Germany.

There is increasing criticism of the latter activity in America, among neutrals, in France and at home, while the Germans are said also to be laughing at it. I am sure it is a mistake to continue this business, which is becoming ludicrous, while the Poles are being bombed to pieces. Either we should drop bombs or not fly over at all. But Campbell Stuart[1] backs the idea as if it was going to win the war. In addition, each time we carry out a raid we seem to fly over neutral territory and infuriate either Holland, Belgium or Denmark – all three have now protested.

I quite see it is wrong to dash off against the Germans, either by land or air, merely to relieve the Poles, when by conserving our effort we should be able to deal a much shrewder blow later. Obviously we must not be led into any false move by quixotry. We can, in any case, do little to relieve Poland at present – she must go down now to rise again as a result of allied victory in the west, perhaps not till two years' time. On the other hand, there is Western morale and French morale to think of, and war conducted on go-slow principles may strain relations with the French who are already in heavy action on the Maginot Line, may lower our stocks in America, beside leading to criticism and pressure "to do something" over here. It is going to be a difficult line to follow. But above all we must avoid the insensate slaughter of 1914 and 1915.

The peace machine has turned over to war with surprising smoothness, all things considered. The new Ministries are getting down to their work and the War Cabinet is making long-term plans. But obviously there must soon be further changes in the Cabinet. It is absurd that Amery, Duff Cooper, Lloyd should have no posts in a national emergency and such people as Macmillan[2] and Cross[3] should be in. Harry Crookshank should also be in a more key position.

Some indication that Daladier is about to enlarge his Government,

1. Director of Propaganda in Enemy Countries 1939–1940.
2. Lord Macmillan, Minister of Information at the start of the war.
3. R. H. Cross, M.P. Minister of Economic Warfare.

possibly with Herriot as M.F.A. We are doing all we can here to ease Bonnet out.

Great dissatisfaction at Ministry of Information which is stopping *all* news, though this is really due to the Service Departments who wish to keep everything secret so that the enemy shall not know.

September 15th

Turkish negotiations still hang fire. Cabinet today decided a sharper reply should be sent to the continuous demands for more money and more supplies. Cabinet took a sinister view of Turkish attitude, which they thought resembled that of Molotov. They felt Turkey should be asked whether she still wanted a treaty or not. Halifax had meeting to discuss this. It was felt that Turkey was waiting to see what Russia intended to do before committing herself. If Russia invaded Poland, as it now seemed she might, Turkey would not want to come in against her.

Halifax also discussed question of arranging for Polish Government to emerge through Rumania if they were driven to the frontier, so as to enable them to set up and carry on in France or Great Britain. We are going to inquire at Bucharest whether they would arrange safe passage.

Belgian neutrality also discussed. Chiefs of Staff very anxious, as British Army is on northern end of line, some staff contacts should exist with Belgium in case Germany violates Belgian neutrality as in 1914. But the Belgian Government, under the lead of King Leopold, refuses flatly to discuss anything for fear of compromising themselves. Moley Sargent and Alec Cadogan believe the Belgians intend to allow the German armies to pass through Belgium as *force majeure* rather than fight again. It is felt that no approach through Ambassador or Minister for Foreign Affairs is likely to shift Belgium to agree to any staff talks. It has been decided therefore that King George should write personally to King Leopold and point out that if Belgium is attacked and no preliminary discussion with Great Britain has taken place, it will be too late for us to help. This will be bad for us but worse for Belgium.

September 18th

Lunch with Weizmann. He did not take Russian invasion of Poland too tragically. First of all the population were Ukrainian in that area, not Polish (W. himself came from Pinsk), and it meant that the Ukraine was lost to Hitler – a warning to Hitler, in fact. Weizmann afterwards saw Halifax who was immensely impressed with him. He asked me my views about W. and his reliability. I said I would trust him absolutely and he said he would too but he only wanted to check his judgment against mine. He was very impressed by the possibility he had of good work in America and also for obtaining and trans-mitting information to and from Germany through Jews. W. said he thought the Rhineland might crack as being very anti-Nazi.

The Turks also do not take the Russian invasion too badly, their views are much the same as above.

September 22nd

Russian business working out slowly, so far not too badly. Russians have cut off Germany from direct access to Rumania by occupying up to the Hungarian border. They are moving into all Eastern Poland, almost up to Warsaw. I cannot believe this suits Germany's book, although of course she is saying it does.

Rumanians are behaving very badly over Polish Government, which they are seeking to intern. The Polish Government is to be set up in France where we shall recognise it. Meanwhile Warsaw sur-rounded by Germans and Russians is still holding out.

Turkish treaty not yet signed, but the signs are that it is now very near signature, though the Turks have driven a very hard bargain over the financial and economic clauses. Turkish Minister of Foreign Affairs just off to Moscow about Russo-Turkish Non-Aggression Pact. He, too, does not think Soviet action will do us much harm – "a warning to Hitler".

What will Germany do next? Crash down over Hungary, who would resist, into Rumania after the oil, or concentrate all her forces against France and ourselves in the West? Nobody can say yet and we must be prepared for either. Arrangements and concentration in France are being completed smoothly and relations between us and the French could not be better. At sea we are slowly mopping up submarines, which in turn are taking a steady, but not too great, toll of our shipping. As the convoy comes into being, this should diminish. Nobody here knows where the *Bremen* is, but we think she may be in Murmansk.

All German weapons – superiority in man-power and in aircraft, in tanks, etc. – are designed for quick success. All ours – blockade, sea power and world financial and economic resources – are long-term ones. If Germany cannot win a quick success, she cannot hope to win a long drawn war. Our problem is to hold up and contain early German onslaughts while our long-term weapons come into play and the German population and German resources are worn down. The role of our army, navy and air force must therefore be essentially defensive. The blockade is our offensive. The danger is that we shall squander our military resources in costly offensives instead of keeping the military, except for local action, strictly on the defensive while the blockade is worked up. I gather Gort[1] and Gamelin are both sound on this.

The question of a Salonika expedition is being considered. If Germany goes into Russia then it is thought a base of operations must be organised there. We should warn Italy that we have no designs on her. On the other hand, such a new theatre would mean a dangerous diversion of our own forces, although it would also mean a dispersion of German forces. The Balkan armies, though brave, have little first-class equipment and we have but little to spare them. A difficult problem.

Italy remains on the fence. We get more and more accounts of the anti-German and pro-peace feeling of the Italian people, the House of Savoy, the Church, the army, and of the increasing unpopularity of the regime. Musso himself is reported to be in failing health, with what truth we do not know, but I doubt it. The Italian people still have a pathetic faith in him to pull them through. Ciano is all over Loraine, but one cannot believe him. On the whole it looks less and less likely that Musso could or would bring Italy into war against us and France. She stands to gain a good deal, financially and economically, by staying neutral. We can buy much from her, even if we prevent her from selling much to Germany. Francis Rodd is going out next week to take preliminary soundings for an all-in economic agreement to meet our requirements under the blockade. All to be done very delicately. Italy has agreed like a lamb to a reversion to

1. Lord Gort, C.-in-C. of the British Expeditionary Force (B.E.F.).

Nyon procedure as regards her submarines – none to submerge except in certain pre-arranged areas.

On the whole, the Government machine has really turned over from peace to war remarkably smoothly. Plans for three years' war being worked out and, as far as one can see, on sound lines. The problem is to square our maximum military with our maximum economic effort and *both* with our finances. The last is going to raise very big problems – without war loans from U.S.A. It looks as if we might have to restrict our effort for financial reasons.

The one big uncertainty is the effect of air power. How much harm can the Germans do with their superiority in air power? Can they deal a crippling blow to our industries, shipping or London? And again, how strong is the Maginot Line? Gort has said "the war may be lost in France, even though it cannot be won there".

And what about Hitler's threatened new weapon? We think it may be some chemical or bacteriological business. Weizmann spoke to me about this. A German Jewish chemist friend of his, now in Switzerland, mentioned to him some time ago that the Germans were up to some new devilry of this kind and W. has offered to go out to Switzerland to see him. I have passed this offer on to the hush-hush people.

September 26th

More and more evidence accumulating of bad aspects of defensive tactics on Western Front – among neutrals and in U.S.A., where it is thought we don't mean business, at home, where public opinion cannot understand it, having never been told the facts of German air superiority, and among our allies. The leaflet-dropping adds fuel to these flames.

Poland now quite rolled up except for Warsaw. Soviets in occupation of over half, including the oil. Polish Government practically interned by Rumanians, but this is of less consequence, as they are all quite discredited on their own side.

Kingsley Martin (*New Statesman*) told me yesterday that there was a great deal of pacifism among his readers. This will certainly be fed by a stalemate type of war.

September 27th

I saw Clifford Norton who had just returned from Poland by way of

Rumania – with the Embassy. He spoke of the absolutely ruthless and deliberate bombing and machine-gunning by the Germans of civilians – women and children – well away from any military objectives. He said the Polish Higher Command are bad, and Beck and Smygly-Rydz were now discredited. The Rumanians were determined to intern the latter as they were terrified of doing anything which might bring German wrath upon them. The Poles are trying to persuade the President, Mosciki (who is also interned), to appoint a successor outside Poland and then resign, the continuity of the Polish state would then be preserved, before the Germans can appoint a puppet Polish Government. In the parts of Poland which Soviet Russia has occupied, a regular *jacquerie* is proceeding.

September 28th

Ribbentrop and the Turkish Minister of Foreign Affairs both now in Moscow. We all feel rather doubtful about the Turks standing out against their blandishments.

Our guarantee to Rumania covers aggression from any quarter, if Rumania resists. This means that we should in certain circumstances have to fight Soviet Russia if she goes into Bessarabia. (The Polish Treaty was limited by a secret protocol to aggression by a European power, i.e. *not* Russia.) H. is determined not to do this. Our guarantee was unilateral and can therefore be modified – as of course at the time it was made we only had aggression by Germany in mind. Nor can we, in fact, help Rumania against Russia even if we would, as Turkey would not help us against Russia.

September 29th

Dahlerus, the famous intermediary, has turned up again. He sought out Ogilvie-Forbes[1] at Oslo and asked if he could come over with a "peace offer" from Goering. He arrived today and proposes apparently peace and disarmament on basis of an independent Czechoslovakia and Poland. But yet today in Moscow Ribbentrop and Stalin have agreed to partition Poland finally!

1. Sir George Ogilvie-Forbes, Ambassador to Norway.

October 3rd

German divisions steadily rolling up from East to West, but we are debarred from any serious offensive action on trains or concentrations because of our air inferiority and the need of gaining every month we can before the real fighting begins. I suppose this strategy is all right?

October 5th

Two very strong peace feelers are out at present. Our old friend Dahlerus, who came over last week, is anxious to come again. He then told us that Goering would be ready to meet a negotiator in neutral country and to consider independent Poland, Czechoslovakia, disarmament. We have now heard much the same thing from Ankara, where Hugessen has had it via his Dutch colleague from Papen who is Ambassador there. Latter went further and intimated that Hitler would have to be side-tracked or eliminated altogether. He claimed to be working with Goering and to be moved by the Bolshevik turns which Nazi policy is now taking. This may well be true. He also talks very big about an independent Poland and Czechoslovakia, a parliamentary regime for Germany herself, disarmament and guarantees. We are keeping both these sources in play to see what they may produce, but otherwise there is no intention of contemplating a patched-up peace with Hitler. "Hitler must go" is the slogan, and the P.M. has now said in the H. of C. that we cannot negotiate with the present German Government.

October 6th

A.E. dined last night. He complained of lack of imagination in War Office in only calling up 20-year-olds upwards and not letting 30-year-olds at least volunteer. He said how inspiring and refreshing Winston was in Cabinet. P.M. still looked at everything personally and would not consider using anybody whom he disliked on personal grounds, e.g. Amery. Speaking of war aims, A.E. holds strongly we must work for the Briand ideal of a United States of Europe – all arms under international control, otherwise disarmament.

On all sides I hear the view that the present Government isn't

324

broad enough or strong enough to last very long, probably up to Christmas after the first shocks of war.

Weizmann dined tonight. He is just off to Switzerland to see a German-Jewish chemist friend of his to try and find out if he knows anything about Hitler's "secret weapon". He sent Namier[1] to see me just after Hitler had referred to it, to say this friend, when last he'd seen him, had made some reference to this possibility: he wondered whether we knew anything about it and offered to go at once to Switzerland if necessary to interview his friend again. I passed this on to our hush-hush people and now they've arranged for him to go.

October 18th

Dined with Weizmann last night on his return from his visit to Switzerland. A most interesting evening. W. had succeeded in seeing his German-Jewish chemist friend – Velsteter – at Zurich. The latter gave as his opinion that the Nazis had no *new* chemical discovery with which to surprise us (as there were no decent chemists left), but that they had got very large quantities of a mustard gas (liquid form) for dropping in large bombs: this stuff was nothing new but the quantities were the new feature. Had we the means of retaliating because that was the only means of defence? Velsteter impressed on W. the great danger of underrating "totalitarian" war: he thought we were in for a very stiff job indeed. Bad as internal conditions in Germany were, food shortages, etc., we must not underrate capacity of German people to tolerate conditions which would never be accepted in G.B. or France.

Weizmann had also seen Paul Reynaud in Paris and formed the definite impression that he was grooming himself to be President of the Council in Daladier's place. He had also seen Dautry[2] and thought highly of him. The latter had asked after possibility of repair shops and powder factories in Palestine (for armies in Syria) which W. said could certainly be erected.

October 25th

Luncheon today for Bastianini,[3] new Italian Ambassador. P.M., H.,

1. Sir Lewis Namier, the historian.
2. Raoul Dautry, French Minister for Armaments.
3. Bastianini had succeeded Grandi on September 18th 1939.

Clarendon, R. A. Butler, Crolla and myself. Rather an obvious wooing of Bastianini. P.M. and H. discussed Ribbentrop for benefit of B. – how he had never understood this country – how he announced on his arrival that he had come to fight Bolshevism. His vanity, his stupidity. H. confessed that he rather liked Goebbels and Goering. The former was very quick and the latter a mixture of the Duke of Devonshire, his head gamekeeper and Al Capone, all topped off with a schoolboy.

October 30th

A.E. dined last night. He is most disappointed with Winston's attitude over Eire – latter wishes to seize the ports and drive Eire out of the Empire! A.E. says De Valera is doing all he can for us and it would be madness to drive him further and start up all the trouble again. And what would U.S.A. say? Apart from that, Eire even now is our best recruiting ground. Winston's attitude over India is just as bad. Here he is up against Halifax. A.E. is beginning to doubt whether Churchill could ever be P.M. so bad is his judgment in such matters.

I rubbed into A.E. how necessary it was for him to remain at Dominions Office in such circumstances.

November 1st

Musso's purge of pro-Nazi Ministers very significant. It looks as if Muss has had his hand forced or else why should he make such a blatant change which is all against his policy of sitting on the fence but leaning slightly over to the German side? Perhaps the King and the Army have forced it owing to the known incapacity of the latter to wage war owing to shortages.

U.S. Ambassador Kennedy is engaged in defeatist propaganda with Beaverbrook. I'm afraid he only thinks of his wealth and how capitalism will suffer if the war should last long.

Van very active with various "contacts". All his geese are swans – but their song is much the same as Dahlerus and all purport to come from Goering. I think the feelers for peace are genuine as far as those in the background are concerned, but I don't trust Goering. Anyway, I don't believe any of these elements will do anything. They expect

326

us to fight their battles for them. They represent the anti-communist element of the Nazi party who are veering towards the moderates among the officials, the army and business.

November 3rd

Discussion in H.'s room (Loraine, R. Campbell, Van, Alec C., Lloyd (who is just going on a tour of Balkans), Strang, Nichols,[1] R. A. Butler and me) on possibility of encouraging a neutral Balkan bloc. All agreed this would be ideal. P. Loraine very anxious that we should not initiate it but let it go ahead if it can on its own and then encourage it from outside. He was opposed to our inviting Italy to organise it but favoured leaving her to try if she wished. Campbell also thought movement must come of itself – spoke of Yugoslav-Bulgarian contacts designed to bring this about. Yugoslavia less mistrustful of Italy than she had been, but still very suspicious. Yugoslavs determined to keep neutral if possible and therefore rather resentful of Turkey's action, as a member of Balkan Entente, in concluding Anglo-French pact, i.e. with belligerents.

Rumania has now proposed to fellow-members of Entente a scheme for formation of a neutral bloc to which Bulgaria, Hungary and Italy should be invited. All turns on whether Bulgaria can be satisfied by concessions and by how much, e.g. in Dobruja or more. It was decided to adopt attitude of passive encouragement and offer to support any such plan if it could be brought to life.

November 9th

Great nervousness in Holland and Belgium who now fear Germany is about to invade them. This was the reason for the joint offer of mediation by Leopold and Wilhelmina which was launched so suddenly yesterday.

We are inclined to doubt Germany attacking them now that there is a great accumulation of divisions opposite Belgian and Dutch frontiers.

Belgians still refuse any staff conversations with us. This is due to Leopold. Spaak and Co. are veering in favour of closer contact with us and France.

Fresh feelers are being put out to us all the time from Germany –

1. Sir Philip Nichols, then Counsellor at Foreign Office.

this time from some generals who say they are prepared to take over regime.

Bomb outrages in Munich last night. Hitler narrowly escaped. Is this the work of "the generals"?

P.M. ill with gout.

A great row between the Air Ministry and the War Office over the provision and control of aircraft for the B.E.F. Gort wants masses of small mass-produced aircraft under his orders. Air Ministry say they can only be provided at expense of Air Offensive and Defensive Force which is none too strong, and they don't believe such small and cheap aircraft would be of any use anyway. And where are the pilots to come from?

Charles Peake tells me that the Duke of Windsor has sent a message to Monckton from France to say he is flying over during the weekend in a private aeroplane and wants to see Winston but that the King is not to know! Monckton, after taking Charles' advice, has warned Winston, who is saying that he has to visit fleet over this weekend and is telling Hardinge about it. He is also telling Belisha and will ring up the Duke tonight to tell him he cannot come. The D. of Windsor has some nebulous job at Gamelin's H.Q.

November 10th

Great nervousness still about Holland and Belgium. Former quite sure now that she is to be attacked. A further telegram sent last night to Belgian Government urging importance of immediate staff conversations if we were to be able to help.

Our Passport Officer at the Hague was shot last night apparently just when he was conversing or waiting to converse with emissaries of the German generals referred to above. The Nazis dashed over the frontier and shot up the whole party – details still awaited.

I had a message via our Consul at Geneva today from Riesser who had gone to see him urgently last night to say he had learned from a trustworthy source that the Germans intended to make a mass air-attack on England within the next few days; probably over Holland and on November 11th. I attach importance to this as I regard Riesser as absolutely sincere though, of course, he may be misinformed. Anyway, the warning has been passed on to those concerned.

1. Walter Monckton, later Lord Monckton, the Duke's legal adviser.

328

November 10th (contd.)

According to telegram from Paris tonight Belgians have now asked for staff talks with French.

November 11th

No bombing after all today!

Slight *détente* on Dutch and Belgian frontiers – yet it only looks like lull before the storm. Belgian Government have now asked to be told through our Military Attaché at Brussels what help would be sent to Belgian army in case of appeal to British guarantee. Belgian M.A. has also been received by Gamelin. We are concerting our reply with Gamelin as C.-in-C., but I understand his view to be that unless he has three days' notice he cannot and will not take up positions in Belgium.

There is a difference of opinion between us and French (Gamelin) about use of airpower. We think that if Germany invades Belgium and/or Holland we should use our airforces, not only to bomb invading German forces but also to bomb Ruhr, thus disorganising German production and affecting civilian morale. Gamelin wishes to concentrate all on German advancing forces and to spare Ruhr because of danger of retaliation on French air factories which are inadequately protected by French Air Force. This is to be discussed by Supreme Council shortly.

November 13th

Still no further move against Holland or Belgium. King Leopold still holding out obstinately against committing himself to conversations, but he has gone so far as to authorise his people to ask Gamelin and us what we would do in first 48 hours *if asked.*

Poor Leopold is in a desperate dilemma. If he commits himself to a military agreement, the Germans will say he has violated his neutrality and so justify German invasion. If he doesn't get agreement with us and France we cannot afford him proper help if he is attacked – a vicious circle. Moreover, it can be represented as an allied interest that Germany should *not* invade Belgium and therefore that Belgium should not provoke Germany. The answer is, I suppose,

329

that Germany will invade Belgium if it suits, whatever Belgium does.

I hear our Passport Officer and his companion on the Dutch frontier were shot and dragged back into Germany by the raiding party, together with the German representatives of the generals they were talking to!

November 17th

Daladier and Gamelin came over today to Supreme Council meeting at No. 10 to decide difference about bombing policy. It was agreed to accept French view of not bombing Ruhr unless and until Germans bombed our towns, regardless of whether they invaded Belgium or Holland.

Lull persists on Dutch frontier – many rumours of trouble with German generals.

Weizmann has had a very satisfactory interview with Ironside about Palestine and the punitive and savage measures being taken there against the Jews. Latter disagreed profoundly with this policy and favoured a strong Jewish Palestine as a British interest.

November 22nd

Charles Peake dined last night and told me more about A.E.'s visit to France with the Dominion representatives. He also emphasised as did A.E. to me on Sunday the exiguous character of the defences in front of the British Line in comparison with the Maginot, and also the very wide front being held there by each British unit. We agreed that A.E. should bring this to the notice of the Cabinet, who have asked him to lay a report on the visit. Charles will press him to do so and after dinner we drafted a note for him. It seems absurd to run any risk of the Maginot being turned by leaving the defences for the Franco-Belgium frontier dangerously weak.

November 23rd

The new German magnetic mines which are being dropped by aeroplanes are causing considerable havoc. This seems possibly to be Hitler's new weapon, adopted when it looked as if we had got the better of the attacks on merchant shipping by U-boats through convoys, etc.

330

November 25th

One of the new German magnetic mines has been found in fact at low tide, having been dropped too near the shore by an aeroplane. It is now being examined by our experts. It appears that they can only work in shallow waters.

The *Rawalpindi* – armed merchant cruiser – has been sunk by the *Deutschland* near Iceland.

I'm afraid my growing forebodings in the past about the Admiralty may be proving all too true. They've been incredibly slack over all their preparations. They had even neglected the Scapa defences! We are now in this position: the Grand Fleet is in Clyde, German aircraft are continually over our coasts, and Germany can claim with some truth command of the North Sea. Only Churchill could hold the position with his courage and prestige. The Government are lucky indeed to have him to cover up their criminal neglect of the Admiralty in the last two years. But we may yet have to pay for it with some heavy disaster.

December 7th

A.E. dined. He told me that there was a great move to get rid of Belisha whom the soldiers hated and to put himself into the War Office. Kingsley Wood had even told him of this and said he had spoken to the P.M. of it.

December 24th

We go to Paris on 28th and I've been on leave since early in December when I handed over as Private Secretary to Ralph Stevenson. Very sorry to leave London.

The Government seem to be losing face in all quarters – even where their stocks, e.g. the City, stood highest, and there is a general feeling that the P.M. is too old and must go, but also general confusion as to who can take his place and how he can be got rid of. At the secret session last week Burgin and Belisha were both on the mat and the P.M., winding up, made a very poor impression. The chief criticism now is against the supply and economic side of the war programme, all of which cries out for co-ordination and greater drive.

An M.P. who is an officer made a most damaging attack on the Government over the state of his regiment which was just off to the front. I understand it is now most likely that changes will be made in the Government over the recess but that the P.M. will stick on. Halifax is still favourite for next P.M. – if only *ad interim* – though many are doubtful if he could hold it. Winston is a good second, but everybody is nervous of his instability. Recent naval successes have, of course, put his shares up. A.E. is lying pretty but might well get the War Office *vice* Belisha and he would certainly adore to get it. Belisha is loathed by G.H.Q.

I saw Clement Davies[1] here today. He has withdrawn his support of the Government because of its economic inefficiency – violently anti-Simon but also anti-P.M.

The heroic and effective resistance of the Finns against the Russians[2] is surprising and heartening everybody. It might well precipitate a revolution in Russia against Stalin himself. The naval victory at Montevideo[3] has also had the most beneficial effect on neutral opinion. It was a magnificent affair and nobody in Germany can feel pride in it. I have a feeling that these events must be having a profoundly disturbing effect on German opinion. No German except an absolute extremist can feel anything but acute discomfort at seeing the Russians attack the Finns – the Nordic race *par excellence* – whose independence was originally won by German aid. Nor can Soviet advanced bases in the Baltic be regarded as anything but a disastrous result from Ribbentrop's diplomacy. Again the Van Spee affair and the scuttling of German ships must be shocking to German naval and military opinion. May this not precipitate an internal revolution? I doubt it, although I don't think it impossible that the war may fritter out sooner than we expect into a series of unco-ordinated local efforts. But what would be worst would be for Hitler to disappear and for Goering and Co. to take charge and then come to us with offers of peace conditional on a joint crusade against Russia. Many here would be foolish enough to fall into such a trap, the P.M. and Horace Wilson first of all, I believe. Germany, we can never sufficiently insist, is our only enemy. Once we have defeated her roundly, Russia will cease from troubling. I saw Hardinge before I left

1. Clement Davies, Liberal M.P. for Montgomeryshire and Leader of the Liberal Party 1945–1956.
2. Russia had invaded Finland on November 30th.
3. The Battle of the River Plate.

London and he was absolutely clear on this point. What a good influence he is there!

The Balkans for the moment look safe, but if Russia defeats the Finns, Bessarabia will come next. I think Germany would then push down too so as to get to the oilfields first, and then even Italy might move in – though on which side I don't know – to pick up what she can. I hope and trust when the hour of settlement comes the sins of Italy will not be forgotten. Mussolini is every bit as bad in his Italian way as Hitler. How can we fight for the reconstruction of Poland and Czechoslovakia and condone the rape of Abyssinia and Albania? His system was the father of Hitler's and is equally based on militarism, suppression and robbery. Mussolini is also hostile to us and sympathetic to Germany. But he hopes to bide his time and come to the help of the victor – as Italy always does and will. And meanwhile he hopes to coin money by selling arms to us, thereby rehabilitating his tottering finances. We should firmly resist any extension of Italian influence to the Balkans. As we get stronger we shall speak a different language to her.

Part Five
February 4th 1940 - June 24th 1940

When O.H. arrived in Paris just before New Year 1940, the Government of Edouard Daladier had been in power since April 1938. On the outbreak of war Daladier had shunted Bonnet – the arch appeaser – into the Ministry of Justice, but political rivalries prevented him from finding a suitable replacement. He himself therefore, as well as being Prime Minister was bearing the additional burdens of the Foreign Ministry and the Ministry for War. Paul Reynaud was his Minister of Finance, while Georges Mandel was at the Colonial Office. Daladier, the leader of the slightly Left of Centre Radical Party seemed a more credible wartime leader than Mr Chamberlain. But with men such as Herriot, Blum, Chautemps, Delbos, and Marin, outside it, his Government was equally criticised for not being a National one. He was expected to be on the point of reconstructing it when a bad fall off his horse on January 7th temporarily put him out of action and to some extent appeared to affect his prestige.

The great problem during the winter for the French Government was the Russo-Finnish War which cast a more sinister shadow on France because of its large Communist Party who had opposed the war against Germany ever since the Nazi-Soviet Pact, and the militant Right which seized on the Russian invasion as a pretext for a complete break with the Soviets. The news of the Armistice on March 13th was a blow to the Government which was blamed for not having provided more assistance to the Finns. The situation was hardly helped by Sumner Welles' peace-feeling mission to the warring capitals in the same month which afforded opportunities for intrigue by the Bonnet faction in the Government.

On March 19th in a crucial debate, though the Government won by 239 votes to one, there were more than three hundred abstentions. Daladier resigned and was succeeded by Paul Reynaud.

Reynaud's position was always weak, for, as an independent, he did not have the backing of any single party. He could count on Socialist support from Blum, but to remain in power he needed the votes of the

335

Radicals – the party of the man he had just ousted from the Premiership. He felt obliged to make Daladier Minister for War, whilst keeping the Foreign Office for himself, though his talents were more needed in the other post. These two politicians effectively cancelled each other out by their rivalry and mutual antipathy. Reynaud's other disadvantage was the defeatism and interference of his mistress Hélène de Portes.

But the scene was changing from the lobby to the battlefield. On March 28th Reynaud signed the Agreement with Great Britain by which both countries pledged themselves never to sign a separate peace. On the same day the British mined Norwegian territorial waters to prevent their use as cover for German iron-ore ships from Narvik.

On 9th April the Germans invaded Denmark and Norway. In reply, the British landed at Namsos and Andalsnes. In spite of naval victories, the British were forced to evacuate by May 3rd. This was the end for Chamberlain. In the debate on a vote of censure, his majority fell to 81. An attempt to continue by widening the existing Government failed when Labour refused to serve under him. On May 10th the Germans invaded the Low countries, Chamberlain resigned, and by the evening Churchill was Prime Minister. Reynaud survived by the skin of his teeth in Paris, preserved by the German onslaught at Sedan.

On May 14th Sedan fell; by the 20th the Germans had reached the Channel ports. The rout had started.

"My God! what a pass those bloody old men have brought us to!" wrote O.H. to a friend on 21st May, "We were never ruthless enough with them I'm afraid. What a responsibility both S.B. and Neville bear . . . !"

British Embassy, Paris.

February 4th 1940
P.M., Halifax, Winston, Stanley, Kingsley Wood and Alec Cadogan
arrived for Supreme Council meeting tomorrow.

Long talk between Halifax, Alec and Ambassador[1] about Finland
and French plan of sending support to Petsamo. H. does not like idea
of expeditions unless militarily sound. Doubtful if we can do anything up there without Swedish and Norwegian consent (which unlikely to be forthcoming). What we want to do is to stop Swedish
iron ore to Germany, doubtful if Petsamo expedition could help
there. French think that our appearance at Petsamo would make
Germany invade Sweden. Very doubtful. Danger in France of effect
on morale if inactivity continues indefinitely.

We impressed on Halifax importance of continuing after war the
present relations with France – the greatest lever we have.

February 29th

I saw Beaumont-Nesbitt today here for a conference with the
French. Gort, Ironside and Macfarlane[2] also here.

Beaumont-Nesbitt said he did not believe the Norwegians and
Swedes would ever allow us to go through their territory to Finland
and that our whole expedition would have to be called off. He
thought it quite likely that Finland would have to go – presumably
Russia would take what she wanted and leave the rest. He did not see
any quick successes for us anywhere, but he doubted whether Hitler
could sit still and do nothing – more difficult for him even than for us.
He does not favour isolated attack on Baku. The important thing is to

1. Sir R. H. Campbell.
2. Lt.-General Sir N. Mason Macfarlane, D.M.I. with the B.E.F. 1939–
1940.

defeat the Germans before they can reorganise Russia and defeat the blockade.

We spoke of need for taking action now to continue the Anglo-French Alliance after the war and get it tied up before the strain of peace came; the difficulty of getting French and English to like and understand each other. Vast improvement in this respect in relations between British and French troops and staffs since last war. Peter Loxley,[1] who left here yesterday, said that he had heard disquieting news about the P.M.'s determination to continue the war to a resolute end. According to his information, the P.M., who writes regularly to a sister in Birmingham, had told her that it would be a mistake to beat the Germans too hard and create chaos which would open the door to Bolshevism. Victor Gordon Lennox told me the same story last week.

March 1st

Lawford[2] rang up from F.O. about 5.30 p.m. to ask us to find out immediately French views on following. The Finnish Minister had just come and asked if we could send 100 bombers plus 50,000 men and if we could get Norwegians and Swedes to agree to passage of men, and if they would not, would this alter our decision to help. Cabinet was meeting at six and wished for immediate reply.

H.E. (His Excellency, i.e. the Ambassador) was ill and so I went at once to Léger who rang up Daladier's Chef du Cabinet then and there and told me that Holma[3] here had made a similar *démarche* this morning, and that Daladier had been in agreement with all requests. French contingent of men were ready to start: instructions had been sent to French representatives at Oslo and Stockholm to support our *démarche* there, and finally if Swedes and Norwegians refused, it was agreed that we should *passer outre* and make a forcible entry.

F.O. have not been keeping us well informed and Léger told us that the Finns had received a Soviet peace offer and been about to accept owing to their discouragement at the poor character of the help which the British had been able to propose to them. Apparently their figures were inexact and Daladier had begged them to postpone decision for 24 hours. Since then matters had been discussed with Halifax by Corbin and above decisions reached.

1. Of the Ministry of Economic Warfare.
2. Nigel Lawford, Assistant Private Secretary to Halifax.
3. Finnish Ambassador in Paris.

I am astonished at decision to make forcible entry, if necessary, and feel it will have worst effect on U.S. opinion, Sumner Welles[1] being in Berlin!

I saw Paddy Beaumont-Nesbitt again this evening dining with Gort at the Crawshays'. He, B.N., was also very surprised and still thought it a mistake. He thought Winston had stampeded the Cabinet. We none of us think the Swedes and Norwegians will give way.

March 3rd

Gort and Pownall[2] dined at the Embassy last night. H.E. was ill and so Maudie[3] and I entertained them. I talked to Gort after dinner. He felt the Scandinavian expedition was a mistake, a very difficult operation, not enough destroyers, and might, as I suggested, prove a Gallipoli. I said the French were naturally eager, as we were, to carry the main burden and it would stimulate our interest in the war. Gort thought Winston had an unlucky star and, all things considered, it was wise to back a lucky man.

I asked Gort how Gamelin and Georges[4] were getting on. He aid "Not too well". He thought it was jealousy and it was a great pity as both were good men. He said the French soldiers thought Georges the bigger man. Foch had said he had discovered two men – Weygand[5] and Georges, but possibly Gamelin got on better with the politicians. He, Gort, was very careful to retain the confidence of both. He was determined the B.E.F. should not become a bone of contention. He knew Gamelin well in his days as C.I.G.S. and he talked very confidentially with him. His relations with Georges were equally confidential.

March 14th

Acceptance by Finland of Soviet terms. I cannot help feeling a sense of relief that after all we are not committed to a Scandinavian expedition. I feel certain that our resources are not adequate and we

1. On his peace-feeling mission.
2. Lt.-General Sir H. Pownall, Chief of General Staff, B.E.F., 1939–1940.
3. Lady Harvey.
4. General Georges, Gamelin's Chief of Staff.
5. Weygand was then C.-in-C. of the French forces in Syria.

should have risked another Dardanelles campaign, possibly prolonging the war an extra year. We *must* go slow until our resources in
men and material are far greater, this means staying on the defensive
the whole of this year. Next year we should have air superiority and
then we can allow ourselves the luxury of attack. To have gone into
Finland across a reluctant and possibly obstructive Norway and
Sweden with two divisions and lines of communication stretching
right across the North Sea, always seemed to me madness. Fortunately the Finns did not appeal to us to send men and under strong
pressure from Sweden who was squeezed in turn by Germany, they
decided to accept terms.

Great Britain and France do not come well out of it because whatever way we look at it, it is a defeat for democracy. It is shaking up
Daladier badly here, but I do not think it will bring him down. I do
not know what the effect in England will be but in any case we are at
war "against evil things" and for strategic reasons it may be, and is I
think, necessary for us to go slow at this stage and eschew dissipation
of effort. Norway and Sweden are contemptible and lose all claim to
be representatives of that higher international morality which they
have so long preached at us. I am not sure whether Germany has in
the long run much to be pleased about, with Russia at Hangoe, etc.

Daladier, speaking in the Chamber on Tuesday, spilt all the beans
about the 50,000 men ready to go, our waiting for a Finnish appeal,
the unwillingness of Sweden and Norway. He even spoke of the
possibility of appealing to the Scandinavian workmen to aid us
against their Governments. This part was censored from the official
record but seems to have surprised and rather shocked the deputies.
Now tonight he has a secret session in the Senate where Flandin's
friends are going to attack him – for showing insufficient energy,
though really in the interests of ultimate defeatism. Daladier still
suffers much from his foot. He is having an extremely painful treatment to accelerate its re-setting so that he can again visit the armies,
which is almost an obsession with him.

March 25th

In London on leave.

Charles Peake dined. He said the P.M. last week had offered the
Labour Party three seats in the Cabinet, the Admiralty, Supply and,
he thought, some new post as economic co-ordinator. Attlee would

not come in, but Alexander, Greenwood and Morrison[1] were seriously considering it.

My first reaction was, what fools they would be to go in. We then thought if they should refuse they would take a big risk of being labelled unpatriotic, possibly having to wait a long time before a fresh chance occurred. P.M. might go on a long time yet as his stock was still pretty high. On the other hand, the Government stocks were very low indeed, especially Simon and Hoare. For Labour to go in without undertakings as to the conduct of the war, etc., would be fatal for them. Nobody trusts the Prime Minister's resolution. I suggested that they might say they would serve with the Prime Minister but not with Simon and Hoare. This would put them in a very strong position either way.

Paul Reynaud[2] got a majority of one only what with abstentions in the Chamber on Friday, but he is going on and will meet the Chamber again on April 2nd. He has annoyed the Radicals by his intrigues against Daladier, and the Right by his inclusion of three Socialists (a good move in itself). He is of course a Parisian, a bourgeois and well-to-do, and not the type of French politician who easily becomes a President of the Council. Daladier has all the qualities required and has an immensely strong hold over the country, but he lacks quick decision and has neglected both Chamber and Senate who are sulky with him. If Reynaud does fall next week I should hope Daladier would come back, stronger and wiser. What is essential is that both Daladier and Paul Reynaud should be in any Government. The bad men, Laval (whose attack on Daladier in the Senate started the landslide), Flandin (very anxious now to display his patriotism), and Bonnet (always double-crossing) are raising their heads and will become a danger if there is a prolonged Government crisis coupled with a peace offensive.

Paul Reynaud has sacked his Chef de Cabinet and henchman, Palewski, who had been working so hard to make him President of the Council, because Hélène de Portes is jealous of him. But he could be invaluable to him in keeping him *au courant* with political currents. One of the reasons for Daladier's fall has been, I am sure, the fact that *his* henchman, Jacques Kayser, has also gone to the army.

There is no doubt a strong demand in France for a more vigorous

1. Herbert Morrison (later Lord Morrison), Labour M.P. and Chairman of L.C.C.
2. Reynaud succeeded Daladier as Premier on March 22nd.

policy. Daladier himself knows it and wants it too, but has not been able to achieve it, mainly because of our slowness and hesitation over Finland. Paul Reynaud has become identified in the popular mind with vigorous action, like Winston here. But the attacks on the Government for lack of vigour are also being made by those who are defeatist at heart because they know that at present no other line of attack is possible and they hope to discredit the sound men and so drive in a wedge for themselves. That is the danger of these crises and jealousies. For Paul Reynaud has undoubtedly intrigued against Daladier – egged on by his entourage and by his own vanity – whilst Daladier undoubtedly mistrusts Paul Reynaud as a peasant distrusts a bourgeois.

March 26th

Moley Sargent dined last night, gave very depressing account of what Air Ministry[1] were doing, declining production, etc. On the other hand, he was encouraging about prospects of Anglo-French union after the war. There is to be a Supreme Council on Wednesday or Thursday and the idea is to make a declaration then about our joint intention of continuing after the war our existing arrangement. This declaration would be followed, according to Moley, by a regular treaty covering customs union, military unified command, common finance and foreign policy, etc., which, however, would require considerable preparation in public first. Moley is thinking already on the lines of a common Anglo-French nationality and of the perpetuation of the Supreme Council as the organ of the dual Anglo-French State.

He was also very gloomy about Mussolini whom he thought might well now come in against us. Sumner Welles apparently told Halifax that he thought he had had a stroke or very near to it. In any case he was not the man he was, and all his prejudices were on the side of Hitler and his regime.

I saw A.E. for a moment this evening. He said Winston had told him he thought he might get the post of co-ordinator and if so would A.E. take on the Air Ministry? A.E. was much tempted by this as he feels he is insufficiently occupied at the Dominions Office. A.E. did not think any offer would be made to Labour or that they would accept. He felt the old men in the Cabinet were hopeless.

1. Under Sir Kingsley Wood.

March 27th

Breakfasted with A.E., walked down to Dominions Office (D.O.) with him. Alec Hardinge had told him he thought the time had come now for the P.M. to go. A.E. seemed to think that if there was a re-shuffle he might be offered D.O. plus Colonial Office, Malcolm MacDonald going to another post in the Cabinet. I rub in on every occasion how well placed A.E. is at D.O., "in, but not of, the Cabinet", seeing all that goes on but not being responsible for the conduct of the war and so becoming discredited, having very useful and important work keeping the Dominions straight on foreign policy and representing their point of view in the Cabinet. But he chafes at the relative inactivity of the D.O. and grieves for an executive Department; he was disappointed at not getting the War Office and would certainly now like the Admiralty or the Air Ministry. The whole problem is to keep him calm. I also urge in and out of season that he should use all his spare time cultivating the House of Commons – he has been naughty about that. I also go at him for being too nice about the P.M. to whom he always feels, quite unjustifiably, a certain gratitude for giving him office when war began. I tell him that the P.M. hates him but was forced to take him and Winston in by public opinion.

March 30th

Jim Thomas lunched. Rather worried about A.E. and his chafing – he had been beating up the D.O. Also his neglect of H. of C. and his group and also of Bobbety. I am afraid he is going through a trying time, and great patience and complacency are not in his nature. He hates not being more actively on the job, and rightly so, with the sight of all these old dotards before him.

Jim said Government stocks and P.M.'s were very low everywhere. (I also hear from another source that the last Government loan has gone very badly, largely because of the unpatriotic conduct of the bigger City banks and firms.) Dick Law's attack on P.M. in debate was most courageous.

March 31st

Toby[1] came to see us. Much concerned about scope of Anglo-French Declaration[2] – was it merely a military alliance and did we commit ourselves to support *any* French Government and policy? He said there were two tendencies in Labour and T.U.C. circles: one isolationist and even pacifist, the other League of Nations and bellicose. The Whitsun meeting would be critical. The P.M. was mistrusted and such a declaration involving future policies should not have been made without careful preparation with Labour.

I explained the genesis of the declaration and Moley's idea of it being first step towards a real union between the two countries – customs, finance, military, etc. – which could serve as the main plank of a future federation of Europe and meanwhile be a powerful deterrent to Germany and the warmongers. I said I believed the P.M. approved of the principle but was going slow as he feared preliminary education was necessary at home. I suggested that Labour could for once give a useful lead by urging advance on really comprehensive lines.

Toby thought it very necessary to encourage Labour who were fearful of the Right in France and at the whittling down of the Blum programme. There would be great difficulty for instance over retaining conscription as part of this Anglo-French policy unless the confidence of Labour could be gained in respect of the *bona fides* of the policy and that it was not just a military alliance in the interests of the *Comité des Forges*[3] and English imperialists.

I had tea with Tyrrell today. He has at last come to the conclusion that we cannot win the war with the present P.M. and he must go. He says it was like with Asquith in the last war. People felt that however respected the P.M. was, he just had not got it in him to win the war. He did not think it would take much to upset him now. Halifax was the man to succeed. He was glad Finland had not materialised into an expeditionary force, which would have been very difficult to maintain. He was very anxious that we should not

1. J. H. Martin, Labour M.P. for Central Southwark 1939–1948.
2. By which Britain and France pledged themselves never to negotiate a separate Peace.
3. French Steelmaster's Federation, a body tainted for the Left with Kruppsian associations.

344

attack Russia or apply pinpricks. She would not, he was convinced, attack us. She wanted neither side to win, she would not help the Germans or us, but if we attacked her, then she would be forced into Germany's arms.

Winston, broadcasting on Saturday, I see, has now said that we did not intend to attack Russia.

April 1st

Dined with A.E. and Beatrice at Café Royal. He told me that John Simon was anxious to leave his present post and receive another, and that great difficulty was being found in getting a new Chancellor. He wondered whether it had ever occurred to them that he, A.E., might fill the bill and we discussed whether or not he could do so. We thought "Yes", though the chances were all against his being offered it. But it would be a great opportunity, valuable training, and if he succeeded, leave him obvious heir to the throne. A.E. said Dick Law had suggested it after a conversation with S.B. who had told him that A.E. must be at No. 10 for the peace and "that it was up to the young men of the party to see that he got there!"

A.E., apart from this possibility, seemed much more happy in his work at the D.O. and was hoping for a trip to Canada if Mackenzie King[1] agreed – which we all doubted.

April 2nd

Went to F.O. and saw Halifax for a moment. He said the French were tiresome people – this because, whereas they were willing to agree to the Narvik operation at our expense and cost, they were refusing to agree to the *Royal Marine*[2] operation because of possible reprisals on them. Yet at the Supreme Council on Thursday everybody had agreed to the combined operation.

I also saw William Strang who agreed with me, with relief, that we had not become involved in Scandinavia. He, like Tyrrell, was opposed to our attacking Russia.

Charles Peake and Leeper came in late. Leeper very keen on Anglo-French co-operation in future and setting his brains trust to

1. Canadian Prime Minister.
2. A plan to sow mines in the River Rhine.

345

work at it. I told him of what Toby Martin had said of Labour attitude and he promised to attend to it.

April 4th

British Cabinet reconstruction announced, a very poor affair, same old faces in new offices. Simon still at No. 11. Sam Hoare to be Air Minister. Chatfield is dropped – that at least is something for he had ceased to be useful. Poor De La Warr, who is now here, has been pushed into the Office of Works just when his good work at the Ministry of Education was bearing fruit merely to make way for Ramsbotham.[1]

Here trouble between Daladier and Paul Reynaud is rising afresh. D. having consented to serve under P.R. in the new Government is now intensely jealous of the latter's success in London when he brought back the Anglo-French Declaration, although it was not in any way due to P.R.'s efforts. In London agreement was reached on two operations to stiffen up the war – Narvik and the Royal Marines – but when P.R. returned to Paris he had to report that the French Government could not agree to the Royal Marines because of the risk of reprisals. But the fact is, we believe, that Daladier is putting a spoke in P.R.'s wheel by supporting the objections which Lebrun is known to feel to the Royal Marine operation in view of the likelihood of reprisals in Lorraine.

Deadlock having been reached and H.M.G. being fed up, the first idea was for the P.M. to send Daladier a personal letter, but when this was suggested to P.R. he refused to allow it and now Winston has come over to see P.R. and Daladier himself.

P.R. dined at the Embassy last night and met Winston, but P.R. now professes dislike of the operation also, but he would agree if Winston could convince Daladier and all three are invited to dine at the Embassy tonight. But Daladier will not come.

Meanwhile I dined with Camrose where I met Margerie, who told me P.R. was most anxious for the operation as were Gamelin and Darlan[2] and it was only "that old fool Lebrun" and Daladier who opposed it. Reynaud in very difficult position. No party behind him and Margerie very doubtful indeed of Daladier being got to give way, but Margerie hoped H.M.G. would help him by carrying out their

1. H. Ramsbotham, M.P., later First Viscount Soulbury.
2. Admiral Darlan, C.-in-C. of French Navy.

side of the bargain – Narvik – in spite of the French failure, at which he felt nothing but indignation. P.R., if helped now, would get stronger and would be able to do more later.

Camrose outraged at British Cabinet changes, especially Sam Hoare. He would like the P.M. to stay on but to jettison his unpopular colleagues. He was in favour of the closest Anglo-French cooperation after the war.

April 7th

In spite of Winston's visit, the French Government would not agree to the Royal Marines and H.M.G. have reluctantly consented to do their part alone. Reynaud was very grateful for this and this should much strengthen his position. Meanwhile Daladier is playing politics disgracefully, sulking and evidently determined to get P.R.'s blood. Senate and Chamber both meet next week and P.R.'s fate will be decided. It all depends on the Radicals who are angry about Daladier's resignation yet hesitate to overthrow P.R. because of the evident disapproval of public opinion in France at such exhibitions in wartime.

April 9th

News received this morning of German invasion of Denmark and Norway as a reply to our laying of mines in Norwegian waters at dawn yesterday.

P.R. and Daladier have gone off to London for Supreme Council. Daladier in a very bad mood, like a bear with a sore head, the Ambassador said who saw them off.

H.M.G. and French Government have offered all support to Norway.

No other news during the day, except reports of a naval engagement off Norwegian coast, no details. It also appears that the German expedition must have started before our mines were laid; i.e., the gathering of troops and the expeditions to Trondheim and Bergen.

P.R. told H.E. this morning that he would urge the immediate occupation of Belgium.

April 10th

P.R. and Daladier returned from London last night. It was agreed to call on the Belgian Government to allow us to occupy the country – useless, I fear. Belgium will never ask us in, we must go in without asking leave.

Still no reliable news yet of naval battle. Two British destroyers reported lost.

April 11th

Belgian Government have again refused to invite us in, though the Belgian Ministry of Foreign Affairs made a half-hearted suggestion that if we could promise to occupy the Albert Canal line, it might make a difference. We asked the French about this and Gamelin and Daladier have authorised the reply that we would do our utmost to achieve this.

A mission is being sent by air to Stockholm of Coulondre[1] and a French general, to be joined by British representatives in London. This was Reynaud's idea as our representatives in Sweden have not got their instructions owing to German control of communications. Mission is to promise full support to Sweden if she resists and joins Norway.

April 12th

Winston's speech in the H. of C. gave details of naval actions. Nothing about land.

Bad reports from Italy, she looks as if she may be preparing a coup against Dalmatia. Troop concentrations reported. If Mussolini does this, he will be taking what Giolotti was promised in 1916. Léger told me yesterday that Mussolini had been immensely impressed by Germany's blitzkrieg and it was most important to keep him informed of facts. Goering was pumping false reports into the Italian Ambassador and Mussolini might well be tempted to take a fatal step on falsified information.

1. Previously French Ambassador in Berlin.

348

April 14th

Very busy yesterday. Telegrams in and out all day. Daladier is behaving disgracefully, crabbing and cramping everything out of jealousy of P.R. We are trying to get hold of Jacques Kayser to bring his influence to bear.

No more news tonight. Charles Peake telephones that in London there is some anxiety about Belgium and Holland being violated tomorrow.

In Scandinavia the Anglo-French mission in Stockholm are urging the paramount importance of the recapture of Trondheim rather than of Narvik, where the Germans are isolated anyway. The Admiralty and War Office (and Winston) wish to clear up Narvik first and make it a base. But meanwhile the Germans are also consolidating themselves in south Norway. There has been some difference between the C.-in-C. on the spot who wanted to go into Trondheim at once, and the Admiralty who insisted on Narvik being taken first.

The Swedes very shaky. It looks just possible that they will defend themselves and that is all that can be said of them. King Gustavus has always been pro-Nazi. Norway holding out bravely, but she cannot do so long without help.

Reynaud-Daladier friction here at its worst.

April 19th

No more news from Scandinavia, except that we have landed near Narvik. About Trondheim, where attack is also imminent, all is silent. I have a feeling we are being too slow and should have gone smack at Trondheim before the Germans could push in reinforcements, leaving Narvik for later. I am afraid the Germans may succeed in cutting off and encircling Haakon[1] and his army. We are getting pathetic appeals from them all the time. We hear that a British transport has been sunk near the Shetlands. An early success in Norway may decide Musso to keep out, as certainly as a defeat for us will decide him to come in against us – which he is longing to do. I only hope that we and the French agree to go straight for him if he so much as touches Yugoslavia or Greece.

1. King Haakon of Norway.

349

We are always slow and late and I am convinced we must change this Government before we can win the war. We are losing time and men because of the Government. No neutral trusts us, nor does the U.S.A. The P.M. and his personal following in the Cabinet must go before we shall really get the best out of our position.

We are now discussing with the French Government and Turk our attitude *vis-à-vis* Italy. We have decided to go into Belgium at once, with or without invitation, the moment she or Holland is invaded. That is something.

April 22nd

Supreme Council here today. We lunched at Embassy, P.M. and Winston there. I saw Ironside after. He said we landed 9,000 men in Scandinavia without a single loss. German aircraft not very accurate or persistent. They had bombed an empty transport of 20,000 tons for an hour without hitting her. There has been some trouble with the French Admiral who had escorted the transports with Chasseurs Alpins to Namsos. He had skedaddled with his ships when a bomb (which did not explode) hit his deck, taking with him the anti-aircraft ship. Ironside has now got Gamelin to agree to all French troops there being under our command. He said P.R. was being very fussy and nervous, not nearly so calm as Daladier.

The Italian Ambassador here is going about saying we should not pay so much attention to what the Italian press says. "Italy is not neutral but non-belligerent." It was the Italian way of keeping the Germans quiet.

I saw Nevile Henderson today. He has turned all the profits of his book, present and future, over to a trust fund to assist British refugees from Germany. He expects it will bring in some £40,000. He has now retired from the Service and is going to the south of France to try to get fit. I am afraid he is not very well and also that he realises it himself. Rather sad.

April 23rd

Supreme Council ended today. Fairly good *stimmung*.[1] Relations between Daladier and P.R. seem better for the moment. St George's Day luncheon at the Inter-Alliés. We listened to first-rate speech by

1. Atmosphere.

Duff Cooper[1] relayed from London. What a pity he is so lazy. He might get to the very top.

Sir Stafford Cripps[2] called to see me this morning in Ambassador's absence. He is now returning from a trip which has taken him to Japan, China, Russia and America. I asked him his impressions of the Russian situation. He said that he had seen Molotov, but not Stalin, but that he had obtained the very definite impression that the Soviets were extremely nervous about their situation and were very anxious to come to some agreement with us. Ever since the blockading of the Baltic and their Western frontiers, they had become particularly touchy about their Eastern port of Vladivostock which had become their life-line with the outer world. Any action by us designed to blockade that port might have a disastrous effect upon them. On the other hand, they were nervous at the expansion eastwards of Germany and would certainly not wish to bring her any help if they could avoid it. They would wish to be more or less neutral as between the belligerents and disliked their present position by which they were linked up with Germany and might well be attacked by us. Among the increased supplies which were going into Russia through Vladivostock, it must be remembered there were now considerable quantities of goods for Russia herself which in ordinary times would have entered through the Baltic. Cripps thought that the time was now ripe to make an economic agreement with Russia in order to secure with their willing consent what we must otherwise obtain by force, namely an undertaking against re-export to Germany.

Cripps gave a good account of Chiang Kai-Shek's position in China and said that he was more than holding his own in the military sense. His great danger was the currency. If he failed to maintain the currency he would lose control. The Russians were not interfering with him and had in fact abstained from absorbing Sinkiang as they might have done. The Chinese Communists had no connexion with Soviet Russia and were being dealt with effectively by Chiang Kai-Shek himself.

A real danger was if Russia and Japan should come to terms to divide China. This was the danger which he foresaw if we ourselves were to attack Russia. From what he had heard at the United States

1. Still not in the Government.
2. Sir Stafford Cripps, M.P., had been expelled from the Labour Party in 1939 for trying to organise a Popular Front of the Left against Fascist aggression.

Treasury he believed that America would be prepared to join us in supporting the Chinese currency. He said our name was mud in China owing to our refusal to really do anything to help her which might offend the Japanese.

In Japan, Cripps said that he formed the opinion that Mr Grew, the American Ambassador, was doing more good by his blunt words of criticism than Sir R. Craigie who was always suggesting that an Anglo-Japanese agreement was only just round the corner. Mr Grew received numbers of letters from Japanese liberals thanking him for his words.

Finally, Cripps said that he had seen M. Paul Reynaud at the outset of his journey and the latter had expressed a wish to see him again on his return. He naturally had not asked to see him today, but he asked if we could let him know that if he was interested to hear his views he would either fly over at any time or, alternatively, would send him a copy of his report. Cripps will be seeing Lord Halifax as soon as possible in order to acquaint him with his views.

April 26th

The Ambassador was with Léger this morning when P.R. rang up and told the latter that it had been decided by the British Cabinet this morning to clear out of Norway because our positions there were untenable! Léger and P.R. both horrified, and Gamelin had been packed off to London to protest. We have no details ourselves. If this is true, it is bound to have a most tremendous moral effect on all neutrals. It may well decide Mussolini to take the plunge against us. This round goes to Hitler.

All one can say is that if our positions were so precarious, then it is clearly wise to evacuate at once rather than use up our resources, as at Gallipoli, in a hopeless struggle. It appears that lack of anti-aircraft protection is our trouble. I also suspect confusion and jealousy between the three services. It will certainly bring Reynaud down, it may bring Chamberlain down too, and if it does that, at least some good will have been done.

Herbert Morrison is here. I lunched at Sandford's with him, Blum, Monnet[1] and Sir Alfred Baker.[2] He dined with us tonight. He makes a very good impression, vigorous and independent in outlook. I did

1. M. Jean Monnet, economist and politician.
2. Legal Adviser to the Labour Party.

my best to stir him up to take more interest in foreign affairs. I told him to think of what the Lord Mayor of Birmingham had done. He favours an altogether more drastic conduct of the war – quicker decision, more punch and more plain speaking and hard hitting in politics. How right he is!

April 28th

We heard at midday yesterday that Reynaud, Daladier, Darlan and Vuillemin[1] had left for London for a Supreme Council in the afternoon.

A depressing day, but I saw Hoppenot[2] at dinner. He said the party had got back from London at eight and the situation was a little better. Gamelin had given a masterly appreciation of the situation and it had been decided to stay at Narvik, strengthening our base there and gradually to withdraw from the south of Norway.

Our trouble is lack of anti-aircraft protection and lack of aerodromes. Wherever we go in Norway our troops are exposed to ruthless bombing. The force near Dombas has suffered very badly and may not be able to get away.

H.E. saw Reynaud this morning and found him calmer.

April 29th

P.R. sent for H.E. late last night. He found him with Brantes, Assistant Military Attaché in London, who had flown over to Namsos where he had found a far more favourable situation than had been depicted at the Supreme Council. Quays in good order and fit for landings. Troops there quite happy and not being troubled by aircraft. P.R. wanted to have the Supreme Council decision (to clear out of south Norway) suspended. He also wanted to know why the Supreme Council had not had this information and generally gave the impression that we had got into a panic and were making a mess of things. Gamelin is still in London.

All very odd. We know nothing for certain here. Naturally P.R. will do everything to prolong our presence in Norway because his position as President of the Council depends on it. All seems to turn on whether or not we have command of the air. Unless we can

1. Chief of French Air Force.
2. Henri Hoppenot, Under-Secretary at Quai d'Orsay.

D.D.O.H.—Z

protect our troops against German aircraft, it is folly to try and stay.

April 30th

Still very little news. Situation in Norway seems a little easier and H.M.G. a little calmer about it. They seem to have been badly rattled two days ago.

Dined with the Fellowes.[1] Duff Coopers and Windsors there. H.R.H. (I had not met him before) was very friendly and asked a lot about conditions in the Diplomatic Service, in which he always took a great interest. He also asked me about Horace Wilson and how he got there – which I did my best to explain. The Duchess was also looking very friendly, though I did not get near her. Lady Diana [Cooper] curtsied very low to her!

May 1st

Depressing day. We hear 2,000 men were successfully evacuated last night. They hope for more tonight but expect bombing. News that things have not gone well has not so far leaked out. Mandel has said that it will have a disastrous effect here. Hoppenot takes the same view. P.R. will almost certainly fall, but I hope Daladier will be able to take his place without too much ado. But the rot may go further. Laval is active in the background. P.R. is in a nervous state and inclined to blame us and Gamelin and the two General Staffs for what has happened.

Lecture by Duff Cooper on opinion in the U.S.A. He wound up with a most rousing speech in English about the danger of France and Great Britain being defeated by German propaganda. He said we should doubtless have defeats before victory and then voices would be raised in France blaming Great Britain and in Great Britain blaming France. "These voices would be those of fools, cowards or traitors!" Nothing could have been more timely. He was cheered to the echo.

Many rumours and warnings coming to us from all sides about imminent operations against Holland and/or Belgium.

1. Hon. R. Fellowes and his wife Daisy.

May 10th

Awakened by air raid about 5 a.m. At 8 a.m. Mack[1] telephoned from the Embassy to say Germany had invaded Holland and Belgium.

Last night P.R. had resigned in view of differences and obstruction in his own Cabinet, but resignation had not been made public. He wished to substitute Weygand for Gamelin!

At home, after the debates of Tuesday and Wednesday,[2] Neville Chamberlain has at last been severely shaken and his resignation is also expected. Labour refuses to serve with him and the country wishes above all National Government. But doubt seems to exist as to who should succeed – Halifax or Winston. Herbert Morrison's was most effective attack on the Government and I hope he will be brought in.

Later news this morning is that P.R. will not resign for the present and will probably enlarge his Government and that N.C. will also carry on for the present. I only hope to God that N.C. and Co. do not get away with it again.

Holland and Belgium at once appealed for our help and Anglo-French forces are advancing into Belgium.

Six p.m. Charles Peake telephoned that N.C. has resigned and that the King is thought to have sent for Winston; Labour has agreed at Bournemouth to accept full share of responsibility in a new Cabinet.

P.R. here has arranged his troubles and has taken in Marin[3] and Ybarnégaray[4] on the Right; I do not yet know what is happening about Gamelin. Meanwhile our troops are advancing well and so far without opposition towards the Antwerp-Louvain line. The Dutch are reported to have done well against German aircraft and parachutists and the Belgians to be holding them up well too.

1. Sir H. Mack, then Counsellor at the Paris Embassy.
2. The Government majority had fallen to 81.
3. Louis Marin, Right Wing Catholic politician, leader of the Republican Federation.
4. Jean Ybarnégaray, Right Wing politician of the *Parti Social Français*.

May 11th

News tonight not so good. Germans have succeeded in getting bridges at Maastricht over the Meuse which the Dutch and Belgians had failed to blow up. Troops are now pouring over the Meuse there. German fighters and anti-aircraft guns are there in force and prevent bombing.

Otherwise British forces advancing well. The French have got a motorised division into Holland north of Antwerp. The Belgians are said to have given way in the Ardennes. Germans said to be attacking with 72 divisions.

The Dutch have shot down many aeroplanes. Rotterdam aerodrome, which had been captured by parachutists, has been recaptured.

At home Winston is P.M. I hear A.E. may get either War Office or Leadership of H. of C. Simon and Sam Hoare are to go.

Germans bombed Orléans Air Experimental Station last night without resistance. No aircraft apparently there to defend it.

May 12th

Another day of anxious waiting. We hear the Germans have got not only Maastricht but also Vize bridge over which troops are pouring. They have also captured a fortress near Maastricht "by a new method which made the occupants incapable of defending it," – as the German communiqué claims. We do not know yet what this is, but it looks as if it was gas. Our troops have got on to a line in advance of Louvain-Dyle running through Dyst, and the Belgians are falling back from the Meuse on to this. Our 10 divisions are wedged in between the French on either side. North of Antwerp a French cavalry division has reached Brede in order presumably to attempt to link up the Dutch and Belgian lines and prevent the Germans wedging their way through. German parachute troops still holding out in Rotterdam, though the aerodrome is clear. Our R.A.F. aircraft have bombed important German marshalling yard station behind Maastricht with great effect and also German troops advancing into Belgium.

R.A.F. doing wonders. Wherever they encounter the enemy both

356

fighters and bombers seem superior. Let us only hope there are enough of them. So far our losses not great.

Germans bombed Bourges last night. French have report that Hungary and Italy are about to advance against Rumania and Yugoslavia respectively in connivance with Germany.

The Pope's message to Belgium and Holland should give Mussolini something to think about, if he is still able to think. New factors are the use of parachutists and air-borne troops and "the new method" employed at Liége. What will be the importance of these? Everyone now on the look-out for the former which have had considerable effect in Holland.

The next problem is where the main thrust is to take place; probably at Longwy where the Maginot ends and the newer, less good, line begins.

May 13th

Bad news from Italy. It looks almost certain as if Mussolini were now coming in against us, possibly in conjunction with a German-Hungarian drive against Rumania. Incident in Rome last night when Virginia Cowles and party from Embassy were attacked in the street. Two air raids over Paris last night. Our R.A.F. brought down a great number of German machines yesterday, morale of latter does not appear high, all very young boys.

Germans, however, reported to have recovered aerodrome in Holland.

British Cabinet still cannot decide to bomb *behind* the German lines *in* Germany or German military targets. (This from Air Attaché who got it from Air Ministry.) This seems incredible as roads and railways must be thick with troops and transports.

May 14th

News this morning not too good. German thrust has reached Sedan faster apparently than French command expected. Latter are also worried about their reserves of aircraft and have begun to appeal to us for more. Two more squadrons were sent yesterday, but Newall[1] anticipates attacks on England shortly and will not want to denude our defences.

1. Air-Marshal Sir Cyril Newall, Chief of Air Staff 1937–1940.

In Belgium our lines, Louvain-Dyle, are holding.

Gamelin's position is still precarious. P.R. cannot sack him whilst battle is in progress and Daladier still wants to keep him. But relations between Gamelin and Georges seem also to be awkward.

News from Italy ominous. Musso is heaping insults on us in his papers, and by organised demonstrations against consulates, etc., and by exploiting the effects of the blockade is doing everything he can to excite Italian opinion against us. Loraine thinks he is trying to provoke us into declaring war on him and that we should be careful to swallow the insults so as not to play into his hands. I think he will come in when our fortunes look darkest like a bully and a jackal. The Pope has sent telegrams to the King of Belgium and the Queen of Holland, but of rather a perfunctory nature, and refuses to come out with a round moral condemnation.

U.S. opinion, on the other hand, is more and more helpful. Our new Government will help us there.

By God, if and when we do win this war, I hope we shall have a day of reckoning with those who did not help us. No excuses, no consideration.

May 15th

News still disquieting. German penetration at Sedan serious. French counter-attack yesterday unsuccessful. Fresh counter-attack to take place today. P.R. rang up Winston at 6 a.m. and demanded 20 more R.A.F. squadrons saying *Tout est perdu*. Howard-Vyse,[1] who is in London, returns today. Gamelin has gone up to Georges' G.H.Q. and Reynaud has put Giraud[2] in charge of operations opposite Sedan. (He had been further north.) Front between Louvain and Antwerp is also uncertain. Belgian divisions here between French at Antwerp and British line which ends at Louvain being none too sure.

Threat to Paris has become a reality and we are considering our plans in case of evacuation being decided. Bullitt[3] heard from Phillips, U.S. Ambassador at Rome, last night that Italian Government had decided to come in against us.

1. Major-General Sir R. Howard-Vyse, Head of Military Mission to French High Command 1939–1940.
2. General Henri Giraud.
3. W. C. Bullitt, U.S. Ambassador in Paris 1936–1940.

May 16th

Bad news again. 100 German tanks have broken through the line although, as far as we know, the line is still fairly firm behind them.

P.R. has appealed for more aeroplanes, but Winston has refused on the ground that this is only a temporary reverse such as were common in 1914 and it is desirable to draw the Germans on to the U.K. To this P.R. has replied that the war is different from 1914 and the Germans may be in Paris tonight!

We are burning our archives, arranging to get the female staff away by train today to Havre, packing our suitcases for a sudden flit if necessary ourselves.

The 100 tanks are heavy tanks against which our anti-tank ammunition is ineffective.

No signs of alarm in Paris yet.

Afternoon

Winston arriving here this afternoon. I went to Quai at 5 p.m. and Rochat[1] told me the news a bit better. He thought the breakthrough of tanks was being held on either side.

Winston arrived at five full of fire and fury, saying the French were lily-livered and must fight. After conference with P.R. he took graver view and agreed to telegraph to the Cabinet, which he summoned to meet at 10 p.m. to put before them the French appeal for more aeroplanes. He recommended this being granted as it might turn the scale and enable the French army to recover. Gamelin badly shaken, has got his reserves in the wrong places. Reply received at midnight that the Cabinet agreed to send aeroplanes.

Meanwhile the Embassy ladies were evacuated by car to Havre at 11.30 p.m. This was decided at short notice with Winston's emphatic approval. "This place will shortly become a charnel house" he said consolingly to Lady Campbell as she was saying goodbye to Ronnie. Maudie and Co. protested loudly at being sent away. They could only take suitcases with them.

The typists were packed off earlier by train, 7.30 p.m. We are now prepared to flit ourselves at short notice tomorrow, if necessary. Burning archives all day.

1. Charles Rochat, of the Quai d'Orsay. He later became head of the Vichy Foreign Office.

May 17th

Hal, Mack and I slept at the Embassy last night. I next door to
Winston who woke me up with his singing and splashing in his bath
while he was getting up to catch his aeroplane at six.

A quiet night except for sounds of distant bombing and artillery.

News first thing was that situation was slightly easier on Laon
front, but that fresh German attack had taken place at Wavre at the
south end of British line and tanks had broken through there too.
Our aeroplanes must now be *en route* and should begin their attack
on the German thrust without delay. Two nights ago we dropped
bombs on the Ruhr and it is believed we exploded large petrol re-
fineries. It is reported that columns of smoke 10,000 feet high
stretched from Essen to Brussels. This area has been bombed for the
last three nights. We all expected a raid on Paris last night.

May 14th was evidently a very bad day for the French. No air
protection and German planes could bomb and machine-gun them at
will. French troops coming up to reinforce were caught before they
arrived. One regiment practically wiped out. It is hoped that now
with greatly increased R.A.F. this will be stopped and the tide
turned.

Bullitt is being magnificent. He rings up Roosevelt two or three
times a day and gives him the latest news. Roosevelt has been weigh-
ing in heavily with Musso to keep him quiet.

News this evening not so good again. According to the Air Attaché,
when Joubert[1] saw Georges today, the latter admitted the French
troops were not fighting as they should and seven months of inactivity had weakened their fighting spirit. Our advance air striking
force is being taken back to rest and re-form – only enough for two
squadrons left. The push has now turned away from Paris towards
the Channel ports. The B.E.F. communications are therefore
threatened.

May 18th

News a shade better according to the Military Attaché. German advance said to be held on Oise. He thinks it probable that Weygand
will be brought in to replace Gamelin. His is now the only big

1. Air-Marshal Sir P. Joubert de la Ferté, Assistant Chief of Air Staff.

military name in France which commands respect, and he might provide the *coup de fouet* necessary to pull the troops together. The country itself is calm but does not yet realise the imminence of the threat.

Very quiet night. No air raids. The Government have decided to defend Paris to the last and to stay themselves as long as possible. We remain too therefore. We have sent all the ladies and typists home; we are now going to send away the non-essential men and keep those necessary to run the Embassy and who would go to Tours if we evacuate.

I have seen the map of the line. What has happened is that some 100 tanks which over-ran Blanchard's[1] army are now held between some fresh troops and Blanchard's people who have risen up again, and are being destroyed. The bulge is still an ugly shape pointing towards Paris. We hold Laon still and the Oise. To the North the B.E.F. have fallen back to conform (through Peronne and Cambrai, I think) and are doing very well. To the South the Maginot holds good. Fresh troops are coming up from the South, and these combined with those from the North should be able to pinch off the bulge if they have spirit and numbers enough. All the German tank divisions are in the push, which is really a giant raid, and have far out-stripped the main forces. It is *just* possible, therefore, that the situation might be turned into a victory for us, but it all depends on French morale.

R.A.F. bombed the Ruhr last night. The Germans have bombed Le Touquet.

Pétain[2] is being brought into the Government. Mandel becomes Minister of Interieur to deal ruthlessly with the Fifth Column and Weygand will probably also be given a post. Gamelin is being side-tracked by Georges. The situation has great possibilities for either side if they can be seized and developed. Atmosphere slightly better. Refugees from North and North-East pouring back.

May 19th

Night quiet. News this morning less good. Dill[3] over here to see

1. General Georges Blanchard, Commander of French 1st Army.
2. Marshal Pétain, the hero of Verdun, came into Reynaud's Government from Spain, where he had been French Ambassador.
3. General Sir John Dill, Vice-Chief of Imperial General Staff since April.

Paul Reynaud and French G.H.Q. German push now resuming towards Amiens. H.E. saw Reynaud, not in very good spirits. Dill brings letter from P.M. to Georges with ominous reference to the safety of the B.E.F.

P.R. has sacked Léger and put in Charles Roux! This is monstrous and quite indefensible from every point of view. I am amazed that Daladier, who now becomes Minister of Foreign Affairs again, consented. The Entente had no greater or better friend. For years and years he worked for it. He has moulded his Department into a magnificent instrument. It is shocking that he should be used thus. Charles Roux, hitherto Ambassador to the Vatican, knows Italy well.

Wilson Broadbent of the *Daily Mail* came to see me. Very interested and very determined. He spoke of defeatism in London among the richer classes. He had been greatly impressed by the spirit of the French in Paris. He thought Morrison might win the war for us and be our Lloyd George. He said Archie Sinclair was proving no good at the Air Ministry. Dill would probably replace Ironside. He reiterated how badly London was reacting though the provinces and the North were very sound and would fight. He was very pleased with the Government.

Broadbent a good man. Attractive. But he thought A.E.'s stocks were low and he had not forgiven him for not having come out against the old Government when he originally resigned.

Werth[1] of the *Manchester Guardian* tells me Bonnet has been seeing much of Daladier lately and darkly suspects Bonnet of bearing peace messages from Berlin. I wonder! I can believe Bonnet capable of anything, but not Daladier capable of listening. Werth thinks Musso may come in as *entremetteuse* with German proposals for a separate peace if things go badly on the Western Front.

We are certainly at the very edge of the precipice again as, I suppose, in August 1914. Can the French save themselves again as they did then? Have they a Foch or a Clemenceau? Much depends, if not all, on the psychological aspect. Great Britain can do little for them except do what we are doing, lending almost all our R.A.F.

Indeed the B.E.F. is in a parlous position. The Germans must have deliberately lured us far into Belgium by non-resistance as indeed they lured us into Norway earlier, though we did not get badly caught there. We have now to execute another strategic retreat. But why on earth had not Gamelin a vast reserve North-East and

1. Alexander Werth, their Paris Correspondent.

East of Paris? He had seven months to do it and he knew and always said that it was here the German thrust must come. Indeed a child could have seen that the area between the Maginot and the sea was the only possible place for an attack. Now our B.E.F. communications are gravely threatened and Paris is dangerously exposed.

News from Italy extraordinarily contradictory.

May 20th

Big news today, or rather last night, is the appointment of Weygand as Generalissimo, *vice* Gamelin. The shortcomings of Gamelin are being brought to light more and more – so P.R. told H.E. yesterday – all sorts of obvious precautions neglected. The reconstructed French Government (with Mandel as Interior, Pétain as Vice-President) has a good press. There seems a slight improvement in tone in the air today.

Good broadcast by Winston last night. I told our press people to drop a hint to Frossard[1] that Weygand should broadcast a message to France tonight. These broadcasts are invaluable.

News tonight confusing. The B.E.F. has orders to retire on Amiens. This was the decision of the War Cabinet yesterday. The German bulge much the same and held to a great extent though apparently two further irruptions of light tanks have taken place, one towards Paris at Chamy, the other towards Amiens where two weak half-trained British divisions had been thrown in. Margerie came in with a message from P.R. to the P.M. asking from Weygand that the R.A.F. be ordered to provide all help required by Billotte[2] who is co-ordinating the British, French and Belgian armies in Belgium.

May 21st

All quiet still. We hear Havre and Dieppe were bombed yesterday. And today that a fresh drive towards Abbeville has begun apparently from the North. The idea obviously is still to get to the sea and cut the B.E.F. communications, leaving Paris *pro tem.* Evidently great confusion of enemy and our elements on the front. We are on the edge of a great disaster or a great victory! Important to remember *both* possibilities are there. But what a mess the French soldiers

1. André Frossard, French Minister of Information.
2. General Pierre Billotte. He was killed in a car accident on May 22nd.

have got us into in spite of eight months to prepare for it! Weygand is now our great hope.

H.E. was told this morning by P.R. that the Germans were now in Arras and Amiens. The Millitary Attaché confirms this and says he thinks they are light machine-gun lorries and adds that parachutists had been used. Weygand is supposed to be preparing a counter-attack.

I went with H.E. to the Senate to hear P.R. make his statement. *"La patrie est en danger"* he began. The words have a familiar ring. He gave the brutal truth about the military situation and paid a great tribute to the R.A.F. at which all present rose and applauded. He spoke of the incredible neglect of certain French army commanders and said that those responsible would be made to suffer. He said new methods must now be adopted. Weygand and Pétain were united with him as one man and he believed France would again save herself.

Slightly better feeling tonight. French reserves being got together and plans for counter-attack taking shape.

May 22nd

German aeroplanes dropped leaflets on Paris last night, urging the French to make peace as the English alone were responsible for their troubles.

Winston arrived here 10.15 with Deputy Chiefs of Staff. Position on coast seems somewhat better. Although advance guard of tanks had reached coast, they had been badly bombed and held up, while at Boulogne a Guards battalion had been put in.[1] Also Arras is reported to have been recovered.

Luncheon at Embassy with Dill, Peirse,[2] Phillips,[3] Ismay[4] and H.E. (Winston lunching *à deux* with P.R.) All immensely impressed by Weygand's grasp. "Here at last is a man with a plan," they said. But we are in a pretty poor case it seems, and all depends on counter-attacks now to come. Our people amazed at way in which French

1. Two Guards Battalions were sent in, but were withdrawn the following night. At the same time a Greenjacket force had been sent to Calais.
2. Air-Marshal Sir Richard Peirse, Deputy Chief of Air Staff 1937–1940.
3. Admiral Sir Tom Phillips, Vice-Chief of Naval Staff.
4. General Sir H. Ismay (later Lord Ismay), Chief of Staff to Minister of Defence (Churchill).

364

have allowed themselves to be cowed by tanks. The B.E.F. were not at all rattled by them. Ismay said he had gone through five days of hell over the B.E.F. being cut off. Now it seemed the tanks on the coast have been bombed and held.

May 23rd

Duke of Windsor came to see Ambassador. He is up from Biarritz and is returning to Antibes "to settle the Duchess in".

No news yet of battle, no pushes south of the Somme, but tanks reported to be working up the coast northwards. Many ugly stories of demoralisation among officers and men and of incredible slackness.

Considerable anxiety over advance of tank divisions up the coast round behind Gort and B.E.F. It is hoped that the counter-offensive agreed upon yesterday to come from north and south will cut these off. Havre and Dieppe temporarily blocked by mines.

News from Italy still contradictory. Charles-Roux wants to try and appease Musso by concessions; fatal policy, I should have said. We also hear from Berlin of considerable shortages and anxiety. I am certain that if we can repel the present attack we shall win. The Germans are putting their all in because they cannot wait. It all depends on our standing up to this and on the French standing up, because it is their army rather than ours which is engaged. Have they still got the spirit to do this? If the French fall, we shall fight on alone, a defensive battle at first, until the resources of America, and perhaps America herself, are here. But this will be decided in the next few days.

The ambassador has three or four of us to luncheon and dinner each day. I am a standing dish and the rest of the party is made up of Mack, Colyer, Malise Graham[1] and Barclay,[2] with occasional variations. After dinner we listen religiously to the B.B.C. news for such crumbs of comfort as can be got, especially air raid news. In the afternoon he and I go for a short walk together, round the block, that is into the Faubourg St Honoré, down the Rue de l'Élysée, up the Champs Élysées to the Crillon and then home again by the Boissy d'Anglas. He daren't go further in case of urgent messages arriving. Such glorious weather – never did the trees in the Champs Élysées look so lovely.

1. Brigadier Lord Malise Graham, Military Attaché.
2. Sir Roderick Barclay, then Second Secretary at the Embassy.

Last news this evening far from reassuring. Position of B.E.F. increasingly precarious with their communications cut off and only one day's rations and 100 rounds per gun. C.I.G.S. had telegraphed to military mission with Weygand to say the Cabinet this evening were considering instructing Gort to do what he could to cut himself out. Malise Graham could get no further news from French G.H.Q. tonight, but there seems no special anxiety there and it could only be hoped that Weygand's plan was being carried out. Earlier in the day in reply to an appeal from Winston to P.R. for immediate operation of the plan as arranged yesterday (it appeared that the northern part of the offensive was sticking), Weygand said the plan was being carried out and "You can cut off my head if I fail, but do let me get on with it!"

Poor Gort, he is in the hell of a position. Through no fault of his 160,000 men are cut off. Malise is very anxious as he feels the French soldiers are not fighting.

Offensive from the south going forward, Amiens recovered, but Germans hold Boulogne.

May 24th

Further message from P.M. to P.R. tonight saying that Gort had reported a complete lack of co-ordination in northern armies and urging Weygand to send details of plan he was carrying out. P.R., rather stuffy, asked whether Gort was not under French orders. Ambassador is seeing P.R. again now with Weygand.

H.E. saw P.R. and Weygand. The latter said his plan was only possible hope for B.E.F. and it was being put into operation. Gort should endeavour to get supplies through Dunkirk and endeavour with Blanchard's troops to fight his way through southwards and join hands with the French forces pushing via Amiens and the Somme to the north. Weygand was not in communication with Blanchard direct, but he believed Gort was, but Weygand was in communication with the Belgians who were in communication with Blanchard. German columns still working their way along the coast towards Dunkirk which was covered by two French divisions.

No news at all tonight except that some food and ammunition has been got to Gort, presumably via Dunkirk. No big push yet. After dinner Margerie came round with a fresh message from P.R. to Winston saying that Blanchard reported that Gort, contrary to the plan arranged and orders given, had retreated forty kilometres towards the coast and Weygand had now to alter the whole plan. We cannot make it out. It seems incredible that Gort should retire without orders or that H.M.G. should order Gort to retire and not tell the French Government also. It must be some misunderstanding, but why on earth cannot such misunderstandings be prevented by more efficient communications?

Douglas Colyer tells me a dozen parachutists or so have been dropped singly round the south and east of Paris today.

May 25th

Reply to P.R. from Winston came early this morning. Winston says, as far as he is aware, Gort is still going on with the plan as arranged. All he had done was to throw out two divisions as a flank guard towards the sea to protect himself from enemy pressure from that quarter. Dill was with Gort today and he was convinced that the plan was the only possible course. H.M.G. would not order any change without letting the French know and they hoped offensive from the south would begin without further delay.

Yet Malise Graham this morning confirms that Gort *has* fallen back to a line further back behind Arras. Spears[1] has arrived with a personal letter to P.R. from the P.M. and hopes to straighten this out. Daladier's plan for buying off Italy has progressed. He has now proposed that Roosevelt be asked to inform Musso that the Allies would be willing to consider his problems provided he kept out of the war and to ask what he claims. I like this idea better than that of our going direct to Musso. F.O. agree to this and we are approaching Roosevelt accordingly. Roosevelt is empowered to say that we would agree to Italy having a seat at the Peace Conference as if she had been a belligerent. I hate to see us reduced to this, especially as the first requirement of a Peace Conference must be the abolition of totalitarian forms of Government. Musso is the father of all our present troubles and no peace will be stable which does not destroy and discredit him. But Roosevelt may refuse to touch it.

Spears lunched at the Embassy today. He came straight from meeting at the *Ministère de la Guerre*. His account most depressing, an officer had been present from Blanchard's army of which he gave

1. General Spears became the Prime Minister's personal representative to the French Prime Minister.

a very bad account. Spears says there is no chance of a big push from the south because there are not enough French troops; meanwhile the gap has increased in size, and the French and British divisions from the north are in a regular bag. What of the plan? Spears says it cannot be carried out and Gort's only hope is to get to the coast. Dill was with Gort today and Spears – who has sent home his report by air – is staying here. Thus at least liaison is assured. Weygand seems to be engaged in building up the line of the Somme and the Aisne. Yet our aircraft yesterday had a better day than ever – 150 Huns down. It seems clear there are not enough French troops to counter-attack, even though the Germans must be well nigh tired out. No more news late tonight, except that P.R. has to go over to London tomorrow morning.

May 26th

Malise Graham this morning says he hears Gort and Blanchard are after all making a push southwards today with two divisions each, though in a slightly more south-easterly direction towards Cambrai, while from the south a push is also being made in conjunction from Péronne across the Somme. Dill is staying with Gort. The idea of making for the sea abandoned, if it ever existed, while the enemy columns still seem held up at Calais.

Information so conflicting and changing it is impossible to follow situation. Malise and I wonder whether Spears did not convey a wrong impression and was not unduly depressing. He was very tired and is, I should say, rather liable to be up or down.

Our move to buy off Italy has gone a stage further. Roosevelt is now being asked to inform Musso that the Allies are prepared to consider his Mediterranean grievances and negotiate a settlement of them, to be put into force at the end of the war, Italy also to have a seat at the Peace Conference. Muss, of course, if he plays at all, will put forward monstrous demands for a new Treaty of London. News from Italy itself seems to be more definitely pro-war than before, but where attack would come, on the Jugs, the Greeks, on us, Egypt or France, is completely uncertain.

Malise told us tonight that the British Cabinet (when P.R. was there today) finally took the decision to order Gort not to attempt to advance south, but to withdraw, together with Blanchard and hold a sort of redoubt with their backs to the coast, stretching in a semicircle from Dunkirk round to Ostend. The Belgians let the Germans get into Courtrai and Gort was obliged to send one of the two fresh divisions destined for his push southwards to their help. This rendered proposed offensive impossible. We understand Weygand is quite satisfied with the decision and he will build up the Somme and Aisne front. He too had not enough troops for a real push up north to meet Gort. Malise much happier in consequence, and I too must confess to a feeling of relief. The southward push was at best a most desperate course and now we can probably get our people gradually away and bring them round again and in on the Somme, using our old bases. The only fear is how far it may react unfavourably on French morale. Daisy Fellowes told me today how much harm the women were doing by spreading defeatism in consequence of the stories of refugees now spread all over France, and also by the accounts of their menfolk who have returned wounded from the front and bring tales of the muddle of the Generals.

May 27th

Poor Lancelot Oliphant is lost.[1] F.O. have no news of him or of his Military Attaché since May 21st when they left Belgian G.H.Q. in a car.

H.E. saw P.R. early this morning, found him very depressed and saying that he would now soon be swept away and his place taken by those who had wished to make peace. It will be necessary for us to try and strengthen the Aisne-Somme front as soon as we can – to hearten and encourage the French. The Canadian divisions must now be ready, can we however afford to denude the U.K. just now? At the same time we must do everything possible to increase the air force. If we can dominate the air the Germans are beat.

But now all depends on the civilian and political morale. *Pourvu que les civils tiennent* and do not infect the troops with defeatism. The General Staff with Weygand in command must now be assumed to be doing everything that is possible and probably that is enough to hold the Germans. The situation is in no way worse, but much the same as in 1914. We know the Germans cannot face a long war, that their resources of petrol, material and of technical trained troops must be severely tried. They cannot carry on an offensive for long,

1. The British Ambassador to Belgium. He had been captured by the Germans and was interned from June 1940 until September 1941.

but we can carry on for ages, provided our morale, especially French morale, is equal to it. We are all struck at the lack of holy wrath among the French. No blood seems to be boiling at the thought of the invader on French soil. Our blood at home is boiling all right to judge by what one hears, but not the French.

What have the French to hope for by not fighting? A fool's paradise now and amputation later. Their only hope is to fight on with us and then, what is more, we are bound to win.

I saw Sandford today, just back from Touraine. He gave the most encouraging account of morale there in spite of the refugees. I am having Blum to lunch on Wednesday to find out what he thinks. I also saw Cadett of *The Times* who is very close to Paul Reynaud to tell him of what I heard of the latter's depression so that he can try and put some fresh heart into him when he sees him.

No other news until dinner time when H.E. and Spears came from P.R. to say the King of the Belgians had asked Germany for an armistice and proposed to cease fire at midnight! P.R. and Weygand furious at this treachery and latter sent orders at once to Blanchard to *se désolidariser* from the Belgians and wanted Gort to be told like-wise. P.M. was rung up and agreed at once to this. Gort and Blanchard are being told to do what they can to *sauver l'honneur des drapeaux*. Meanwhile Pierlot[1] and Spaak of the Belgian Government, who are in Paris, have disavowed the King and the former broadcast tonight telling all to continue resistance. What a mess! We do not seem very lucky in this war yet, but it will turn in the end. We cannot imagine what Gort and Blanchard can now do. O. Archdale was dining at the Embassy – he is a liaison between Blanchard, Gort and G.Q.G. and was over here to report. He said Blanchard was not much good and very shaken, but Gort and Co. were magnificent. But they are in a hell of a position. What can they do but withdraw fighting to the coast ports where they must be terribly congested. The only bright spot remains the R.A.F. which continues to bring down phenomenal numbers of German aircraft.

May 28th

P.R. broadcast at 8.30 a.m. about the Belgian treachery. He sent for H.E. this morning to tell of an idea he has for a direct appeal

1. Belgian Prime Minister.

to Roosevelt by King George and President Lebrun. He put it to Bullitt who favoured it and it has now been telegraphed to London.

The news of Belgium leaves people absolutely aghast. The Belgian Government – all of whom are here – are determined to carry on. On the French it has had an infuriating effect, they are really angry. They have found a real traitor at last and not a Frenchman. This will help us to get over the next difficult days. I understand the troops are already being got away.

Today P.R. proposed that Great Britain and France should now make a desperate appeal to Roosevelt to come in and help. H.E. asked Bullitt about it and he thought it should be submitted to Lothian. I fear this is asking too much of Roosevelt, who is moving as fast as he can, or rather getting himself pushed by U.S. public opinion as fast as he can. It would be very dangerous for him to take the lead too much, though his last broadcast was absolutely unneutral.

I saw a lot of people today. Lunch with Madame Schreiber – all very stouthearted. They said P.R. was gaining ground in the country. Cadett told me he had seen Spaak, the Belgian Minister of Foreign affairs, who hoped to raise an army of 300,000 from refugees in France. The King of the Belgians had tried to get his Ministers to stay with him in Belgium and they had tried to get him away, but he refused. They are now hoping to depose him if they can get enough Deputies to pass the necessary Act of Parliament. Meanwhile no act of his was valid as he had no Minister with him. I also saw both Madame Tabouis[1] and "Pertinax"[2] – the latter very low and sad at our present pass. Madame Tabouis, on the other hand, very buoyant. It was generally agreed that Daladier would soon be forced to resign from Ministry of Foreign Affairs.

I feel slightly less depressed tonight. I do not know why. The French are taking this better than I had expected. P.R. however is desperately anxious and so is Daladier to buy off Italy even though Roosevelt's *démarche* has met with no response and Halifax's broad hint to Bastianini has also been unsuccessful. Charles-Roux's daughter is a great friend of Ciano and he is a wild appeaser.

1. Genevieve Tabouis, French diplomatic correspondent of *l'Oeuvre*.
2. Pen-name of André Geraud, an influential French journalist.

May 29th

We have had P.M.'s reply to Reynaud's appeal for further direct approach to Musso. He turns it down on the ground that it would be useless in view of rebuffs to Roosevelt and Halifax. He says we can only stay Musso by showing ourselves resolute. I quite agree. I am slightly worried however by text of telegram which seems to envisage possibility of Musso mediating at a later date. It looks as if Halifax may have evolved some scheme for mediation by Italy on an offer of terms to Hitler. Incredible though it sounds, I cannot put it past him. It would be fatal.

P.M. also dislikes tone of suggested appeal to Roosevelt to come in and help us, he thinks – I am sure rightly – that we must not say "come in and help us because we are at the last gasp", but rather "we are going to fight on whatever happens – even if we lose – are you going to help us or stand aside?" All this however, has been put to Lothian.

I saw Bargeton[1] today, very gloomy. Had no news of Lancelot Oliphant. Last saw him at Bruges last Monday a week ago. He said the King had made no attempt to see the Allied Ambassadors while at his headquarters at Bruges in the last few days.

Spears is being very useful after all. He bucks up the French and is a useful contact to have with the P.M. He feels, as we all do, that French morale is important thing now. We discussed the possibility of speeding up the arrival of fresh British troops in France. If it has been decided that we can send more troops to France in spite of the threat to the U.K., which naturally we here cannot assess, then the sooner it is made known here the better for French morale. Spears spoke to London about this (to P.M. I think) and learnt that we were sending more men, but that to begin with they would be very ill-equipped.

H.E. saw P.R. at dinner time again and returned with the depressing news which has become customary now. P.R. had read him a letter from Weygand saying that the French army had been ordered to stand on the Somme-Aisne-Maginot line without thought of retirement. If there were a breakthrough here however, it would be difficult to prevent a raid reaching Paris and if Paris were lost with 70% of French industry, it might be impossible for France, in spite

1. Paul Bargeton, French Ambassador to Belgium.

of her will to resist, to carry on the struggle. This was to be brought to the notice of H.M.G. who were to be asked to furnish more divisions, artillery, A.A. guns and tanks and to afford full air protection.

Loraine also reported today that Ciano had told him that it was now certain that Musso would come in against us, but that the exact hour had not yet been fixed and that he would not consider any offers because of his loyalty to Hitler.

May 30th

Only news is that we have already got 53,000 away from Belgium and it is hoped to get another 25,000 away today. Contrary to expectation, this operation is proving easier by day than by night.

H.E had Pertinax to lunch. Pertinax very interesting as usual. He has a high opinion of P.R. but wished to be reassured that he had not shown signs of weakening. H.E. assured him that this was not the case. P. warned us against Baudouin[1] (his Chef de Cabinet), a sinister man, ignorant of foreign affairs and very weak about Italy. (We already felt this to be the case.) There is an intrigue on foot to get rid of Margerie, who in turn is accused of weakness, but I am sure this is not the case and that he has a good influence with P.R. Hélène de Portes is having a bad influence as owing to social ambitions she is pushing people like Baudouin.

Daladier wishes to make one more effort to buy off Musso – we are trying to suppress him – it is quite useless after the failure of Roosevelt and only humiliates us. This is the doing of Charles-Roux, he is a poor exchange for the robust Léger. The odd thing is that P.R. disapproves of further approaches to Musso, yet will not put his foot down.

I saw Spears this evening, he is still disappointed at lack of fight and organisation displayed by French. Ghastly stories of German shootings in northern France. Gestapo already set up.

Eighty-five thousand have now been got away from Belgium.

Record day for air victories.

Late tonight we heard P.M., Attlee and C.I.G.S. (Dill)[2] are coming over tomorrow for Supreme Council. I welcomed these visits for their psychological effect. I am already arranging with

1. Paul Baudouin, later Vichy Minister of Foreign Affairs.
2. Sir John Dill succeeded General Ironside on May 27th.

Charles Peake[1] for Duff Cooper and George Lloyd to come. We must do all we can by personal contacts to hearten the French.

May 31st

Winston, Attlee, C.I.G.S. and Ismay arrived about 12.30, rather late owing to detour taken by aeroplane. They all lunched with H.E. and me at Embassy before beginning their talks with French.

We heard during lunch that 150,000 had been got away to date – of which 15,000 French. P.M. said he would be content with nothing less than 200,000. Every sort of boat is being used from beach and harbour. Amazing operation. All the badly wounded are having to be left behind.

All were convinced that the next three months were vital and if we could hold out this period, we should win. But all very doubtful of the French. Dill said we had practically no troops to spare for them on the Somme. P.M. spoke of the need for anti-tank guns and anti-tank methods: in the U.K., special anti-tank corps are being formed. P.M. also spoke of the heavy responsibility borne by Daladier; all agreed he ought now to go. He strongly favoured sending Cabinet Ministers over here in relays to stiffen the French. He said how well A.E. was doing at the War Office.

Attlee strikes me as being very determined, but he is a man on a small scale. He has a good military mind, I should say. Spears is most useful as A.D.C. and nurse to P.M. on these occasions; he packs him off to rest before dinner.

I saw Georges de Castellane, who was with General Billotte when he was killed in a motor accident returning from a staff conference at Ypres. He complained of lack of liaison with Gort and said that in early stages of Meuse battle if we could have thrown in more aircraft it might have turned the scale.

I saw Charles-Roux and Hoppenot this evening. The former said if we had put a *mise en demeure*[2] to Italy in September last, Musso would probably have been upset or at least obliged to share power with Badoglio. The extent to which Italy was now run by Germans was appalling. He regarded Musso as a complete cynic whose politics

1. Attached to Ministry of Information, of which Duff Cooper was now Minister.
2. i.e. to challenge or put on the spot.

were those of a heavy gambler. I said we had always *manqué d'audace* in dealing with Musso; he agreed. He doubted if Musso would attack France direct, more likely to go to Egypt or Greece. Hoppenot said how sorry he was that Daladier's last attempt to buy off Musso had not been stopped by us. (We told him that we would not associate ourselves with it as we thought it useless and an unnecessary humiliation.) Hoppenot said it was a manœuvre by certain *milieux politiques*, (he mentioned Monzie[1]) to start up conversations having as their objective negotiations with Germany for a separate peace. P.R. did not want to get rid of Daladier until Italy did come in or he would make political capital of it. Daladier ought to be got rid of as soon as possible.

I wonder what the next week or ten days will bring forth, a disaster or a victory. We have all the cards for a long war, the Germans must win quickly or not at all. But the French are terribly weak and they are like an ill man who will not fight for his own life. Yet this is one of the decisive battles of the world – like Charles Martel's Poitiers. Will the next few days bring out some Frenchman of destiny? If only they had a Winston, I would not fear, but neither P.R. nor Weygand approach him in personality or determination. He is like a giant. The French do not seem to have the will to fight. Even in Paris here people are still loafing about, strangely apathetic. They should be digging trenches or drilling or doing something. I am only too afraid in my heart of hearts that we shall end by having to fight Germany alone. But that we can and shall do if necessary and perhaps Roosevelt will eventually help us.

June 1st

Winston and Co. went off early this morning.

Last figures for evacuation 200,000, of which 20,000 French. Winston very encouraged by this and says he may now be able to do more for the French on the Somme.

I hear that it was agreed yesterday that if Italy did come in against us we should immediately bomb her industrial areas in the north. Bombers are already getting to the south of France for the purpose. I am sure that is right and the mere knowledge of it may keep Musso out. There is in any case some slight hint of further procrastination by

1. Anatole de Monzie, Minister of Public Works, Independent Socialist French politician – very pro-Italian.

Italy. All very odd. I doubt if Hitler wants Musso in yet, and that is probably the reason. If Hitler thinks he can beat France without Musso, he will not want him to come in and absorb spoils. But if Hitler gets stuck, then he will probably insist on his coming in. In either case he will want Musso to look as ugly as possible, so as to immobilise British and French forces. Musso, on the other hand, does not want to be left out and have no pickings, but he will be afraid of coming in until *quite certain* that France is beaten. Again, Musso by keeping out and looking menacing may hope to play the role of mediator between France and Germany, which is the Monzie-Laval idea, and leave Great Britain isolated for a combined attack by the two ruffians. That is how I see it. How the different cross-currents will work out, it is impossible to say.

We hear Marseilles was bombed today – that is to scare the *Midi*. A British transport is said to have been hit in harbour. The local French aircraft seem to have done nothing.

Weygand sent a further message to P.M. today *via* Spears to say he had certain information that a German attack was to be expected on the western front either from Amiens or Rheims towards Paris between June 3rd and 6th. He appealed again for further British assistance.

Daladier's last appeal to Musso has met with a snub, the fate it deserved and as we foretold.

June 2nd

Figures for evacuation this morning 245,000! Of these 45,000 are French. We shall have trouble over this disproportion though it is more than justified.

Germans have made a move at Villers-Bretonneux preliminary to push for Paris. Spears says Weygand is still clamouring for more of everything and P.R. is inclined to be nasty. Spears, I am glad to say, bites back. He says, however, he thinks we are sitting in Paris behind a paper screen.

Duff Cooper and Charles Peake arrived this evening on a two days' visit to Frossard. I met C.P. and we had a gossip in the car coming back. He says P.M. has had a row with Chamberlain and is going to get rid of him and wants to bring Lloyd George in instead. Would the French mind? I said "Certainly not." A.E. doing very well at War Office. He had overruled Ironside over British brigade at

Calais. Ironside had wanted to withdraw them but A.E. said they should hold on and had appealed to P.M. who had supported him. In consequence, although practically the whole brigade had been destroyed and only 20 got away, two German divisions had been held up and evacuation of B.E.F. greatly helped. In consequence of this, Ironside had been replaced by Dill. A.E. now wants to send Canadian and Australians to France, but is encountering much opposition from those who wish to keep them at home.

C.P. said that Halifax, as I suspected, had been anxiously exploring possibility of peace proposals à la Lansdowne, but P.M. had flatly turned them down.

Another piece of hair-raising gossip is that Kennedy's cypher clerk has been caught sending copies of his telegrams to the Italians. Of course we have been telling Kennedy everything. The clerk has now been imprisoned.

C.P. also told me that it was Campbell Stuart who had prompted the idea that Roland de Margerie was defeatist and a bad influence for P.R., about which Cadogan had written to the Ambassador. I said we none of us shared that view here, indeed the contrary we thought was the case. I told him that Hélène de Portes was out for Margerie's blood as well as for Corbin's, and I warned him against Baudouin who is the real villain of the piece, I believe. Probably Campbell Stuart has been got at through Baudouin or Hélène de Portes.

C.P. said there had been an idea of sending some super Englishman to reside in Paris in addition to the Ambassador. He was combating this idea as much as possible and welcomed any bits I could give him about the strength of the Ambassador's position here.

June 3rd

Frossard dined at Embassy last night to meet Duff. Not a very impressive man, but energetic.

I lunched with Suez Canal Company today for their annual meeting when I have to produce certificate of H.M.G.'s shares. In the middle of lunch *alerte* went and a man with a steel helmet appeared from the roof to say aeroplanes were dropping bombs on the Eiffel Tower! We went on with our lunch very stoically and eventually the all clear sounded. We then heard Citroën works had been set on fire, several houses hit and Villacoublay aerodrome had been bombed. Charles Peake and I motored out to see Citroën works on fire and also a house which had been shattered in Boulevard de Versailles. Two hundred German aeroplanes are said to have taken part. I haven't heard what casualties yet.

Malise Graham said latest figures for evacuation now were 210,000 English and 65,000 French, i.e. all B.E.F. except wounded. Some 25,000 French remained. They hope to get more off today.

He also said signs of German concentration for attack were going on behind Rheims. The question of help by our fighter aircraft was most important and French wished to have them located in France. We agreed that it was vital that we should meet them if possible over this as this would be a decisive battle for both of us.

Dined tonight with Daisy Fellowes for Duff to meet Mandel. Duff said he hadn't been much impressed by Paul Reynaud whom he had seen today and found very dispirited.

June 4th

Jackie Crawshay arrived by the aeroplane from England. He had been with Gort all the time and gave most vivid accounts of evacuation. All B.E.F. except wounded and nearly 100,000 French now off. He gave great accounts of Gort and Pownall.

Charles Peake told us that Winston was proposing to impregnate the beaches of the U.K. with mustard gas. When some coldfoot in the Cabinet expostulated, he replied, "Can't we do what we like with our own beaches?"

Both H.E. and I very doubtful of French standing up on the Somme and continuing to fight even if we do send more aircraft, which is badly needed at home. The next weeks will decide.

June 5th

We have decided to re-impose full blockade measures against Italy – good!

We hear German offensive has begun on the whole line, not with tanks so far, but with artillery and dive-bombers.

Later news that 300 tanks have nonetheless broken through at Amiens.

Paris today is extraordinary. The Germans may well be here in 48 hours if things don't go right, and yet there is no sign of it in the faces of the people in the streets. Far from panic, it is like an ordinary afternoon in August. Emptyish streets, otherwise men, women and children as usual. Is it *sang-froid*, or ignorance, or apathy? I really can't say. An hour after our raid children were playing again in the street next door to houses which had been shattered.

Luncheon with Blum. He seemed calm but anxious. He didn't see how the war could continue for France if Paris fell, but he refused to contemplate it. He agreed with me that there should be more broadcasting by different political leaders. I have written to Margerie to suggest this.

Further exchange of acrimonious messages today between P.M. and P.R. Latter asking for more and more, former pointing out what we had already done and promising to do what more was possible without jeopardising ourselves in U.K.

P.R. told H.E. that old Pétain , when told of how little we could do, had said "Then there is nothing left but to make peace, and if you don't want to do it, you can leave it to me."

June 6th

P.R. has reconstructed his Government. Daladier goes and so do Monzie and Lamoureux.[1] P.R. becomes M.F.A. again, Frossard Public Works instead of Monzie, and Prouvost[2] Minister of Information instead of Frossard. These are good changes. Thank goodness both Daladier and Monzie are gone – they were appeasers. The only danger is that now the bad men are all out and can get together. The alternative French Government is there!

Ambassador tells me that Spears had an awful interview with P.R. and Weygand last night, so much so that Spears is now off home till next Wednesday. They attacked him again about our failure to do more than we are doing by way of sending all our fighters to France. Bullitt said much the same thing to H.E. himself this morning, while Brousset[3] tells me Mandel's one nightmare is that the importance of this battle isn't realised in London. Brousset said Mandel was like a rock and I said he might still be another Clemenceau to France. He will be ruthless and will fight on till literally the last ditch. He is certainly the staunchest of them all.

Malise Graham reports that the battle is proceeding fairly happily

---

1. The Minister of Finance.
2. The newspaper proprietor, later held office under Pétain.
3. Mandel's *Chef de Cabinet*.

and the French are fairly satisfied. But the English division on the lower Somme had yielded a bit in front of German tank attacks and was back on the Bresle. It had been put in hastily and had probably not had time to prepare its reserves, etc. Brousset said that since 10 a.m. heavy tank attacks had been launched, but the tanks were being held in the second line while the troops' front line had not been broken.

Madame Tabouis came this afternoon to ask for news. She warned me again of the dangerous activity of Madame de Portes, who is now out for Margerie's blood, after having got rid of Palewski and then Léger. Baudouin is her favourite and he is a black defeatist. She confirmed what Brousset told me today about the likelihood of Mandel finishing the war as a second Clémenceau. She said Hitler she knew was asking Muss for use of his aerodromes but wanted no more from him. He didn't want Italy to attack France herself.

News tonight not so good. Our 51st division on extreme left of Somme front has fallen back to Tréport-Bresle line. When Ambassador saw P.R. this evening, latter complained bitterly of this and asked at whose orders general had retired when Weygand had ordered that it should stand fast on the Somme line – had the general got orders from the War Office? Amb. had very difficult interview with P.R. who again went over all the old ground about necessity of sending at least two-thirds of our air force to help in the present battle. Spears was also there. We all at Embassy here feel supreme importance of this battle, but decision for H.M.G. is very difficult, involving as it does safety of U.K. itself. H.M.G. are nevertheless sending three more divisions during this month and promise to do all they can in the air.

Weygand is in a carping and defeatist state of mind; P.R. is really the stoutest of them all. What hell it is having to fight battles with Allies! Yet if the French do lose this battle, it will make future infinitely more difficult for us fighting alone. Trouble is over losses of pilots even more than of machines. Canadian training scheme will not turn out really large numbers till November.

On main streets and at bridges in Paris tonight large dustcarts are drawn up ready to block roads, also mysterious holes are being dug in the middle of the Champs Élysées. Douglas Colyer says parachutists are expected tonight.

June 7th

Germans are putting in very heavy push now from Amiens with armoured divisions. When Ambassador saw P.R. this morning he seemed fairly calm.

Twenty-three parachutists have been rounded up. We had an *alerte* last night; though a number of bombers came near, no bombs were dropped here.

I saw Vanier,[1] Cadett, Pertinax and Maurois.[2] Last-named came to speak of ill-feeling over alleged report that B.E.F. would not be returning to France and over eternal question of air support. It looks as if every Frenchman who knew an Englishman had received a *mot d'ordre* to go and see him and urge necessity of greater air support. Anyway H.M.G. are now sending all they possibly can every day for operations here.

June 8th

News this morning, according to Malise Graham, fair, but there is what he calls a nasty hole in the lower Somme, which unless stopped, may prove serious as a threat to Rouen or Paris. He says there is a good deal of ill-feeling between French and British armies at the moment owing to 51st division withdrawing on extreme left coming after Gort's withdrawal from Arras. The French are terribly anxious to discover scapegoats. Gort is to come over next week on a goodwill visit.

Our supply of R.A.F. for the battle seems now satisfactory and a new division is now arriving.

Midday

Ambassador has seen P.R. who tells him that two armoured divisions have got through and reached Forges les Eaux, making for Rouen. Usual appeal for ever more air effort. But the situation is again very serious, our 51st division and remainder of our armoured division is pressed back against the coast, cut off by these two German divisions.

1. Georges Vanier, Canadian Minister to France 1939–1940. Later Governor-General of Canada.
2. André Maurois, French journalist and writer.

Some Lines of Communication troops are making stand in front of Rouen, but the shortage of French troops is appalling. It is in fact troops, not fighters, that are wanted now. I fear also tendency to blame it on us will increase because of original retirement of 51st division. If German push continues, Paris will become untenable.

I hear by telephone from Charles Peake that he is taking steps to bring the letter I wrote him yesterday about the vital importance of our battle from the point of view of keeping the French in the war "to the highest authority" – presumably through Duff to Winston.

Ambassador saw P.R. again at 8 p.m. News very grave. German divisions now advancing from Forges les Eaux towards Gisors, i.e., towards Paris. At the same time, another break has occurred at Soissons across the Aisne. P.R. was nonetheless not too depressed and said he was discussing plans for defences south of Paris.

We received an alarming message after dinner from Noble Hall[1] to say that it was reported that the whole line had given way from Abbeville to Soissons. Later Malise Graham confirmed that the French troops were falling back from the Somme to Aumale to conform with movements on the wings and that the extreme left wing on the sea had also now had orders from the French to fall back. The famous Somme-Aisne line has collapsed.

In this gloomy situation we discussed our own movements. If P.R. intends to stay to the last, the Ambassador should have an aeroplane to get him and staff away as roads by then may be very difficult. At the same time, all but absolutely necessary staff should be got away at once. We are to discuss this tomorrow morning early.

Berlin bombed by French naval aircraft. We must expect a raid here tonight.

June 9th

News today is that German push continues towards Gisors to northwards and from Soissons to south east, whilst further east and north of Rheims another big offensive is starting. French troops are falling back to cover Rouen, the citadel of Paris, and thence to the Marne. Threat to Paris imminent. French however seem to be adapting themselves to a less rigid and more mobile form of warfare and this is to the good. If they cannot stop the Huns, the next best thing is to

1. Henry Noble Hall, temporary 1st Secretary at the Embassy.

retreat stubbornly and not get surrounded. The important thing is to keep the armies intact.

Ambassador has gone to see P.R. to try and ascertain the Government's plans as to moves.

French Government have now decided to move away all but essential services. We are doing likewise therefore and party leaves tomorrow. The remainder (about 14) will stay with H.E. who will stay till the Government itself goes, possibly by air. We are warning the F.O. therefore that they may have to send an aeroplane soon.

Musso's intentions still shrouded in mystery. My guess is that he is going against us, not France, and in Egypt. He has sent increasing forces to Libya. He may also attack Corfu. But he will spare France. Heavy bombing very audible south of Paris this evening.

No more news tonight except that Vanier told me German motor-cyclists had now reached Creil, 40 kilometres from Paris.

P.R. actually asked H.E. tonight when and where he proposed to go. H.E. said he had reduced staff to a minimum and they would go when P.R. went. He urged P.R. however not to stay too long and be caught. This P.R. said he would not do. Various Government Departments are actually moving today: Ministry of Information, Ministry of Supply, Air Ministry, and all but skeleton of Quai. P.R. in fairly good fettle – less complaining.

June 10th

Very heavy bombing and firing near Paris last night.

Today, Germans reported to have reached Seine at Rouen where bridge is blown up and to have crossed at Les Andelys and near Evreux, also to be at Pontoise and Isle d'Adam. On Soissons-Argonne front French are putting up magnificent resistance.

I am trying to ginger up H.E. to insist on getting adequate warning from P.R. of his departure. All the other ministries have been slipping away without a word to anyone, after giving all assurances to the contrary. We shall probably not be able to go by air as the aerodrome staff is packing up today. The roads are getting more and more crowded. H.E. is seeing both P.R. and Charles-Roux this morning.

P.R. told H.E. that the Government had left, but that he, P.R., was staying in Paris and would then leave for an army headquarters. He thought it prudent H.E. should leave tonight, "though he would miss his conversations". We learn that Quai all left this morning, *sans mot dire.* We are therefore hoping to get H.E. away about eight tonight.

4 p.m.

All more or less settled now. H.E. and I and Lloyd (who arrived this morning to ginger up the French) and Malise Graham go off last about eight. Hal Mack a little before, about 7.30, the less importants before that.

Hardly had I written this when we received a telegram from F.O. to say Winston was intending to arrive here at 6.15 and stay the night. The local aerodromes have been evacuated and so this had to be stopped at once. We just got through on the telephone in time. But he now threatens to come tomorrow. Lloyd is strongly opposed to his flying about in this way and says the Cabinet is too. He and Ambassador are going to speak to Halifax and urge that he be dissuaded from coming. Apart from the danger, it is quite unnecessary as P.R. at present is in very good form.

Lloyd was immensely impressed by Mandel, who said there are hundreds of Dunkirks in France and millions to defend them.

6.15 p.m.

We hear Italy has declared war against Britain and France.

Almost all shops in Faubourg St Honoré closed today. H.E. went down to say goodbye to P.R. at 7.30. We had a final meal about eight and eventually got off about nine, leaving Spurgeon and Christie[1] in charge of the Embassy, which is under Bullitt's protection. The Ambassador also went to say goodbye to Bullitt who told him he believed all the Paris police were being withdrawn at midnight.

It was very difficult to get a move on; we ought to have started an hour earlier, but H.E. got slower and slower. We were all in six cars: Military Attaché in first car, Ambassador and I in second, Lloyd and his secretary in mine. The roads were very crowded leaving Paris, but there were no very bad blocks. Everybody seemed to be in cars piled high with luggage, very few on bicycles or on foot. We passed a number of barricades on the way consisting of farm carts ready to push across the road. But there was no air activity and no bombing,

1. The Chancery Servants.

fortunately, because we were an easy target. We drove all through the night, getting on faster as it got later, because all those in cars seemed to have drawn up on the roadside to sleep. We did not reach Tours till 3 a.m. and then took an hour to find the Château de Champs Chevrier near Clerey where we were billeted. Barclay was already there to welcome us and we fell exhausted to bed.

June 11th

Woke up late. Lovely morning, and found ourselves in a most charming 16th century château with a moat. We are entertained by the Baroness de Champs Chevrier in person who wears a black dress, a white band round her throat and white tennis shoes. Her son is at the war and she has a daughter-in-law with her in the house. The château must be quite unchanged since at least the 18th century and Louis XIV himself could step into it and find nothing strange. Full of very fine furniture and tapestry and good panelling, but no running water, no *confort moderne* whatever. There is only one bathroom, which the Ambassador has, but it has no *conduite d'eau*. This is of course exactly how the French provincial nobility live and it is their strength. Such people never go to Paris, except for a horse show. Lovely park and woods all round. We are like a little camp with our lorries, our wireless and R.A.F. and R.E. personnel.

Ambassador and Mack went off to see Ministry of Foreign Affairs in their château about 10 miles off, and heard very confidentially that the French Government did not expect to be here more than two or three days and after that they might take up a final stand in Brittany. P.M. had flown over after all to see Weygand and P.R. at former's headquarters today.

After tea Ambassador and I went over to Ministry of Foreign Affairs again and I saw Hoppenot. The Ministry's château is smaller than ours, hidden among a lot of woods. Everybody was unpacking out of cars while diplomats drove up from other châteaux to find out what was going on. All rather like a country club.

Even here roads are full of people fleeing before the invader. After dinner, we listened to the B.B.C. 9 o'clock news from a wireless in the attics. This is our chief, and almost only, link with the outside world. A German bomber over our head this evening. No war news tonight except that Germans are on the Marne, but Paris quiet. Our 51st division has been very badly hit. Frère's army very exhausted.

June 12th

I went with Ambassador to Tours this morning where he saw Mandel and I Brousset. Tours crowded with refugees in cars piled high with luggage. Streets very blocked. We also saw Kerillis[1] and Delbos. After that we went on to Ministry of Foreign Affairs and saw Charles-Roux, Hoppenot, etc. No one working, but everyone standing about talking on the lawn. Not much news, Germans making a fresh attack at Rheims. Paris all quiet still. German plan, I was told by Kerillis, was to concentrate now on Orleans from the two wings, and at the same time to capture as many ports as possible so as to cut France off from Great Britain. These were apparently the plans found on a captured German officer. We heard that Winston and A.E., who came over yesterday to Weygand's G.H.Q., stayed the night and P.R. is holding a Council of Ministers at Tours this evening.

According to reports tonight, Germans are now near Dreux and at Colombes. A big bridge near Rouen was blocked with refugees when German tanks arrived and tried to cross too. Thereupon the whole bridge was blown up, refugees, tanks and all.

Spears turned up this evening from attending the Supreme Council at Weygand's H.Q. He gave a most gloomy account. French completely exhausted, no reserves, not even a battalion left. Yet if only France could hold out another two months situation might change owing to Germany's own difficulties.

I am afraid it is becoming more and more evident that we shall have to fight this war practically alone. I do not believe the French can possibly hold out more than a month and then we must bear the full brunt ourselves.

Spears said the French were so anxious about the Italians that they had actually prevented our bombers from leaving Marseilles to bomb north Italy by placing lorries across the aerodrome just before they should have taken off, although the plan for this had been agreed and co-ordinated with them beforehand. The French navy had also refrained from carrying out the operations against Italy which had been intended. H.M.G. were furious at this.

1. Henri de Kerillis, French Right Wing politician.

June 13th

I went early with H.E. to drive to Reynaud's headquarters. We arrived after about 2 hours at a château at Chissay on the side of a hill. We found there a state of great confusion and depression. Pouring rain and dripping trees added to the atmosphere. Madame de Portes and Mademoiselle Eve Curie[1] were in the courtyard. Spears came and told us that P.R. had asked for Winston to come again that very day and he was expected in the evening. He gave, however, a rather better account than the day before. A telegram had been sent to Roosevelt (which the latter wanted to publish) declaring that "France would fight on before Paris and behind Paris and if necessary in North Africa", and another telegram was to follow it asking if the U.S.A. would not come to her help. Spears had also talked to de Gaulle[2] (who is the only calm and intelligent soldier left) who had agreed that the plan of using our new divisions piecemeal even by battalions, was thoroughly unsound and should if possible be prevented. (I must say Spears is very good and at once on to such questions – Howard Vyse's mission seems quite useless.)

I had a word with Margerie who said the plan was to withdraw part of the army south to Lyons and the other part to Brittany and for the Government to go to Bordeaux and be concentrated as the present system of scattering is quite unworkable. This is certainly true. He said the Germans were now at Bar-le-Duc, behind the Maginot, the position in Paris getting very difficult owing to food scarcity and riots were expected. The position of the French armies was nearly impossible as there were absolutely no reserves. Even to defend Brittany would require 20 divisions, we were providing two or three, but it was very doubtful if the rest could be found in the remainder of the French armies.

The scene at the château seemed completely chaotic. Everybody, Ministers, secretaries, all talking and telephoning in the same room. Margerie dictating a telegram to Roosevelt in one corner; Ambassador and Spears and me talking in another; Madame de Portes rushing about with untidy hair.

1. Mlle. Eve Curie, daughter of Mme. Curie, was a journalist working at the French Ministry of Information.
2. He had become Under-Secretary of Defence.

After this we set out with Spears to return to our own château. We stopped on our way at Chenonceaux for an excellent lunch and then continuing to Tours suddenly passed P.R.'s car there. Thinking that he might have news of the time of Winston's arrival, we went to the prefecture to discover that P.M., Halifax, Beaverbrook,[1] Alec Cadogan and Ismay had just arrived and conference was then in progress.

I waited about in the courtyard among a crowd of journalists and politicians, all extremely depressed and full of rumours (e.g. that the Germans were at Chartres!) At the meeting, P.R. was less satisfactory and asked whether, in the event of the U.S.A. declining to come in, H.M.G. would make it easy for the French if they made a separate peace. Winston said we must await Roosevelt's reply before giving an answer. Afterwards Herriot, Jeanneney and Marin had made speeches declaring that France would fight on.

The truth is that the French are completely beat. I doubt if they can hold on any more effectively, though we may succeed in bolstering them up another 10 days or so, but there is nothing now to stop the Germans going where they like. Disorganisation is almost complete. It is just possible, however, that we may induce the French Government to leave France and carry on like the Dutch from abroad. We finally saw P.M. and Co. off from the aerodrome at 6 p.m. and returned home.

June 14th

Late last night Spears came over and said that Mandel had advised him that we should go to Bordeaux and be off by 10 a.m. as German elements were pushing towards the west and were near Le Mans. He also heard that Paul Reynaud was wobbling again, though Marin, Mandel and Campinchi[2] were firm. There was a majority for an armistice. Madame de Portes bad defeatist as usual.

Great scurry therefore as we were to be off early in the morning. We left our château after a pathetic farewell from the poor old Baroness and her daughter-in-law who stood weeping on the steps. We drove through Tours, more and more crowded with refugees, cars and carts and bicycles, and made our way south. But after Angoulême appearance of country changed and evidence of war much

1. Lord Beaverbrook had become Minister of Aircraft Production.
2. Minister of Marine.

scarcer, and indeed scarcely existent. We reached Bordeaux at 7 p.m.
to find that protocol had allotted us a château fifty kilometres from
the town. This couldn't be tolerated and I went to see Brousset who
at once and most kindly requisitioned ten rooms for us at Hotel
Montré. I saw Margerie for a minute; he showed me Roosevelt's
reply which he found far from corresponding to Winston's enthusiastic description of it which we read late last night and in which
he called it a moral commitment to go to war. Margerie said the
Germans were in Dijon and I later heard they entered Paris today.
French armies deadbeat.

H.E. saw Mandel, and Spears did so too. We later all dined at
Chapon Fin.[1] Spears thinks all depends on view they take of U.S.
reply. Portes' influence at its worst; she never leaves P.R. alone, but
Mandel, Campinchi and Marin are firm as rocks.

Yet what has France to gain now by a separate peace? Germany
will remain in occupation because we shall carry on the war, whilst
France must also make peace with Italy at a high price. But if she
carries on from North Africa, she has there a complete French
administration and French army; she can fight Italy, rebuild her air
force with safe and open sea communications and at the same time
keep her navy and her empire.

Pathetic appeal from Tabouis on behalf of herself and Pertinax to
come to the United Kingdom.

Ambassador and Spears saw P.R. late after dinner. They found
him very undecided, so tired in fact as to be incapable of thinking.
What is doing the greatest harm is idea encouraged by P.M.'s generous words when he was here that even if France did fall out, it would
make no difference and we would set her up again. This plays directly
into the hands of the defeatists and needs to be severely dealt with.
France becomes a second-class Power if she now gives up.

June 15th

Greatest confusion in Bordeaux, nobody knows where anybody is or
the way anywhere. We spend hours driving up and down, losing our
way and finding no one to guide us – a nightmare! I eventually found
G.H.Q. this morning where P.R. now is and saw Margerie. He gave
me text of second telegram sent to Roosevelt (on June 10th) saying
that whether France went on fighting or capitulated must now de-

1. Restaurant in Bordeaux.

pend on U.S.A. coming in. Her armies were incapable of further resistance here. The telegram went on to say that Great Britain would "possibly or probably" also be defeated if U.S.A. did not come in. I drew his attention to this and said it in no way represented our point of view and would furthermore have worse effect on U.S.A. who would hesitate to help at all if they thought we were both sunk. French Government were awaiting reply to this and Council of Ministers to meet at 2 p.m.

Spears trying to see P.R., while Ambassador saw Baudouin and found him not unsatisfactory. I also saw André de Fels, found him very defeatist and, when I pointed out all that France might preserve by North African solution, he said while that was no doubt true, psychologically French people wouldn't admit that their Government should be overseas and anything might happen in France if they went.

Ambassador feels that situation is slipping very fast and unless definite promise by Roosevelt to intervene comes, French Government will soon now ask for armistice. He has telegraphed in this sense to F.O., adding that he presumes now no question of Winston again seeing P.R. owing to distance. (We also hear H.M.G. have decided to send no more troops to France.)

We are working at Consulate offices in considerable difficulties, stairs and passages packed with refugees clamouring for visas and evacuation.

Palewski came in to say he had just been to see P.R. to encourage him before the Council. He said that he and a number of airmen would come to England if necessary. He spoke bitterly of the defeatism of the soldiers Weygand and Pétain. I saw poor Hoppenot this afternoon very anxious that the French Government should take the right decision. He asked whether, if need be, we could take Léger to U.K.

F.O. telegraph that light cruiser is arriving for us tomorrow with very limited accommodation but provision of a larger ship very difficult and being examined. This is impossible solution; we can't sail away and leave all other British subjects behind.

Late this evening Ambassador and Spears were sent for and handed a document by P.R. This said in effect that French people would not understand that their Government should abandon them and go abroad unless it were first established that peace conditions were unacceptable. Therefore the Council had decided (a) to ask H.M.G. to release them from obligation not to conclude separate peace, and (b) if H.M.G. agreed, to ask Roosevelt to ascertain Hitler's and Musso's terms. If these were unacceptable as French Government expected, then they would continue the struggle – demand for surrender of fleet would be regarded as such. If H.M.G. refused, then P.R. implied he would resign and there would be no knowing what new Government would do. Roosevelt had meanwhile replied to F.O. telegram and said he could not at once go to war.

Discussion late with H.E. and Spears as to telegram to F.O. Spears saw Margerie who thought greater possibilities than might appear of Hitler playing into our hands and rallying opinion to P.R. by asking for preposterous terms or continuing advance. If we don't agree, fairly certain P.R. will resign and he is our best friend.

Message from F.O. about midnight saying that Ambassador must resist any proposals for armistice.

Meetings and telegraphing till 4 a.m.

June 16th

Continual rush today.

Message from P.M. in reply to P.R. saying that we would release French Government if they first sent fleet to U.K. and as many aircraft as possible as well; also they must keep us informed of terms of armistice. No sooner was this delivered by H.E. than instructions came to cancel it. While Ambassador and Spears were with P.R., de Gaulle telephoned from London a declaration of Anglo-French solidarity of such strength that P.R. was quite encouraged by it. As far as we can make out, it amounts to the completion of Anglo-French union. There is to be meeting tomorrow at Concarneau between P.R. and Mandel and Winston. Ambassador and Spears go from here.

I went out of the Consulate to see the Prefecture about arrangements for evacuation and when I came back an hour later I found all had gone wrong again. The visit cancelled and P.R. resigned.

There had been a Council of ministers in the afternoon when P.R. had read to them Winston's declaration. While the council was proceeding, I was actually with Brousset, Mandel's *Chef de Cabinet*, who said to me how much better the situation was. Yet at that moment the defeatists had jockeyed P.R. into a ministerial crisis, the object being to make Pétain President of the Council to make a disgraceful peace. Ambassador and Spears disgusted as we all were. How the gods do mock us!

France is choosing tonight whether she sinks to a third-class Power or whether she fights on and becomes greater than ever. Hélène de Portes and the defeatist Baudouin are working their hardest to bring about the first alternative. The younger France is frantic at the idea that it may be betrayed. Palewski is determined to fly to England with his airmen. The soldiers Weygand and Pétain are also doing their best in the wrong sense, defeatist and old.

The new Government has been formed – Pétain President of Council, Baudouin Minister of Foreign Affairs, Chautemps Vice-President. Baudouin sent for the Ambassador at 1 a.m. to say that it was impossible for the country to continue the war or for the Government to leave it; General Weygand could no longer answer for discipline and the Germans could soon be masters of the whole country. The sufferings of the civil population and of the refugees could not go on. The new Government had therefore asked General Franco to ascertain terms for an armistice. He gave, however, a solemn assurance that the fleet would not be handed over to Germany, and if this were demanded by Germany, it would be refused.

The flight of Frenchmen from France has begun. Madame de Fels came to me about poor Léger. Hoppenot also spoke about him to me. Pertinax and Tabouis also wish to escape, so do de Gaulle, Rothschilds and Henri Bernstein. I hope to get them all away in a ship which has arrived today. Poor Léger they may try to stop, we must get him aboard surreptitiously. All this I must do tomorrow. De Gaulle leaves anyway tomorrow by air for London. So does Spears.

I wonder how long we shall stay ourselves. A cruiser is to take us.

Laval appeared at dinner at the Chapon Fin tonight – a bird of ill-omen.

Everybody dines and lunches at the Chapon Fin – we all have our tables – the Americans, the Spaniards, Mandel and his lady, etc.; everybody one can think of turns up sooner or later – all Paris.

June 17th

Ambassador went early to Pétain and found him completely gaga. He gave, however, formal assurances that the fleet would not be handed over but declined to agree that it should be given to us.

I spent the morning rounding up the French who were in danger from the Nazis or the new Government. I collected and packed off Pertinax and Mme, also Geneviève Tabouis and Elie Bois.[1] These were put on H.M.S. *Berkeley*, a small sloop which had tied up in the river here and was to take them down to the *Madura*, the big ship waiting for refugees at the Point de Graves. Finally I arranged for the great Léger himself to be brought up from Arcachon by the Fels, and I met him myself on the quay – they were nervous lest he might be stopped and so I promised to wait for him myself and escort him personally on board. Poor man, he was absolutely miserable at the humiliation of his country. He and Geneviève embraced on the deck. Whilst this was going on, a terrific storm of thunder, rain and lightning broke and I thought we should all be struck dead.

A hellish day. All day long the Consulate office is besieged by wretched British subjects and refugees fleeing from the terror to come. The stairs were almost stormed and at one moment one couldn't move up or down. Poor people clawed at one to get some special attention. Both Huysmans and Julien Cain, Pierre Cot[2] (who said he wanted to join the British Army) came and begged for visas and chits for the boat. We decided to give them. A number of young officers wanted to come, but these we advised to wait to see how things went. After all it is still possible, though improbable, that Hitler's terms may be rejected. I never saw so much human anguish.

After lunch, as he was leaving the Chapon Fin, Mandel was arrested. So the patriots are being rounded up!

I went to see Hoppenot later, quite miserable. The faces of the Quai people are ashen. H. said old Pétain was completely taken in about Hitler and his speech had created a lamentable impression. The *mous* of the late Government would be the *durs* of the present and he thought two tendencies would develop themselves soon. Even Baudouin would draw the line somewhere. No reply had yet been received about the peace terms. The French Government had also asked the Nuncio to ascertain Musso's terms. Hoppenot fears that Winston's final offer was too much for the suspicious *Français moyen*. But we both agreed the tragedy was that these fatal decisions were being taken when public opinion was quite unaware of them. No newspapers, no wireless. Hoppenot terribly afraid Hitler would treat France like Czechoslovakia and gradually nip pieces off.

1. Editor of the *Petit Parisien*.
2. French Air Minister 1937.

Spears went back to England today, fed up.

At dinner Mandel suddenly reappeared, having been released with an apology. What a ridiculous Government!

June 18th

Quiet night and fairly long one at last. Air raid woke us up. We hear First Lord and First Sea Lord arriving at 10 a.m. about fleet question.

Fels tells me German wireless has been hostile to new Government, especially to presence of Chautemps, whilst Childs learns stiffening here towards idea of resistance and departure for North Africa.

Germans at Lyons and Anjou. Still no reply to armistice proposals.

I saw Brousset for a moment and promised that if possible at last moment, we would take Mandel off. Latter did not want to leave until all hope was lost. I also had a talk with Campinchi who thought the French Government should see to it that a number of responsible French Ministers left at once for Algiers or London so as to be able to set up an alternative Government in case this was captured. We have promised to take him and Delbos off also. He said Pétain was *gâteux*[1] and that other elements (he hinted at Pomeret[2]) were sinister. Hoppenot told me Herriot and Jeanneney were working hard on Government and had brought about a certain redressment. He said Herriot and Jeanneney had protested vigorously against Mandel's arrest. The country without papers or radio was quite ignorant of the Government's intentions or state of war; they thought Pétain Government meant more vigorous war. P.R. would like to see present Government decide on continuation of struggle. He thought fleet should be handed over now and given back later. Blum was in Bordeaux.

Ambassador working hard all day on fleet question. Baudouin fairly satisfactory this morning. Fleet could not be handed over now because war was still continuing, but orders had been given for its ultimate departure for U.K. or for scuttling. Alexander[3] and Pound[4]

1. Senile. 2. Minister of Labour. Independent Socialist.
3. A. V. Alexander (later Lord Alexander), First Lord of the Admiralty 1940–1945.
4. Admiral Sir Dudley Pound, First Sea Lord.

arrived about 4 p.m. and went to see Darlan whom they also found satisfactory about this. Roosevelt has sent a telegram about it too.

Georges Monnet, the Socialist leader, came to see me.

Dinner with First Lord, First Sea Lord and staff. Alexander went and spoke to Mandel after dinner, a good idea. After dinner John Fitzgerald[1] appeared in state of great excitement and said Ambassador should get on board destroyer along quay tonight as Germans might arrive at any moment; they were at Angoulême; we were endangering whole ship's company, etc. Ambassador very angry, refused to budge.

We really must find out tomorrow exact military situation. I certainly believe Germans will turn up sooner or later like this while French are still talking.

Zog came to see me to ask for visas and boat for himself and party of thirty-five. He said he would go anywhere the British Government wished. A gentle, rather ineffective man. I said we would consult the F.O. and let him know – he is at a villa near Royan.

June 19th

Very quiet night in spite of Fitzgerald.

This morning Ambassador had heard from Pétain and Baudouin that the German Governments had asked for plenipotentiaries to be sent. No indication of terms. Representatives were being sent but not as plenipotentiaries. French Government had also decided that as enemy approach Bordeaux, President of the Republic, Presidents of two Chambers and two or three Ministers should be sent overseas. Others would remain here for the present.

Meanwhile de Gaulle is broadcasting from U.K. for French officers and technicians to go there to continue the struggle. Vienot[2] came to see me about this. We are telegraphing about need for boats being sent to take such officers, etc., off. Margerie spoke also about it. No more British boats here but if French Government decide to go themselves, then they must provide French boats.

I think all these factors – hints of mass desertion to U.K., calmer reflection after some physical repose, increasing number of those arriving who express contempt at idea of capitulation – are having

1. Naval Attaché.
2. Pierre Vienot, Under-Secretary at the Quai d'Orsay.

effect in stiffening up the defeatists. Herriot and Jeanneney are being magnificent.

At this point we learnt Lloyd was arriving on a special mission and Jean Monnet (of the Anglo-French Purchasing Board) walked in, having started before him. His plan was to offer French Government all shipping facilities to evacuate French soldiers, equipment, individuals, etc., provided French Government went at once and set up fresh Government overseas. They were of course unaware of situation today, viz. that French Government have gone some way to anticipate this. Anyway Lloyd has a personal message from War Cabinet which he and H.E. are to deliver to Lebrun regarding this and offering at same time Anglo-French union. Monnet seemed a mixture of gangster and conspirator and wants to get busy collecting suitable men for an alternative Government. I don't care for him and I don't trust him, though in England they think him the cat's pyjamas.

Mandel came at last today to ask to be got away, himself, his daughter, his mistress and his black servant. So off he goes on H.M.S. *Arethusa* tonight from Point de Graves. Delbos and Campinchi still here, old Alexander with us too, a sensible old thing, rather portentous but full of sense. He is no trouble.

We still don't know when we go ourselves. H.M.S. *Berkeley* has gone down the river which is no longer thought safe and is to lie off Arcachon. We can motor down there.

Lloyd arrived at length, three hours late, then lost his secretary and his papers and wasted more time.

June 20th

Last night Ambassador took Alexander and Lloyd to see President of the Republic and then Pétain. Results inconclusive. Nobody can make up their minds about anything. Later Ambassador and Lloyd saw Herriot and Jeanneney whose departure had just been cancelled pending ratification by Council of ministers this morning.

Terrific air raid during the night just when we were trying to write telegrams. We heard one bomb drop quite close. H.E. refused to go down to the *abri*, but we finally persuaded him to sit in the passage where, by candlelight, we went on with our drafting.

Herriot asked us for a ship to be sent to take off about forty marked men. We have done this and also asked for a ship to take off officers who wish to respond to de Gaulle's appeal.

Government decided today that they would leave in a body, all of them, for Perpignan today. They would await there the German conditions, hold a council of ministers, and then President of the Republic and two Presidents of Chambers would go off to North Africa.

We discussed our movements and divided into two parties. Ambassador and me, Naval Attaché, and Air Attaché to go to Perpignan and North Africa, the rest to go by *Berkeley* to England. We hastily wrote farewell letters to our families and were all ready to start at five when message came to me from Ministry of Foreign Affairs "that departure no longer urgent, French Government probably not going where we thought, and Ambassador to get in touch with Charles-Roux".

Ambassador and Hal Mack went off at once while we are left to speculate. How can there be no hurry? We were bombed last night and will certainly be again tonight. Can it possibly be that they have accepted armistice terms? It seems hardly possible, but I feel it in the air.

Ambassador eventually returned to say that French Government had decided to stay another night so as to enable them to learn terms here. Delegates are to meet Germans at Tours this evening and terms will be telephoned.

It is reported that Weygand is saying it is no good France fighting on as Great Britain cannot resist invasion.

We agreed that after dinner Ambassador and I would go round and try to ascertain terms before French Government had decided on them as H.M.G. insist they should be consulted on terms. This the French Government may refuse to do on the ground that Germany won't allow time. Added to this, Germans are jamming our wireless from the destroyer so communications are very difficult. We set off in cars about 11 p.m. with Canadian and South African Ministers in tow in order to be the more impressive in insisting on previous consultation. It was a fruitless errand. We went first to the Presidency of the Council where Baudouin had told H.E. the Council would be held. It was dark and empty and even the orderly officer had gone to bed and could only be produced after 10 minutes' delay. He said *le Général Weygand se repose* and nothing was going on there. We then went to the Ministry of Foreign Affairs which was quite empty except for the sentries – not even a resident clerk. By now we had made up our minds that the French Government had gone. We then went to Marshal Pétain's residence where again all was dark. But we insisted on going in and were received by an extremely disagreeable *chef de cabinet* who seemed astonished that we should be so disturbed at having no information. Ambassador was very acid with him. However it appeared that Pétain had also gone to bed (we could hear him overhead), that nothing had been received yet from the delegation and we were promised to be told at once. So we came home to bed about midnight, having arranged to be ready for a summons at any moment.

June 21st

About 6.30 a.m., Ambassador, being anxious, sent Military Attaché round to Baudouin who told him plenipotentiaries had been unable to cross some bridge and had only reached Tours at 4 a.m.; nothing had as yet been received but the Germans south of the Loire were being withdrawn to the north. M.A. also communicated a formal note to Baudouin from H.E. to the effect that H.M.G. were expecting to be consulted. At 9.45 a.m. when we were still waiting, Ambassador received formal reply from Baudouin that French Government had always intended to have exchange of views with H.M.G. on terms but that they did not expect to receive them before the late afternoon.

Off with H.E. at ten to see Herriot. We found him sitting alone smoking his pipe. He complained that Jeanneney had been sent off to Perpignan and then the Government had decided not to go. He had a number of deputies waiting on a boat at Point de Graves to go to North Africa. Thus in Bordeaux itself there were only the defeatists. Pétain had received a deputation from Laval and Bergery,[1] and had given out that there would probably be no departure from Bordeaux. He thought this most significant. He was turning over in his mind what to do. He thought that if worst came to worst, he would reserve the rights of Parliament without whose consent no French territory can be alienated. He said all the soldiers and civil servants in the cabinet were for capitulation, the civilians were for resistance and they were still a majority. He told us how Madame Herriot had got up in the middle of the night and insisted on returning alone to Lyons so as to be there when the *boches* entered as he

1. French politician and journalist.

was obliged to stay with the President. Yet others were thinking too much of their wives and children.

It looks more and more as if there will either be a general move to North Africa in agreement with French Government or else a revolutionary government will be set up there. The local government will most certainly resist and the stiff ones from here will join them.

Bad signs are that the French censorship (Prouvost) is now suppressing news about America's war effort and our operations against Italy. When Childs protested, Prouvost said nothing must be allowed which might interfere with Pétain's peace effort.

P.R. is being pressed to go to U.S.A. as Ambassador. Hoppenot has become Minister at Lisbon, Margerie Consul-General at Shanghai. A purge. I am convinced they are going to sell out on us.

June 22nd

Message received late last night that terms received and would be considered in early hours of the morning. Ambassador went round and found complete confusion and eventually extracted copy of terms from Baudouin who was both badly rattled and rude. Terms had been considered and it had been decided to reply with certain questions. About fleet German Government proposed that it should be interned in French ports under German control but not used by Germans. Baudouin said French Government were to propose that it be interned in North African ports. Other terms were occupation of whole North and West coastline, small free zone for French Government in centre. Musso's terms not yet received. No French subjects to leave or serve elsewhere or they would be treated as *francs-tireurs*.[1] We worked from 4 a.m. onward drafting telegrams.

Our difficulties are increasing rapidly. Ambassador finds it more and more impossible to get any information out of the French and indeed feels himself treated even with suspicion. He saw Pétain for a moment this morning and was again reassured about the fleet.

Our position is becoming a problem. Our ship is at Arcachon and we must not be cut off from it by staying too late. We can hardly wait for Italian terms although two armistices are tied together.

H.E. went before lunch again to see Charles-Roux and obtained with great difficulty text of French reply. Most serious change pro-

1. i.e. shot on capture.

399

posed refers to fleet – it is now suggested that fleet should be disarmed under German or Italian control and then sail to North
African ports.

When Ambassador protested at this on ground that once Germans
had hold of ships they would never release them, C.R. said most of
ships were already in North Africa where German controllers would
have to go; as for the remainder in French metropolitan ports, scuttling clause would apply if necessary.

I saw Pierre Lyautey,[1] now decided to return to Lorraine and stay
with his people there. He has old *Madame la Maréchale* with him who
is horrified at being away in Bordeaux and not amongst her peasants.

Later H.E. was sent for and shown text of German reply. Germany
rejected French fleet proposal but said it was a matter for application
of the control commission.

Armistice signed at 6 p.m. The French Government did not even
bother to tell us. H.E. only learned of it when he called on Weygand
tonight.

Much discussion as to what we should do. Finally decided we
should go at midnight to Arcachon (a) because it was no longer safe
from German advance, and (b) because it was henceforward *infra dig.*
to remain, and (c) because of danger to cruiser. H.E. went round with
Military Attaché to say goodbye to Baudouin and Pétain. Latter in
bed. We finally left at 11 p.m. for Arcachon taking with us the
Canadian and South African Ministers as well as all that remained
of the Embassy party, Attachés, service personnel, etc. We arrived
about midnight at the Dupuys' villa where beds had been prepared
for us.

June 23rd

Here we slept till 6 a.m. when we were called and started off again to
go down to the pier and be taken off to the *Galatea*. We embarked in
an open sardine boat, the whole lot of us, with our suitcases and
official boxes and then made our way down the lagoon to the open
sea. It was very rough and soon began to rain, but fortunately some
far-sighted person had taken a tarpaulin off our lorry and put it up
over our heads in the boat. But when we reached the open sea, the
cruiser was nowhere to be seen. Our boat slowed down and it rolled
more and more and the rain increased. We could only suppose that

1. Writer and journalist.

the cruiser had been circling round waiting for us and would be back at any minute. But time went on and our position was really rather parlous – exposed as we were to submarine or air attack in an open boat. The Canadian Minister got sicker and sicker and was quite collapsed. The Naval Attaché had a portable wireless set which eventually got the *Galatea* but she didn't say where she was and only told us to wait. At length another ship altogether, the *Fraser*, a Canadian destroyer, appeared and we received instructions from *Galatea* to embark on her. This we did with great difficulty as the sea was very heavy. Poor Vanier had to be hauled up practically dead, no easy task as he is a large man with a wooden leg.

The destroyer could not have been kinder to us and fed us and dried us. It was explained that *Galatea* had remained at St Jean de Luz where we arrived about 6 p.m. We then transferred to the cruiser *Galatea*. St Jean de Luz very full of shipping embarking refugees, British subjects and Poles.

We received a telegram with a message for Lebrun from the King appealing to him not to let us down about the fleet. This we could only send on by telegram from St Jean to Bordeaux. We heard also that the Germans were at Royan just north of the Garonne and that Laval had joined the Government. We finally set sail about midnight and proceeded to sea at full speed as apparently a submarine was known to be in the vicinity. Very rough. Too tired to be ill.

June 24th

A long day at sea, very fresh and reviving after all we had gone through. The weather improved as the day went on and we finally reached Plymouth about 9 p.m. after an uneventful journey. We were met by the Admiral's barge in the harbour and taken up to the Commander-in-Chief's house where we found him entertaining the Duke of Kent and party consisting of Lord Birdwood,[1] Stephen Gaselee[2] and Chatfield who were just off on a special mission to Portugal. We were finally put on the midnight train and left for London. Thanks to an air raid which delayed the train, we weren't turned out at Paddington till 10 a.m. instead of seven – Hitler's only service to us!

1. Field-Marshal Lord Birdwood.
2. Sir Stephen Gaselee, former Librarian in the Foreign Office.

Appendices

A

O.H. to Secretary of State (Anthony Eden), March 1936 *(Extract)*

. . . You cannot base a long-term foreign policy on a dictatorship which always lands itself sooner or later in an Abyssinia. Our ultimate objective must be a prosperous democratic Germany not a prosperous Hitlerite Germany, any more than an impoverished democratic Germany (that was the mistake made after the war) . . .

The great question is whether if we help Hitler now by economic or any other concessions we should, in effect, strengthen his regime or begin to undermine it . . .

B

O.H. to Secretary of State (Anthony Eden), March 7th 1937

[See page 22 Note 2]

I know you are rather concerned, naturally enough, about our German policy and our failure so far to get any response from Germany or to get her into any settlement. I honestly cannot see any alternative to our present course of re-armament combined with continued invitations to co-operate. Although both Hitler and Mussolini still go on re-arming and refusing to co-operate, it is early days yet to expect our policy to have any very definite effect. After all, it is only in the last year, or more particularly in the last six months, that we have had a foreign policy at all. You have had to carve it out yourself in your speeches and the re-armament has only become manifest in the last six weeks. I think we must be prepared to wait a good deal longer before it sinks into the German mind. There have been many wobbles in British foreign policy in the past years and the Germans must be forgiven if they are a little slow in appreciating our new-found firmness and determination. An important date will be the change of Government here when Stanley Baldwin goes and they find that you are still Foreign Secretary as we know they may be pinning some hope to a change of policy then. I think we must wait at least a year or more whilst we continue firmly but calmly on our present course.

We none of us believe that Germany is quite certain yet what she wants – whether it is colonies or Czechoslovakia or war or peace or what. On the other hand, we know what we want – peace and no aggression – and we should not ignore the psychological effect of our determination backed by strength on an undecided Germany conscious of obvious economic and strategic weakness. This may not be of very rapid effect, but in the long run it may have considerable influence on a people of slavish political mentality like the Germans. (We may compare the psychological effect of America's entry into the last war in breaking the German spirit.)

Incidentally, I heard yesterday from somebody who knew Germany well that the German Government are much worried by the Soviet Wireless Service which, working in conjunction with the German Communists (who are now a very efficient underground organisation), broadcasts a most embarrassing news service in Germany.

This year is the worst from the armament point of view and the chances of a knock-out blow being successful are highest, but from all indications we have it is improbable that Germany would attempt it because of the doubt of a knock-out blow ever proving successful and of the fact that she too is not yet ready. Even this year, short of a successful knock-out blow, we and our friends should more than hold our own in a war. If we get through this year, then next year, while the German machine will be more nearly ready, the prospects of a successful knock-out blow will be definitely lessened by our better A.A. defences and our own general re-armament will really be becoming formidable. In any war which is not over in a few weeks, the advantages would be increasingly on our side. Nor does it seem likely that Germany will attack Czechoslovakia this year, again because she is not ready and because she cannot be certain that France and Great Britain would not intervene.

But while we must go on re-arming as rapidly as possible and go on offering Germany reasonable terms of settlement (as we are doing now over Locarno, etc.), it is equally important that we should keep the "peace-front" together. We must expect that Germany, as she becomes more convinced of our determination to re-arm and to resist aggression, will redouble her efforts to disintegrate the peace-front. We see her at it now with Belgium. She will also continue her efforts to detach *us* and we must be careful in any developments arising from

the Schacht–Leith-Ross conversations that we keep our friends informed and do not allow the suspicion (which Germany will naturally
foster) to grow that we are contracting out. Our relations with France
must remain what they are (and here Phipps should be invaluable in
case of trouble there). Our relations with the Soviets, though perhaps
they need not be any warmer, must never be allowed to cool off, for
Germany would be able to face us with an absolute instead of only a
relative superiority if there were a Soviet-German rapprochement,
and this cannot be regarded as absolutely impossible. And finally, we
must retain and develop the goodwill of Roosevelt; it is very difficult
to see what positive steps can be taken to this end as it seems that
very little can be done over the trade negotiations because of Ottawa.
(I would like to suggest our asking Lindsay for a full report on what
if any positive steps he would advise our taking to retain American
goodwill in view of the paramount importance of the U.S. being at
least a benevolent neutral in the event of a European war.)

The same also applies to the small states of Europe, but here it is a
question more of indirect rather than of direct action. So long as
Great Britain, France and the Soviets are strong and united in
defence of democracy and small nations, with America as a benevolent
supporter in the background, they will be with us. They can only
hope to survive by backing the winning side and they will be with us
so long as we are strong and determined. Our relations with Turkey,
for instance, are now very satisfactory and there seems no danger of
a German-Turkish alliance so long as Ataturk is there. He is also on
good terms with the Soviets, but he must be restrained from quarrelling with the French.

I have not said anything about Italy as I do not think we should
treat her at present any differently than, or separately from, Germany.
Though her interests may clash with those of Germany, their systems
are alike. Italy at present stands for the law of the jungle, we cannot
work with her so long as she upholds the principles which Mussolini
himself announces. We have offered her friendship through the
Anglo-Italian declaration;[1] I do not regret that, because although it
has led to no material result so far, it has been useful for educational
purposes and has silenced those who would now be saying that if you
had not refused the proffered Italian hand, Italy would not have
persisted in the Berlin-Rome axis. Italy will betray her friends when
she thinks it will pay her. Her policy is based on blackmail and it

1. The Gentleman's Agreement of January 2nd 1937.

would be folly to try and buy her off. We do not believe she is comfortable in Germany's arms, we believe she is in considerable economic difficulty – let us leave these factors to work. Her chief nuisance value is her disturbing effect on the minor Mediterranean powers. I do not think we can do anything about this except, as in the case of Germany, by convincing them that we are both strong enough and determined to resist aggression.

I was very interested by what you were saying to W. Strang and me the other day about the Protocol, that in two years' time British opinion might be ready for it. I am convinced myself that the Protocol policy is right and that a system of automatic military guarantee for all Europe would prove the one effective deterrent against a local war breaking out which would almost inevitably today spread everywhere. But it would only be a deterrent if everybody believed that a sufficient number of great Powers were determined to make it work. There must be no doubt about it, and at present British opinion would certainly introduce a doubt. I myself hope, however, that steady pursuit of our present policy (Leamington[1]) which is as far as we can go at present, with the popular education given by your speeches, our increasing armament and influence, may make it possible as the next step. I do not think we ought to contemplate any arms limitation without it.

My hope is that Germany, confronted by the overwhelming force and solidarity of the Western Powers plus Russia, with the knowledge that America is also against her, will end by accepting our terms of settlement. But our position would be fatally turned if Germany succeeded in buying us off or in otherwise splitting the peace front. It is unfortunate but a fact that Europe is now divided into two camps, but that is the fault of Germany not of us. She destroyed the Locarno Treaty and refused the Eastern Pact. Nor can we be reproached for not standing for reasonable terms of settlement.

C

O.H. to Secretary of State (Anthony Eden), April 6th 1937 (Extract)

. . . 1. We cannot offer the Central European and Balkan States that direct guarantee through the League which would bind them to our policy.

2. We can nonetheless influence them considerably by re-arming

1. A speech of A.E.'s in his constituency, November 20th 1936.

to an extent which must obviously make us and the League group patently stronger than Germany and Italy.

3. We can also bind them to us to some extent by financial and commercial facilities, which if supplied systematically and in co-operation by all the League group of Powers should go far to make them independent of Germany and Italy.

4. We can impress them greatly by the indirect method of a resolute policy towards Germany and Italy.

Our policy towards the Little Entente and the Balkans is closely related to our policy towards Italy. How far are Germany and Italy really united? Should we lump them together or try to separate them? . . . It is very doubtful, however, whether we could detach Italy without paying a price which would defeat our main purpose of organising the League front. Mussolini is anti-League and always has been and always will be. If we make friends with him on his terms, we stultify ourselves; it is certain that he will not make friends yet on League terms. Yet although his political system is ideologically the same as that of Germany, Italian national interests conflict with those of Germany in Austria, in the Balkans and in the Mediterranean.

. . . It comes to this, therefore; we can only buy off Italy at the cost of our principles, and when once we had bought her we could not be certain that she would fight for us against Germany except at a price which we should be unwilling to pay. If, therefore, on a long view, the League policy is the best for our interests, we must be prepared, on a short view, for the possibility of hostilities with both Germany and Italy at the same time. Provided that our own re-armament has been adequate, that our public opinion has been carefully educated (hence the infinite value of your speeches) and that the League from (primarily France, the Soviets and the more important Mediterranean states) has been kept together, this prospect need not unduly alarm . . .

D

O.H. to Secretary of State (Anthony Eden), May 8th 1937

[See page 35 Note 2]

The more or less emphatic oppositions of the French Ministers to the idea of colonial retrocession by France obliges us to reconsider our own attitude of conditional surrender of the pieces of the Cameroons and Togoland which we hold.

I have always felt convinced that any surrender of colonies to Nazi Germany, however small, would arouse passionate opposition in this country, among the Left even more than among the Right. I think the Cabinet, in discussing the question as it has, is somewhat out of touch with the force of public opinion on the question not only in the House of Commons but even more in the country.

Then there is the mandate difficulty. Germany would not thank us for a mandate colony. Yet to demandate a territory (apart from the legal difficulties) would be such a retrograde step, striking at one of the foundations of the League, that I really cannot see how His Majesty's Government could seriously countenance it for a moment. I know that certain mandates are now almost indistinguishable from colonies, but the principle has been preserved and is, I believe, of vital importance for the future of colonial administration.

Finally, there is the Dominion aspect. We should, I feel sure, take the opportunity of now sounding Dominion opinion on the colonial question. I always have felt that we have gone rather far in raising it with the French Government as we have without ever having actually consulted the Dominions.

Moreover, we have decided that *we* cannot in any case surrender Tanganyika, but only the West African colonies, and these only if France does so too. I think it is most important that we should not wrangle with the French Government over this, and still more that we should not let Germany know what our attitude is and so allow her to drive a wedge between us.

After all, what is the position? We will not return the only good German colony we hold; we will only give up a few strips. France is not disposed to give up her one good German colony; her attitude (based on strategy) is as justifiable as our own attitude over Tanganyika. We may be certain, moreover, that to Germany the return of the West African colonies alone (*pace* Dr Schacht) would be received with scant gratitude. Even if all were returned it would only be regarded as mere justice. But even Germany's pre-war colonial empire was not regarded as sufficient place in the sun for her.

The question is how now to proceed. Should we tell Germany flatly that we cannot consider the return of the colonies but would offer her economic concessions, etc., instead? This has the merit of honesty and would, I am convinced, be popular in this country. It has the disadvantage of slamming the door noisily at a time of tension when we do not want to upset Hitler more than we can help. It would also, moreover, be calculated to have a depressing effect on the Central and Eastern European States, who would fear that they would then be cast for the role of satisfying Germany's hunger. On the other hand, to leave the question open by implying in reply to Germany that in certain circumstances we might consider retrocession would be rather dishonest and cynical in view of our own and the French attitude towards the return of the larger colonies. On the whole, it may be wiser perhaps to send no reply either to Dr Schacht or to Baron von Neurath. After all, there has been no official demarche and we do not owe them any formal reply. At the same time, other channels of negotiation are open and functioning, e.g. the Five-Power Conversations and van Zeeland's economic mission, both of which afford us ample opportunity of letting Germany know what we want of her and what we can do for her in the political and economic spheres, without it being necessary to bring up the colonial sphere at all unless and until we have a definite German official demand for it.

E

O.H. to Secretary of State (Anthony Eden), June 20th 1937

[See page 45 Note 1]

1. The German conditions are quite unacceptable for us (Naval Demonstration, Surrender of Submarines and Threat of Immediate Reprisals Next Time). British opinion would not tolerate acceptance by H.M.G. for one moment. There is some reason to suppose, however, that these conditions are Ribbentrop's and not based on instructions from the German Government (see Mounsey's conversation with Corbin, according to which the German Ambassador in Paris did not mention them to Delbos although he communicated the German note).

2. The evidence is one-sided and flimsy. No submarine was actually sighted; the evidence is based only on the "detector", although the track of a torpedo is alleged to have been seen from the ship. As some proof of Spanish Government intentions, however, there is the Basque broadcasts.

3. Nonetheless, this incident following on the *Deutschland* incident is certainly suspicious and we cannot exclude the possibility that it was a deliberate attempt by Government Spaniards (or Russians or even anti-Nazi Germans on the Government side) to sink the ship and embroil Europe. It is almost incredible that it should be a German "frame-up" in view of what we believe fairly reliably to be Hitler's wish to liquidate his liabilities in Spain.

4. We must admit therefore that the Germans have a very serious case and also that by invoking the Four Power consultations they have acted so far according to the rules. What can we offer by way of immediate satisfaction and in order to diminish the risk of further incidents?

5. The least that we can do is to press the Valencia Government to give the assurances as regards respect of foreign warships which we have asked for. (This is being done.)

6. Valencia should also be asked if they can give any explanation of the incident. Can they account for the movements of their submarines? It should be possible also to get some corroborative evidence either for or against the German case from foreign warships engaged on the patrol. Did any of them sight a Spanish submarine on those days in that area? The Admiralty should also be able to say exactly how many Spanish submarines there are and what is their capacity. (I cannot believe that any Spanish or Russian submarine can be very efficiently navigated: it must have spent much time on the surface.)

7. But supposing the Valencia Government gives the required assurances and is able to give evidence that their submarines were not in that area, it is difficult to see what more the Valencia Government can be expected to do.

8. The placing of neutral observers on board the control warships is a matter for the Four Naval Powers themselves. This would certainly be helpful in providing outside evidence; but, although valuable where in air attacks ocular evidence is required, in this particular case a neutral observer could hardly have added much to our knowledge. Nonetheless, this would be a contribution towards prevention. (It may be noted in passing that if the Cabinet had agreed to your original proposal for an all-British control, such an incident as this would probably never have occurred.)

9. Are there any measures which we might ask of or impose on both sides in Spain as a means of prevention? If the Germans insist on more drastic sanctions against Valencia than we can accept, it will be easier for us if we can insist on their covering both sides. Here the proposal of the German Ambassador in Paris that both sides should be asked to surrender their submarines is suggestive. A still more drastic proposal would be for the Four Naval Powers to say that they would not tolerate any Spanish naval activities by either side outside territorial waters on the ground that they were a menace to foreign shipping. They might ask both sides to agree to this and,

failing acceptance, impose it. This would, of course, be very high-handed and illegal and at present it would help Valencia more than Franco, I suppose, but on the other hand the peace of Europe is at stake and it is intolerable that it should be jeopardised by a Spanish civil war. I am sure that public opinion here would approve and even welcome any measures, however drastic, which applied equally to both sides and which were clearly humanitarian and intended to limit the dangers of a general conflagration.

10. Finally, we could bring out our offer to supervise the immediate evacuation of volunteers on a pari passu basis from both sides. As the presence of volunteers is the real source of all these troubles and we alone are guiltless, we could perhaps make our acceptance of the German conditions (after they have been suitably modified) dependent on agreement as to an immediate beginning of withdrawals.

11. I fear that it would be futile to suggest any form of mediation at this stage, although the more we can merge the settlement of this German incident in some fresh big attempt to limit and terminate the war in Spain the easier it will be for all of us to make concessions to each other.

12. I cannot help thinking that Neurath's visit may be very useful. In the first place I should have thought that Ribbentrop will be very anxious to reach a settlement before he arrives. In the second place, unless Neurath runs out (in which case we must turn all our guns on him) it may be easier to take up with him both the immediate snags and the wider scheme for evacuation of volunteers. An Anglo-German agreement on Spain would be well worth his while if he could get one. In talking to Ribbentrop we can take the line that German insistence on such conditions as he has suggested, which public opinion here would never understand, could only have the most disastrous effect on Anglo-German relations on the eve of the Neurath visit which we are all hoping will improve them.

F

O.H. to Secretary of State (Anthony Eden), July 25th 1937
[See page 46]

Spain. The longer the war lasts the more expensive, unpopular and damaging it must be for the dictator countries. We know that Soviet aid now at least counter-balances, if it doesn't actually exceed that of Italy and Germany – hence, other things remaining equal, a long war, if not a stalemate, seems probable. At the same time the longer it lasts the more unpopular should foreign aid become in Spain itself, where it will be seen that foreign aid is prolonging the civil war – hence in the long run our own genuine neutral attitude should be increasingly appreciated.

If, therefore, our object should be, as I think it should, to prevent either side from winning a quick victory with foreign aid and to neutralising if we cannot eliminate the foreign aid on either side, then we should endeavour to hold the present situation as long as we can. We should insist on linking the grant of belligerent rights with withdrawal of volunteers, and if the compromise plan breaks down on this, as it very likely will, then I think we should revert to our original task of trying to restore the control system either by appointing observers on Spanish soil (if the Spanish parties will agree, but this is improbable without a *quid pro quo*) or by reviving Ribbentrop's idea of an international trawler patrol under the Dutch Admiral.

I feel sure we should give no encouragement to the idea of denouncing Non-Intervention and opening frontiers, as that would open up entirely new and dangerous possibilities, the outcome of which we cannot possibly see. Whilst Valencia could theoretically buy and import arms through France, I believe that Mussolini would seize this last chance of one final massive intervention to force the issue in Franco's favour. Such an outcome would be most damaging to the democracies and would leave Franco Musso's slave. The Labour Party are suffering from a most dangerous illusion in this respect.

It may perhaps be argued that to give belligerent rights without insisting on withdrawal of volunteers wouldn't affect the issue as most of the Soviet material is coming in Spanish ships, although the ships of Panama and Mexico, etc., would probably be covered by belligerent rights. This may be true, but against this we must consider that it would involve a very great strain on Anglo-French relations; it would cause great parliamentary trouble with the Opposition; it would increase risk of incidents between pseudo-Spanish ships (camouflaged Italian, German or Russian) and other ships, besides being a tremendous triumph for the dictators. It is always possible that Franco may end by quarrelling with his backers and expelling the volunteers.

Germany. On the whole, it seems unlikely that Germany is contemplating foreign adventure this summer. She has, all things considered, been reasonable about Spain. While she has undoubtedly got several irons in the fire, in Austria, in Czechoslovakia, in Danzig and Memel, any one of which she wouldn't hesitate to make use of if provoked or if the watchfulness of ourselves and France were relaxed, she doesn't look like *making* trouble. I think her policy in this respect is largely opportunist at present, but liable to sudden changes if Hitler's nerves are provoked or opportunities are too tempting. From all accounts our present policy is still best calculated to keep him calm and to gain time, viz. to insist on our readiness for a Western Pact as a prelude to a wider European settlement, to maintain a friendly tone in speeches but to make it clear that economic easements (which we are always ready to contemplate) must be accompanied by political easements, to continue to consult Germany and work with her where we can, whether in Spain or the Far East, and to give Ribbentrop all the credit we can. Finally, in the autumn we might revive the idea of a visit here by Neurath.

One point which will come up for decision during your leave is that of Henderson's attendance at Nuremberg in September. He is very anxious to go. Perhaps you might discuss this at a meeting before you go away? I am divided in my own mind. I can see the Ambassador's argument and see certain advantages if we want to get on Hitler's soft side. On the other hand, it would increase Labour suspicion of Henderson although Parliament will not be sitting. We might ascertain what is the practice of H.M. representatives in the other totalitarian states, Russia, Italy and Turkey, as regards attendance at these national party celebrations. I feel the case isn't on all fours with that in democratic countries and needn't necessarily have the same treatment. *We should, in any case, act in conjunction with the French*, I think, and whatever decision we do reach should apply to all totalitarian states, Black or Brown or Red, and that would be the answer to the Labour Party.

Italy. This is certainly for the moment our most immediate danger and our most difficult problem. We have her military preparations in Libya, her behaviour in Spain, Mussolini's insulting and bellicose speeches and articles, his apparent conviction (substantiated by the Embassy, by Graham and even by Grandi) that we are harbouring thoughts of revenge. Against this we have to set the Anglo-Italian Declaration (to which Mussolini still seems to attach importance), your friendly references in recent speeches, your talks with Grandi, and now comes the offer to Hore Belisha of a military agreement. Much of the bellicosity is no doubt intended for internal consumption to maintain excitement and to overcome the lassitude and discontent caused by the strain of the regime. Yet even when this is allowed for, the regime is admittedly militarist and expansionist and he is a gangster. I feel therefore that while we should do all we can both publicly and privately to eradicate the fallacy that we mean to fight Italy when we are strong enough, we should be very careful not to be lulled into a false security. But, like the other dictator, he ought to be kept in play, for time is on the side of the democracies.

One thing I feel convinced that we should not do is to sign any military agreement to limit our forces in the Mediterranean. This would be far too dangerous as we can never trust an Italian signature in a vital matter. The offer to Hore Belisha, with its reference to the Rome-Berlin axis, is strangely like Italy's attitude in 1914 when she put herself up to the highest bidder. I do not think, however, that it should be absolutely turned down; it should be explored further and it might perhaps be possible to arrange for exchange of information about military movements (if the C.I.D. see no danger in this) as opposed to a limitation agreement.

Then there is the idea of a personal letter. If sent by the P.M. (which would be more normal as Mussolini is P.M.) it would, I fear, revive the legend that you alone are intransigent. Then what could be put in a letter which hasn't already been said in public? The one act which would do more than anything to show that we had closed the Abyssinian chapter would be to grant *de jure* recognition, and I think this ought to be done, in conjunction with the French, after Geneva this autumn if by any means possible, but we cannot speak of it now.

All things considered, I feel that there really is very little that we can do beyond keeping calm and keeping prepared, doing what we can by speeches and conversation to emphasise our determination to let bygones be bygones, co-operating wherever we can, giving them previous notice when we can of our intentions, finally, recognising Abyssinia as soon as we can.

Here, as in the case of Germany, time is on our side and I feel that we must seek to gain time by riding the dictators on the snaffle. If we bring them up short we might get away with it, but it would be a great and unjustifiable risk, not only from the military point of view but from the domestic point of view, as I am quite sure the country – as apart from the Labour Party – are in no fighting mood. But equally, if we let the dictators get away with it too much and too easily, they will end by going one too far and we shall have a war even so. I'm afraid it is a very difficult and delicate course for you to steer – between their hopes and fears and their ambitions legitimate and illegitimate, but I will only say that you've succeeded in doing so so far in our *worst* period of weakness and I for one am quite confident that you will be able to go on doing so now.

G

O.H. to Anthony Eden, November 7th 1937

[See page 57 Note 1]

I keep on getting evidence of the immense effect of your speech, in the City, in the street and in the country and among all classes. The reason given for such a profound impression on all these diverse elements is always the same. Here at last you had said what the country wanted said; here was one person at least in the Government who had dared to speak out to the dictators what the country felt about them. The effect was the greater because of the long period of waiting and also because fears were developing that you too had succumbed to the cloying methods of the Government as a whole.

For the Government is not popular. How can it be? The P.M. is not regarded with any enthusiasm. He cannot inspire affection like Stanley Baldwin, nor is he a "younger man", indeed, with his gout he is liable to be put out of action at a moment of crisis. The Simons, the Hoares, the Hailshams are regarded with contempt as the old gang. Everybody now realises what Simon and Hoare have been responsible for in foreign affairs and the country is shocked that these unsinkable politicians should go on from Government to Government. It is not with such men that the democracies will win. Neville Chamberlain had his chance of making a clean sweep last July, and the country would have responded to him, but he wasn't big enough to take it. I believe this opinion is widespread among the younger members of the House and with many older ones too who feel that the qualifications of the second eleven to promotion were insufficiently considered. The only satisfactory feature in the Government from the point of view of the H. of C. and of the country is yourself. As Foreign Secretary you were the country's choice two years ago; since then you have steadily built up a solid reputation very different from the somewhat artificial peak of popularity you reached in the Simon period.

The country is watching you very closely. It suspects that your colleagues are trying to damp you down and it is wondering whether they will succeed. Lloyd George at Caernarvon spoke for large sections of the country. The Government, on the other hand, while jealous of your personal position is very content to use you for its own publicity purposes while obstructing your policy.

The first point I want to make is this. You are the only Foreign Secretary in sight. If you left the Cabinet the Government would fall. The Government is living on your popularity and reputation; you are not only entitled to but you are able to impose your terms.

The second point is this. You are, rightly as I think, profoundly disturbed at the slowness and inadequacy of our re-armament and the general administrative and financial obstruction which it is encountering. What is required is a great speeding-up of immediately available equipment, and this must include purchases from abroad. You are also receiving insufficient support in the Cabinet for your foreign policy; indeed, far from supporting you many of your colleagues, even the P.M. on occasion, seem mainly concerned in obstructing you. If you had shown them the text of your speech they would have prevented you making it. Yet that was the speech the country has been demanding for months. Far from provoking the dictators, it has had a sobering effect. It is intolerable that you, the only member of the Government whose resignation would bring about the fall of the Government, should be in this position. In fact, the position is that the Cabinet is the *only* place where you are in a minority.

We know how dangerous the international situation is likely to be in the next two years. It is no time for drifting. We must have more rapid re-armament and a vigorous because unhampered foreign policy. From the purely parliamentary point of view, I am certain there will be a revolt sooner or later from the old gang. It is most important to preserve you from becoming involved in their discredit because it will be a very serious thing for all concerned when the country discovers that our preparations are inadequate if we drift into war. That is the sort of opportunity that Winston and L.G. will instantly profit by.

I feel most strongly therefore that while the effect of your speech is still present, you should speak to the P.M. with some "appalling frankness". You should say that you are profoundly disturbed at the slowness of our re-armament and at the complacent attitude of your colleagues, that you personally feel unable to share responsibility any longer for their delays and ostrich-like behaviour which may cost the country a disaster; similarly, that you feel you are not receiving the support from your colleagues in foreign affairs to which you are entitled. You stand for vigorous methods; they stand for flabbiness. You feel moreover that the country and the House support you. From your F.O. experience you know the dangers which may beset us if we falter and you must therefore ask for more effective immediate re-armament, including purchases abroad and more solid support of your policy, otherwise you must leave the Government and warn the country.

This would be very plain speaking, but I honestly believe the hour has come for it. The times are too dangerous for niceness and the lesser loyalties. I feel you must mark out your position now or else your colleagues will involve you in their ruin. It may be fatal to hang on too long, and after all it must be remembered that in spite of personal feelings it is the country and the House which have certainly given you their confidence, to which you owe the first loyalty. You owe none to those colleagues, the principal obstructionists, who would gladly have kept you out of the Cabinet if they had been able. Your position is so strong now that the Cabinet would not dare let you go. They are imposing on your good nature because they do not think you will ever turn on them.

H

O.H. to Secretary of State (Anthony Eden), November 7th 1937
[See page 57 Note 5]

You will have been reading a number of papers on Palestine. From the point of view of objectivity it is worth remembering that Rendel is a Catholic and a passionate anti-Zionist and that the question is also viewed from the Eastern Department angle only.

There is another F.O. aspect. The Balfour Declaration was made during the war as a gesture to secure the support of international Jewry. The Arabs also received promises which were largely implemented by the liberation as free nations of Irak, Arabia and Syria. Any suggestion that we may now be seeking to go back on or water down our promises to the Jews would excite intense indignation in all countries where there are Jews, especially in America. On the whole, it must be admitted that the Jews have deserved well of us.

When Rendel suggests a fixed percentage of 40% purposely to prevent the Jews from ever becoming a majority in Palestine, I feel myself that this would be regarded as arbitrary and unfair. Such a percentage should be at least 50% and it would be far better to have no cut and dried percentage at all but to secure the liberties of both parties by constitutional safeguards. It would be a poor exchange to placate the Irakis and the Saudis only to incur the hostility of the American Jews. Sympathy for the Arabs can, I think, be overstated. All the Arab lands are now freed apart from Palestine, and vastly underdeveloped. The present trouble has largely arisen, I am sure, from the fumbling of the C.O. and the failure of the local administration to keep order. The moderate Arabs have been killed or terrorised by the Mufti's party. The partition scheme has much to recommend it, but its prospects were prejudiced by lawlessness and delay. Whatever eventual decision is taken, the first thing now is drastic action against murder and intimidation. Here again Rendel's plea for further latitude seems to me misplaced.

I

O.H. to Secretary of State (Anthony Eden), December 29th 1937 (Extracts)

[See page 67 Note 1]

It seems to me that the situation *vis-à-vis* the two dictatorships, Germany and Italy (to which Japan must now be added), is becoming clarified and hardened. The contrast between the dictatorships and the democracies is more marked, not through the fault of the latter, and recent conversations and speeches prove cumulatively that *for the present at least* we must give up hope of either the general European settlement with Germany which is contemplated or any settlement with Italy which would include a return to satisfactory co-operation with us and France and the League . . .

. . . I think we must not disguise from ourselves that no *real* agreement such as that between France and ourselves is possible between us and Fascist Italy (or for that matter Nazi Germany). Mussolini's system is diametrically opposed to ours. It is not that we cannot co-operate with dictatorships, e.g. the Soviets or Turkey: we can co-operate with any regime which wants peaceful relations and respect for law. But Mussolini (like the Nazis) openly glorifies war and violent change. Any agreement which the democracies concluded with him would be no more than a temporising one – accepted by him for purposes of prestige or of blackmail or because of weakness.

That being so, I think we must approach the problem of recognition on severely realist grounds with our eyes open to the limited and temporary advantages to be obtained.

. . . The advantages to be obtained by according recognition in return for a hard bargain seem to me very doubtful; indeed, apart from settling the tiresome question of Ambassadors and of the Abyssinian frontiers, I doubt whether we should get any. If Mussolini is sufficiently alarmed by Germany's expansionism to overcome his natural leaning towards Nazism, we will get him on our side anyway; so long as he thinks the two dictatorships can co-operate usefully, he will take what we give and remain where he is.

. . . Yet, obviously, the grant of recognition would lessen the tension between the two countries and should finally convince Mussolini that we do not intend to go for him ourselves. It may still be thought worthwhile to do this, even though we cannot hope for much more.

. . . My own conclusion is that there is a fundamental incompatibility between the systems of Hitler and Mussolini and the democracies, and I do not believe that any permanent composition with them is possible for us on terms which would not involve suicide, either for them or for us!

. . . Is there not a risk that we shall reinforce Mussolini just when he is feeling the strain and perhaps even cracking under it? If we could be sure of making a reliable friend of him, we should not hesitate to recognise, but we cannot hope to do this. All we can hope for is a temporary *détente*.

One thing is certain and that is whatever we do must be done in conjunction with France. I suppose we couldn't consult the U.S. too? . . . it would be at least worth ascertaining that the U.S. Government would not be shocked if we and the French recognised. Knowing Roosevelt's views about the dictators, we cannot be sure that he would not be and that would be a fatal bar having regard to the paucity of advantages which we stand to gain by recognition anyhow.

J

O.H. to Anthony Eden, February 18th 1938

[See page 94 Note 1]

My Dear Anthony,

In the paper attached I have tried to analyse the position as I see it, but I would like to say a word about the more personal side.

Your speech last Saturday[1] has had a better press than any other. It has been welcomed as a stand for vigour, the long view against the short view, for principle against mere expediency – what the country wants in its leaders but isn't getting. That is what you stand for personally in the country's eye and that is what you represent in the Government.

This Italian business is very sticky and the country will hate giving *de jure* recognition. I doubt whether the country will have it at all except in return for a genuine settlement. Such a settlement must include some striking proof of better behaviour such as the evacuation of Spain. The country loathes Musso and all he stands for. You said only last week that we must not sacrifice principles for quick results. I do not see how you could possibly defend in the House of Commons what the P.M. is asking of you. You must insist on getting your own way in foreign affairs or you cannot continue in the Government. The P.M. has treated you abominably – whatever you may say! There is, I daresay, a genuine difference of view between you, but that is a reason for one of you going. If he cannot approve *your* policy, you cannot approve his. Democratic Government depends on issues being faced relentlessly, even though Governments fall, but there isn't really anything so terrible in that when it comes to questions of principles – the fact that the idea of your going should so upset the P.M. and would, in fact, endanger the Government shows how important you are, important exactly because you represent these principles which the P.M. wishes to violate – what kills democracy is when the country loses faith in its leaders. Where there is conflict of loyalties, the wider must come before the narrower. Again and again the P.M. has intervened against your known views (Musso, letters, Halifax, Roosevelt) – he really cannot have it both ways – i.e. keep you and run his own foreign policy. It is too much to ask any man to carry the burden of your office unless he has full and confident support from the P.M. and colleagues. But the reverse is now the case – they give you far more trouble than even the foreign countries.

I do not think you should be unduly disturbed at pleas put to you about risks of provoking a Cabinet crisis just now. You simply can't go on in a false position on a major issue – you can't conduct a policy you don't approve. I am myself fairly certain they will give way – as they did more or less over Roosevelt. But I don't think it

1. To the Junior Imperial League in Birmingham.

matters too much if they don't give way and the break comes. You are entitled to say this is one of a series of cases where you feel you haven't the support of the Cabinet, and you must be given that support or you can't be expected to carry on. They must get someone else to carry out *their* policies.

The most I think you could accept would be the announcement of conversations at *Italy's request, acceptance now of Spanish scheme* and *understanding*, clearly stated, that *no goods will be delivered until the Italians are out of Spain*.

This would be a triumph. But to require Italians to be all out of Spain before you start talking would be, I think, asking too much. The only other acceptable alternative I see is method followed hitherto of informal talks concurrently with the settlement of Spain.

Yours,
Oliver.

O.H. to Secretary of State (Anthony Eden), (attached to above letter of February 18th)

The upshot of the conversations between the P.M., yourself and Grandi is:

(a) That Grandi says Italy was asking herself whether G.B. really meant to open conversations with her;

(b) to which the P.M. quotes Ciano and Lady Chamberlain to the effect that an early start should be made in view of possibility of future happenings;

(c) Grandi retorts that as Italy can't have both Germany and G.B. against her, she must make even closer friends with Germany unless G.B. comes along fast;

(d) but Grandi insists that the talks must be in Rome;

(e) that he cannot discuss Austria; and

(f) that he wasn't authorised to accept the withdrawal scheme about Spain.

To all of which the reply was that H.M.G. had reached no decision yet but reply would be given on Monday.

You have previously made it clear to Grandi that we are ready for conversations with a view to ultimate *de jure* recognition provided propaganda stops and Spain is cleared up. Grandi himself admitted the reasonableness of this only a week ago and undertook to refer the Spanish scheme to Rome. We are still awaiting his reply.

At the Cabinet on February 9th the P.M. agreed with your view that you should continue discussions with Grandi on these two points that you should advance step by step in other subjects and that you should have no formal opening of conversations with attendant publicity.

P.M. now says that events in Austria have changed all this, that Musso has received a bad shock and that we have a psychological opportunity for detaching him from the Berlin axis if we go quickly and agree to announce immediate talks. You say, on the contrary, that we must go slow, the boot is pinching Mussolini more and more and that if he wants to join us we can get him to do what we want in Spain, etc., that we are doubtful whether even now he is sincere and that he must prove his sincerity by irrevocable acts in Spain before we can give away our principle of agreeing to conversations.

Why does Musso want immediate conversations? There is no doubt that there is a fundamental hostility between Germany and Italy over Austria and he cannot have liked what has happened in the past week. Has he succeeded in extracting a *quid pro quo* from Hitler for his acquiescence or has Hitler disregarded him completely? If the former, then he must have got a promise of support in the Med. or Spain and his conversations with us would be mere eyewash designed to deceive us and gain time. If the latter, then he must be genuinely anxious and can be reasonably expected to give us what we want in respect of Spain and propaganda.

A third possibility is that in the true Italian fashion he is putting himself up to the highest bidder. Grandi blandly tells us that Italy must choose between Germany and Great Britain, which is exactly what Giolitti told the allies in 1914. (Are we sure that Musso is not saying the same thing in Berlin?) We are told that Italy will be even more bound to Germany unless we agree with her quickly. How can this be? How much closer can the Axis be? Italy has never found any difficulty in betraying her allies when she thought it was in her interests.

What have we to show Musso's real intentions? Grandi has already put out in breach of his understanding with the P.M. a tendentious account of today's conversations for Reuters.[1] In this he emphasises that the initiative comes from H.M.G., that Grandi has

1. Charles Peake to O.H. 18.2.38: Reuters inform me that the Italian Embassy have given out the following account of the conversations which took place at Downing Street. The announcement is semi-official. The

no statement to make about Austria and that Spain must be left to the Non-Intervention Committee. In fact, he asks us to go to Canossa, he refuses to talk about Austria although we are co-signatories of Stresa, and if he is genuine this should be his chief reason for wanting to concert with us, and he doesn't even reply to the inquiry about Spain we made only a week ago. Moreover, one would have thought he should have welcomed an honourable way out of the Spanish bog which will give him 40,000 extra men.

There are a number of good reasons for going slow just at the moment and for refusing to allow ourselves to be rushed into a public announcement of conversations: viz. Hitler's speech on Sunday, Roosevelt's plan possibly due at the end of the week, the general uncertainty in Austria, and the British dislike of dramatic methods in foreign affairs. If Musso is genuinely afraid of Germany then we have already offered him reasonable terms for settlement. If he is blackmailing us or playing for time, then there is additional reason for insisting on our terms, including concrete action in Spain.

It has been suggested that we should agree to the announcement of conversations provided that it was indicated that the initiative came from Italy and that Italy accepted the scheme for withdrawal

---

Press have been told to use it as "it is learnt in authoritative Italian quarters, etc.".

1. The Italian Government welcome the new approach made to them by the British Government.

2. A general conversation took place covering all points at issue.

3. The Prime Minister and the Foreign Secretary raised the question of Austria, but Count Grandi had no statement to make.

4. The Italian Government think that the conversations should embrace every subject, including the recognition of the Italian conquest of Ethiopia.

5. The withdrawal of volunteers is not in the view of the Italian Government a subject to be included in the conversations unless they embrace all points at issue; it should be dealt with by the N.I. Committee.

6. His Majesty's Government have now made it clear that they are prepared to discuss all the subjects together.

After this announcement had been made to the Press at the Italian Embassy, the announcer (the First Secretary) said that in his personal view warm satisfaction was felt that the British Government had now waived the Spanish question and the question of the Bari broadcast which had hitherto been used as a pretext for failure to start conversations.

Reuters, who have received the above, are holding it in case further information should be available.

from Spain. This would undoubtedly be better than an announcement that we had initiated the conversations without any undertaking about Spain. But Italy has violated her undertakings so often that anything less than insistence on positive action would certainly be regarded as fatal weakness. There will be great difficulty in making the conversations acceptable to public opinion. The idea that they will be welcomed is fantastic. Only if they can be based on positive measures of appeasement will they be accepted, and it must be remembered that once we start we must face *de jure* recognition at the end. In any case, why should Italy not clear out of Spain where she has no right to be?

There is the further possibility that we should agree to the opening of conversations now, provided it was made clear that the initiative comes from Muss, that he accepted now the Spanish formula and that it was understood now that no agreements would be signed or *de jure* given until Italian troops were out of Spain. This would be a considerable triumph, but it is also the least that I think we should agree to. What would be fatal would be to consent to open conversations now and say nothing about Spain. Indeed, without liquidation of Spain it is highly unlikely that we can keep our pledge and proceed with the League in this. The League would hardly agree to concur in *de jure* unless Spain is tidied up, and we should risk being unable to deliver the goods ourselves.

What I dislike is that Muss should come to us with a sort of ultimatum in which all the concessions are to come from us and offer nothing to meet our suspicions. If he is genuine then he must be prepared to accept our *desiderata* and timing. We have been made fools of by Muss too often.

K

Notes for Anthony Eden before resignation, February 20th 1938

[See page 96 Note 1]

You don't feel situation is one which can be met by compromise even if one were found. For some time aware of real divergence of view between you and P.M. and many colleagues. Foreign Secretary cannot carry on unless assured of full and confident support – you feel you haven't had that. Particularly is this true of P.M.

Nor is the situation satisfactory for Government or country. Foreign policy must be strong and united – now there are two policies and the country and Europe is increasingly aware of it.

You believe in one policy – P.M. in another – a real difference of view – yet now *neither* of these two policies is being carried out effectively.

Instances original letter from P.M. to Mussolini in August when you were away from London – you did not approve of that letter and you were not consulted before it was sent – this was origin of our present difficulties. A decision of such importance should have been taken surely by P.M. and Foreign Secretary in agreement, if necessary after consulting colleagues.

Halifax visit – original idea approved by you but disapproved both moment and conditions of visit. Visit was hurried on again while you were away in Brussels, and conditions which you sought to attach, viz. that Hitler should receive H. in Berlin and that Hitler should *invite* H., were overruled – H. finally went to Berchtesgaden, not on an invitation but at his own request – humiliating conditions.

Third instance. Roosevelt plan here again decision taken in your absence on major issue – R. submitted plan – P.M. without sending for F.S. or consulting colleagues sent chilling and discouraging reply which you felt fatal mistake – on your return you sought to reverse effect produced by original reply.

You don't say your view is necessarily right and P.M.'s wrong, but you quote – all having occurred in six months – to show that real divergence exists between you and P.M. and that you have made real attempt to co-operate with him. But each fresh instance convinces you more that there is no common policy between you. There really are two policies and we are now having worst of both. Only honest thing is to have a Foreign Secretary who believes in and can carry out P.M.'s policy – it will then have fullest chances of success. (You cannot defend in H. of C. a policy which you don't believe to be the right one.)

L

O.H. to Secretary of State (Lord Halifax), June 30th 1938
[See page 159 Note 1]

Foreign policy must be regarded as a whole. It is not possible to take a strong line in one quarter and an apparently weak one in another indefinitely. There is some danger, as it seems to me, that our policy in Spain may react eventually and unfavourably upon our policy in Central Europe and in the Far East.

Up to now Czechoslovakia has been the outstanding success of His Majesty's Government in foreign affairs. Our action stopped the overwhelming of Czechoslovakia in May, but our further success in maintaining peace combined with justice depends on the continuance of the German belief in our determination to see a settlement through and our refusal to be bluffed; otherwise Hitler may be expected to revert to the extremist policies urged upon him by Goering and the Party leaders. Equally, our success depends on the Czechoslovak belief that we are worth listening to and can and will make our influence felt and respected in Berlin, otherwise Benes will in turn yield to his reactionaries.

In the Far East the Japanese are watching us closely. If we appear to them to be kicked about by the Italians and Germans over Spain, they must be expected to start doing the same with British shipping and interests, etc., in China and the China Seas. If we can follow up our initial success in Czechoslovakia and also put a stop to the attacks on our shipping in Spain, the Japanese will view us with the more respect. Again, if we show our determination to help China where we properly can (i.e. over a currency loan or the building of railways, etc.) without paying overmuch attention to threats of Japanese resentment, this may be expected both to impress the Japanese and indirectly to strengthen our prestige in Europe.

The trouble about the Spanish situation is that it is equally bad for His Majesty's Government from the external point of view and from the home point of view. The Opposition have little other cause for attacking the Government, but Spain in itself constitutes a very large and vulnerable target for allegations of failure to protect British shipping and British imperial interests, failure to stand up to dictators, proof of fascist tendencies, etc., etc.

Apart from the technical difficulties of what form stiffer action in Spain should take, there arises the political difficulty of the effect on the Anglo-Italian Agreement. The whole value of that Agreement depends not on the wishes of His Majesty's Government but on its relatively cordial acceptance by the British public. Unless its ratification is genuinely approved here, still more if its ratification were the signal for an outcry, Anglo-Italian relations would be no better, if not worse, than before and our gesture of recognising Abyssinia would have been wasted. The continuance of the present situation in Spain is increasing anti-Italian feeling here and causing the gradual evaporation of any appeasement value in the Anglo-Italian Agreement. On the other hand, a stiff attitude in Spain which led to effective cessation of attacks on British ships would put up Government stocks at home and make the eventual ratification of the Agreement far more palatable. Indeed, it may be said that until the British public is convinced that Mussolini is no longer at the back of these attacks, it will never regard him again as a friend.

There remains the question of what the effect of firm action would be on Mussolini himself. This is certainly a matter of doubt. If stern action were taken and Italian airmen were killed, the risk must be faced that Mussolini would go off the deep end. He might, on the other hand, behave as he did over Nyon and prevent any awkward situation arising by effectively withdrawing his people from the danger zone. It is at least arguable that a stiff attitude on our part would earn the respect of one who is himself a fanatical advocate of firmness and force and make us the more attractive to him.

If we could recover our prestige in Spain by the effective stoppage of such attacks, this would strengthen His Majesty's Government's position not only at home but also *vis-à-vis* Germany and the Far East, and finally America. Although opinion in the last country is not to be taken too seriously in view of the unlikelihood of any immediate action resulting, it is, on a long-term view, of vital importance that we should appear as upholding democracy in Europe, especially as our stocks have recently slumped there somewhat on this account.

There is also this consideration. We have no wish to engage in ideological wars or to help the division of Europe into two camps; at the same time we do stand for constituted authority and are opposed to aggression. The Russians, now that we have damped down the French, are the only supporters of Government Spain; they are also almost alone in helping China. There is therefore a danger that these two countries – Spain and China – *faute de mieux* – may become the prey of Bolshevism. We cannot obviously support Government Spain, but the fact that we appear to be weak *vis-à-vis* Franco encourages the belief that we do in fact favour his side.

M

O.C.H. to Secretary of State (Lord Halifax), October 27th 1938

[See page 219 Note 1]

I cannot help feeling that Sir E. Phipps is getting into dangerous waters if he lends himself in any way to the encouragement of the removal of high officials in the Quai. Reports are already too current in Paris that the Embassy has been intervening overmuch in French internal politics during the recent crisis. Sir C. Mendl was certainly far too active in particular.

M. Bonnet has now got rid of M. Massigli. Whatever may be said against Massigli, he has always been in season and out of season a good friend of Anglo-French relations. Likewise Comert, who also at the time of the Laval Government stuck up for our point of view. In earlier days Comert was very nearly sacked for being pro-German. The trouble is that he is not anti-German but anti-Nazi. If now Léger is to be removed, we may find ourselves badly short of friends in the Quai.

I feel one of the dangers which must be faced as a result of the agreement at Munich and the Anglo-German Declaration is that those elements in France who are more pro-German than pro-British and, or rather perhaps, more pro-Nazi than pro-Left, will be encouraged to reach direct agreement with Germany behind our backs and at our expense. Such an agreement would be on the basis of France accepting a German guarantee of non-aggression, dropping the Soviet Pact and disinteresting herself in Europe entirely, on the understanding (probably mistaken) that *her* position (not ours) in the Mediterranean and the colonies should be left undisturbed. There is a school which favours France abandoning the struggle and becoming a second-class Power. This is the school of Flandin and Caillaux. (We remember Caillaux's treacherous activities in 1914 and 1915.) If the Front Populaire can be broken, if the Quai can be purged, the way will be clearer for action by this element. I don't think they will succeed because Caillaux is old and ill; he is also identified with high finance and his past reputation stinks. Nor does Flandin seem to possess the particular qualities necessary for a French leader. But Daladier, though not a strong man, has personal leanings towards a direct Franco-German Agreement and could be pushed further. Bonnet is light.

French politicians being what they are, and French public opinion being easily influenced, I do not think one can exaggerate the importance to us of the Quai d'Orsay. The politicians come and go, the Quai remains. It represents the permanent element in French diplomacy. If the basis of British policy remains close friendship with France and no separate agreements with Germany, and if our aim is to see France strengthen herself, then we must beware of weakening the position of those like Léger and Massigli. They are absolutely sound on this policy, but if replaced they might be succeeded by a very different type of man.

Secretary of State (Lord Halifax), to O.H., October 28th 1938 (In reply to above)

We have discussed. I don't see any evidence of Phipps acting unwisely in his letter. As regards the general question, it is, I think, inevitable that recent events and German strength will affect French policy in the sense of making it more restricted and more defensive on narrower lines. But if the ultimate choice for France is between that and an attempt probably not very successful and potentially very dangerous to obstruct German expansion in Central Europe, the French may well think the first is the wiser.

N

O.H. to Secretary of State (Lord Halifax), January 8th 1939
[See page 237 Note 1]

I had luncheon yesterday with Lord Tyrrell who had some interesting views about the international situation.

As regards the Rome visit he took the view that Mussolini was in a difficult position and that we should lose nothing by being very firm with him. We should say that where we joined issue with him was in respect of his methods, so long as he sought to use force rather than persuasion as his method we could never restore the old relations of friendship with him. What had really shocked this country both in respect of Germany and in respect of Italy was the flagrant breach of undertakings and the use of force and threat; our difference with the dictators was a moral issue, not a political one at all. We were always ready to listen to and aid in redressing legitimate grievances if reasonably presented. So long, however, as they put force first, we could never deal with them.

He said that it was important that steps should be taken while in Rome to see both the French and the American Ambassadors. The Italian press would insinuate that we were sympathising with Italian claims far more than would be the case, and such press reports might do untold harm abroad unless corrected by such contacts.

Speaking of the audience with the Pope, Lord Tyrrell said that he very much hoped that you would be able to have some private conversation with him apart from the P.M. I think he thought that the

Pope would be more likely to open out to you. In him we now had a passionate collaborator in the task of re-establishing a moral order in international affairs. His anxiety over the dangers to civilisation of the dictatorships was the one thing that was keeping the old man alive. The fact, moreover, that when Hitler, the leader of one of the largest Catholic countries, went to Rome, the Pope refused to see him and ostentatiously went away, whilst he should receive yourself and the P.M., leaders of the greatest Protestant country, would have an important effect on the German people in opening their eyes, also on the Italians.

Of Germany Lord Tyrrell spoke again of the vital importance of keeping our issue with the Nazis on the moral plane. We were not concerned to block German claims; we were concerned with their methods; we could not tolerate force. That was the issue which the British public saw and which the German people might be made to see. We had an opportunity afforded by Nevile Henderson's illness to prolong his absence from Berlin and so keep in step with the recall of the American Ambassador. The German people would notice that both Ambassadors were away from Berlin and would realise that something was wrong. The Germans had a natural inferiority complex.

He thought the Germans were likely to go East and they were satisfied that the French would not fight. If they went East, they might be led on into Russia and then they would be lost. But we were Public Enemy No. 1, and unless we were adequately armed they might be tempted to go for us first. He endorsed my view that really impressive A.R.P. was probably the greatest guarantee of European peace we could furnish because the dictators could not face a long war, but so long as London was apparently an easy target, they would always be tempted to believe that we never could intervene or else to try a knock-out blow. If we were really well defended, the Germans would hesitate long before precipitating a situation in which we might intervene.

O

"The Times", May 3rd 1939

[See page 286 Note 1]

THE REICHSTAG SPEECH

CHOICES BEFORE THE WORLD

LORD RUSHCLIFFE'S VIEW

To the Editor of *The Times*

Sir,—Now that sufficient time has elapsed to study the speech which Herr Hitler made on Friday last to the Reichstag, I think the great majority of the people of this country will consider it a profound mistake to dismiss it with the superficial comment that it leaves matters exactly as they were and that it is, therefore, unnecessary to pay any particular attention to it. It was the deliberate, carefully prepared utterance of the man who has it in his power to plunge Europe into war – or, on the other hand, to make the greatest contribution to peace.

As you, Sir, truly say in the leading article of *The Times* of April 29th, the choices before the world at this moment are three only – namely, conference, indefinite deadlock or war. If it be assumed that neither the leaders nor the peoples of any country in Europe desire either of the latter two alternatives, the first one remains as the only hope of avoiding war, since indefinite tension would in the end almost certainly lead to it.

It is, of course, idle to pretend that the invasion of Bohemia and Moravia has not created a new situation of great difficulty; but from the welter of charge and countercharge – claim and counterclaim – certain definite issues seem to emerge. If Germany, realising our strength and our reason, and recognition of both is imperative, is prepared to enter upon a general negotiation covering all matters in dispute, I cannot believe that any one of them is so intractable that accommodation is impossible, assuming, of course, that it is the genuine desire of all parties to avoid war and that they are prepared to give sufficient guarantees of good faith. There is the question of Danzig and the Polish corridor. According to the Poles (as stated in your issue of April 29th) agreement had actually been reached before the invasion of Bohemia and Moravia between Germany and Poland that Danzig should be under joint German and Polish guarantee, but afterwards Germany put forward wider proposals which Poland felt she could not accept. What were those proposals? Have they been formally presented or considered at all? Now that England has undertaken serious obligations in respect of Polish independence, she is at least entitled to be satisfied that any wider proposals are so unreasonable that they would constitute such an infringement of Polish independence as would justify armed resistance or, in other words, a European war.

There are the Italian claims in the Mediterranean. The serious claims of the Italian Government must, of course, be distinguished from the irresponsible demands of a section – probably a small section – of the Italian population. Have these claims been officially promulgated? If so, to whom? And is there among them any demand so hopelessly unreasonable that discussion is out of the question?

There is the question of the German demand for the return of her former colonies. Herr Hitler, while making it plain that he will never abandon his claim for their return, has stated in terms that this question would never become the cause of a military conflict. Mr Chamberlain has repeatedly said that the British Government is prepared to discuss with Germany trade relations in all their aspects with the object of increasing that trade to the mutual advantage of both countries. Is it impossible to say what is the nature of the trade facilities we are prepared to offer and what we expect in return? This, at any rate, seems to me plain, that efforts at this stage to increase Germany's economic difficulties by import duties will, so far from bringing that country to reason, drive her to despair. If this short-sighted policy were pursued she would indeed be entitled to complain of economic encirclement.

Perhaps, however, the most serious statement in Herr Hitler's speech was that "a war against Germany was taken for granted" in this country. I believe this to be profoundly untrue and that perhaps the most valuable result of Munich was the striking manifestation in all countries of the intense desire for peace. There can, of course, be no relaxation of our defence preparations, but it cannot be too often or too strongly emphasised that the object of these preparations is to secure peace and not to make war. There is too much evidence at the moment of a feeling of fatalism and inevitability which, if allowed to develop, may largely contribute to a result which all are anxious to avoid.

All these outstanding questions between ourselves and Germany, including their claim to a sort of Monroe doctrine for Central Europe, appear to be capable of settlement and, if discussed on both sides by those in a position to arrive at decisions, actuated by a mutual desire to reach agreement, the position can surely be satisfactorily adjusted. The various questions would no doubt, in the first place, be investigated in relation to each other, and when that relationship had been ascertained the outstanding and remaining questions would be discussed in relation to the main objective – peace.

I am not in a position to judge whether the present is the best moment for such discussions; but I am sure they must take place sooner or later, and I am anxious lest the well-founded uneasiness created in all our minds by recent happenings should lead the Government to feel that public opinion here would object to their attempting presently to make one more effort to ease the state of tension in Europe, the continuance of which must inevitably expose the whole of Europe to the ever-recurring danger of an outbreak.

Yours, &c.,

RUSHCLIFFE.

House of Lords, May 2nd.

P

O.H. to Secretary of State (Lord Halifax), 3rd May 1939

[See page 286 Note 2]

There are one or two aspects of the Government's policy which account, I think, very largely for a certain mistrust which still surrounds them at home and even abroad.

Henderson's return to Berlin has set everybody thinking, those who want it and those who don't want it, that fresh "appeasement" is in view. He is the symbol of appeasement and so long as he is at his post, whatever his instructions may be, he will cause mistrust in our new policy, especially among the Poles and smaller nations, who identify him with British policy over Czechoslovakia. On the other hand, it is to be feared that he has no restraining influence on the Germans and likewise to them spells a policy of weakness.

The failure to enlarge the Government by the inclusion at least of Eden and Winston Churchill also causes misunderstanding at home. Why, it is asked, does not the Government now widen the basis to include those who have always supported the present policy,

if the Government is really sincere and does not contemplate fresh
"appeasement"? There seems no answer to be given to this. (See
Lord Rushcliffe's letter in today's *Times*.)

Again the Government will shortly have to contemplate three rather
awkward decisions; the recognition of Albania and of the extinction of
Czechoslovakia, both of which are doubtless inevitable, and also
the new Palestine policy, which rightly or wrongly will be represented
as a betrayal of the Jews.

All this being so, I come to my final point, namely the great danger
of any suggestion of "Muniching" the Poles over Danzig or the
French over Tunis. The former danger is twofold. If we do bring
pressure on the Poles, which they resent as excessive, still more if
we suggest that we won't fight for them if they don't accept a certain
settlement, it will at once dissolve all our eastern peace front. The
Poles know their Germans and Beck, it must be remembered, is
the pro-German statesman in Poland, himself a representative of
appeasement, as illustrated by his policy over recent years; he can
be trusted, I think, not to go too far in unreasonable or provocative
opposition to Germany. I am convinced that German strength is in
inverse proportion to the degree of resistance it meets. If we press
or fail to support the Poles over Danzig, German pressure will
become stronger, our guarantee will be regarded as a purely "moral"
one and having won a favourable settlement over Danzig, Hitler
will press on to a next step, e.g. Silesia, until Poland is surrounded
and isolated. Hence I feel real anxiety over the idea of invoking
Mussolini's aid. It will not be possible to keep it private; it will
arouse great nervousness and misgiving in France and Poland, besides
intense opposition and suspicion at home. However it is dressed up,
it would, I fear, look exactly like the preparation for a new Munich
conference, with dangerous consequences to national unity at home.
I really feel we must trust the Poles to handle their own case in this
matter and only bring in Mussolini if the Poles themselves would
welcome it.

Finally, there is the Franco-Italian situation. I am rather nervous
at the extent to which we are using Bonnet against Daladier. Bonnet
is a broken reed and would certainly not stand up for us in the hour
of need, whereas Daladier, though far from being a Poincare or
Clemenceau, is of stiffer and straighter material. I believe a more
direct and frank approach to Daladier instead of manoeuvring
through Bonnet would be more likely to be effective with him. I

quite agree that the three points raised by Ciano in the François-Poncet conversation are susceptible of reasonable discussion and settlement and I think it would be wise to get them out of the way. They would not weaken the actual French military position in any way as far as I can see. I would suggest your having a heart-to-heart talk with Daladier yourself on your way to Geneva next week. He is a frank and honest creature and I feel sure would respond.

Q

O.H. to Secretary of State (Lord Halifax), July 15th 1939
[See page 302, Note 1]

The almost hysterical note of Henderson's letters, quite apart from the defeatist nature of their substance, does seem to me evidence that he is no longer physically equal to the strain of the coming months.

I'm afraid I do regard him rather as a public danger! Although you at this end can discount what he says, we know he is the most indiscreet of men and certainly talks to others as he writes to you.

Moreover, he is the symbol of "appeasement", and so long as he is at his post Berlin will believe that "appeasement" is not dead. His withdrawal would be a piece of that ocular evidence which we are always being advised to give in order to convince Hitler that we mean business.

Nor is it quite fair to Henderson himself, who has always believed sincerely and passionately in appeasement, to expect him to carry out with conviction the complete reversal of policy which has come about.

R

O.H. to Secretary of State (Lord Halifax), August 27th 1939
[See page 308, Note 1]

If I may summarize my own views, they are that
(i) The Soviet-German Pact was a measure of desperation by Hitler, done from knowledge of increasing weakness internal and external.
(ii) It has not had the effect on his enemies he hoped, *vide* signature of Anglo-Polish Treaty and general firmness of Great Britain, France, Poles, etc.

435

(iii) It is having a catastrophic effect on his allies – Spain going neutral, Japan reconsidering her attitude, Mussolini very wobbly.

(iv) He must therefore fear that in return for the doubtful help of the Soviets, he has lost all his other friends.

 (v) The firmer we are now, the more desperate his position becomes: if we are weak, he will recover his prestige and be able to steady his old allies.

(vi) It is essential also if we are to steady our own allies and American friends and impress Hitler's wobbly friends that there should be no sign of wobble here, still less any hint of selling out on the Poles. A straight and steady course is the only line to take when everyone else is shifting theirs.

Glossary

A.E.	Anthony Eden.
O.H.	Oliver Harvey.
Bobbety	Lord Cranborne (Lord Salisbury).
Van	Sir R. Vansittart.
Alec or A.C.	Sir Alexander Cadogan.
Moley (Moly)	Sir Orme Sargent.
Jim	J. P. L. Thomas, M.P.
W.T.	Lord Tyrrell.
H.W.	Sir Horace Wilson.
H.	Lord Halifax.
S.B.	Stanley Baldwin, M.P.
Muss	Mussolini.
C.P.	Sir Charles Peake.
N.H.	Nevile Henderson.
Harry	Captain H. F. C. Crookshank, M.P.
Sam	Sir Samuel Hoare, M.P.
P.R.	Paul Reynaud.
H.E.	His Excellency (i.e. the Ambassador).
D.P.R.	Defence Policy and Re-armament Committee of the Cabinet.
C.I.D.	Committee of Imperial Defence.

Index

Ministry of Supply, 145, 219, 221,
282, 340
Minorca, 52, 252
Molotov, V., 289, 294-296, 301, 304,
319
Monckton, Walter, 328
Monnet, Georges, 395
Monnet, Jean, 352, 396
Montevideo, 332
Monzie, A. de, 375, 379
Moreno, Admiral, 82
Morgenthau, Henry, 17
Morrison, Herbert, 341, 352, 355, 362
Morrison W. S., 78, 95, 96, 99, 103,
128, 131, 135, 175, 249, 259, 315
Mosciki, President, 323
Mounsey, Sir George, 24, 26, 37, 107,
111, 119, 170, 255-256
Munich, 201-203, 207, 209, 220-223,
227-228, 238, 251, 255, 260, 285,
288, 299, 307, 328
Munters, 139
Mussolini, Benito, and Spain 28-32,
33-34, on withdrawal of volunteers,
35, 45, 48, and non-intervention, 50,
57, 65-66, 79, 81, 83-86, and Austria,
90-92, 94-95, 102-103, 105, 107,
108-109, 112, 115, 117, 122, 130-
133, 137, 139, 149-150, and Anglo-
Italian Agreement, 154-159, 161,
and Czech crisis, 176-181, at
Munich, 201-202, and Spain,
209-211, 214-215, 219, 221, and
Franco, 224, 227, 229, 231-232,
234-235, receives Chamberlain,
238-244, 245, 247, 251, 258, 265,
speech of, 270, and Albania, 274-
277, 282-283, 286, 288, 293-294,
and French negotiations, 296, 299,
and Danzig, 302, and Polish crisis,
304-314, 317, 321, and war time
policy, 326, 333, 342, 348, 352,
357-358, 365, 367, 372, 373, 374-
376, 380, declares war, 384, 391

Namier, Sir L., 325
Narvik, 346, 349, 353
Nashville, U.S.S., 176
Negrin, Juan, 254-256
Neurath, von, 21, 35, 116, 161, 164
Newall, Sir C., 357
News Chronicle, 103, 163, 234, 302, 303
Newton, Sir Basil, 18, 142-144, 146,
168, 173-174, 188-190, 192-193
Nichols, Sir P., 327

Nicolson, Harold, 97, 142, 210
Niemöller, Martin, 112
Noel-Baker, Philip, 52, 156
Nogues, General, 223
Non-Intervention Agreement, 19, 35,
154
Non-Intervention Committee, 31, 37,
39, 45, 50-52, 52-54, 107, 125, 149,
160
Norman, Montague, 226, 234-235,
237, 243
Norton, Sir Clifford, 287, 322
Norway, 337-339, 340, 347, 349,
352-354, 362
Nuremberg, 169, 173
Nyhtens, General, 42
Nyon Agreement, 45, 47, 82, 152,
322

Ogilvie-Forbes, Sir George, 34, 323
Oliphant, Sir Lancelot, 294, 369, 372
Ormsby-Gore, William, 40, 51, 74, 95,
140, 147
Osborne, D'Arcy, 241, 287
Osusky, Stefan, 145, 167, 190
Ovey, Sir Esmond, 41
Oxford, Lady, 233
Oxford by-election, 215, 219

Pacelli, Cardinal, 241, becomes Pope,
258, 287-288, 357-358
Palairet, Sir Michael, 90, 115
Palestine, 29-30, 45, 105, 219, 298,
325, 330
Palewski, Gaston, 223, 341, 380, 390,
392
Panay, U.S.S., 64
Papen, von, 90, 324
Paris, 358-363, 378, 382, 384-385, 389
Patenôtre, 136
Paul, Prince, 24, 41, 251-252, 284
Peake, Sir Charles, 41, 92, 101, 136,
138, 140, 222, 238, 241, 245, 291,
328, 330, 340, 345, 349, 355, 374,
376-377, 378, 382
Peake, Osbert, 154
Peirse, Air Marshal Sir R., 364
Perth, Lord, 16, 86, 101-102, 107, 111,
115-116, 119, 121-122, 125-126, 154,
156-157, 181, 195, 209, 227, 239,
245, 277, 282-283, 288, 292, 294,
296, 317
Pertinax, 371, 373, 381, 389, 392-393
Pétain, Marshal, 361, 363, 379,
390-396, 398-400